TRANSPORTATION AND TOWN PLANNING

TRANSPORTATION AND TOWN PLANNING

KURT LEIBBRAND

Professor Dr.-Ing. habil.
Zürich

Translated by
NIGEL SEYMER

THE M.I.T. PRESS
CAMBRIDGE, MASSACHUSETTS
AND LONDON, ENGLAND

© *Birkhäuser Verlag, Basle, 1964*

First published in Great Britain 1970 by
Leonard Hill Books
A Division of International Textbook Company Ltd

First M.I.T. Press Edition, November 1970

ISBN 0 262 12040 2 (hardcover)

Library of Congress catalog card number: 70-138300

Made and printed in Great Britain

FOREWORD

Town building and traffic cannot be separated. One without the other is unthinkable. There is no such thing as a town without traffic; and human settlements grow up at every transportation node. Towns determine the axes along which traffic must move. Transportation gives towns their form and confines their layout. It makes no sense to establish an order of priorities. If transportation is subordinated to town planning in our thinking, or vice versa, there will inevitably be shortcomings in our judgement of facts or in the planning of new facilities.

Our generation is faced by the task of guiding both the rapid growth of towns and the great progress of transportation technology along orderly paths, and reconciling one with the other. This difficult task can only be performed if it is tackled with all their energies by experts, equipped with sound knowledge and experience, and above all with the ability to see beyond the confines of their own professional fields.

Recognized rules of town planning and of transportation planning have long since emerged, and these must be observed without question. They should serve as the basis of all deliberations. But unfortunately they are again and again ignored. These mistakes threaten the structure of towns and settlements and cause either once-and-for-all or continuing economic disbenefits.

This book is designed to ensure the avoidance of such disbenefits. Using numerous examples it sets out the fundamentals of town planning suited to modern traffic, and shows the process of formation of plans from the basic concept by way of the scientific investigations and the necessary calculations to the constructional details. Final answers cannot of course be given to certain questions because things are in constant flux. Development never stands still.

The present volume is based on my book *Transportation Engineering*, published in 1957 by the Verlag Birkhäuser in Basle. The thoughts set out in that book—which are in part more theoretical—will not be repeated here. The present volume was also first published in German by Birkhäuser.

My collaborator of many years, Mr. H. R. Furter, Dip.Tech., deserves special thanks for the outstanding knowledge and thoroughness which he has devoted to the plans and drawings which are used as examples. I would also like to thank warmly Mr. Nigel Seymer, M.A., for the great care with which he has translated the text, and also for many valuable suggestions.

LEIBBRAND

Zürich and Frankfurt/Main

CONTENTS

vi

A. GENERAL CONSIDERATIONS

We DON'T *need self-advertised experts with patented transportation nostrums. We* DON'T *need abstract and utopian planners of future dream cities. We* DON'T *need the noisy publicity of those who simply wail at the walls of Megalopolis.*

Austin J. Tobin, Executive Director, The Port of New York Authority, in a lecture on *Balanced Transportation—Metropolis—1980* (1961)

1. The overall task

The transportation engineer must carry a steadily growing responsibility in the design of towns and settlements. For this reason it is clearly necessary to concern ourselves more closely with the relationships between transportation and town building.

Modern transportation is in the eyes of many fellow human beings a great nuisance:

It swamps the roads, defiles rivers and lakes and pollutes the air.
It robs us of contemplative peace and quiet, and destroys sociability and human dignity.
It desecrates places of art and culture, invades peaceful residential areas, ruins recreational areas and carves up open spaces.
It maims thousands and annihilates more and more human lives.

Transportation is indeed the most powerful expression of modern technology. Its rapid development is still looked upon—or is increasingly looked upon in recent years—with the eyes of the machine-wrecker of the last century, who saw nothing but evil in technical progress.

It is therefore no wonder that transportation engineers are frequently met with suspicion. Are they not the sorcerers who have lost all feeling for beauty, peace, townscape, human scale, protection of the home and care of monuments? Is it not they who, without taste or feeling, heedlessly demand every sacrifice in town and country which their wretched calculations and drawing board designs indicate would be beneficial to the 'traffic moloch'?

It is many years since Pascal saw in traffic the source of all mankind's misfortunes: 'ne pas savoir se tenir en repos dans une chambre' (not to know how to have peace and quiet in one's room). How much unwholesomeness would have been avoided if mankind had not left his study!

But this 'source of all evil' has ruled mankind's destiny from time immemorial.

Well-meaning citizens often remind us that traffic is our servant, not our master: its needs and desires should be catered for last of all, because 'man is the measure of all things'.

It is not by chance that such thoughts are mentioned at the beginning of this book. They are part of the daily bread of the practising traffic engineer. Only too often he has to come to terms with the objections which councillors, journalists or laymen raise against his proposals. The same game is repeated in many places. First there are loud complaints about traffic congestion, growing into an avalanche of wishes and suggestions. Overcoming traffic difficulties is the talk of the day. Finally some serious traffic planning is started. Publication of the first proposals sparks off public discussion. For some the proposals are too large-scale; for some they are too small-scale. This one looks unusual; that one is too expensive. Parking should be forbidden here; there ought to be more trees there. Constructive thinking is opposed by aesthetic feeling. Opinions are bandied about. One person has heard that they do things quite differently in the U.S.A. Examples from other cities are quoted: examples of things which were either done in quite different circumstances or are outmoded, or were simply wrong-headed (as a result of a similar process).

And so the fight sways to and fro for a time, until someone raises the battle-cry: 'The city is for people, not vehicles.' Traffic congestion can easily be solved—at any rate on paper—by closing streets to motor traffic and creating big pedestrian-only areas. This would solve everything, and much public money would be saved.

But after a while the game starts from the beginning again because traffic congestion is hindering economic activity more and more. It injures trade. Something must be done.

Meanwhile much valuable time has been lost. Traffic has increased further. Year after year it increases by a few per cent, without pause. The carrying out of the essential measures has become more difficult. Some solutions have been made impossible by new buildings or installations. Now the engineers are blamed for not having foreseen this development.

Especially harmful is the universally held opinion that traffic is something so simple and obvious that every man knows enough about it from his own observation to enable him to pronounce a sure judgement on traffic questions; that traffic requirements and the effects of traffic measures can be so easily observed that they can be assessed correctly without taking any special trouble. Some people even doubt whether traffic engineering should be regarded as a separate branch of engineering. They brusquely challenge the necessity for scientific handling of traffic questions.

Many people think up plans for their own homes; why should they not also design a plan for traffic?

Generally speaking the inhabitants of rural areas are too keen on railways, and those of towns are too keen on roads. When the transportation engineer delivers his judgement, as it is his duty to do, he is told that he is prejudiced and partial, that he keeps changing his tune. Similarly he is often not understood if he calls for a rigid restriction on floor space in the city centre, and for a greater residential density in outlying areas of a city.

An extreme example of what can happen was the case of the big city where people had to vote on whether the public transport system should be operated with trams or buses. Catholics and Communists came down in favour of one alternative, right-wingers and Social Democrats showed an equally rare unity in favour of the other. A bare result would have satisfied neither side, so an overall transportation plan was called for. It was scarcely finished when a rival plan was prepared by outsiders. There has been endless talk; and in ten years a decision has still not been reached. And time presses.

In another city a transport plan was produced by consultants. The councillor responsible for transport did not think it was any longer necessary to look at it, because he knew already what decision was to be expected on the basis of the voting strengths of the parties. But when he had finally had a look at it he was amazed to discover that the study was politically neutral. He had not thought this was possible. He then explained that he would use the plan as a weapon, but in the meantime the report ought not to be published because of various elections. The consultant's proposals were finally adopted by a large majority, and have since been carried out at a cost of several millions.

A city in North America has, in the opinion of its traffic engineer, far too many traffic signals. This is because every newly elected councillor wants more signals in his ward. The same men would never dare to express an opinion on many detailed questions concerning transportation, such as the design of a roadway on a bridge, or of a tunnel cross-section, or the drainage of a road where frost was a hazard, or the provision of a rail siding, or the method of operation of a blind landing device or the switching of a green wave signal system. Similarly they would not presume to take issue with a chemist, a lawyer or a doctor in his own field.

The engineer cannot avoid such confrontations. If he can succeed in gaining trust then he has created the most important basis for his work. But he must remember that he is not paying the piper, but only suggesting what tunes should be called. A 'Plan' with many-coloured drawings achieves nothing. The planner must become the advocate for his proposals and seek to win over the public.

The city council has the right and—being responsible to the public— the duty to make wishes known, to state requirements and to demand precise information. If then politician and engineer pull the same way they cannot help succeeding. There are a gratifying number of examples one can point to. I need mention only one: the big traffic installations in

Baden bei Zürich, whose genesis was due to the far-sightedness of an outstanding mayor. This was built at a cost of forty million Swiss Francs in a small town of less than 20,000 inhabitants. This way lies success in carrying out the proposals of traffic planners and gradually relieving traffic congestion.

2. The engineer's role

The engineer ought not to be content with being a mere technician. So long as he claims to possess 'ingenium' he must surely give thought to the basis of his calling and the moral foundation of his practice.

'Man is the measure of all things!' Let us take this saying of Protagoras as a starting point. It is this very Man who demands year by year more transportation. And it cannot be otherwise if his needs are to be satisfied in a situation of increasing population density, rising standards of living and increasing division of work. Transportation is just as 'good' or 'bad' as technology as a whole; it is necessary. It all depends on what mankind does with it.

Human life without transportation is unthinkable. Most activities and processes are impossible without moving men, goods or news. Every loaf of bread contains 'transportation'. Sheaves, corn, flour and finished bread have to be transported in a variety of vehicles. Oil, coal and ores are fairly valueless at the points where they are produced; they are only useful when they have been transported to users.

In conurbations most men would find it impossible to pursue their occupations without transport. Similarly education, pleasure and recreation usually give rise to transport needs. More and more workers earn their livelihood in the provision of transport—every fifth worker is thus employed in the industrialized countries of Europe, and every fourth worker in the U.S.A.

The return of the mail coach and the horse-cart is impossible. Conditions during and after the Second World War, and likewise those which arise when transport is interrupted by nature or by a strike, give us a fore-taste of what life without transport would be like.

Without modern means of transport only as many people would be able to live in each area as the land in that area could support. Destruction of all transportation in an industrial country would compel millions of people to emigrate. Even in an agrarian country there would be famines, because it would not be possible to bring in food from areas producing a surplus to areas where the harvest has failed. It is not mere chance that Central Europe experienced its last famine in 1846. At that time it was thinly populated in comparison with today, but there was no coherent railway network available. In 1967 starving China was able to import grain from Australia, Canada and Argentina.

Transport technology has overcome hunger. In so doing it has created an important precondition for the rapid increase of population first in Europe and then overseas. It started a chain reaction. There is no way back. But the 'traffic moloch' has not just ensured mere life; it has helped decisively in improving living standards.

Transport plays not a servile but a dominant role in making further progress along this road. Transportation engineers work in the service of their neighbours, their nations and mankind as a whole. Thus their activities are recognized as a public service. They are called upon to make ever greater efforts to ensure that their fellow men enjoy the basic amenities of life.

But where does this road lead to? As a child of his time the transportation engineer must give thought to this. The engineer influences the future of our civilization and in particular of our technology. Was Oswald Spengler right in what he wrote in 1922 in the last pages of the second volume of his *The Decline of the West*? He wrote:

> The intoxicated soul wills to fly above space and time. An unutterable longing beckons him towards boundless horizons. Man would free himself from the earth, rise into the infinite, leave the bonds of the body and circle in the universe of space amongst the stars. . . . Hence the fantastic traffic that traverses continents in a few days, crosses oceans in floating cities, bores through mountains, rushes about in subterranean labyrinths, discards the steam-engine, the potential of which has long since been exploited to the limit, in favour of the internal combustion engine, and finally rises above roads and railways and flies in the air . . .
>
> Not merely the importance but the very existence of industry depends upon the existence of the hundred-thousand rigorously trained brains who are the masters of technology and who develop it further and further. It is the quiet engineer who is the true captain of our technological destiny. His thought is as possibility what the machine is as actuality. There have been fears, thoroughly materialistic fears, of the exhaustion of the coalfields. But so long as there are technological pathfinders of merit available, dangers of this sort need not worry us. When, and only when, the crop of recruits for this army fails—this army whose brainwork forms an inner unity with the work of the machine—must industry flicker out despite all that managerial skill and the workers can do.

A different view is expressed by Eugen Diesel, son of the creator of the diesel engine:

> For thousands of years men have had at their disposal only their own muscle-power, the strength of animals and the power of the wind. Since the beginning of the industrial revolution, whose offspring is modern transport, the power at man's disposal has increased ever more

rapidly. Already individuals can control surely and with ease thousands of horse-power. But this is only the beginning of a development which will lead us on to a further sharp upswing.

Are we at the beginning or are we nearing the end? Who is right, Spengler or Diesel? Every engineer must seek his own answer to this question of man's destiny. He cannot alter that destiny; it will govern his actions and reactions.

3. Scope of transportation engineering

One often hears it said that traffic engineering is something entirely new, for which there was no precedent. We would have to start right from the beginning, and could at best use American traffic engineering as an example, despite the fact that it was based on different circumstances.

This is not correct. The dynamics of vehicle movement have long been scientifically studied. Generations of civil engineers have laid the foundations of modern traffic engineering. We may remember the names of Launhardt (Hanover), Lill (Vienna) and Cauer (Berlin). In classical fashion Blum (Hanover)—who died in 1944—built up his work in the wide field of traffic, town planning and regional planning on the basis of fundamental principles of traffic design and operation, and worked out the relationships very clearly. Transportation engineering must progress in the direction in which he led us if the pressing traffic problems of our cities are to be correctly solved. Only in this way can the design of towns and settlements be restored to health.

What then is transportation engineering? It must be described as follows:

> Transportation engineering is concerned with the operation of all trafficways, and their design as it affects traffic operation. Since this involves structural design it is a branch of civil engineering. Over much more than a hundred years it has however become increasingly independent as it has developed out of civil engineering.

The first major task which modern transportation set the civil engineer was the building of railways. At first it was hardly a matter of providing usable connections between city and suburb. General wonderment was excited by the bold mountain railways through the Alps, and the long-distance railways through scarcely explored areas, like the railways across North America and Siberia, and the Cape-to-Cairo railway which will wait a long time yet for completion.

As traffic density increased, the centre of interest gradually shifted from civil engineering questions to problems of operation and traffic characteristics. The expression 'capacity' became more and more important. Today it dominates all fields of transportation—on land, on water and in the air. But civil engineering has remained the foundation because the operation of a vehicle cannot be divorced from the way on which it runs. For this reason it is worth considering what position civil engineering has reached and how it can develop further.

4. Technical style

Each age has its own style, even in technology. Since traffic planning is always directed towards the future we must venture to take a view regarding the future development of engineering science.

The unity of building design, so completely personified by Erwin von Steinbach, builder of Strasburg cathedral, or by Albrecht Dürer, the 'engineer' of the mighty round towers of the Nuremberg city walls, has long since ended. The splitting of building design into architecture and engineering is extremely regrettable, but it cannot now be undone. The two branches have grown too far apart. Anyone with insight will always try to promote close collaboration.

The oldest field of civil engineering is water engineering: the damming of streams, the protection of sea coasts, the irrigation and drainage of fields and meadows, the building of harbours and canals. In the last century railway construction presented engineers with a big, new task, and led to a great upswing in civil engineering. The building of the railway network in most parts of Europe was interrupted in 1914. Since then shortage of capital and changes in transportation have meant that large-scale new works have seldom been undertaken. Railway administrations turned their attention to operational questions.

But now the civil engineer was given important tasks to perform in factory and power-station building and in the construction of roads and motorways. The building of hydro-electric schemes in the Alps and on the rivers of Central and Western Europe is already approaching finality.

The new fields of increasing importance are sanitary engineering and transportation engineering. At the same time questions of operational economy are gaining in importance, and with them developments such as the automation of construction work and prefabrication of buildings.

The basis of civil engineering is statics, which has undergone marked changes in the course of time. In the first half of the past century building statics were separated from theoretical mechanics. Gradually graphic statics developed as a fundamentally new aid to the engineer. The graphic method is distinguished for its clarity. It sharpens the wits of the young engineer and helps to awaken in him a 'feeling' for statics.

From about 1920 onwards graphic statics were pressed harder and harder by analytical statics, which represented a big step forward but which broke the direct relationship between the appearance and the statics of a structure. Creative design and static calculation gradually grew apart. Statics were practised independently by specialists as an auxiliary

science. The link with questions of materials, of constructive and architectural appearance, and even of practical experience became weaker and
weaker. Abstract calculation supplanted constructive perception. In the
view of Sedlmayr, expressed in his book *Verlust der Mitte* (Loss of the
centre), this process has been comparable with the substitution among
architects of geometrical pattern-making for a *feeling* for style.

The outstanding transportation engineer Blum once warned that 'the
best engineer is not the one who can calculate best but the one who can
guess best'. And we may recall the saying of Goethe: 'It is one of the oldest
sins to think that calculation is invention.' Calculation is not creative.
The true essence of the work of the engineer is to design for utility and
beauty. Only in this field can he show true mastery of his art.

Now a new revolution is on the way; and it is not by chance that it has
started in the U.S.A. Analytical methods are being replaced with statistical
ones. Series of observations take the place of mathematical calculations.
Evaluations can be made with great rapidity with the help of electronic
computers operating largely automatically.

With this new process the gap between creative design and anonymous
calculation becomes even wider than ever. An even deeper chasm is fixed
between the thinking through of design questions, which requires a high
degree of mental culture, and the drawing out of approximate values
statistically obtained.

As an indicative example from the field of transportation engineering
we may take the determination of travel time and fuel consumption of
vehicles. Exact graphical methods of calculation for these values were
developed as long ago as 1920 by Wilhelm Müller. They have been used
for over thirty years by railway administrations, and for a shorter time
also by highway authorities. They were adapted in such a way that they
could be used for mechanical calculations. The methods can be used even
for vehicles still on the drawing board. They have proved very reliable.

In 1960–61, trial runs were carried out for the same purpose by the
University of Washington. The results of the observations were fed into
a computer, which was to determine statistical average values which will
enable travel time and fuel consumption to be predicted. This is the new
approach to a clear problem.

It is astonishing that in such a basically different field as economics
similar worries are being expressed. Thus Röpke wrote in 1960 in his book
Jenseits von Angebot und Nachfrage (Beyond supply and demand), as
follows:

> He was formerly considered a good economist who knew how to
> estimate the relationships between economic forces operating at a
> given time; and power of judgement and sound understanding of men
> was considered more important than formal finesse in the application
> of methods. But now a different type of economist is coming more and

more to the fore, a man who knows how to express in mathematical formulae and curves hypothetical statements about functional relationships in the economy. I am thinking above all of the tendency to treat the economic process as a mechanistic one, which can be quantitatively measured using mathematical-statistical methods and finally predicted.

Linked to this is a series of other questionable tendencies: the specialization of research, carried ever further and further, which promotes the fragmentation of the social sciences and takes an unmistakable pride in the use of mathematics.

These sentences could easily be altered slightly to fit transportation engineering as it is today. They are valid as regards traffic prognosis, the estimation of future traffic volumes. But they are valid equally as regards the handling of technical questions. We should be especially on our guard against influences which work in this direction. The engineer is not a mathematician, important as mathematics may be as a basic skill. His mental work and his experience cannot be replaced by a computer programme—although electronic computation undoubtedly greatly facilitates the engineer's work. We cannot dispense with graphic and analytical methods in the further development of traffic engineering and the training of future engineers; on the contrary these methods must be brought up to date and refined for use in this field.

With their help the young engineer must develop a 'feeling' for traffic and operational questions. He must gradually learn to recognize where intuition must take over from calculation.

5. Planning

The word 'planning' must be mentioned. In the last few years we have heard it more and more frequently. The word has become almost a slogan; but it hides many different and often muddled lines of thought.

Many seize their pencils at once and see the true task of planning as the preparation of plans and drawings. Others take fright at the word planning and think that it means measures to create a planned economy, which would circumscribe the free play of economic forces and is therefore incompatible with a market economy. Neither view is correct.

In a free economy every large concern practises planning. Manufacturing or wholesaling concerns conduct market research, which corresponds to basic research in the field of town or traffic planning. They observe changes in the consumption of their product, shifts in the social class of consumers, changes in habits of life and in taste. From this they draw conclusions about increasing their production, the setting up of branches or alternatively cuts in the production and distribution of goods.

In this process political questions are not excluded but are of course brought into the deliberations—e.g. trade treaties, the reduction of tariffs, the creation of wider economic areas or the effect of international tensions.

Series of numbers can be set up from the many figures for population, standard of life, income growth, consumption, age structure, births, deaths and migration. 'Econometrics' seeks to express the series as formulae, and hence to derive values for the future—i.e. for ten, twenty or thirty years hence.

But the most thorough basic research can never detect the influences arising from way of life, the economy (good or bad harvests, industrial activity, monetary conditions), technology, taste or even politics. There is no doubt that such influences play a very large role, if not a decisive one.

They influence all data concerning the population and its living conditions. No one could have foreseen thirty years ago the social changes which have been caused by rapid motorization or by television. No one would dare to guess what shifts there will be in the coming years in the balance of power between nations and alliances. All of which shows that planning cannot consist of setting forth so-called laws for the future. Planning must above all be flexible and supple.

But this recognition means that it is never possible to set up plans which cannot be altered. No generation is cleverer or more far-sighted than its predecessor; and each generation has different wishes, different needs and different cares. Planning must continually adapt itself and take account of the necessities of its time.

The industrialist frames, on the basis of market research, a long-term programme for gradually increasing, step by step, the capacity of his plants. The plan will be continually adjusted to present market conditions, and executed only so far as it is truly needed. Any work carried out too soon incurs capital charges unnecessarily.

Planning includes plans for finance and execution. It takes visible form in engineering designs. Here the method of operation in the production process plays a dominant role. Physical extension of production plants is an especially important and striking part of planning, but does not constitute the whole of it.

Traffic planning is not a matter of planned economy measures for the compulsory distribution of traffic between different modes of transport and the control of free competition between modes. What is meant is purely technical planning, by which alone traffic flow can be improved. The economic return from proposed solutions should of course be tested —as in any other technological field.

The method of work of traffic planning corresponds exactly to that adopted by industry—even though transportation has peculiarities which are unknown in other economic fields. Its product consists of person-miles and ton-miles of very different kinds, which differ from goods in that they are 'invisible' and 'easily spoilt'. This product cannot be stored. For instance with commuter traffic there is a short-lived demand for person-miles which can hardly be satisfied. A few minutes later, after work has begun in the factories, trains and buses run empty; their capacity has become unsaleable.

In transportation, as a general rule, every demand ought to be met at once, so that installations must have generous dimensions and consequently will not be very fully utilized. This is especially true as regards urban peak traffic. In transportation, construction is only a means to an end. The operation of the system is the decisive thing. Traffic planning must operate within budgetary constraints.

In a wider context the word planning has become confined to the field of town and country planning. With increasing population the use of land can no longer be left to chance. Good housekeeping is necessary with regard to the earth's surface. On human and social grounds, excessively large concentrations of population in favoured areas must be avoided, and the economically weaker areas promoted.

According to the political conditions, national planning has various ways and means for introducing or carrying through the measures which are considered necessary. In states with a planned economy, the needs and wishes of national planning find their expression in a national plan which controls the activities of the entire population. In western countries, national planning must adapt its methods to the market economy, and take account of the free play of economic forces. Here the planner cannot dictate, but can only lay down standards and promote or deter development. He has more or less influence according to the legal and political conditions. His methods of work and his success therefore differ from country to country. In states with a free economy national planning can use the following methods:

The method of *financial inducement*, e.g. tax concessions to economically backward areas or industries, equalization of tax revenues between municipalities or regional authorities, building subsidies for particular places, direction of public building projects.

The method of *development control*, by means of building regulations, prohibitions on building, or compulsory purchase which the law permits in certain cases—especially for the building of transportation facilities.

The method of *transportation policy*, meaning either *economic discrimination*, e.g. special fares on public transport for the improvement of local conditions, or special fares for certain classes of the population; or *technical discrimination* in the provision of roads, railways, canals or airfields, bus lines, bus stops or railway stations—in short traffic planning measures.

Town and regional planning uses the same methods as national land use planning to carry out its aims, but on a smaller scale.

The transportation engineer has a big planning responsibility. He must concern himself in detail with legal decisions and the practical possibilities of local, regional and national planning. It is his duty to call the attention of the public and of the authorities to the relationships between transportation and town planning and national planning, and to give warning in good time about the detrimental effects of wrong decisions. The aim of all planning is after all to maintain society and the economy in good health and to promote their development.

6. Transportation science

Hitherto we have spoken only of transportation engineering. But it would be better and more correct to assess this field in the framework of a comprehensive science of transportation. This question has a considerable practical importance, for the question must be considered whether independent training centres ought not to be established in the West modelled on the Institute for Transportation in Dresden, which is independent of the Technical University there, or other Institutes in the East. Creation of such an independent institution would not be anything very unusual, since there are special training establishments in other fields: for world commerce in Vienna, for commerce in St. Gallen, for economics in Mannheim, for politics in Berlin, for agriculture in Hohenheim.

On the basis of general considerations any splitting away from the University is to be regretted, for in this way the '*universitas*' will be lost. This is true of the Colleges of Advanced Technology (known in Germany as Technische Hochschulen), whose students have far too little contact with other fields of knowledge and experts in those fields. A further fragmentation into different fields of application—and transportation is such a field—would certainly have even bigger disadvantages.

Transportation science covers widely separated areas, such as:

> Traffic law
> Transport economics as a branch of economics
> Operating economics of traffic undertakings
> Town and country planning
> General civil engineering
> Transportation and traffic engineering
> Mechanical engineering (vehicles)
> Electrical engineering
> Medicine (relevant to accident research, aviation medicine)
> Sociology
> Transport geography
> Statistics

It is not in dispute that the traffic lawyer must be a fully trained lawyer and the transportation doctor a fully-trained doctor. It is the same in the engineering profession. And no one will have complete mastery of even two of the fields listed above. Thus there cannot be such a thing as a transportation man possessing thorough knowledge of all fields. And so there is no suggestion that we should depart from the method followed hitherto, whereby every person employed in transportation should first have a thorough grounding in his particular field.

To what extent particular fields will be deepened in the course of time and made independent is another question. There are strong arguments against excessive specialization. Each little field is fenced off from the others, and understanding of the larger relationships suffers. Such considerations argue likewise against making town and country planning a separate profession alongside architecture and civil engineering, as has been done in the U.S.A.

Further fragmentation would also have the effect of lengthening the training period, which must be seen as a disadvantage. Between the ages of 7 and 57 (many do not reach pensionable age) there are fifty years available. As a result of longer schooling, national service, practical instruction. lengthened studies and further training (dissertation, second state examination) there is in some cases a ratio of 25 years of learning to 25 years of practising one's profession, a ratio of 1 : 1. This cannot be justified economically and must lead to heavy social costs. Young men enter professional life far too late. They sit too long on the school bench and too often lose their keenness for their profession, their drive and joy in holding responsibility. They must wait far too long before they can stand on their own feet financially and start a family.

With a taut education and training, confining itself to essentials and occupying altogether seventeen to eighteen years, the ratio mentioned above could be improved to 2 : 1. At 24 young men would still have youthful enthusiasm for their profession. They would take pleasure in deepening their knowledge during the first few years of independent activity. A large part of the so-called shortage of engineers would be removed, and the overcrowding of the Colleges of Advanced Technology would be considerably eased.

If for these compelling reasons any extension of the education and training period is to be rejected, voluntary further education after entering on a career becomes more important. For this purpose the German, the Austrian and the Swiss Transportation Science Societies are available, similar institutions exist in the Netherlands and in Scandinavia and likewise the famous Institute of Transport in Britain. Here the transportation scientists from the various professions are brought together and receive further training. This promotes readiness to collaborate and mutual understanding, which are so indispensable if the representatives of so many different fields wish to serve a common cause.

7. The main sub-divisions

(a) Overall planning

In view of the close relationship between the various means of transport, the transportation engineer must not confine himself to a narrow field— e.g. to bus transport, rapid rail transport or private road transport, with which the road traffic engineer concerns himself in detail. The engineer must rather keep in mind the totality of transportation needs and requirements. It is his task to evaluate, organize and improve total transportation in an entire area, and to design the channels of movement required for this purpose. He must find solutions at the especially difficult 'transport interface' points at which travellers change from car to aircraft or from train to bus, or where goods are transferred from ship to road vehicle. He must so knit together the networks of the various means of transport that they will form a balanced whole.

Often separate plans are worked out for the different means of transport. For instance, road networks or parking facilities or public transport networks are often dealt with independently of each other. Sometimes local and long-distance roads are designed without relation to one another.

The intermeshing of the different networks becomes closer and closer. The interchange points between them call for closer attention because their capacity and convenience is often inadequate for the transfer of persons and goods. The weakest link determines the capacity of the entire chain. In the case of an airport for instance, the vehicle parks, the passenger and goods handling facilities, the customs facilities, the departure lounges and the freight sheds must have as great a capacity as that of the runways. The total transportation task must always be considered.

The effects of transportation on national, regional, city and local planning are more and more apparent, so that the interaction with these fields must be constantly taken into account. Purely technical solutions are usually no longer adequate. Economic, social and political questions are of increasing importance.

(b) Speed

The public takes a great interest in supersonic aircraft, trunk motorways and long-distance express trains. But the question of maximum speed has on the whole been solved by the mechanical engineers and is only of real significance for military and scientific tasks. As far as can be foreseen, no ocean-going craft will travel within the next fifty years at more than 100 km/h (63 mph), nor will a speed of 200 km/h (125 mph) be reached regularly on any heavily used motorway, nor will any railway line be operated at more than 300 km/h (185 mph). There is little point in operating aircraft capable of more than 1,000 km/h (625 mph) between say London and Paris. An increase of speed by 50 km/h (31 mph) brings the following time savings on a journey of 1,000 km (625 miles):

from 50 to 100 km/h (31 to 63 mph) 10 h.   = 600 min
from 450 to 500 km/h (280 to 311 mph)   = 13 min
from 950 to 1,000 km/h (594 to 625 mph)   = 3 min
from 1,950 to 2,000 km/h (1,229 to 1,250 mph) = 0·8 min or 47 sec

For further increases in speed the relationship between expense and utility becomes less and less favourable. Building and operating costs set a limit to further acceleration.

It is far more important to concentrate on raising travel speeds for important transport links, especially in cities, where present speeds are quite inadequate.

(c) Long- and short-distance transportation

While public interest is concentrated on long-distance travel, far too little attention is paid to the millions of trips which are made day after

Figure 1: Traffic flow diagram of the town of Freiburg, Switzerland (35,000 inhabitants) after the opening of the planned National Road Berne–Lausanne. From the Berne direction 56 per cent of the cars will branch off to Freiburg, and from the Lake of Geneva direction 58 per cent. The multi-lane National Road will have much less traffic to cope with than the narrow alleys of the town centre.

day over short distances, and for which the standards of speed and comfort
are quite inadequate. Even a cursory observation of car registration plates
confirms that everywhere—except in holiday areas in the peak holiday
season—local traffic predominates. In Germany it has been established

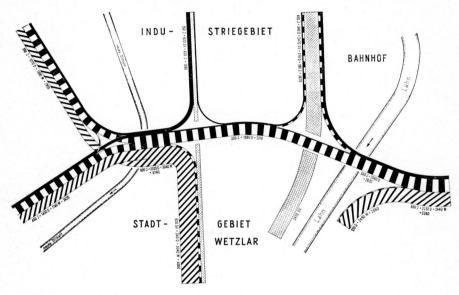

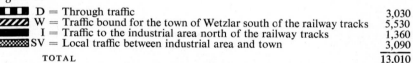

Figure 2:

	D = Through traffic		3,030
	W = Traffic bound for the town of Wetzlar south of the railway tracks		5,530
	I = Traffic to the industrial area north of the railway tracks		1,360
	SV = Local traffic between industrial area and town		3,090
	TOTAL		13,010

In Wetzlar (38,000 inhabitants) terminating traffic is heavier than through
traffic on all trunk roads. Through traffic includes traffic between municipalities immediately adjoining Wetzlar.

that 85 per cent of traffic is local and neighbourhood traffic and only 15 per
cent is long-distance traffic. A study carried out on the motorway between
Duisburg and Kamen in the Ruhr area in 1960 showed that 46 per cent
of the cars were making trips of less than 15 km (9 miles) and only 7 per
cent were making trips of more than 40 km (25 miles). These figures should
not cause surprise. In most places the volumes of long-distance traffic
are far smaller than those of short-distance traffic (Fig. 1). Everyone makes
short trips far more often than long ones.

It is pointless to argue about whether long-distance traffic is of greater
economic value than local traffic. The two types of traffic cannot be substituted for each other. Each has its own important. But it is not in dispute
that local traffic, composed of countless trips to work, school, shops and
colleges, and for social and recreational purposes, is by no means satisfactorily catered for and that greater attention must be paid to it (Fig. 2).

(d) Congestion

Congestion is far more evident in local traffic than in long-distance traffic. The overloading of trafficways has four causes:

Increasing population
Increasing travel *per capita*
Increasing traffic peaks which get sharper and sharper
Increasing space required per unit of travel, i.e. per person-mile

Population is increasing mainly in the big cities and the areas around them. In country districts it is increasing only slowly or is even declining. Thus cross-country links are becoming relatively less important. On the other hand traffic volumes in the conurbations are growing incessantly. Most of the people who are moving into the conurbations could hitherto reach their places of work on foot. They are now compelled to travel more or less far every day. As the urbanized area spreads out, so people are obliged to make more and longer trips.

Travel to work shows the highest and most inconvenient peaks, especially inside the cities. At the boundary of the city or urbanized area traffic is fairly constant throughout the day. It declines very little around midday and only increases slightly in the evening. Long-distance traffic is fairly well spread over the whole day. The worst delays in cities are caused mainly by trips to and from work. This traffic is of great social as well as technical importance. Observations in various European cities have shown that it has grown faster than other kinds of traffic owing to all available labour being drawn into the cities, and that only a moderate degree of staggering of working hours is possible. Thus traffic congestion arises mainly in local traffic.

Another cause of congestion must also be mentioned: the transfer of more and more social classes from public to private transport, which requires much more space. While the transportation engineer must take the other influences as given, he can influence the 'modal split' between public and private transport within certain limits.

The biggest difficulties arise in the cities and conurbations. They are a threat to the objectives of town and country planning. They detract from the increased leisure time which has come with the shortening of the working day. They make ever greater demands on health, time and money. More attention must be paid to them, since the conurbations are assuming an ever more predominant position in the economic and political life of the people. Traffic operation and geometric design are both especially complicated in these areas. Transportation planning in such areas is the true high school of the transportation engineer.

(e) Methods of work

The transportation engineer sets about his task in a similar fashion to the civil engineer. The individual steps in the design of a structure or of a traffic facility correspond exactly:

DESIGN OF STRUCTURE	DESIGN OF TRAFFIC FACILITY
Static loading	*Traffic loading*
Fixed values according to regulations or standards	Estimates based on surveys and expected increase in traffic
Choice of system	*Choice of system*
Beams, curves, frames, determined statically or non-statically	Network, outline road plan, rail system, line or directional operation, 2-way or 1-way traffic
Design	*Design*
Construction drawings	Plan and sections
Appearance	*Appearance*
Design from the architectural point of view	Design from the town planning point of view
Check on design strength	*Check on capacity*
Static calculation	Capacity calculation
Requirement in terms of strength per unit area	Load in terms of vehicles per unit time
Economy	*Economy*
Calculation of building costs	Calculation of building and operating costs

The biggest differences are in the first and the two last stages. While the civil engineer can take given loadings as his starting point, the transportation engineer must first of all calculate his loadings; and this requires a considerable statistical expenditure. This is the first main sub-division of his work, for the suitability of the entire design will depend on the correct estimation of future traffic volumes. Here political, economic and social influences play a part; and these can only be assessed with difficulty. They may well change over the years, and for this reason the design must afford considerable scope for possible later adaptation.

Capacity means not only the volume of traffic which can be handled, but also the quality of transportation service provided. Here type of vehicle, speed, safety, economy and comfort must be taken into account, and it is difficult to find a common denominator for these.

With traffic facilities the calculation of economy is much more extensive than it is with structures. It embraces quite different quantities. Both construction and operating costs must be assessed at the same time; and the minimum total cost for both together should be the ruling criterion.

B. THE DEVELOPMENT OF TRANSPORTATION

He who would plan for the future must be familiar with the past. Only thus can he form any judgement as to whether his plans have any prospect of being carried out, and are therefore sensible, or whether they will remain Utopian. We should learn from history, even from the far too little known history of technology. The development of transportation will be sketched in this section, if only with a few broad strokes.

Transportation is movement. The possibility of moving about is one of the most important conditions of human life. From time immemorial mankind has sought to develop this facility further. The distance a man can cover on his own feet is too short; the loads which he can carry on his own shoulders too small. He wants to enlarge his area of operation. He wants to overcome the 'friction of space'.

Even in prehistoric times man made use of horses and caravans, carts and sleds, rowing boats and sailing ships. From the outset they were tools used for trade, politics and war.

It cannot be disputed that culture and civilization are unthinkable without a high standard of living. So long as all men lived out their earthly existence in bitter poverty they could not execute large works of art or technical creations. Spiritual achievements are supported by the political strength and the wealth which trade and industry bring. Neither can develop without good transportation links. That is why peoples in all ages have fought over access to the sea and to large rivers. In our own century roads and motorways, railways and air bases are the bones of contention.

1. Water transport

(a) Ancient times

From time immemorial waterways were the most important channels of movement. It was only on rivers, lakes and seas that heavy loads—grain, timber, stone—could be carried in large quantities. Only light, valuable goods were sent over long distances by land—as is indicated by such names as 'Salt road', 'Amber road' or 'Silk road'.

One of the oldest of man's monuments is the Tower of Babel. Babylon, one of the most beautiful and largest cities of the ancient world, was in about 2300 B.C. the capital of a mighty empire. The Tower, which was really a stepped pyramid, is said to have consisted of six mighty steps with a total height of about 100 m (330 ft). It was an extraordinary transportation achievement to have procured the stones for this structure.

Babylon is said to have covered 14 sq km. If we assume it had a high residential density of 500 persons per hectare the city could have had a population of 700,000. The inhabitants could only be supplied by means of transport which depended on the muscle power of men or animals or on the powers of the waters or the winds. The big loads which had to be brought in day by day for the feeding and clothing of the large population, and the wares which were exported in exchange for them, could only be carried on the River Euphrates. The transportation network of Babylon must have been very extensive. As long ago as 3800 B.C. the Babylonian ruler Sargon of Agane is said to have travelled from the Syrian coast to Cyprus. 'Guest workers' were brought in from distant lands. The Bible speaks of the 'Babylonian confusion of tongues' which prevailed in the city and was thought to presage the end of the empire (Genesis xi).

In the year 2525 B.C. the Egyptian King Cheops had the largest pyramid erected, with a height of 146 m, an area of 233 × 233 m and a cubic content of 2·5 million cu m. According to Heroditus (writing about 460 B.C.) 100,000 men took twenty years to build it. For the feeding of this work force and the transporting of the stones there was no other means of transport available other than those of Babylon. Such a task could only be accomplished with the aid of waterways. The importance of shipping also found religious expression: the dead King Cheops was given 'Sun ships' to transport his soul into eternity; and one of these was found in 1954 in a rock crevice close to the pyramid.

The size of the transportation task is better appreciated if the stone mass of the pyramid is compared with modern structures. The earth dam built for the Marmorera hydro-electric scheme in Switzerland required the moving of 2·7 million cu m of earth. Some 2·1 million cu m of concrete were used in the Grande Dixence dam in Valais. But for both these structures the bulk of the materials was obtained close to the site.

In the 14th century B.C., under the Pharaohs Sethos I and Ramses II, a canal was built for the fleet from the Nile via the Lake of Timsah to the Red Sea; this later fell in. Necho (619–604 B.C.) began the building of a new canal from Bubastis on the Nile to Patumos on the Arabian gulf; and this was completed by Darios Hystaspis in 517 B.C. Around 260 B.C. it was improved by Ptolemy II by constructing locks. The canal is said to have silted up in Cleopatra's time, but to have been reopened under Trajan. The canal was renewed in the 7th century A.D. by Amr, the Caliph Omar's commander-in-chief, and used for transporting grain. But in the 8th century the waterway became unusable.

Around 1200 B.C. Egyptian ships 67 m (220 ft) long are said to have crossed the Indian ocean to Sumatra to fetch gold. On the orders of King Necho Phoenicians starting from the Red Sea made a circumnavigation of Africa, which lasted three years. The Phoenicians were known as the foremost seafaring people. Their most important colony, Carthage, developed on an excellent harbour in a favourable location and attained world importance. The ships of Carthage are said to have reached the fabled land of Ophir. They certainly made many, many voyages to the ends of the then-known world; but only one single major feat of overland transportation by Carthaginians is recorded, Hannibal's crossing of the Alps into Italy. It was a foolhardy enterprise to cross the Alps by mule tracks with the elephants, the armoured units of their day. There was no proper road available. We do not know exactly where the crossing was made. Hannibal cannot have had any supply route by land that was worthy of the name.

Carthage is said to have had 700,000 inhabitants at the beginning of the third Punic war, but was destroyed in 146 B.C. after the war was won by Rome. Because of the attractive transportaton situation the Romans soon started to plan a new settlement on the site. The city was rebuilt under the Emperor Augustus, and thanks to its excellent sea communications soon enjoyed a new blossoming, so that it became the third most important city of the Roman world, after Rome and Alexandria. From 439 to 533 A.D., Carthage was the capital of the Vandal empire, and was then part of the Byzantine empire until it was destroyed by the Saracens in 697. But the favourable transport situation still had a magnetic effect. The big city of Tunis stands today on almost the same spot.

The power of the Greek city states and their wealth and culture were based on shipping too. It is no coincidence that Athens, with the fine harbour of Piraeus, soon excelled all other cities—including the brave Sparta, which lay inland. As an inland city without direct access by water Athens reached a population of something over 400,000 inhabitants. The vital link between Athens and the Piraeus was guarded by walls on both sides.

The chain of Greek colonies extended from the harbour town of Rostov on the Don and Odessa via Syracuse and Naples to Nice, Marseilles and Spain. Many of these settlements, the locations of which were chosen to meet the requirements of trade and transportation, are still important cities to this day. Pytheos of Massilia (Marseilles) sailed in 350 B.C. via the Irish Sea to Norway, and back via the North Sea. The lighthouse built in 279 B.C. at Alexandria, and called Pharos, counted as one of the seven wonders of the world. But while Greek shipping traded far and wide, history does not record any roads built by the Greeks.

The most important Greek colony, Byzantium, won, thanks to its unique transport situation, huge wealth and mighty power. The city covered an area within the Theodosian walls, which were built in 413 A.D., of about 13 sq km, and had perhaps 800,000 inhabitants. After the city, renamed Constantinople, had been captured by the Turks in 1453 A.D. it became the capital of the Turkish Empire. Now named Istanbul, the city is not nowadays the capital of Turkey; but with its population of about two millions it is the economic centre of the country. There will always be an important city on this site.

For the Roman empire, as for its predecessors, sea transport was much more important than road transport. The basis of Rome's power was the Mediterranean basin, which was completely under her control. The city of Rome was supplied with its main requirements by sea transport in the form of sailing ships and rowing ships (triremes and quinquiremes) which brought grain from North Africa to the harbour of Ostia or even up the Tiber right into the city. Roman triremes were rowed up the Danube and the Save. Tacitus reports that the Germans towed a captured Roman trireme up the Lippe. In 5 A.D. a Roman fleet under Tiberius appeared off Jutland. By 100 A.D. Roman seaborne trade extended to China. A first attempt to dig the Corinth canal was made under Nero in 59 A.D. (The canal was finally dug in 1839.)

(b) Middle ages and modern times

After the stormy period of the migration of peoples, the first cities of Western Europe grew up once again on waterways. The three 'Queens of the Mediterranean', Barcelona, Genoa and Venice, dominated the commerce of the South. Florence too was a seaport; it was in a unique situation in that ships could reach it up the Arno, and yet it lay so far inland that the Arabian pirates could not attack it. This put it as far ahead of the harbour city of Pisa as it was of the inland city of Siena.

In the North there arose the Hanseatic League, whose chief member cities were Lübeck, Hamburg, Cologne, Visby, Brunswick, Danzig, Bremen, Rostock and Stralsund, and which had 'counters' in Bruges, London, Bergen and Novgorod. Its members carried on trade from Portugal to Russia, and the League waged war on Denmark over fishing rights and the control of the entrances to the Baltic Sea. The Treaty of Stralsund in 1370 marked the zenith of its power and prosperity.

In the year 1106 the boatmen of Worms formed the first German guild. In 1254 the cities of Mainz, Worms, Oppenheim and Bingen joined together to form the Rhenish League, in order to secure peace. It was soon enlarged to include more than fifty member towns from Cologne to Basle. Traffic from Flanders and the Netherlands to North Italy and beyond to India increased rapidly. The traffic across the Alps could not have been large in terms of volume, but it consisted of high-value goods which yielded a high profit. Until the beginning of the 13th century the only road across the Alps was that via Chur. Then the shorter route over the St. Gotthard pass was opened. The traffic over this pass was the reason for the rapid strengthening of the original Swiss cantons and the founding of the Swiss Federation in 1291. Conversely the collapse of Swiss power at the beginning of the 16th century should not be seen as a purely military and political event; it must be ascribed to the sudden shifting of the transportation routes and the resulting impoverishment of the country—in 1492 Columbus discovered America.

The competition for the trade of the New World was so sharp that already in 1493–94 the overseas territories in the western hemisphere were divided between Spain and Portugal, and in 1529 the lands acquired in the East were similarly divided. In 1497 Vasco da Gama succeeded in rounding the Cape of Good Hope and pressing on to the East Indies. In the course of the next thirty years the Portuguese, in fighting against Arab traders and natives, brought one East Indies harbour after another under their control, and took over the trade in spices and other valuable products of the East on which the wealth and might of Venice had hitherto rested. The route to the East Indies no longer lay via Italy and Arabia but via Lisbon.

This example illustrates vividly how commerce and transportation determine the course of history.

Italy and South and Central Germany were hard hit by the shifting of the trade routes. From then onwards they lay to the side of the world's main trade routes. The most important trade routes in Europe were no longer north–south but east–west. Precious metals streamed in from the Spanish colonies in Central and South America into Europe. Wares from the East Indies were unloaded in Spanish and Portuguese harbours.

This reorientation influenced strongly the position and development of cities and was followed with concern. In 1528 the Welsers of Augsburg, with the permission of the German Emperor, fitted out three ships in Spain which, under the command of Ehinger of Ulm, took possession of Venezuela. They wanted in this way to arrest the annihilating blow which the discovery of the sea routes to America and the East Indies had dealt their burgeoning city. This first German colony was given up in 1554.

After the destruction of the Spanish Armada in 1588 the Netherlands, England and France attracted more and more overseas trade to themselves. The Spaniards had to withdraw from North America. Formosa, Indonesia, Tasmania, Ceylon, the Cape of Good Hope and Guyana came into Dutch possession, and so for a brief period did New York and Brazil. The Portuguese possessions in the East fell mostly into English hands. France conquered Canada and Louisiana, the islands in the Caribbean Sea and certain colonies in the Far East.

The fight for world trade never ceased. Napoleon imposed the continental blockade against British trade. After his fall Britain took over the lead not only in politics and economics but also in technology and especially transportation technology. The British Empire was the empire of the steamship and the railway. Britain ruled the sea routes to the Far East with her coaling stations at Gibraltar, Malta, Egypt, India, Ceylon, Singapore and Hong Kong. The Cape-to-Cairo railway was intended to be another axis of imperial power. In the First World War Britain blockaded the German seaboard; in the Second World War Britain and Germany fought the Battle of the Atlantic.

B

Russia's 'push to the sea' is marked by the foundation of St. Petersburg in 1703 and Vladivostok in 1860, the constant pressure on Turkey over the Dardanelles and the annexation of Königsberg in 1945. The importance of shipping in the 20th century has been underlined by the conflicts over the harbour cities of Port Arthur, Danzig and Trieste and the nationalization of the Suez Canal in 1956.

(c) Canal building

The importance of water transport over the centuries can be read from a list of the canals that have been built:

540–1320   Peking–Hangchow canal built by Chinese Emperors
Since the
11th century—The Naviglio Grande from the Adriatic to Milan
1390–97   Elbe–Trave canal with simple locks
1604–42   Briare canal built to link Seine and Loire
1667–81   Canal du Midi from Garonne to Mediterranean (279 km long, 20 m wide, 2·00 m deep)
1732   Ladoga canal from Petersburg to Volga (110 km long)
1783–1834   Rhine–Rhone canal, Strasburg–Mulhouse–Burgundy
1810–24   North Sea canal to Amsterdam
1817–25   Erie canal, Buffalo to Albany (544 km long)
1836–45   Ludwigskanal linking Main and Danube (172 km long)
1838–54   Rhine–Marne canal via the Saverne gap
1859–69   Suez canal (112 km long)
1894   Manchester Ship Canal (64 km long)
1887–95   Kaiser-Wilhelm or Kiel canal (99 km long)
1906–14   Panama canal (80 km long)
1905–38   Mittellandkanal linking Rhine and Elbe

and in recent years the Great Alsace Canal, canalization of the Moselle and Neckar rivers, and construction of the St. Lawrence Seaway enabling ocean-going ships to reach the Great Lakes.

(d) Ships

Some manuscripts in the archives of Salamanca appear to prove that, in the year 1543, a naval captain, Don Blasco de Garay, invented a machine moved by steam, and capable of propelling ships by means of paddles, independently of oars or sails. The apparatus was fitted to a vessel of about 200 tons, called *La Santissima Trinidad*; and an experiment was conducted in Barcelona roads which resulted in the ship attaining a speed of one league per hour.

In 1736 Jonathan Hills took out a patent in England for applying the steam-engine as a motive power to propel ships. Steamboats were built in France from 1774. In 1802 a steamboat built by Symington was demonstrated on the Forth–Clyde canal (it was not used commercially for fear of the wash damaging the canal banks).

In 1803 the American Fulton, in collaboration with Livingstone, tested out a steamboat on the Seine. Later he went to England to promote his plans for building a submarine. In 1806 he returned to the U.S.A. and built there a usable steamboat, for which Watt supplied the engine. In 1807 this boat made its first trip on the Hudson from New York to Albany. In 1812 he built a steam ferry for service between New York and Jersey City.

The new means of propulsion made rapid strides. In 1816 the first English steamer appeared on the Rhine; and in 1818 another appeared on the Elbe. In 1819 the paddle-steamer *Savannah* crossed in 26 days from America to Liverpool. In 1824 the first steamer services started on the Lake of Constance. In 1829 Ressel built the first screw-driven steamer in the Austrian port of Trieste.

In 1911 the first diesel-engined ship appeared. In 1930 the German remote-controlled target ship *Zähringen* came into service. In the 1940s pusher tugs, already much used on the Mississippi, made their appearance on European inland waterways. In 1962 the first regular hydrofoil services were started.

It must be remembered that the fastest ship in 1881 ran at 32 km/h, the *Bremen* in 1929 at 53 km/h and the *Normandie* in 1935 at 54 km/h. Even the newest ships do not have a very much higher speed—apart from hovercraft. Only warships are faster. The world water speed record, which rose to 228 km/h in 1939 and to 258 km/h in 1950, is of no significance for transportation.

Coal has long been replaced by oil as fuel for ships. The first nuclear-powered ships are already running. But the new forms of propulsion are not causing any revolution in sea transport. Operational questions are the subject of the closest attention, e.g. the most economical size of ship and the shortening of loading and unloading times.

2. Road traffic

(a) Roads

The Assyrians, Babylonians and Egyptians built fairly good roads. According to Heroditus the Persian empire had a road 2,300 km long from Sardis in Lydia to Susa in Iran, on which Darius Hystaspis introduced a postal service in the 5th century B.C. The pontoon bridge which Darius I built across the Bosporus in 514 B.C. and the two which Xerxes built across the Dardanelles in 480 B.C., are well known. Only now, 2,500 years later, a fixed bridge over the Bosporus is planned.

Road-building also began very early in China, India and Peru. Everywhere roads served mainly for defence purposes. A realm without such power axes, the empire of Alexander the Great, was bound to fall apart rapidly.

The Roman roads are well known. But these, too, had to carry very little goods traffic. They were first and foremost military links, along which troops could be rushed to restless provinces and threatened frontiers. Messengers and riders conveyed important news along them. The best-known Roman road was the Via Appia, which was completed as far as Capua by 312 B.C. and was extended to Taranto by 270 B.C. From 170 B.C. onwards the streets of Rome were paved. In 55 B.C. Julius Caesar built a pile bridge over the Rhine at Bonn. In 36 B.C. a road tunnel 700 m long was cut through for the Via Flaminia between Naples and Pozzuoli. In 313 A.D. the first Rhine bridge at Cologne was erected. In the 2nd century A.D. the Roman road network was between 60,000 and 120,000 km in extent. The roads were between 4 and 7 m wide, and generally had no gradients steeper than 10 per cent. They were built as straight as possible and preferably on high ground.

Apart from this planned network of roads, the amber road must be mentioned. This ran southwards from Samland in East Prussia. Nero sent a Roman knight there. The amber coast was probably brought into the Roman trading world as a result of this expedition. There were salt roads in several areas. A frankincense road ran south from Gaza in Palestine via Mecca. The names of these roads are a sign that they were used mainly for transporting very valuable goods of low weight. The technological means were not available for bulk transport of goods by road.

An important road was the silk road which in about 270 B.C. ran from Seleukia on the Tigris eastwards via Ebbatana (now Merv), Baktra and the southern edge of the Gobi desert. In A.D. 165 a Roman embassy is said to have visited China. Since then the link with the Far East was never entirely broken. A Christian priest is said to have travelled from Rome to Peking in the year A.D. 630. In 1245–47 the Franciscan Plano de Carpini travelled, on the orders of the Pope, via Hungary, Kiev, Rostov and the northern shores of the Caspian and Aral seas to Karakorum, where he visited the Great Khan, ruler of the Mongolian empire which at that time included the whole of China. In 1253–55 he was followed by the Fleming Wilhelm van Ruysbroek, who used a similar route. Between 1255 and 1269 the brothers Niccolo and Matteo Polo of Venice carried out a trading trip to Peking. Niccolo's son Marco accompanied them in 1271 on their second trip via the silk road to China, and returned with them by the sea route via Indonesia and India. In 1298 he wrote his celebrated account of the journey.

As world population increased and living standards rose, transportation gradually increased. In the 13th century the Arabs, who controlled all trade from Spain to the southern part of East Africa, Ceylon and the Sunda islands, transported cotton to Europe. It was transported by sea across the Mediterranean and then across the Alps to Augsburg, where it was processed.

It was only in the 16th and 17th centuries that road-building in Europe was appreciably improved, especially in France and in Great Britain. Napoleon I built his roads with the same objects in mind as the Romans, and therefore they were made as straight as possible and mainly for military purposes. In the first decades of the 19th century, road-building increased in tempo. In 1819 Macadam described his new road-building method. But soon the railways took over the long-distance traffic. Main roads lost their importance. Only local road traffic on the feeder routes to railway stations continued to increase.

(b) Vehicles

The origin of wheel and wagon is not known. Around 3500 B.C. the Sumerians are said to have used, for military purposes, four-wheeled vehicles with disc wheels drawn by four donkeys. Spoked wheels were used from about 2400 B.C. About 1700 B.C. horses and carts are said to have been brought from Mesopotamia to Egypt. Around 1300 B.C. the Egyptians were using two-wheeled war chariots.

The Romans used many types of two- and four-wheeled vehicles for the transportation of persons and goods. In urban transport the sedan-chair was gradually replaced by the vehicle. The German tribes possessed carts which they used to form barricades. At the time of the Merovingians the princes used ox-drawn carriages. Charlemagne had one hauled by four oxen. From the end of the 12th century, vehicles were drawn in Central Europe by horses.

In the 15th, 16th and 17th centuries, experiments were made in China, Britain, Holland and Germany with other types of propulsion. In 1447 there is mention of a man-propelled vehicle in Memmingen. Sailing-cars are mentioned at the end of the 16th century. In 1649 the Nuremberger Hautsch built a man-propelled car. From this is said to have developed the scooter which Drais introduced in 1817 in Mannheim. This vehicle disappeared into oblivion until Michaux equipped it with pedals and exhibited it at the Paris Exhibition of 1867. Thus was the pedal-cycle born.

Public transport also started fairly early. In 1657 De Givry received permission to run a service in Paris using two-wheeled four-seater vehicles. From 1662 for the next fifteen years a service was maintained on five routes using six-seat and later eight-seat horse buses, the 'Carrosses à cinq sous'. In Vienna an 'Order concerning hired vehicles' was promulgated in 1720. In Berlin in 1739 King Friedrich Wilhelm I authorized fifteen vehicles to ply for hire.

The first omnibus services of modern times were those introduced in Nantes in 1826, in Bordeaux in 1827 and in Paris in 1828. The buses had fifteen seats to begin with and were drawn by three horses. Buses were introduced in London in 1829, in Berlin in 1837 and in Hamburg in 1839.

The use of steam power brought a big advance. The engineer Cugnot began building steam-propelled road vehicles in Paris about 1760. Like so many other technical innovations this was adapted first for military purposes. In 1769 Cugnot built a steam-driven vehicle for transporting cannons.

This thinking was taken up in England. In 1785 Murdoch, a collaborator of Watt, built a steamcar. A whole generation of engineers took this thinking further. Evans built an amphibious steamcar, to run on land or water. In 1793 in Vienna 'some crazy man made experiments' with an invention which he called a railway. Trevithick built a large steamcar in 1801, long before the first railway. In 1830 there were twenty-six steamcars in use in London. A few steam buses were still in use in 1900 in London. They had thirty-six seats and travelled at 16–19 km/h (10–12 mph).

The well-known German economist Friedrich List wrote in 1834:

> The steam-driven road vehicle will never be suitable for the transport of goods and still less for that of people. Fifteen km/h (or 9 mph) is the fastest that it can travel over uneven rural roads. Even at this speed it is liable to fall to pieces, and if it does so the traveller is helplessly stranded and must take up his walking-stick. No time should be wasted on these vehicles.

The building of railways encountered formidable opposition from various sides, but its victorious progress was continuous. For decades it relegated road transport to a subordinate role. The reversal of this process was due not only to Daimler, who patented his first car in 1883, or Benz, with his three-wheeled car of 1885, or Diesel, with his new type of engine of 1893, but also to Dunlop who, with his pneumatic tyre of 1885, at last made comfortable suspension of road vehicles possible. Road building also made great progress. The way was open for modern road traffic.

(c) Motor traffic

The new development of transportation is often wrongly described as motorization. But the essential feature of this development is not the introduction of a new form of propulsion, which has happened to a large extent on water, on rails and in the air: it is rather the invention and rapid popularization of vehicles which every individual can own and operate himself. Motor-cars, motor cycles and also pedal cycles have brought an astonishing improvement and extension of transportation possibilities. But they have also brought with them traffic congestion: shortage of space for traffic.

Travel speeds increased rapidly. The memory of this development is so fresh in the minds of the present generation that there is no need to describe it here. By 1910 quantity-produced cars were capable of 80 km/h (50 mph). Racing cars were already doing more than 150 km/h. In 1934 the racing driver Rosemeyer died while making a test run at 440 km/h on the Frankfurt–Darmstadt motorway when a side wind forced him off the roadway.

But maximum speed has long since lost its significance. Interest is turning more and more away from motor racing towards tests for reliability, durability, beauty of form, winter safety and, last but not least, economy; for these are the qualities that are most important to the car owner.

The question of propulsion is now of secondary importance. Steam engines were followed by petrol and diesel engines, electric motors run off overhead wires or batteries, gas turbines and rotary engines. If one day nuclear power is introduced for heavy vehicles, traffic flow will hardly be affected. Engine technology makes very high speeds possible; but very high speeds cannot be permitted from the traffic engineering point of view.

In most countries maximum speed is limited by law. Where no such limit exists the number of accidents is not very much greater, but the severity of accidents is much greater. The force of impact increases as the square of the speed. This well-known physical law means that the same accident will cause only light property damage at 40 km/h (25 mph) but will cause serious personal injury at 60 km/h (38 mph). Unfortunately there are always know-it-alls who do not want to recognize this fact, even though it has been unequivocally confirmed by the experience and the accident statistics of many countries. But the limitation of speed is not only of value for safety reasons; it also increases road capacity. Every channel of movement has the greatest capacity when all vehicles are travelling at the same speed. The greater the differences in speed the smaller is the capacity. Recognizing this fact many countries have set minimum as well as maximum speed limits on motorways and expressways.

The adolescence of motor transport is over. It has become an established part of economic life. The industry produced the following numbers of motor vehicles in the years shown:

	1898	1906	1965
France	1,631	55,000	1·6 million
U.K.	682	27,000	2·2 million
Germany [in 1965 Western]	894	22,000	3·0 million
Italy	0	18,000	1·2 million
U.S.A.	0	58,000	11·1 million
Russia	0	0	0·6 million
Japan	0	0	1·9 million

Altogether over 24 million vehicles were produced in 1965.

The number of registered vehicles throughout the world is already well over 180 million.

3. Rail transport

(a) Development

As long ago as 1430 an illustrated manuscript on techniques of warfare mentioned wooden rails fixed with iron. In German mines in the 16th century hollowed-out ways were used and also rails made partly of iron to facilitate the movement of trucks in the coal-drifts. In the first half of the 17th century wooden railways were used in England as a substitute for ordinary roads. In 1765 rail tracks were used in Newcastle for bringing coal from the pits to the quays where it was shipped. In 1767 the Colebrook

Dale iron works laid a track made of cast iron rails, apparently because there was for the time being no demand for its iron owing to an economic crisis. The rails proved very successful owing to their low rolling resistance. From them the modern type of rail gradually developed.

In the middle of the 18th century, stationary steam engines were being used in the coal-mining areas of Wales and Scotland to haul wagons up steep gradients by means of chains or ropes. In 1784 Watt patented a steam locomotive—but the first usable steam locomotive was put into operation by Trevithick and Vivian in 1805. The former had experimented for years with steam-propelled road vehicles, making use of Cugnot's experience. At that time it was feared that the adhesion between wheel and rail would not be sufficient to pull a heavy train. This opinion was represented by the physicist Arago, who proved 'scientifically' that heavy loads could never be moved on a railway. For this reason Blenkinsop in 1811 equipped his machine with a rack and pinion.

In 1814 George Stephenson started hauling coal trains at Newcastle with smooth wheels. The steam engine needed less power on smooth rails than on a rough road surface, or alternatively much heavier loads could be transported with the same power. Moreover the engines lasted longer. Thus the railway was born. A combination of steam propulsion and iron rails provided a land transport system of great capacity, such as had never existed before. The first railway for public transport was opened in 1825 between Stockton and Darlington.

This short account shows that the railway was not suddenly discovered. It was the result of the dogged efforts of engineers over many decades, who went forward step by step. This is stated not to detract from Stephenson's reputation, but to counteract the popular idea of sudden development of technology. No one will make a sudden breakthrough which will solve present-day traffic problems at a single stroke.

On the continent of Europe there were already in 1826 more than 250 km of iron railways with horse-drawn vehicles, of which about 60 km were in the coal-mining areas of the Ruhr and the Saar. The building of iron railways started in 1827 in France (for horse-drawn traffic between St. Etienne and the Loire) and also in the U.S.A. In 1830 the 45-km line from Prague to Lana was opened. It was followed in 1832 by the 127-km line from Linz to Budweis in Austria. At that time Austria had a marked technological lead. The next lines to be built were Nuremberg–Fürth (1835), Paris–St. Germain (1836), Dresden–Leipzig (1837–39), Vienna–Wagram, Berlin–Potsdam and Petersburg–Zarskoje Selo (all in 1838). The total length of railway lines throughout the world grew as follows:

1840	7,679 km
1860	108,000 km
1880	372,000 km
1900	790,000 km

1920   1,160,000 km
1938   1,330,000 km
1960   1,500,000 km

Important dates in the history of railways are:

1856   Baden Black Forest railway Offenburg–Triberg–Constance opened
1863   First underground railway in London
1867   Brenner railway Innsbruck–Bozen opened
1869   First transcontinental railway in U.S.A. completed
1850–57   Mont-Cenis tunnel, 13 km long
1872–81   St. Gotthard tunnel, 15 km long
1878   First elevated railway in New York
1879   First electric locomotive built by Siemens in Berlin
1881   First electric trains in Berlin
1891–1900   Trans-Siberian railway built
1900   Paris metro started
1900   First trolley bus in Bielatal near Dresden
1898–1912   Jungfraujoch railway built
1913   First diesel locomotive
1938   First 'push-pull' trains in Germany
1962   First remote-controlled underground train in New York

(b) The battle of the gauges

A significant event at the beginning of the railway age deserves to be mentioned. The first railways in England were built with different gauges. Stephenson had chosen a gauge of 1,435 mm (4 ft $8\frac{1}{2}$ in) because of the construction of his locomotives, and this later became the standard gauge. Other gauges were used by other companies, the largest of them, 2,100 mm. (6 ft $10\frac{1}{2}$ in) by the Great Western Railway (hence its name). Similarly on the continent differing gauges were used, e.g. in Baden 1,800 mm was used at first.

The battle of the gauges brought considerable economic disadvantages, until it was finally ended in 1845 by a decision of the British Parliament which laid down the standard gauge as compulsory and compelled railways in Britain to make a costly conversion. The railway networks of India and Australia are fragmented to this day into systems with different gauges.

The present century has witnessed a similar battle over types of electrification. In 1912 the Union of German Railway Administrations, whose membership included all railways from Austria–Hungary and Switzerland to the North Cape, decided in favour of electrification with 15,000 volt A.C. and $16\frac{2}{3}$ cycles. The electric Trans-European Express trains between Switzerland and Holland now start off with this current, and then run across France using 25,000 volt A.C. and 50 cycles, across Belgium using 3,000 volt D.C. and finally into Holland using 1,500 volt D.C.

The confusion over the gauges could have been a lesson that small-scale measures in competition with other transport concerns are generally damaging to one's own concern and to the public at large. But in the event this lesson went almost unheeded. Some railway companies deliberately set out to place other carriers at a disadvantage or to hinder interchange between different systems. An example is the Berlin underground station called Stadtmitte, at which interchange between the platforms of two different companies whose lines intersected there was deliberately made difficult. The warring companies have long since been merged; but the mistake can no longer be made good, and everyone changing from one line to the other must make a time-consuming, uncomfortable trek through the long connecting tunnel. Many other examples exist, above all of poor interchange between road and rail. This should be an awful warning. The engineer must think big!

Things are no better, despite the demand for standardization, in other fields of technology—e.g. in television. Mention may also be made of the 'keep right' and 'keep left' rules on roads and railways in different countries. Engineers would like to see uniformity in this matter, but this would now be extremely expensive to achieve, and has also now become an economic and political question.

(c) Speed

On railways, high speeds were reached quite early on. Milestones in the development were the following trips:

Stockton–Darlington railway, George Stephenson	1825	20 km/h
Locomotive competition Manchester–Liverpool, George Stephenson	1829	47 km/h
English steam train, Robert Stephenson (son of George)	1851	104 km/h
Experimental electric railcar on the Marienfelde–Zossen line, Siemens and Halske (Berlin)	1902	211 km/h
'Rail Zeppelin' with air propeller, Kruckenberg	1930	230 km/h
Opel's rocket car, wrecked during test on Lüneberg Heath	1935	450 km/h
Electric train of S.N.C.F., Bordeaux–Hendaye	1955	331 km/h

After the 1955 test run the French stated that this was only a test of wear and safety, and that they were not thinking of pushing speeds up so high. Sixty years after the Berlin high-speed tests a speed of 200 km/h was attained in normal operation on Japan's New Tokaido Line, a standard-gauge line from Tokyo to Osaka.

A further raising of maximum speed is hardly to be expected. Thus development in this direction is just as complete on railways as it is on water and on the roads. In this respect no more great tasks will be set for mechanical engineers. And things will be no different even if nuclear power should replace 'conventional' diesel and electric traction.

For several decades the railways, under the impetus of sharp competition from road transport, have been concentrating their attention on questions of operating economy. Costs rise with rising speed, except for manpower costs per train-mile which decrease. A study of operating economy on the German State Railways in 1925 showed that the most economical speed for passenger trains, at which total costs per train-mile (material and manpower costs) are minimized, was 60 km/h. Since then, wage costs have risen faster than material costs. The most economical speed must therefore be considerably higher. The railways are therefore compelled, as a matter of urgent necessity, to force up speed for the mass of trains, which for many routes is no higher than it was in 1914. Requirements of traffic and operating economy are now of the first importance; questions of building and mechanical technology are less important than formerly.

4. Air transport

Flight has been a dream of mankind's since time immemorial. Greek mythology tells of Dädalus and Ikarus, the Norse sagas of Wieland, who fled from the court of King Nidung in a flying suit which he had made himself. Archytas of Taranto is said during the 4th century B.C. to have prepared a dove which lifted itself into the air with 'aura spiritus'. In the 9th, 10th and 11th centuries of our era, the Arabs carried out attempts at flying and gliding, which failed. In 1670 the Jesuit Lana described a proposed airship which was to be supported by metal balls emptied of air.

The first man to fly was the Portuguese Don Gusmao, who at Lisbon in 1709 made a flight in an airship. The discovery was forgotten until in 1783 at Annonay Montgolfier had a balloon filled with warm air lifted into the air. In 1785 Blanchard crossed the English channel from Dover to Calais by balloon. From 1794 to 1799 the French Army already had two companies of balloonists.

Between 1812 and 1816 the German Leppich built in Russia an airship shaped like a fish, which was to be used against the Napoleonic armies. In 1852 Giffard produced a dirigible airship with a 3-hp steam engine, which reached a speed of almost 10 km/h.

In 1898 Count Zeppelin began his airship experiments. In 1924 his ZR III crossed the Atlantic. The building of airships for transportation purposes ended in 1937 with the destruction of the *Hindenburg* while landing at Lakehurst. Airships never attained any appreciable economic importance. Aeroplanes virtually drove them to the wall.

A few dates in the development of heavier-than-air aircraft may be mentioned. A vain attempt at heavier-than-air flight was made in 1811 by

Berblinger, the 'tailor of Ulm'. From 1894 onwards Lilienthal made gliding flights of up to 300 m. He was killed while gliding near Berlin in 1896.

In 1903 the Wright brothers made the first flight using an engine. In 1907 the first helicopter flew. In 1911 Hirth reached a record height of 3,900 m. In 1912 the first parachute descent from an aeroplane was made. In 1915 Junkers built the first all-metal aircraft. The first jet aircraft flew in 1940.

The speed of aircraft increased rapidly. The records set up were as follows:

1909	77 km/h
1913	200 km/h
1925	486 km/h
1939	755 km/h
1963	more than Mach 2·5

Maximum speed is of importance only for military aircraft. The speed of airliners rose from 250 km/h in 1932 to 500 km/h in 1952. In 1952 the British introduced the first jet airliner (the Comet). In 1956 the Russians introduced jet airliners (Tu 104) with a speed of 800 to 900 km/h. The American 707 followed in 1958. Supersonic airliners can be expected to enter service in 1970. This date is determined less by technical than by financial considerations. The airliners need a breathing space to enable them to write off the jet airliners purchased in the past few years.

The use of supersonic airliners makes sense only on long routes. A study in the year 1960 assumed an average non-stop flight of 5,600 km (3,000 miles). On short routes a marked increase in speed is not likely. But traffic on these routes has increased especially fast in recent years, and will probably in the future also increase faster than long-distance traffic. The overloading of roads and railways in the conurbations is causing a switch of passengers and high-value goods from land to air transport. On the shortest routes the competition between helicopters and fixed-wing aircraft has yet to be fought out.

Apart from airline traffic private transport by air is increasing. In the U.S.A. there are already many more than 100,000 private aircraft. In the town of Anchorage in Alaska, which had at the time 45,000 inhabitants, 800 take-offs and landings took place daily in 1953. In the conurbations of Europe such intense air traffic *per capita* is hardly imaginable. Air space is limited. Every air lane and every runway has only a certain capacity. Air traffic control is confronted with extremely difficult tasks. Even with this new means of transport, questions of operating methods are coming more and more to the fore.

Air transport has fundamentally altered our view of the world. Distances are no longer measured in kilometres but in hours. Today it takes longer to reach certain places in one's own country than distant airfields in foreign lands. This can be illustrated by the following examples of comparative travel times in 1967:

FASTEST PLANE		FASTEST TRAIN OR SHIP	
Berlin–Frankfurt	55 min	Berlin–Leipzig	3 h 0 min
Hamburg–Frankfurt	55 min	Hamburg–Kiel	1 h 12 min
Copenhagen–Düsseldorf	1 h 10 min	Copenhagen–Malmo (boat)	1 h 45 min
Copenhagen–Athens	4 h 10 min	Copenhagen–Fridericia	5 h 0 min
Brussels–Geneva	1 h 10 min	Brussels–Ostend	1 h 19 min
Frankfurt–Rome	1 h 35 min	Frankfurt–Cassel	2 h 10 min
Zürich–Düsseldorf	1 h 15 min	Zürich–St. Gallen	1 h 19 min
Zürich–Athens	2 h 25 min	Zürich–St. Moritz	4 h 30 min
Zürich–New York	7 h 30 min	Zürich–Zermatt	6 h 0 min
Vienna–Istanbul	2 h 10 min	Vienna–Salzburg	3 h 50 min
Prague–Moscow	2 h 30 min	Prague–Eger (German border)	4 h 0 min

To the flight times must be added of course the longer time taken to reach the airport and the longer 'despatching time', and also the more frequent delays. Also flights are usually less frequent, so that waiting times are longer. Nevertheless the cities with airports are strongly favoured.

Similarly towns served by motorways or fast train connexions are at an advantage compared with more remote places. On the branch railway lines and lesser roads commercial speed drops to one-third of that on main connexions between big cities, and to one fifth if the trip involves changing trains. Places with good transport links grow faster than the average town and generate especially heavy traffic. In 1958 in Zürich there were 1·4 air trips per 1,000 inhabitants, in the neighbouring town of Winterthur only 0·4 and in rural areas of Switzerland less than 0·1. This preferential treatment for a few cities is not desirable from the planning point of view. Other areas must be served by air.

The transfer of persons and goods from one airline to another and likewise transfer from plane to ground transport and vice versa is becoming more important. Attention is being paid more and more to shortening ground travel and despatching times, to the improvement of reliability, punctuality and regularity, and to operating flights to more places more frequently. In air transport as in other fields of transport the mechanical problems have largely been solved, with the exception of V.T.O.L. or S.T.O.L. But a host of tasks still awaits the transportation engineer in this field.

5. Transmission of news

In the 5th century B.C. Greeks and Persians transmitted news over long distances by means of bonfires. Roman troops on the borders of the empire also communicated by fire signals. Napoleon I also made use of a similar light-telegraph for his communication system. Uniform signals were exchanged between signal towers erected within sight of each other on hills (some of the towers are still standing). In the decisive battle of Water-loo in 1815 Blücher made a quick decision to march his army towards the sound of gunfire, and arrived just in time to help the hard-pressed British army under Wellington, and turn the tide of battle. Neither commander had any kind of technical aid for the transmission of news.

In 1809 Sömmering invented an electro-chemical telegraph which however proved impractical. Morse developed the electro-magnetic tele-graph in 1836. The first telegram was transmitted between Washington and Baltimore in 1844. In 1849 Wilkings described a device for transmitting signals without wires by induction from England to France. Other important dates are these:

1855   Hughes telegraph
1858–66   First transatlantic cable laid
1862   First telephone by Philip Reis
1876   Bell telephone
1893   First wireless telegraphy by Preece over 8 km
1897   Wireless telegraphy by Marconi over 12 km
1901   First wireless transmission across the Atlantic
1910   Wireless telephony over 400 km
1921   Public broadcasting
1922   First picture telegraphed from Europe to U.S.A.
1936   Public television (Berlin Olympic Games)
1962   Telstar; transmission of news via a satellite.

Wireless telegraphy is another example of the fact that technological progress is never made simply by an individual making an unexpected dis-covery. Even in this field it required the efforts of several generations of engineers to bring an idea to fruition. The distance between Marconi and regular television is very comparable with the distance between Cugnot and the first railway. Both developments took about sixty years.

Postal services must also be mentioned at this point. They are not a means of transport but a transport undertaking. The first postal services in mediaeval times were the messenger services set up around 1425 by the free imperial cities of Strasburg, Frankfurt, Cologne, Constance and Augsburg. These were followed by the public messenger service on horseback be-tween the imperial capital, Vienna, and the capital of the Austrian Netherlands, Brussels, created in 1504 by Franz von Taxis, and the post from Vienna to Rome and Naples set up by Johann Baptist von Taxis in 1516. They were the first reliable and regular links.

Today many ways are open for the transmission of news and the transportation of letters and parcels. The greatest problem for the post office is the organization and distribution of the mail, i.e. the operational efficiency at the main interchange points. Thus the post office is con-fronted by problems similar to those confronting the railways, who have the choice of handling their goods traffic at large transportation cost but small organizational cost via a small number of large shunting yards, or alternatively handling it at small transportation cost but large organizational cost via a large number of shunting yards. Transport itself has long since been solved as a technical problem.

Communication technology has become an indispensable aid for all carriers on land, water or in the air, whether it is in the management of a transport concern, the booking of air travel, television surveillance of road traffic or all manner of other tasks.

6. Special modes of transport

Technology has developed a large number of other modes of transport which must not be overlooked. The following may be mentioned:

Pipelines for
 Water (e.g. aqueducts in ancient times)
 Oil (pre-1900 in the U.S.A.)
 Gas (trunk pipelines Ruhr–Berlin, Saar–Paris)
 Coal dust suspended in water
 Mail (first piped mail in 1858 in London)
 Milk (in Valais)
Overhead and underground cables for electric current
Special types of railway, e.g.
 Cog-wheel railway (1867 in Philadelphia, 1871 on the Rigi)
 Suspended trains (1898–1903 in Wuppertal)
 Monorails of various kinds (trials in Ireland in 1888)
 Cable cars (San Francisco 1873)
 Aerial ropeways, chair lifts, ski lifts
Conveyor belts of all kinds (used for coal transport over 180 km in the
 U.S.A.)
Escalators (the first at the Paris World Exhibition of 1900)
Conveyor belts for people
Lifts, paternosters
Rockets (first Russian space flight in 1961, first American in 1962;
earlier attempts to use rockets for carrying mail)

As a rule these means of transport perform only special limited functions; but they provide a useful rounding out of the transport network. Oil and gas pipelines have attained a big economic importance, strongly influencing the flow of goods traffic, and they cannot be overlooked in the context of overall transportation planning.

7. Interaction of the different modes of transport

(a) Competition

On land, on water and in the air there are nowadays many different means of transport, all of high capacity, available; and their networks are closely interrelated. There is to some extent sharp competition between them, which spurs them on to technical and economic improvements. Each has certain advantages and disadvantages. Each should be used in its proper place. We cannot dispense with any one of them, even though the boundaries between them may be in flux.

In general the newer means of transport—oil pipelines, aircraft, motor vehicles—are increasing their share of the transport market at the expense of the older means. However, the reverse process can quite often be observed. For instance, the Upper Rhine as far as Basle was made navigable for large craft in 1904, when the railway had long held a commanding position. In 1952 more than 43 per cent of all Switzerland's foreign trade was carried via the Rhine waterway.

A large part, if not the major part, of the traffic carried by the new means of transport is new traffic which was formerly served by no other means of transport. This was once true of the railways, when they entered into competition with roads and inland shipping.

The transportation engineer must have some idea of the likely future development of each type of carrier's share of the market. Special attention must be paid to the competition between road and rail, for this has a particularly marked effect on transportation planning.

In all the confused discussion about the future of road and rail transport, three distinct questions must be distinguished:

Public and private transport concerns
Public and private transportation service
Rail and road as technical means of transport

Whether public or private traffic concerns are preferable is not a question for consideration here: it is a question of economic and transportation policy which will be decided differently in different countries.

The clearer expressions 'collective transport' or 'mass transit' are often used in place of 'public transport'; while 'individual transport' may be used to describe 'private transportation service'. Private concerns can provide 'public transport'; and public authorities can operate private vehicles.

(b) Technical comparison of rail and road

In any long-term assessment of the rail versus road question the starting point must be the technical advantages and disadvantages of the two means of transport. The question has little or nothing to do with the type of propulsion. On the roads there were still steam lorries running thirty years ago; there are buses and lorries with electric traction (trolleybuses and battery-driven vehicles); on railways there are petrol- and diesel-engined vehicles from the trolley to the fast railcar. The real difference lies entirely in the track itself.

The steel rail has certain physical and technical advantages. It enables vehicles to follow a fixed line: every wagon or carriage of a long train will follow the same path within a few millimetres. The running surface consists of a high-value material. The 'iron road'—it would be more correct to speak of a 'steel road'—usually has a useful width of $2 \times 60 = 120$ mm (width of the two top surfaces). A roadway on the other hand has to be drivable over its whole width, and to withstand the maximum wheel pressure at every point. For economic reasons it must therefore be made out of a cheaper material. The wheel load of a road vehicle cannot be as high as that of a rail vehicle.

The high-value running surface of the railway track is characterized by a low rolling resistance: with steel wheels it is only 2 kg/ton on a straight, level stretch, and about three times that value with rubber-tyred wheels (such as were being tried out experimentally even on steel rails). With the grooved rails used for trams it is about 4 kg/ton. The best concrete or bituminous road surfaces have a rolling resistance for rubber-tyred wheels of 13–14 kg/ton. Of course road surfaces offering less rolling resistance could be made, but they would provide too little grip to guard against sideways forces and skidding. Shiny asphalt road surfaces are notorious, and snow- and ice-covered surfaces are feared by drivers.

Apart from rolling resistance we must consider also:

Climbing resistance, which is exactly the same for road and rail.
Curve resistance, which has so far not been precisely determined in the case of roads, and is not of great importance with either form of transport.
Air resistance, which is the same for individual vehicles with the same cross-section, but is smaller per unit for trains because each unit is partly 'sheltered' behind the one in front.

As a general average the ratio of total resistances encountered by a vehicle on rails to those encountered by one on a road is 1 : 8, reducing in some cases to 1 : 5. For the same transportation task, therefore, road transport requires as a rule eight times as much power—current, coal, oil or petrol—as rail transport with steel wheels on steel rails.

Since with rail transport the rails absorb all sideways forces, trains can be as long as the operator desires. In Europe goods trains are regularly 650–750 m in length; in America they are sometimes more than 2 km long. Because of inadequate side friction between wheel and roadway, especially when it is raining or there is snow or ice on the road, the length of bus or goods vehicle tractor-trailor combinations is limited by law in most countries to between 16·50 and 22 m (55 to 73 ft). With the maximum permitted loading per metre of roadway, the maximum total loads of a road combination and of a goods train are:

Goods train on rails: 650 m $\times$ 8 tons/m = 5,200 tons
Road tractor-trailer: 18 m $\times$ 2 tons/m = 36 tons

Thus the biggest operating unit on rails can carry 140 times the tonnage of the biggest road unit. This means that the driver's wages are spread over a much bigger tonnage. And a train is simpler to drive since the driver controls only the speed but not the direction; train-driving can even be automated.

As regards passenger traffic the comparative values are:

Suburban railway train (single-floor stock): 1,600 persons.
Articulated bus with standing passengers: 160 persons.

Thus the ratio between the largest units is in this case 10 : 1. That is why the railways are in a weaker competitive position when it comes to passenger traffic. This is confirmed by conditions in the U.S.A. where long-distance rail travel is very small in volume.

But the high friction and the lack of vehicle guidance are not only a disadvantage to road transport; they are at the same time decisive advantages. The steepest gradient which a vehicle can negotiate is determined by the friction. There are for instance gradients as steep as the following:

On urban streets in San Francisco	31%
On the Turracher Höhe (Austrian Alps)	26%
On the Le Havre–Ste. Marie tramway (now closed), formerly the steepest adhesion railway	11·5%
On the Bernina railway (Switzerland)	7%
On the Höllentalbahn in the Black Forest (previously rack and pinion)	5·4%
On the St. Gotthard railway	2·6%

It is no coincidence that on the continent the gradients on roads are usually given in per cent terms, and those on railways in per mille. (For purposes of comparison the values given above are given in per cent terms.)

The gradient on the St. Gotthard line is so small that a pedal-cyclist could ride up it without great effort. In mountainous country, adhesion railways can gain height only with major artificial lengthenings of the route; and these are costly in terms of construction and operating costs and lengthen journey times. The spiral tunnels on the St. Gotthard and Albula railways are well known. There are no spiral tunnels for roads with the exception of one in Northern Italy. A railway requires, mile for mile, many more bridges, tunnels and other works because it cannot fit so well into the terrain as can a road owing to its flat gradients and the big curve radii dictated by its nature. In Baden-Württenburg the railways have fourteen times the length of bridge per mile as have the roads. Even the motorways in this area require only two-thirds the length of bridge per mile compared with the railways.

Because of the high friction, road vehicles are more 'mountain-happy' than trains. In the case of a transition from a level stretch to a gradient of 14 per cent, the combined rolling and climbing resistance of a road vehicle doubles from 14 to 28 kg/ton, while that of a rail vehicle increases eightfold from 2 to 16 kg/ton. It would thus be wrong, in the case of a level crossing elimination scheme to give road and rail the same gradient.

Friction is even more important for braking. Braking distances are short on the rough surface of a road, and long on smooth rails. To that extent railway operation is more dangerous. Train drivers are usually ordered not to proceed at more than 40 to 55 km/h 'on sight' (the regulation speed varies from country to country). At higher speeds extensive and expensive safety devices are necessary to ensure that trains maintain a sufficient headway. Through the division of the line into block sections, which must be at least the length of the 'distant signal' distance or 400 to 1,200 m, and are usually 700 m long on main lines, the number of trains per hour is reduced. On trunk lines only ten to twelve trains per hour are generally possible; on modern suburban lines with automatic block systems forty trains per hour are possible on one track. On roads on the other hand there is no regulation of vehicle headways by means of signals. On well-designed roads and motorways drivers drive 'at sight' at well over 100 km/h. An uninterrupted traffic lane can take 2,000 cars per hour. That is about fifty times as many 'units' as on the best railway.

Lack of vehicle guidance means freedom of manoeuvre. On railways, trains can usually only pass and overtake each other at stations, which are miles apart. These therefore are 'compulsory points' for time-table planning. Road traffic is free of such fetters. It knows of no time-tables.

Freedom of action means that a road vehicle can reach almost any house or other point at almost any time. Railways and trams mean a more or less long walk or drive for persons and goods to the railway station or stopping place. The advantage of such direct service by road should not however be overvalued in the case of goods traffic, because in Central Europe about two-thirds of all tonnage transported by rail starts and finishes its journey on sidings, so that it is transported 'door-to-door' by rail.

Marshalling trains entails heavy construction and operating costs for the railways. In the case of goods trains these costs amount to about a third of total costs. Road transport knows nothing of such tasks.

Road vehicles are also much better at negotiating curves. Even heavy tractor-trailers and articulated buses can drive round curves of 12 to 15 m radius. The railway requires, with standard gauge, a radius of at least 100 m for sidings. With special rails, the curve radius may in exceptional cases be dropped to 35 m; on sharper bends turntables must be installed. Road vehicles can negotiate a given curve about twice as fast as standard-gauge railway trains.

The physical characteristics regarding friction and vehicle guidance create unequal basic conditions which cannot be eliminated by any technical development and will still be fully effective in the future. They indicate that the mass transport of goods and persons is the proper province of the railway, while the road can best serve individual transport. From the economic and planning points of view it would be of great significance if a clearcut frontier between the two could be found which would make possible a healthy division of work. But this is not possible for various reasons.

(c) Economic assessment

If the prices charged for transporting persons and goods corresponded with the true marginal costs of transporting them, then the relative charges levied for making a given movement by rail and by road might be a suitable yardstick for deciding which of the two modes should be used. But in fact there are considerable differences between the prices charged (fares or freight rates) and the prime costs; and the latter cannot be determined precisely and immutably. The prime cost per passenger-mile or per ton-mile in any particular case depends not only on the choice between road and rail as modes of conveyance, but also on the following factors:

The degree of utilization of the *track*, i.e. on the number of vehicles using a railway track or a traffic lane in the course of a year.

The degree of utilization of the *vehicle*, i.e. on the annual mileage run by each vehicle, powered or otherwise; if the annual mileage run by a 1·5 ton lorry rises from 5,000 to 40,000 km, the prime cost per mile drops by about 75 per cent.

The degree of utilization of the *carrying capacity* of the vehicle, i.e. the load factor in terms of the percentage of seats or cubic capacity occupied; if the load factor on a bus rises from 40 to 80 per cent, the prime cost per passenger drops by nearly 50 per cent.

The size of the *operating unit*, e.g. small railcar or large train, light delivery van or heavy tractor-trailer combination; the prime cost per seat-mile is about half as great for a bus with 120 seats as it is for a bus with 33 seats.

The *despatching* costs—loading and unloading, transfer and train marshalling, costs which do not arise with road transport.

The special burdens on public carriers—obligation to carry, obligation to run a service, tariff conditions, and other obligations which benefit the general economy but not the carrier—need only to be mentioned in passing.

A private carrier can calculate charges in particular cases which are close to prime costs. But a 'mass carrier' must, for practical reasons, use handy tariffs—so much per unit, per length of route, per zone or per mile—which can only relate to average prime costs of all traffic carried during a longish period; and are therefore often unsuitable in particular cases. Moreover political influences lead to the introduction of exceptional tariffs for certain users or areas.

Operational considerations also enter into the picture. A poorly loaded section of a through rail connexion cannot be abandoned by itself in favour of road transport. The requirements of the system as a whole may compel the railways to maintain the more expensive means of transport.

But the price of transport is by no means the only consideration. Other criteria such as speed, comfort and safety play a big role. The expensive taxi finds patrons in competition with the cheap bus. Some people walk in good weather and use the tram when it is raining. Some prefer air travel in summer and rail travel in winter. The trader does not consider freight rates in isolation from other factors; he may be prepared to pay a higher charge for a better service. Machines are often air-freighted overseas so that they are available for use sooner and may perhaps enable a factory to start operating at the right time. Flowers are flown from Holland to the U.S.A. because they would wilt on the long sea-crossing. Tractor-trailer combinations drive right through a neighbouring country in order to save spending foreign currency on rail freight charges. Duration of a journey affects the costs of warehousing or interest charges.

The above is not intended in any way as a criticism of efforts to ensure that fares and freight rates should approximate as closely as possible to prime costs. On the contrary it is highly desirable, from the economic point of view, that they should do so. But there will never be a sharply defined frontier between the competing means of transport in terms of costs. With further technical developments, prime costs will shift in the future as they have done in the past. It is probable that no means of transport will be entirely replaced by another.

(d) New modes of transport

New types of vehicle are likely to make their appearance in the borderland between rail and road. After extensive tests the Paris Metro started in 1957 to substitute concrete for steel rails. This gave rail transport the advantage of high friction, permitting faster acceleration and braking, and also of a reduced noise level. Conversely road vehicles can be more safely guided with the aid of rails, and coupled together to form trains (Uniline in Africa). The 'route guidée' principle (road vehicles following a fixed path) was developed in Germany by Kuch. In Italy, tests are being conducted with such a system (buses guided by a low steel rail); while near Paris tests have been made with an overhead guidance rail.

In the U.S.A. and in Britain, experiments are being made with guiding vehicles by means of high-frequency cables laid in the roadway. Such guidance systems could eliminate 'falling asleep' accidents on long stretches of motorway. But they might also serve to reduce vehicle headways and thus increase the capacity of a traffic lane by a large amount. In Switzerland the possibility of such electrical guidance for bus-trains was tested.

The characteristics of future vehicles could be so selected that they would combine certain of the advantages of road and rail. Their construction must be based on required performance and economy. The latter is hard to achieve with 'road/rail' vehicles which can travel on either rail tracks or roads, but which lose much time at the transfer point and must cart around a large deadweight in the shape of the second set of wheels.

A rapid introduction of new modes of transport is not to be expected.

(e) Land area requirements

In comparing private and public modes of transport in conurbations, one consideration which previously received little attention is becoming of greater and greater importance: land area requirements. A strip of land 3·50 m (11 ft 6 in) wide in an urban area can carry in one hour, with the degree of utilization common in peak hours, the following numbers of people moving in one direction:

700 cars with an average occupancy of 1·5	1,050 persons
150 articulated buses, 160 places each, average load factor 75%	18,000 persons
40 suburban railway trains, 1,300 places each, average load factor 75%	40,000 persons

The figure of 700 cars is appropriate for lanes on inner-urban streets with intersections at grade. For cars used for trips to and from work the average occupancy drops to less than 1·3. With buses a headway of less than 20 sec is ruled out owing to the time needed for boarding and alighting, even if a special bus lane is allocated to them and two-bus stopping places are used.

Trams running on segregated rights-of-way can achieve the same capacity as rail 'rapid transit', e.g. with 120 trains each with an articulated motor-car and an articulated trailer-car, each having a capacity of 220 passengers.

'Mass transit' vehicles are more efficient in their use of land area, though not uniformly so. The individual traveller requires much less space. But what is of decisive importance is that congestion is due to nothing but the shortage of land area. In all other fields of technology, materials have long since been used to the limits of their strengths. Land area, which is also a raw material, must also be more economically utilized.

Development is moving in the direction of combining the advantages of the various modes of transport. Mass transport vehicles are less comfortable than private vehicles; but they are faster where they possess a segregated track. A fairly favourable solution, therefore, is to provide 'park-and-ride' facilities at the edge of the congested area. The interchange facilities, with parking space for private cars and stops or stations for public transport, would need to be very carefully designed. Poor interchange, with long walking distances and appreciable time losses, cancels out all the advantages of 'park-and-ride'. Improvement of interfaces between different carriers is a task of great urgency.

(f) Parts played by the various modes

The development of the various modes of transport can best be illustrated by a few figures from Switzerland, which was spared the direct effects of war. The number of person kilometres per inhabitant by various means of transport in three past years are shown in Table 1, together with the estimated values for 1980; while the corresponding figures for ton-miles per inhabitant are given in Table 2.

Table 1: Annual person-kilometres per inhabitant of Switzerland

Mode	1891–95		1920		1955		1980	
		%		%		%		%
Main-line railways	266	=95	620	=76	1,460	=36	1,850	=20
Trams, mountain railways	7·5	= 3	104	=13	185	= 5	280	= 3
Horse-drawn post van	3	= 1	1	= 0				
Horse-drawn carriage	3	= 1	1	= 0				
Motor bus			1·5	= 0	221	= 5	300	= 3
Trolley bus					40	= 1	70	= 1
Motor-car			27	= 3	1,570	=39	6,000	=66
Motor cycle, motor scooter			6	= 1	330	= 8	300	= 3
Pedal cycle	1	= 0	58	= 7	230	= 6	100	= 1
Aircraft (only over Switzerland from and to Swiss airfields)					24	= 0	300	= 3
Totals	280	=100	820	=100	4,060	=100	9,200	=100

Table 2: Annual ton-kilometres per inhabitant of Switzerland

Mode	1891–95		1920		1955		1980	
		%		%		%		%
Railways	201	= 83	362	= 77	670	= 67	880	= 52
Horse-carts	40	= 17	20	= 4	5	= 0·5		
Motor trucks and vans			86	= 19	327	= 32	780	= 46
Waterway (Rhine only)	0·02	= 0	0·06	= 0	4	= 0·5	5	= 0
Aircraft (as in Table 1)					0·6	= 0	10	= 0·5
Oil pipelines							25	= 1·5
Totals	241	= 100	468	= 100	1,007	= 100	1,700	= 100

The opening of transalpine road tunnels and of shipping on the Upper Rhine (above Basle) could bring about certain shifts.

The figures show what immense tasks the coming years and decades will bring in all fields. The actual traffic requirements in absolute terms will grow even faster owing to the big increase in population—especially in the towns and conurbations with the continued migration to them. The multiplicity of the means of transport will become ever greater.

C. THE DEVELOPMENT OF TOWNS

1. The developer

(a) Town builders

Our generation is faced with the task of adapting towns to the turbulent growth of traffic. Prohibition and direction signs are no longer sufficient for this purpose; they cannot achieve any fundamental improvements. This is a vitally important matter for towns, which must be carefully thought through.

The urban framework must be 'X-rayed' and many parts of it reconstructed. New settlements must be designed in a form which is truly up-to-date and adapted to traffic. New basic principles of town building must be applied. Views and opinions are no longer enough. The new tasks demand that the interaction between transportation and the whole wide field of town and country planning should be thoroughly investigated.

Town building is often thought to be concerned only with buildings. But giving architectonic form to the urban scene and aesthetic form to individual buildings, groups of houses, squares or terraces is only one part of the total task. Town building is much more than this. Of the cost of building a town, fully one-third is for the infrastructure—for public expenditure on roads, bridges, water mains, drainage and ducts and cables of all kinds. Regarding the other two-thirds a uniform guidance and control is only possible to a limited extent, except where public buildings are concerned.

Town building calls for the combined efforts of people in quite different professions, such as:

Financial experts and economists
Lawyers versed in building and property law
Town planners, sociologists, statisticians
Structural engineers, traffic engineers, public health engineers, mechanical engineers, electrical engineers
Architects

Members of each profession can only perform their task correctly if they see it as part of a comprehensive commission and are prepared to work together. No profession is entitled to claim that it should be in overall charge of town building, or should carry more weight than the others. But even all these professions together cannot build a town if there is no developer.

Recently a well-known architect was regretting the fact that, in the reconstruction of German cities after the war, considerations of commerce and public finance had usually predominated; the blame for the transgressions against the laws of architecture lay with the legislator. But this 'urban developer' must inevitably have the last word.

Only a few men or groups of men can lay claim to fame as builders or founders of cities:

The men who, in the colonies of the Greek city-states, Rome and the Western nations, laid out planned cities such as Constantinople, Alexandria, Cologne, New York, Rio de Janeiro, Cape Town, Bombay or Sydney.

The temporal and spiritual princes of the early Middle Ages, like the Zaehringers who founded Berne and the two Freiburgs in Switzerland and in Baden, or the citizens who, in the wide lands from Esthonia to the Siebenbuergen [Transylvania], created cities with German law.

Modern monarchs who founded Karlsruhe, Mannheim, Ludwigsburg, Freudenstadt, Neu-Ulm, the Hague, St. Petersburg.

The various political and economic forces of our time with new capital cities such as Washington, New Delhi, Canberra, Brasilia, Chandigarh.

Harbour cities such as Bremerhaven, Wilhelmshaven, Gdynia, Vladivostock.

Mining cities such as Wanne-Eickel, Oberhausen, Koenigshuette, Magnitogorsk.

Car cities such as Ruesselsheim [Opel], Wolfsburg [Volkswagen], Detroit.

Refugee cities such as Sennestadt, Neu-Gablonz.

Living and dormitory towns around London and other cities.

(b) Responsibility

For a 'polis' to grow up there must be a political will. Town building is an expression of this force as well as testimony to the ability of the professions involved in different ages. A princely capital had a quite different character from a free imperial city. The following pairs of towns illustrate the contrast between generously laid-out capital cities and cramped 'citizens' cities':

The Hague	Amsterdam
Brussels	Ghent
Paris	Dijon
Vienna	Linz
Munich	Regensburg
Ludwigsburg	Esslingen
Mannheim	Heidelberg

Darmstadt	Frankfurt
Dresden	Breslau
Schwerin	Rostock
New Delhi	Old Delhi

Even extensions of such towns look quite different—even those built at the same times.

Similarly the town-building of a democracy can hardly be compared with that of a dictatorship. In a centralized state the capital city is far larger than the other cities of the country concerned (Paris, London, Copenhagen, Oslo, Stockholm, Lisbon, Budapest, Bucharest, Sofia, Athens, Cairo, Bangkok, Tokyo, Buenos Aires); while in a federal state there are many cities of roughly equal size, reflecting the 'political weight distribution' (Germany, Switzerland, Italy before 1870, Yugoslavia, India, Australia, U.S.A., Brazil).

In many towns different political forces were dominant at different periods of history. All of them left their mark. Every town planner and traffic planner is to be recommended to make a thorough study of the history of the building and political development of the town he is working for.

The urban developers in western countries are at present the Burgo-master or Mayor and the elected councillors, flanked by the city officials. They must recognize the far-reaching effects of the decisions they take. Good town building is impossible without mutual understanding and trusting cooperation between the councillors who are responsible to the electorate and the professionals who advise them. Mistakes in town building are still felt decades and even centuries later. The following are examples of unfortunate decisions:

The siting of Cologne's main railway station right next to the cathedral. The way the railway installations cut right through the central areas of Basle, Bonn, Essen, Bochum, Hanover, Dresden, Berlin and Stock-holm.
The poor connexions between the street networks of the old and new towns in Milan, Lucerne, Zürich, Augsburg, Munich, Vienna, Stutt-gart and Düsseldorf.
The siting of disruptive industry on privileged sites in Lausanne, Ulm, Mainz and Wuppertal.

It is only in rare and exceptional cases that anything can be done to correct a badly laid-out settlement or a wrongly located transport artery. In most cases the mistake cannot be rectified. Following generations can clean this or that up a bit, but can seldom, because of legal and economic restraints, carry out a thorough-going revamping. We have only to remember the bitter disappointments encountered in the reconstruction of towns destroyed in the war. Despite the destruction of whole areas of some cities, the planners were not given a 'clean slate'. How many high-flying plans remained on paper, how many hopes had to be buried!

(c) Scale

Much unnecessary work, anger and disappointment can be avoided if the scale on which works should be planned can be determined with careful consideration at the outset. Very often an argument arises as to whether the plans are on too large or too small a scale. Criticism of the order of magnitude of the works envisaged often starts up only at a point in time when considerable work has already been done on a plan. The danger then arises that the work may have to be started all over again from the beginning. The choice of the right scale is undoubtedly difficult, but it cannot be avoided.

A splendid example of a choice of the right technical scale is the St. Gotthard railway crossing of the Alps. For a long time the battle raged to and fro as to whether this line should be built as a rack-and-pinion line, with hairpin curves, with a different ruling gradient or with larger or smaller curve radii. It is astonishing that a solution was adopted at that time which was certainly generous in its design standards, but not excessively so, and is still recognized a century later as being suited to the function the line performs.

In town and country planning it is the human and economic scale with which we are primarily concerned. When a house is to be built, it is not primarily the wishes of the future owner but the length of his purse which determines the size of house—a regrettable but unavoidable fact! It is the same with town-building. Planning must be done within the framework of the resources of labour and materials and the tax revenue likely to be made available within the foreseeable future. This is a prudent saying, but only by recognizing its truth can we get any further.

The scale varies of course from town to town and from country to country, according to the standards of living, the economic situation and the technical and geographical conditions. The following figures are therefore given very tentatively; but we can say that the following sums were spent in 1963 in North and Central European cities on transportation facilities of all kinds:

Population (in '000)	Expenditure *per capita* per annum
20–50	$ 5–10 (£2 to £4)
50–100	$10–15 (£4 to £6)
100–250	$12–20 (£5 to £8)
250–600	$15–22 (£6 to £9)
over 600	$20–30 (£8 to £12)

These figures include all contributions from city and other sources (state, etc.) and all investments by local public transport undertakings, whether private or municipal, other than in vehicles. For comparison we may note that the larger cities spend $1.50 (12s. 6d.) *per capita* per annum on street lighting.

In every town, politicians and professionals must agree on an assessment of future development and make themselves jointly responsible for the proposed order of magnitude of the works to be undertaken. A sensible decision must be based on many years of experience and solid knowledge.

2. Location

'Seldwyla means, in the old language, a delightful and sunny place. . . . The original underlying reason for its location was reinforced by the circumstance that the founders of the town located it a good half-hour from a navigable river, as a clear indication that nothing was supposed to leave the place.'

Gottfried Keller, *The people of Seldwyla*

Transportation has an extraordinary influence on the location of towns and settlements.

The *unplanned* town always lies at a transportation node or at a transfer point between land and water transport. The names of some towns remind us of their location in relation to transport: Strasbourg [Strasse = Street], Frankfurt, Schweinfurt, Oxford, Klagenfurt, Bruges, Brugg an der Aare, Bruck an der Mur, Innsbruck, Zweibrücken [= two bridges], Copenhagen (= trader's harbour) or the frankish places Marktbreit, Marktheidenfeld, Marktredwitz.

A *planned* town which is unfavourably located must integrate itself with the transport network. If it is an industrial town or a source of raw materials attracting or generating sufficient volumes of traffic, it will certainly succeed in doing so. However, a poor location will often hinder the development of a settlement and even lead to its abandonment. Therefore it is a risk to build a 'new town' on virgin ground unless certain conditions are fulfilled. The Australian capital of Canberra has only slightly more than 30,000 inhabitants forty years after it was founded. The idea of building something entirely new certainly has its attractions; but in Europe all locations that are suitable from the standpoint of transport geography have long since become the sites of towns. The enthusiasm for 'new towns' is understandable, but the prudent planner cannot share it.

(a) Water transport

All important Roman towns were on waterways. Already in the early Middle Ages the Roman settlements in Central Europe, with their favourable transport locations blossomed into new life: Cologne, Koblenz, Mainz, Strasburg, Basle and Constance on the west bank of the Rhine, and Regensburg, Passau and Linz on the south bank of the Danube.

Similarly transport was in most cases godfather to the numerous new towns which developed during the Middle Ages. Favourable locations received first the 'market right' and then the 'town right'. But a market is only held at a place which is easily accessible, i.e. which has a favourable transport situation. The trade which a market handles needs a hinterland which is connected to it by transport. The better the transport links the bigger the area can be, and the more important the market.

Figure 3: The free imperial town of Mulhouse in Alsace had only 3,000 citizens in 1642. The scale of the street network was correspondingly modest. Today the same streets must serve the traffic of a town of over 100,000 inhabitants. The irregular alignment of the streets is characteristic.

Since water transport was at the time the only mode of transport of any real capacity, numerous towns grew up on coasts, lakes and navigable rivers. No mediaeval town served only by overland transport reached a population of more than 15,000. Such small towns included the proud free imperial towns of Goslar, Nordhausen, Rothenburg ob der Tauber, Nördlingen, Rottweil, Colmar and Schlettstadt. Their hinterlands could not be enlarged, and no big surpluses could be created. Only where a navigable waterway was available could food be brought in from greater distances and goods be exported in exchange. The further afield the waterway stretched the larger the town could grow. Towns on the coasts could thus develop better than those on rivers, and these in turn could develop better than those on lakes. As examples I would cite:

The harbour towns at river mouths, such as Bordeaux, London,

Antwerp, Rotterdam, Emden, Bremen, Hamburg, Stettin, Danzig, Königsberg, Riga.

The river towns, such as Vienna, Pressburg, Budapest, Belgrade, Prague, Dresden, Magdeburg, Berlin, Breslau and Warsaw.

The towns at the outlets from lakes, such as Geneva, Biel, Lucerne, Zürich and Constance.

Towns which lost their waterways suffered great setbacks. This fate overtook Bruges, Ghent and Ravenna, whose harbours silted up, and Ferrara after the Po changed its course in the 12th century. Ghent improved its position quite recently by building a canal. Bremen recognized the danger to its trade in good time and founded Bremerhaven. Rotterdam is pressing closer to the sea with its Europoort.

The most important towns grew up in the most important trading locations. In the early Middle Ages these were the harbours handling the trade with the East. Thus the following ranking of cities by population in the period 1400–1450 will cause no surprise:

Venice	190,000
Paris	150,000
Palermo	100,000
Florence	90,000
Genoa	80,000
Milan	80,000
Ghent	60,000
Brussels and Antwerp, each	50/60,000
London	40,000
Cologne	30,000
Strasburg, Ulm, Augsburg, Nuremberg, Breslau, Hamburg, each	20/25,000
Frankfurt, Basle, Rostock, each	15,000

Venice had by then grown to be the biggest city in Europe, and controlled a chain of bases as far as Constantinople and the Levant. Paris was in second place. The other towns of the Mediterranean basin were considerably smaller. The big cities of the North were in Flanders. Cities without waterways were far behind.

Following the discovery of the New World and the re-orientation of transport towards the West, by 1575 Paris had grown to 300,000 inhabitants and London to 180,000. These two cities became the leading cities of Europe. The cities of Germany and Italy, far from the new trade routes, fell behind. Vienna, capital of the German empire, did not reach a population of 150,000 until 1720.

In many parts of Europe the cities and states made great efforts to make rivers navigable and to build canals. At that time there was navigation on many smaller rivers, such as the Arno up to Florence and the Danube up to Ulm. Around 1830 the Swabian emigrants to South Russia still travelled downstream on the Danube in the 'Ulm crates'. With the rise of the railways water transport came to an end on many rivers. A new age of town-building began.

In the newly discovered regions of the world the ancient capitals lay inland—e.g. Peking, Kyoto, Delhi and Mexico City. The young harbour towns blossomed quickly: Bombay, Calcutta, Colombo, Rangoon, Singapore, Batavia/Djakarta and Shanghai.

Even internal transport in some towns was predominantly by water, e.g. on the grachten in Amsterdam, Rotterdam and Utrecht, on the fleets in Hamburg, on the canals in Venice and on the klongs in Bangkok.

(b) Rail transport

The railways created for the first time the necessary conditions for the growth of big cities inland. They made possible the industrialization and the tremendous increase of population which began in West and Central Europe and soon spread to the whole world. The last famine in Central Europe was in 1846. After that time the rail network was already so extensive that areas short of food could always be supplied from areas with surplus food. Inland towns, away from waterways, whose size was formerly limited to the area of agricultural production within a few hours' cart journey, could be supplied with food from more distant areas. Their populations grew rapidly. This process faced the experts with unexpected and difficult questions. The architect Wegmann described the new situation in 1854 as follows:

> . . . If we compare the present internal traffic of Zürich with that of 20 years ago, we can see that it has grown phenomenally, and has grown far faster than has the population of the town. Through improved communications, postal and steamship connections, Zürich has become the permanent market serving the needs of an extended area. This will happen to a far greater extent when the mightiest means of communication, the railway, is completed. Then Zürich will become the transport hub for the entire Eastern part of Switzerland . . .

His prediction proved correct. The locational conditions were radically altered. The big railway junctions experienced an unprecedented upsurge. Towns which barred themselves from the new transport mode did not develop. For instance, the town of Tangermünde successfully warded off the threatened construction of the Berlin–Hanover railway across its boundaries. The neighbouring village of Stendal became a railway junction and soon outstripped the old town. It did not help the town that it was later on served by a branch line. The transport planning mistake could not be retrieved. A warning example of another kind is the Swiss National Railway, which was taken westwards from Winterthur, bypassing Zürich a considerable distance to the north. For political reasons it did not follow the line of the main streams of traffic. The financial collapse of the line was not long delayed, even though railways at that time were generally doing very well.

Most towns realized the great importance of railways and actively furthered their construction. The railway policy of the big states was deliberately to orient the systems towards the capital cities. Thus London, Paris, Berlin, Munich, Vienna, Budapest, Leningrad and Moscow, and likewise Chicago and Buenos Aires, became the hubs of railway systems; and the growth of these cities was thereby considerably accelerated.

Several states sought, by means of a parochial building policy, to attract additional traffic onto their own railway systems. For example the five states bordering on the Lake of Constance built their railways quite independently, stopping at the frontiers which Napoleon had arbitrarily created (Fig. 4). Baden's Black Forest Railway had to keep clear of Württemberg and consequently climbs to far too high a summit. Württemberg took its line not to the old town of Lindau but to the new town of

Figure 4: The Lake Constance region, showing the fragmented main railway system. No one town could assume the intellectual and economic leadership of the region—a leadership once exercised by Constance at the time of the Council (1414–18).

Friedrichshafen. Bavaria took its line to Lindau through the narrow, newly formed territorial strip, which entailed big structures and considerable extra distance. Even today through working from one network to another is troublesome. Three reversals are necessary on the main route from Ulm to Chur. Not only was the Lake Constance area torn apart as regards transport, but the emergence of any of the lake towns as the economic and cultural centre of the region was hindered.

Similar examples could be drawn from other areas. If different parties work against each other in the planning of new transportation facilities, all participants usually suffer. This is true in small matters as well as large.

The railways did not in every case follow the old roads and rivers whose traffic they took over. At certain points new settlements grew up. The growth of existing towns was either promoted or hindered. Railway towns grew up at certain hitherto unimportant points. Examples include:

Erstfeld, on the northern approach to the St. Gotthard tunnel.
Olten, where the Basle–Lucerne line crosses the Zürich–Berne line.
Bebra, where the Frankfurt–Hanover line intersects with the Erfurt–Kassel line.
Löhne and Lehrte, junctions west and east of Hanover.

The great marshalling-yard and frontier railway stations are other examples.

At these points numerous railwaymen and customs officials settled. Forwarding firms and ancillary services also grew up. Thus the villages grew rapidly. The railway lines which have been built in recent years in Canada, Siberia and China create the conditions for the birth of new towns in areas hitherto hardly settled.

With the coming of the railways the coal and iron-ore deposits could be and had to be exploited on a much larger scale, for the demand for coal and steel grew rapidly. The biggest groups of industrial towns and the most dense railway networks are to be found in mining areas. But transport benefits other locations, too. The steelworks at Ijmuiden, Bremen, Lübeck, Stettin, Danzig and Narvik are located at the transfer point between land and sea transport, far away from both the coalfields and the Swedish ore-fields. Now the switch from steam to diesel and electric traction on the railways, and their decreasing share of total traffic, is having its effect on the towns located on the coalfields.

(c) Road transport

Modern road transport could not operate to any real effect as a founder of towns in thickly-settled Europe. The most favourable locations already had rail connections. Moreover the road network is much denser than the rail which means less concentration of transport. But industry prefers more and more to locate new plants at points with good motorway and road connections. Such places can expect to grow faster than others.

Overseas certain service areas, workshops and transfer points for long-distance road traffic, for instance on the Alaska highway or the Burma road, could be described as the germ-cells of new settlements. At these points markets grow up to serve the surrounding districts, and these may gradually develop into towns.

c

(d) Air transport

Air transport has influenced settlements only for a short time. It promotes further concentration of population, for only a few large cities can have large-capacity airports. Cities with such airports experience faster growth, because they are chosen as locations for important administrative offices and high-value businesses. Air traffic sponsored the development of many hitherto unknown villages. Extensive settlements grow up close to airports, which have become employment centres for thousands of people. It would perhaps be thought an exaggeration to maintain that air traffic already has a detectable influence on urban development. But its favourable and unfavourable effects on such development can already be clearly seen.

The towns of Dover and Calais have already lost irretrievably a large proportion of the passenger traffic between England and France because the direct air connexions between London and Paris are faster and more comfortable. The special advantages of their locations have been depreciated. The economic basis has become narrower. All seaports are feeling the same squeeze. Their loss is the airport towns' gain. These inland towns are also preferred by certain processing industries whose goods traffic increasingly goes by air. For passenger traffic between Europe and the Far East the airports of Cairo, Damascus and Beirut are far more important than those of Gibraltar, Port Said and Aden. Cape Town, formerly so important as a port of call but already damaged by the building of the Suez canal, is now even more neglected, with most long-distance airlines terminating their South African services at Johannesburg.

(e) Other modes of transport

Locational conditions have been further altered by the special modes of 'transport' used for oil, natural gas and high-voltage electricity. New prerequisites for the location of plants and settlements have been created, others have become less important. Heavy industry is no longer tied to the coalfields. The land use planners have gained in many respects a greater freedom, but have also a greater responsibility. We must bear in mind that a pipeline or transmission line once built will hardly be diverted later.

We certainly cannot dispense with any mode of transport. All have experienced further increases in traffic since the end of the Second World War, but these have been of very different orders of magnitude. Water transport is still the cheapest form of transport for bulk goods. Consequently it still retains its influence on town-building. But changes in modes of transport must be carefully watched. They will be decisive for the further growth of towns.

Conditions of transport geography—the lines of ridges of hills, valleys, rivers and coasts—largely determine the routes followed by land transport modes, and the location of motorway access points, railway stations,

harbours and airports. This is true not only of large areas but also of particular parts of a town.

3. Size and extent

(a) Laws of urban development

The population of a town is limited by the size of the hinterland supporting it, which in turn depends on the modes of transport available. This
first law of town-building has lost its force now that, thanks to the progress
of transport technology, food supplies can be brought in from all parts of
the earth in any desired quantities.

In ancient Rome the citizens could not live at any distance they desired
from the forum, the authorities and offices, the workshops and the harbour.
They had to cover the distance from home to workplace on foot. Only the
Emperor Hadrian was in a position to build his villa far outside the gates of
the city. The mass of the population was housed very badly in cramped,
multi-story tenements. Traffic congestion was already serious at the time
of Caesar. A special law—the Tabula Heracleensis—had to be promulgated, forbidding the use of wheeled vehicles on the city streets during the
first ten hours of the day, i.e. from 6 a.m. to 4 p.m. The only vehicles
exempted were carriages on *official* business, the vehicles of the vestal
virgins during public sacrifices or the triumphal pageant of a victorious
general. The noise of wheels at nightfall was unbearable. The poet Juvenal,
who lived from A.D. 60 to 140, remarked that it would cost a fortune to
find peace to sleep in Rome.

The population of the city is said to have reached 800,000 in 13 B.C.
The same figure has been mentioned for the reign of the Emperor Aurelian
(A.D. 215 to 275). The city covered an area of 12·3 sq km. Estimates that
the population may have exceeded one million are hardly credible in view
of the population density they imply. A spreading out of the town was
not possible since regular 'commuting' on foot was hardly feasible with
walking times of more than thirty minutes.

There is a close relationship between transport technology and the
population of cities. Every citizen must go to work every day and be supplied with the necessities of life. Food and goods have to be brought into
the town and then distributed to every dwelling within it. This is not a
simple matter in big cities. Pedestrians move about within a town—partly
through throngs of people—at about 4·5 to 5 km/h (about 3 mph).
Thus in half an hour they can cover a crow's flight distance of 2 km. A
circle of 2 km radius covers an area of 12·5 sq km—almost exactly the
area of ancient Rome. At an average density of 600 persons per hectare,
750,000 persons can be accommodated. In certain areas of Rome the
density must have exceeded 1,000 per hectare, for the walls enclosed the
Forum, baths, squares and streets. Also the density was not the same in
the different parts of the city. Perhaps the population could have increased

still further through an increase in the residential density; but we know what unhealthy conditions then arise. The residential density of Rome was as high as that in the slums of modern large cities. It is surprising that the other ancient cities of Babylon, Alexandria, Byzantium and Peking had in their heyday almost exactly the same population and area as Rome. There is evidently here a *second law of town-building*: the inner urban modes of transport limit the extent and therefore the population of a town. A 'pedestrian town' cannot grow to more than 800,000 inhabitants.

Paris and London approached this population about the middle of the 18th century. Inner urban passenger and goods transport set a seemingly fixed limit to the growth of these hitherto expanding cities. All citizens had to live very close to the administrations and factories and also the docks on the Seine and the Thames because neither work trips on foot nor delivery traffic by horse-cart permitted larger distances. As in the large cities of ancient times unbearable living conditions were the result, the notorious London slums arose about this time. The French Revolution was probably caused to a large extent by the hopeless conditions that prevailed in the pedestrian city. A huge anger had built up among the population who were crammed together in the narrowest possible space, and this needed an outlet. Everyone knows what severe human problems arose after 1945 out of the housing shortage in the towns destroyed by the war.

It is not by chance that the development of modern modes of transport began in Paris and that engineers turned their attention first to inner urban transport. From 1760 Cugnot was working on the development of steam-powered buses. His thinking was very soon followed in London. And in the third largest city of Europe at that time, Vienna, experiments were made, but with the much smaller population there was at that time no necessity to pursue these ideas.

The railways suddenly enlarged the hinterlands of the big cities in an undreamt-of way. Cities could at last grow beyond their previous boundaries. The first cities of a million inhabitants grew up. The narrow spatial boundaries were at once burst asunder.

The spreading out of towns was the product not of the garden city movement (Ebenezer Howard) or of the motor-car. It was started by the railways. The population of the City of London declined as follows:

1851	128,000 inhabitants
1871	75,000 inhabitants
1891	38,000 inhabitants
1911	20,000 inhabitants

People settled along the suburban railway lines. The railways, which had given rise to the enormous growth of towns, also served to reduce residential densities. The inner urban traffic pressure was so great that in London the first underground railway was opened in 1863.

The second law of town-building was by no means robbed of its validity by the railways, but the essential value, travel speed, was altered. The following table shows the relationships, in terms of the law, for a theoretical town circular in plan with uniform accessibility from the centre to all parts of the perimeter within thirty minutes:

Travel speed	Longest trip within 30 min.	Possible area of the town	Millions of inhabitants at a density of 600 persons per hectare
4 km/h	2 km	12·5 km²	0·75
12 km/h	6 km	113 km²	6·8
20 km/h	10 km	314 km²	19
30 km/h	15 km	700 km²	42

Surface public transport (tram and bus) raises the door-to-door travel speed, including walking, waiting and transfer times, to around 12 km/h. For economic and technical reasons the network of routes cannot branch out so finely that the entire circular area of the town right out to the perimeter is served. The area served might be one quarter of the circular area. On this basis a 'tram town' could reach a population of 1·7 millions. This is the present population of Vienna—which had a population of over 2 millions in 1914, and has long had a segregated-track rail network, albeit on unfavourable alignments—and also of Brussels and Milan. These three cities have started to put their public transport underground in the last decade.

With modern suburban railways and 'rapid transit' rail systems the door-to-door travel speed can reach 20 km/h (12·5 mph). If such lines and their feeder services cover one sixth of the circular urban area, the town can reach a population of 3·2 millions. This was the population of Berlin in about 1930, before large-scale motorization began and before the building of the north–south 'S-Bahn' (main-line rapid transit system). The larger cities of New York, Tokyo, London and Paris possessed much denser rail networks covering much larger hinterland areas.

Cars attain an average travel speed of 30 km/h (19 mph) in urban and suburban conditions—largely because of the elimination of walking links. They have thus greatly extended the boundaries of the area of possible settlement. The boundaries are almost entirely removed when expressways are built. Roads cover the whole area, so that, with the residential density assumed above, a town of 42 million inhabitants could be built—if the road system had adequate capacity and the parking problem could be solved.

Between 1950 and 1960, despite all the efforts of the city authorities the population of New York City declined by 250,000 persons. The limit is apparently reached at 14 million. A larger city could not be satisfactorily served with present-day modes of transport. The additional population must be housed in the urban region surrounding the city. The single large city is replaced by a group of cities or a metropolitan area with several centres.

The figures given here merely indicate orders of magnitude. In reality there is no town with a uniform circular plan; residential density varies from one district to another; public transport service is not uniform; and in the larger cities longer work trips are accepted of necessity. Nevertheless the facts give a meaningful picture of the relationship between town-building and transportation. Increasing traffic difficulties have an enhanced significance. They not only rob the citizens of freedom of movement and good temper, but also threaten to undermine the position and retard the growth of the city. Transportation technology sets limits for town-building which cannot be exceeded, even though the rapid growth of a city's population results in urban sprawl.

(b) Population density

For a theoretical circular city with one million inhabitants, the population density would, to conform with the 'law' discussed above, be as follows, depending on the average speed of transport:

Travel speed	Average residential density (persons per hectare)
4 km/h	800
12 km/h	88
20 km/h	32
30 km/h	13

If transportation engineers call emphatically for an increase in travel speeds, this is not an end in itself but is a prerequisite for better living and housing standards.

The figures show that we must do our utmost to raise speeds from the lowest levels. An increase from 10 to 11 km/h brings far more benefit than one from 30 to 31 km/h. At present the travel speed during peak hours in the central areas of many large cities is only about 6 to 8 km/h—not much higher than in the days of the stage-coach. Comprehensive bans on traffic or the introduction of *large* pedestrian areas can only worsen the situation, because they would push travel speed down to 5 km/h. The areas affected by such measures would become 'isolated from traffic'. They would decline both commercially and socially.

The 'flight from the city centre' is a common phenomenon. The central areas of large cities are constantly losing population, as residents are squeezed out by government offices, businesses and service industries. Work trips are thus lengthened, and cost the inhabitants both time and money. The latter is not very serious if the city authorities are willing and able to subsidize public transport. The loss of time hits the inhabitants much harder; and it can only be overcome by an increase in speed.

But in fact the speed of traffic is continually falling, as a result of the increasing overloading of traffic arteries, especially in the old, densely built-up cities. If it drops by only 10 per cent, then the area within which all points can be reached from the city centre within a given time drops by 21 per cent. The residential density of the city must therefore be increased by 21 per cent if the inhabitants are to be accommodated within an acceptable distance of the city centre. It is obvious that the inhabitants of the outer areas of the city have no alternative but to put up with the lengthening of their travelling time (including walking time).

Gradually, however, the 'flight to the suburbs' is partially reversed. A few people are drawn back into the city. They are prepared to live more expensively and at greater density if they can thereby avoid the excessive time losses and discomfort caused by long journeys to work.

Many people ask for towns to be 'loosened up' by the introduction of green spaces. It is sometimes suggested that existing housing should be torn down and replaced by open spaces, thereby creating 'neighbourhood units' and awakening a new feeling of community. Whether the pattern of life of urban society can be changed by such well-meant measures is questionable to say the least. But from the point of view of transport technology, green areas separating a city from its suburbs, or breaking it up into separate parts, have their drawbacks. They lengthen journeys, and thus work against the desired 'splitting into parts'. One day the political pressure from the population may become so strong that the especially favourably located parts of the green belt close to transport arteries are made available for building. There are numerous examples of this happening. In many cases public buildings have even been permitted in the green spaces.

From the point of view of transport economics and technology a star-pattern development of the city is far more suitable, with development along the radial roads and suburban rail lines and green *wedges* penetrating well into the city.

Cities sprawl over the areas around them (Fig. 5). Extensive areas are covered with low-density housing. Distances become so great that full motorization is downright obligatory for the inhabitants of the low-density settlements. An adequate public transport service is scarcely feasible economically.

It is unrealistic to expect frequent bus services in suburbs if residential densities are pushed lower and lower. In the 'car cities' of the western United States the man without a car cannot live.

Around certain European cities the outer suburbs are already being developed in similar fashion. The result is a considerable increase in the demand for traffic and parking capacity in the central areas. But sufficient land areas for traffic facilities can hardly be made available in the densely-built-up areas to enable a large proportion of the population to be housed in 'car cities'. Therefore higher residential densities must be imposed in the

Figure 5: A 'motor city' in California. The landscape is inundated with houses. Traffic engineering construction dominates the 'urban' scene. A man cannot live here without a car.

new suburbs. Rome and Milan have adopted this policy, thereby reducing the demand for traffic facilities and public expenditure on same.

In earlier times the pattern of settlement was influenced to some extent by public transport fare structures. But this aid to town planning has become fairly ineffective since private transport has increased so markedly.

4. Urban structure

In the Middle Ages, urban form was dictated mainly by the exigencies of defence. In the days of mercantilism and the growing up of large, centralized states, which devoted special attention to roads and internal and external water transport, the towns began to grow. Gradually the restraints imposed by the town defences were shaken off. In the layout of new towns or parts of towns, aesthetic considerations came to the fore, as in Karlsruhe, Mannheim or Nancy. The range of transport increased slowly but steadily.

(a) Railways

The building of railways led to a quite unexpected increase in population. In the first century of railways many large towns experienced a tenfold increase in population. These increases were well above the national average.

Town building was thus set entirely new tasks, for which it was unprepared. The scale of these new tasks was moreover not at first recognized. The population of certain cities grew as follows:

	London	Paris	Vienna	Leipzig	Cologne	Stuttgart	Zürich
1700	675,000	500,000	140,000	21,000	37,000	16,000	18,000
1800	950,000	547,000	231,000	32,000	39,000	20,000	21,000
Growth 1700–1800	41%	10%	65%	23%	5%	25%	17%
1900	4,536,000	2,714,000	1,727,000	456,000	373,000	220,000	168,000
Growth 1800–1900	477%	400%	650%	1,320%	860%	1,000%	690%

In the 20th century the turbulent development has continued, even faster overseas, rather slower in Central and Western Europe. The number of towns with more than 100,000 inhabitants grew as shown in the following table:

	1700	1800	1850	1900	1930	1950
Europe	10	23	48	147	245	348
Asia	30	40	55	91	172	291
America	—	1	9	50	143	191
Africa	1	1	2	7	15	39
Australia	—	—	—	4	10	10
Totals	41	65	114	299	585	879

Within a short period accommodation for the new inhabitants had to be provided outside the gates of the old cities. The pressure was enormous, but the area within a suitable distance of the centres of the cities was at first limited since in most cities the pedestrian was still 'the measure of all things'. Only gradually was mechanical urban transportation introduced, and the boundaries of the area suitable for settlement were thus extended. Thus in most growing towns the land had to be very intensively used and the residential density was high.

The mediaeval alleys and angles were not suited to this urban growth. The new parts of cities were to be more 'reasonably' laid out. Most of the town extensions of this time were laid out with a grid-pattern street network, with occasional diagonals, like the famous plan of Washington D.C.

The new towns, with their often rectangular street networks, could be connected only inadequately with the irregular layouts of the old towns. Thus the seams between old and new towns can often be recognized as a disturbing element in the urban structure, even when the old fortifications have long since disappeared. Such a 'break', the elimination of which is giving much trouble, is the Maximiliansplatz–Lenbachplatz area of Munich, which is not penetrated by any link between the old town and the new. Similar seam lines are to be found in Madrid, Barcelona, Zürich, St. Gallen, Innsbruck, Ulm, Stuttgart, Düsseldorf and Essen. The boundary can be clearly seen in cases where town walls and moats have been retained or converted into green spaces, as in Vienna, Nuremberg, Frankfurt, Mainz, Münster, Bremen, Utrecht and Copenhagen. In many towns important tangential streets run alongside the old walls, or they could be comparatively easily introduced in this position.

(b) Location of railway stations

The location of railway stations has a direct effect on urban structure. In many cases they were located close to the city centre or to the fortifications (Fig. 6).

Passenger and goods traffic, which was hitherto concentrated chiefly on the market place at the centre of the town, now concentrated on the

Figure 6: In Zürich the main railway station was built in 1847 outside the gates of the city—a location which was favourable at that time. The Bahnhofstrasse, now the main shopping street in the city, was laid out only in 1866. Thirty years later it had already overtaken all other streets in importance.

railway station. Around the stations grew up inns, warehouses and workshops which attracted additional traffic. The 'Station Roads' with their heavy pedestrian traffic attracted more and more shops. And so the economic centre of gravity moved towards the station (Fig. 7). The balance of the urban structure was disturbed.

In Berne the traffic centre of gravity moved from the Zeitglockenturm to the Bubenbergplatz. In Munich it moved towards the main station, to the Karlsplatz. In Frankfurt the same sort of thing happened. In Vienna the West Station shifted the commercial centre of gravity to the Mariahilfer Strasse. In Berlin the Potsdamer Platz, next to the Potsdamer Station, became the most heavily trafficked point. The more distant parts of the cities were 'transport starved' and declined economically.

In certain large cities a second centre of gravity grew up. An excellent example is Berlin with a second hub at the Zoological Gardens Station, which in 1928 surpassed the old central area. The merchants' advertising

Figure 7: The railway station of Zürich is still on the old site. The plan of the passenger reception building betrays the old division. But in the meantime the centres of gravity of urban area, residential population, work places and traffic flow diagram have shifted to this spot.

campaign 'Everyone to the centre once daily' had no effect. In New York a new commercial centre grew up, close to the long-distance railway stations, on 42nd Street—several kilometres from the old centre at the southern tip of Manhattan, the old hub of water transport.

The traffic pattern in the central areas of towns shifted more and more away from the main roads. It centred no longer on the market place, but on the railway station place (Fig. 8). The street networks could not be adapted to this change and became more and more unevenly loaded. The re-orientation did not at first bring any perceptible drawbacks because the volumes of street traffic were as yet comparatively small, with long-distance road traffic declining. It was only with the arrival of motor traffic that the astonishing degree to which the traffic pattern had altered became visible.

We can scarcely hope to succeed in bringing the street pattern back to conformity with the road traffic pattern. The shift has taken place over too long a period. If it could be forced back the result would only be new

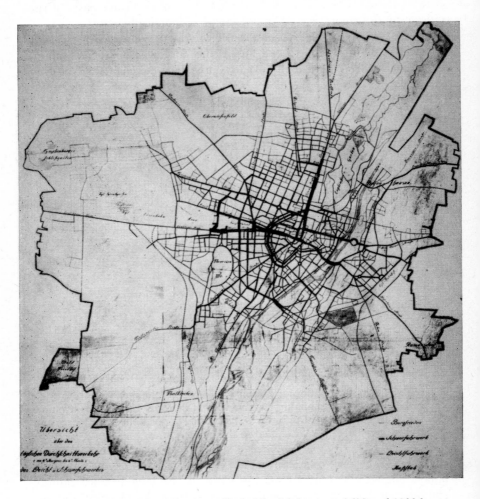

Figure 8: A count of horsedrawn traffic in Munich between 0600 and 1800 hours in the year 1900 shows the marked shift away from the city centre (inter-section of main roads from north, west and east-south-east) towards the main passenger and goods stations to the west (intersection of ring road and western approach) which has already taken place. The north–south traffic streams are bowed towards the west, passing through the area of the railway stations, while the centre of the city has less traffic than formerly.

traffic disturbances and economic losses. The attraction of the big railway stations is still powerful in Europe, for the stations are the entry point for ever-growing numbers of long-distance travellers and commuters. We must watch carefully to see whether and when this trend ceases and the importance of the stations declines. In American cities such as New Orleans and Los Angeles the newly-built stations have hardly any appreciable influence on urban development since the number of trains using them is too small.

In the burgeoning towns, traffic increased. Passenger-mileage and ton-mileage always increased faster than the population because of the rising standard of living. In Berlin the population increased 2·8 times between 1870 and 1902, while the number of public transport passengers increased 42 times. Stations had to be extended, and their forecourts became too cramped. In many cities the stations and the streets leading to them had meanwhile been hemmed in by buildings. The railway installations gradually came to be regarded as 'thorns in the flesh'. The wide areas occupied by rail tracks became an impenetrable obstacle for traffic between the parts of town on either side of them. Level crossings became more and more of a nuisance with the big increases in rail and road traffic. Only a few over- and underpasses were built because of high costs, so that they were often too far apart. Owing to this the parts of the town 'on the wrong side of the tracks' became somewhat isolated. In Zürich, Ulm, Cologne, Düsseldorf, Hanover, Bremen and The Hague there is a particularly marked contrast between the excellent business location on one side of the main station and the truly stunted conditions on the other side. It is thus understandable that the relocation of stations often has been and still is demanded.

In the last few decades the main stations have been moved in Milan, Biel (Switzerland), Stuttgart, Karlsruhe, Heidelberg, Darmstadt, Wiesbaden, Brunswick, Königsberg, Brussels (North Station) and Rotterdam. But the results have been only partially satisfactory. The alterations were advantageous for the operation of the railways. The track layouts could be developed on a grand scale on the basis of new principles. In some towns the terminal stations were replaced by through stations; but this is today only of minor importance for suburban operation. But from the town planning and urban traffic point of view the results have not, in most cases, been very happy. The distances between the new stations and the city centres were so great that the economic strengths of the towns were not sufficient to fill up the intervening space quickly. Where, however, urban development succeeded over a period of time, the new station area started competing with the old commercial centre. The new station was even more 'off centre', so that there was a further shift in the road traffic pattern. Bridging the additional distance made substantial demands on the internal transport system. The structure of the public transport network was complicated because numerous bus and tram lines had to be diverted to serve the station. And owing to the additional time taken to reach the station from the city centre, the traffic value of the railway was reduced. On the basis of such considerations it was rightly decided not to move the main stations in Berne, Zürich, Vienna, Munich, Stuttgart (proposed second move), Frankfurt, Cologne and Berlin.

The present recipe for the reconstruction of railway facilities is: move the operating installations out, but bring the traffic installations right into the town centre! Obviously new urban lines and stations can only be built underground. Important examples are the north–south 'S-Bahn' in Berlin and the 'Jonction' in Brussels. Plans exist for the linking of suburban lines across the centre of the city in Paris, Zürich, Munich, Stuttgart, Frankfurt and Oslo.

Railway stations in the outskirts of cities provide the nucleus for suburban settlements. New centres are built up around them, and then buildings spread out over roughly circular areas. For a given total travel time from the city centre the size of the area that can be settled around each station decreases as the distance from the centre increases, since the rail

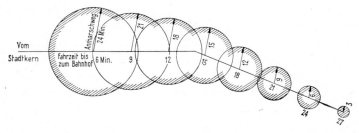

Figure 9: The 'railway-age city' developed along the suburban railway lines. The sum of the rail travel time from the city centre and the time needed to walk to the station from the edge of the settlement is the same for each settlement.

travel time increases and less and less time is left for the walk to the station. Thus the suburbs of a 'railway city' are strung like pearls of decreasing diameter along the railway line (Fig. 9). Between the railway lines wide areas remain unbuilt until they are served by local public transport, with its denser network, and then by cars. The railway city has a few fairly long strings of pearls, while the tram or bus city has many but shorter strings— shorter owing to the lower travel speed. Only private traffic can serve an entire circular area uniformly.

In recent years new traffic magnets have arisen, such as airports, garages and motorway interchanges; but none of these has so far attained the importance of a main railway station. But it is not impossible that in a case like Munich the airport located to the east of the city will in time develop into a town-planning counterweight to the railway station located on the west side of the town.

(c) Inner urban transport networks

In big cities internal public transport has been provided successively by means of horse-drawn trams, electric trams, elevated and underground railways, and here and there by special kinds of railways. The rail networks were supplemented by bus lines.

When trams were introduced, road traffic was so small in volume that no account was taken of it. In the old parts of cities tram tracks were laid in narrow streets, and sometimes single-track sections were laid in alleys. Even in main streets terminals and sidings were permitted. Since 1945 the networks have been considerably altered—especially in the course of the reconstruction of towns destroyed in the war. Many tram lines were replaced by bus routes. The reasons for doing this were of various kinds: economy; fluidity of traffic; simpler layouts of roads and junctions; elimination of ugly overhead wires. The tram network was simplified and partially eliminated, and the spacing of routes in some cases greatly increased. Many stops were eliminated in order to increase travel speeds.

While replacement of trams by buses has no effect on urban structure, changes in the network have far-reaching consequences. The shifting of a stopping place has an effect from the point of view of transport similar to that of shifting a railway station, although on a smaller scale. The old location becomes economically less valuable, the new location becomes more valuable. A shift of even a few metres can make a difference. Anyone who walks through a town with his eyes open can easily spot this effect. Such effects can best be seen in changes in site values, but these are seldom published.

When several tram stops or bus stops are grouped together at one point, the number of passengers at this point increases and with it the number of customers visiting the surrounding shops. Site values and rents rise. Land owners want to use each site more intensively by building higher or covering more of the site.

This sort of thing happened in Stuttgart when several stops were grouped together at the Wilhelmsbau. In Frankfurt shopkeepers complained about the shifting of the tram lines from the Kaiserstrasse onto parallel roads. In Cologne, numerous tram lines were taken out of the old city centre and re-routed round the Ring. As a result commercial activity on the Ring increased and the transport-starved city centre fell behind. Whether the city centre can catch up once again with the Ring when an underground tram link is brought into operation is doubtful. Here the inexorable law applies: the first to open shop gets the custom! In Stockholm a large detour was made in the routing of the north-west branch of the new underground railway, for reasons such as this. Town planning decisions—and every alteration of the transport network is such a decision—have a continuing effect and cannot easily be put into reverse.

However, urban development does not always follow faithfully every shifting of a transport route. The business centre of a city does not extend itself at all easily. Its size is dictated not by planning but by the purchasing power of the inhabitants. Men and women have certain habits as regards driving and shopping. Many people choose their place of work in relation to transport routes. The exercise of judgement on such questions calls for experience and the capacity to get the 'feel' of a place.

In Zürich as a result of pressure from property owners in Limmatquai a tram line was transferred to this street from the Bahnhofstrasse—the two streets run parallel about 300 m apart. But the expected business revival failed to arrive. Many passengers change trams at both ends of the detour because the best shops, including the big stores, are to be found in the Bahnhofstrasse. The service became inconvenient for the majority of passengers—changing vehicles is always inconvenient. In Stuttgart the transfer of tram lines from the heavily loaded Königstrasse to the Neckarstrasse, which runs parallel about 400 m away, had similar effects.

Shopkeepers know very well the importance of a good transport location. Shops are opened at the ends of lines and at interchange points, and these soon develop into local centres. High rents are paid for selling space and bars inside railway stations. In Ludwigshafen in 1960 an important tram stop was incorporated within a new big store. In Brussels, New York and other cities stores and government agencies have themselves paid the cost of providing direct access to their buildings from underground railway stations. First-class shops are to be found in the underground shopping arcades at the underground railway stations in Tokyo and Osaka. The shops in the pedestrian concourse under the Opera intersection in Vienna may also be mentioned.

Thus the siting of bus and tram stops and the location of rail and bus routes is not the sole concern of the transport undertakings; it is a town-planning question of major importance.

(d) Private transport

In contrast to public transport, which directly serves only certain lines and points and concentrates people at a few points such as large railway stations, private transport provides much more uniform service to an entire area. It can use any street or road. It can reach every house. It can pick up and set down people and goods anywhere. All parts of the town are equally accessible to it.

As a result it has at first hardly any effect on the structure of the city, at least as long as sufficient road space and parking space are available. But in many places this is no longer the case by any means. The overloading of streets damages commercial life. Many trades leave the city centre for other locations. The city becomes fragmented. Inhabitants of the northern parts seek work in those parts, while inhabitants of the southern parts seek work in the south. Even in small towns increasing traffic difficulties can be felt, for they too have a shortage of road space.

Private transport too has its stopping places, though most are on a small scale. The construction of a parking lot or a garage is the equivalent of building a 'station' for road traffic, with all its town planning consequences. Vehicles and shoppers are attracted from all directions—at any rate if the location is favourable with respect to the road network, the driver's destination and in some cases to the public transport network.

This phenomenon is used in a planned manner in the modern shopping centres, in which shops and parking lots are merged into a single unit. Occupants of vehicles are converted only for a short time into pedestrians —so long as they do not prefer to be served at drive-in counters.

Pedestrians do not always seek out the shortest route. Often they follow the heavily trafficked main streets. There the shops offer the greatest selection, and there the greatest liveliness is to be found. Comparatively few people walk past even the second or third house in one of the cross-streets; and the next street parallel to the main street is almost unfre-quented.

Many streets have a 'smart side'. Most pedestrians use this side. There they find good shops with a good turnover. The opposite side is somewhat deserted. Despite all efforts it cannot catch up with the other side so long as the cause is not removed. Frequently the cause is a curve in the street, a bus or tram stop, an intersection or the position of pedestrian crosswalks. Pedestrian traffic is sensitive and not easily guided or con-trolled. Good solutions cannot be found solely on the drawing board. In planning we must take account also of such facts and of living and shop-ping habits.

(e) Central business districts and shopping centres

The majority of vehicles pour into the central business district, which often coincides with the old city and has very little road and parking space. Drivers want to park their cars there during working hours or while doing business. In most cases the necessary space is not available. But the access streets also have inadequate capacity. The streets in the city centre can hardly be widened. It is economically impossible to tear down whole rows of houses. This would force more inhabitants out to the suburbs, thus further increasing the transport demand.

If the demand for traffic and parking space cannot be satisfied, the traffic service and the commercial value of an area declines. This gives rise to the burning question of 'town building adapted to traffic', which is close to the heart of the traffic engineer. While the influence of the railways on urban structure can be clearly seen, opinions about the effects of road traffic are still sharply at variance, so that thorough investigations are needed. At the centre of all our thinking is the city core.

With the unequal development of the different modes of transport, locational factors within the city are altered. While public transport led to concentration, private transport leads to dispersion. Certain phenomena are superimposed on each other. There is an interaction between the city and its traffic, so that the size of the city has an important influence on the use of different modes of transport. Early in 1962 the Austrian Road

Society published the following results of an enquiry into modes used for trips to work:

	Vienna	Rest of Austria
	%	%
On foot	30	49
Bicycle	1	17
Motor cycle and Moped	6	17
Car	20	8
Bus	4	4
Tram	43	2
Train	1	5
	105*	102*

*Inclusive of 2-mode trips

If the proportionate use of different modes of transport changes, a favourable business location may slump in value; while other districts may experience an upsurge. The increase in economic activity leads to a flurry of building activity. Such alterations cannot be ordered or forbidden, but only promoted and restrained to a certain extent. But they can, on the basis of careful observation, be predicted over a certain period ahead.

As long as there is a housing shortage—and this is always the case in areas of population growth when the economy is booming—even the least accessible house finds a tenant. Only when there is a surplus of houses do the inaccessible and the expensive houses remain empty. But poorly located shops never find customers. They cannot pay their way and are soon closed down.

Competition between the central business district and suburban shopping centres gets keener and keener. In America such groups of shops are surrounded by extensive car parks, and are located well away from urban development. For example, the Northland centre near Detroit has 12,000 car spaces, one department store and 80 other shops and is about 20 km from the city centre. Many cities already have quite a ring of such shopping centres in their outskirts. There housewives can attend to their total daily needs. But shops catering for specialized demands remain in the city centre. They need a large hinterland and cannot leave the centre of their catchment area.

In Europe new shopping centres are developing at the centres of gravity of the suburbs. These, too, save the housewife many trips into the city centre, so that the amount of traffic in the centre decreases. But the city centre loses purchasing power. This can be carried to the point where —as in the U.S.A.—big economic losses arise and parts of the old town decay.

The outcome of the competition between the old and the new shopping areas is very important for town planning. It depends not only on the position and size of the town, and on the shopping habits and local peculiarities, but above all on transport. The shops which can be reached more quickly and comfortably attract more customers and are at an advantage. The commercial activity in the city centre and its economic strength are largely determined by how well served it is by transport.

In many cities, planning tampers directly with the structure of the city centre, and shifts out of the centre installations and buildings which attract a lot of traffic. Rome has shifted its city administration out to the world exhibition grounds; in Madrid—as in Saarbrücken—the university has been rebuilt well outside the gates of the city; and many authorities moved out of the city centres when the bombed-out areas were rebuilt after the war. These installations lose their immediate contact with the core of the city. Passenger-mileage must rise because of the greater distances to the new locations. There is at first a slackening off in the old area. But other offices soon fill up the artificially created gaps. Therefore the desired result does not always follow, or it is achieved only at the expense of other disadvantages.

Actions of this kind call for care, circumspection and an exact knowledge of the interactions between transport and town planning.

5. Social changes

(a) Expenditure on transport

Increasing traffic calls for more space, more time and more money. Everywhere it makes demands which must be met in order to satisfy the requirements and wishes of a growing population with an ever-rising standard of living.

Expenditure on transportation climbs higher and higher, both for individuals and for the economy as a whole. In central and western Europe it is about 16–18 per cent of the gross national product; in the U.S.A. it is already 25 per cent. In this part of Europe every sixth worker earns his daily bread in transportation; in the U.S.A. every fourth. In towns and conurbations the proportions are considerably higher than these average values, because of intensive local transport and the fact that townspeople travel more and consume more.

It is impossible to discern any end to this growth on social, economic or technical grounds. It is to be assumed that it will continue for the next few decades. An artificial restriction on traffic would result in a lowering of living standards and a shrinkage of economic activity. So long as men strive for an improvement in their economic situation there is no turning back.

(b) The urban scene

Transportation shapes the appearance of towns. This must have its effect on men and women and the way they feel about things. Motor traffic especially has a profound influence on the urban scene. It alters the street scene. Vehicles are in motion everywhere. New roadways, designed on the grand scale, push their way through the urban area. More and more signs and signals are installed. Parking places are demanded at many points. With the scarcity of land and the resulting high site values it is not possible to provide enough parking space at ground level. Thus several multi-storey garages rise up round the city centre.

The appearance of the shop is altered. The parking garage is a concomitant of the modern department store. Banks and administrations are installing drive-in counters, so that traffic lanes penetrate inside buildings. Americans can already visit eating places, markets, banks, cinemas and churches without having to get out of their cars. Many families no longer have a fixed abode, but live permanently in caravans.

Moreover the new house looks different. The car must be parked; and so the house gets a garage. In apartment houses the ground floor or basement is used for car parking since there is not enough open space at ground level. Housing costs are increased by the amount of the garage rent. A four-room flat without a garage costs about the same as a three-room flat with a garage. For a given household income, if the expenditure on transportation is increased through the purchase and operation of a car, economies must be made in other directions. Houses and domestic equipment become more modest. Even in this indirect way motor traffic has a marked influence on town-building.

It is a moot question how much effect small dwellings have on the number of children born. The Frenchman Sauvy, formerly president of the United Nations commission on population questions, coined the bitter phrase that the intelligentsia of Europe would die out because it had embraced the ideal of 1 wife, 2 children, 3 rooms, 4 wheels. We need not discuss here to what extent he was correct.

(c) Urbanization

The big cities will grow even bigger. Where this is no longer possible because of transport technology, as in New York and also in London or Tokyo, the urban region will still grow. Urbanization is a characteristic phenomenon of civilization. But the big cities no longer grow from natural increase. In many cities of north and central Europe the number of births is no longer sufficient to maintain the population at its present level. In a number of large cities the authorities point to a modest excess of births over deaths; but the statistics are misleading. In recent decades the average age at death has been pushed higher and higher. It is now nearly 75, and can, at any rate in the present state of medical knowledge, no longer be pushed up much further.

With an expectation of life of 75 years and a constant population, 1·4 per cent of the population must die every year. If the expectation of life is pushed up by one year in a period of seven years, then only 1·2 per cent of the population will die every year. But the remaining 0·2 per cent must also die at some time, so that the death rate will at some stage exceed 1·4 per cent. For many years the death rate in a large part of Europe has been much lower than 1·4 per cent per annum. Thus it must soon rise steeply. When this happens the drop in the birth rate, which has been most pronounced in Sweden and the German-speaking countries, will at last become evident.

But the big cities will grow further despite this. They will suck in population from the small towns and villages. If not enough labour can be obtained in this way, workers and their families too can, with the help of modern transportation, be brought in from any country in the world. This has been happening for some time. Some people speak with concern about a new Tower of Babel and a repetition of the Babylonian confusion of tongues. So long as there is no economic setback and technical progress does not come to a standstill, men and women will continue to stream into the big city regions from all parts of the world. Thus we must plan for growing cities in which a rising demand for passenger-mileage and ton-mileage must be met.

(d) Human changes

Men and women are becoming rootless. They are hurled hither and thither in their thousands by means of modern transportation. They live as strangers among strangers and have no true home. They do not feel politically responsible for the land or the locality in which they are only temporary residents. It is a difficult task to make them feel they have roots in a new place.

But the life of the indigenous population also alters. One can estimate that the average economically active car owner in an urbanized area covers 20,000 km (13,000 miles) every year. At an average speed of 30 km/h he sits for 700 h every year in his car, or 2 h every day. This is an astonishingly high figure. Part of this time is during working hours, but the car claims the lion's share of leisure time. People practice 'motor sport', some of them on the water or in the air. Before and after work, on Sundays and in the holidays an ever-growing proportion of the population is moving about on the roads. The way of life is profoundly altered. It is a task for sociologists to investigate the results both for the individual and for his behaviour in the community.

We cannot be surprised that the altered way of life is the subject of numerous and perfectly understandable criticisms. But transportation is not to blame. It is in itself neither good nor bad. Man must decide what use he wishes to make of it. And this is not just a question of private motor vehicles. The traffic carried by trains, buses, ships and aircraft is also growing, although at different rates. This traffic is an aspect of that way of life which determines the town building of the future.

The continual increase in travel per head of population is a remarkable phenomenon. No one knows where it will lead us. The shortening of travel times through jet aircraft, express trains and motorways, and the cheapening of fares, induces more and longer long-distance trips. The dispersion of the built-up areas forces people to make longer trips by local public transport. There is probably some maximum value beyond which the number of kilometres travelled annually per head of the population will not grow. But there is no indication that such a figure will soon be reached. As an example, the following are the average distances covered per head of population per annum by all means of transport within the city limits of Zürich, together with index figures taking the 1900 travel figure as 1:

1900	250 km	(index figure 1)
1910	500 km	(2)
1920	750 km	(3)
1930	1250 km	(5)
1940	1500 km	(6)
1950	2500 km	(10)
1960	3500 km	(14)

In the urbanized areas around cities the increase is still more marked, for with the further extension of the settlement 'commuters' must cover ever greater distances. Only wives and children live all day in the suburbs —provided they are not working. The family breadwinner must work throughout the day in the city. Before he decides to go and live in the 'dormitory town' he takes into account how much it will cost him in money and time to make healthier and cheaper living possible for his family. To his rent must be added the price of a season ticket on public transport or the cost of running his own vehicle. The city authorities or the State may step in and subsidize fares on public transport, in order to make them cheaper and thus to promote the decentralization of the city. But the cost in terms of time is a far greater burden, and with increasing congestion on the roads this cost is increasing steadily.

When commuters are spending two hours and more every day in travelling to and from the city we may truly speak of 'suffering commuters'. Thus commuter transport must be speeded by all means in our power. This task is difficult and costly.

(e) Staggering of working hours

Because of traffic congestion the working hours of many concerns are being staggered more and more. One concern may stagger its hours in relation to other concerns, or different departments within a big concern may keep different hours. From the traffic point of view such staggering of hours is a useful measure, because it spreads the main peak traffic demands over a longer period. But an alteration in working hours has an effect on habits of life and on family life. The population would not agree to such suggestions without urgent necessity. But the situation is now such that the staggering of working and school hours must be pushed forward despite the disadvantages. To conform with hours of daylight, working hours can only be staggered by no more than one or two hours, but more and more places and concerns must be brought in. It is not easy to find solutions which the majority of those concerned will accept.

Because of long work trips the practice of travelling home for the midday meal is steadily dying out. Thus does transport alter the way of life of men and women.

6. Town planning

(a) The planning period

Every plan for the future must be based on certain assumptions. It must include certain conclusions and recommendations which of course are valid only so long as the basic assumptions remain valid.

The engineer's recommendations must perforce reflect the limitations of his day. He is familiar of course with the current 'state of the art' and has a certain inkling about future technical developments; but even he can only guess what modes of transport will be in use a few decades hence, and to what extent each will be used. Nobody can predict how men will then live and work and how they will judge town planning questions. We cannot compel our descendants to base their thinking on our own present-day thinking.

Our cities have been built over centuries. A city is never 'finished'. Ideas about building alter again and again.

Planning must have a final target. 'Full development' is often called the planning target. But this is not a clear conception. Development can always become more dense. Men can always huddle closer together, and this they will do in the conurbations.

It is better to plan for a given period ahead. But this period must not be too long. Planning must not be so large-scale that its proposals are just coming to be carried out at a time when the thinking underlying them has perhaps been superseded. It must confine itself to a period which is foreseeable. Five years would be certainly too short a period, since the process of preparation, design work, consultation and decision-making requires many months in the town planning field. Then follows execution which can be far longer, because money, labour and materials are only available in certain quantities and because keeping traffic moving during the construction period often requires the plan to be carried out in stages. What is designed today will not be built tomorrow. It would be short-sighted to plan over so short a period.

On the other hand planning for 100 years ahead is not justifiable since no guesses could be made with even partial certainty for a whole century ahead. Such planning would be pure speculation or even playing about.

He who would be a planner must be clear as to what ten years mean in the life of a city. He will then arrive at the happy medium between excessively ambitious and timidly modest planning.

On the basis of experience, city and traffic planning is usually for a generation ahead—i.e. 25 or 30 years. Designs dating from 1870 were overtaken in 1900, those from 1900 in about 1925. Works carried out in the 1930s are already obsolete.

But even within such a planning period the basic assumptions should continually be tested; and details should often be revised. Actual development can run ahead of the assumptions or it can lag behind. But it can also take another direction or be interrupted through political confusion or economic disturbances. Therefore the overall plan must be flexible within certain limits.

At the time of the Zürich international development plan competition in 1915 it was estimated that the city's population would grow at the same rate as in the years 1888 to 1914—i.e. from 225,000 in 1914 to 442,500 in 1950, an increase of 97 per cent. But in fact it grew only by 71 per cent to 385,300. By contrast the traffic plan for Greater Stockholm drawn up in 1940 was based on the assumption that the number of inhabitants would reach one million in 1970. This population was in fact reached in 1952, so that the plan has become outmoded. While work was underway in 1956 on the transport plan for Bonn, it became known that one part of the city would have to absorb an additional 40,000 people within the foreseeable future; and this resulted in considerable changes in the plan.

(b) The planning area

A town plan should be all of a piece. Too many cooks spoil the broth. Questions of detail should always be seen in their wider context. Any professional one-sidedness or any spatial limitation is dangerous. These basic principles are, alas, often ignored.

A road junction can hardly ever be designed in isolation. It is part of a network. Any change in layout or in traffic control has an effect on neighbouring junctions, since the traffic streams will be diverted from one route to another. Quite often drivers avoid new signals on main streets by using side streets. It would be pointless to expend considerable sums of money merely to transfer a traffic problem from one point to another.

Similarly the design of a parking garage should not merely show the plan of the entrance and exit, but should give an indication of the flows to and from the garage over a larger area.

And in the design of a bus or tram stopping place thought should be given not merely to structural details but also to traffic operational aspects, taking into account pedestrian routes as well as vehicle paths. Its position in the network must be considered as well as local conditions.

In designing an airport, the entrance and exit arrangements for passenger and goods traffic, parking space for vehicles, waiting rooms, counters and areas for passport and customs examination must be related to the capacity of the land transport facilities. The airport is a place of employment for hundreds of men and women and therefore attracts commuter traffic.

Even a town cannot be considered in isolation. It has manifold ties with the surrounding area. Many towns have burst out of their official boundaries. They have coalesced with neighbouring settlements or have merged with other towns to form a conurbation. Planning must look beyond the administrative boundaries, which were drawn in a previous age and for different reasons. It must consider the areas which belong together and together form 'catchment areas'. There are sometimes local, political difficulties about this. Such hurdles can be overcome by means of joint planning committees. Sometimes certain communities are fearful of consultations of this kind or see them as the forerunner of incorporation in the city. If the disadvantages are taken into account—and in planning there are always a few—then such common action is seen to be justified. City planning must be extended to cover city regions. The need for this is fortunately being more and more widely recognized.

7. Administration

'Gouverner, c'est prévoir.' This could be freely translated by 'to administer means to plan'. But administration and planning are two quite different things.

(a) Geographical division

We have just pointed out that planning must reach out beyond municipal boundaries. In some cases it must even jump over land and state boundaries. But administration cannot depart from the present boundaries. This can be seen in the case of population statistics, which is why such data are often not comparable, since one city may have several neighbouring places within its boundary, and another may have few or none, while both cities may have similar traffic conditions. In the Ruhr area, big urban districts were created in the 1920s. In Switzerland, however, city boundary extensions are a rarity. Thus the traffic volume in the heart of Dortmund, with its 630,000 inhabitants, is smaller than that in Zürich with 440,000. Brussels, a city of a million inhabitants, consists administratively of a whole string of large and medium-sized towns. In the centre of Copenhagen is to be found the independent municipality of Frederiksberg. English planning recognizes a Greater London which embraces several planning authorities. The Americans use the term 'metropolitan area', which is however used in more than one sense.

Transportation planning must take a comprehensive viewpoint, but the administrative set-up makes a comprehensive policy difficult to apply. Different authorities are responsible for different means of transport. Only in the case of railways is the same administration responsible for track, vehicles and operation. In water and air transport the harbour and airport authorities are separate from the shipping companies and airlines, in road transport the road building authorities have nothing to do with the licensing of vehicles or the policing of traffic. Even the road-building service is not run by a single authority. The road network is fragmented. Following certain administrative principles it is divided between national, land (or county or cantonal) and local authorities. In some areas there are two tiers of local authority.

These multifarious authorities apply different planning principles and design standards. Their financial power varies widely. In the continuous, urban road networks certain routes are given preferential treatment as regards improvements, because they are designated as trunk roads. And yet long-distance traffic forms only a tiny proportion of the traffic using them. This makes an evenly-balanced, uniform programme of improvements difficult. It is not surprising that different sections of roads are often in very different states.

One might perhaps imagine a situation in which all long-distance rail lines belonged to the state; but the main stations including their approaches, with their extensive track layouts including sidings and marshalling yards, belonged to the cities. The cities would in this situation be carrying an unfair financial burden since the big stations serve the entire country. The citizens would through their taxes be helping to maintain the long-distance tracks, without receiving from the state or land any compensating contribution to the maintenance of the extensive rail installations within the city. Yet this is the position with regard to the road system, which is technically and from the point of view of traffic as much a unit as the rail network.

The result of this is that in many European countries the improvement of urban and local roads lags behind that of the rural main roads. Moreover in towns the widening of 1 km of road is much more expensive than it is in the country—because the site values are considerably higher, and substitutes must be provided for the houses which are demolished. Yet the urban road usually carries far more traffic than the rural. Financial means should be made available at those points where the traffic load is greatest.

A memorandum published in 1963 rightly described the classification of roads as a decision which was pregnant with disastrous consequences.

In every traffic network the overall capacity depends on the three components: roads, junctions and parking space. The capacities of all three must be kept in balance. An autobahn cannot carry more traffic than the interchanges and junctions in its catchment area can handle and the parking space available at the destinations served can absorb. Unified planning must be matched by at least partially uniform financing of all elements in the system. This principle does not in itself lay down to what degree the user of parking space should pay for its provision.

The numbering of long-distance roads is not a happy arrangement, although it helps the motorist to find his way. In certain cities these roads go round remarkable kinks and detours. In order to link up long-distance routes, routes are sometimes sign-posted which only a few vehicles follow. For instance the European Highways (Fig. 10) have a very variable significance. Many sections of these routes are far less heavily trafficked

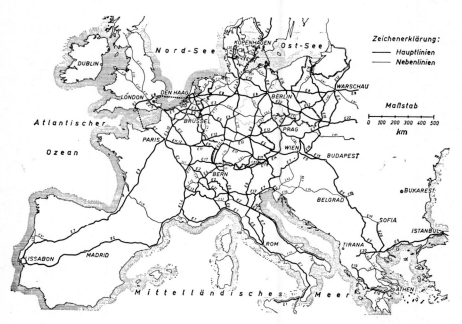

Figure 10: The European network of international highways. To a large extent the direction and volume of the traffic streams bear little relation to this network.

than many unnumbered streets in the cities they pass through. Urban traffic solutions should not be distorted on account of the classification of roads.

For the same reasons the public transport systems—urban transport undertakings, railways, cross-country buses—should work as closely together as possible. Sharp divisions and partially useless competition— e.g. between underground and main-line railways—have drawbacks.

(b) Technical sub-division

In the big cities various departments and authorities—city engineer, city architect, planning officer, police, transport undertakings—are involved in traffic planning. The comparison with the railways can be used again here. The city engineer's office has much the same task as the railway administration's bridges and permanent way department. But it must concern itself more and more with the dynamic or operational tasks which arise in the design of urban traffic networks—tasks akin to those performed by the railway operations department. The city architect's office—like the railway administration's architect's office—is concerned with problems of building structure and appearance.

The planning office is responsible for preparing development, land use and economic plans. In many cities the planning office started as an offshoot of the city engineer's office. At present they employ mostly architects to whom traffic planning is often foreign. With the increasing importance of this field the planning offices should be staffed increasingly with civil engineers. Alternatively independent traffic planning offices could be set up. Several city administrations have already followed this course. But it leads to a further fragmentation and can only be successful if clear direction and willingness to co-operate closely are present.

The traffic police performs more or less exactly the same function as the safety department of a railway company or the air traffic control service at airports. These services are indispensable if vehicle movements in traffic lanes or air corridors are to be free of friction. They have great experience in continuous supervision. But they scarcely concern themselves with the planning or the economy of traffic facilities or with structural questions.

The municipal transport undertakings correspond closely with the operations and traffic department of the railways. But of course they are only responsible for public transport. The operations department has a decisive voice, for they are responsible for capacity, safety and operating costs. At the same time the transport undertakings must be concerned with economy. They often have a partial or complete independence and are thus more or less outside the city administration. This has both advantages and drawbacks. They represent the wishes of their passengers. There is no such representation for other traffic participants—pedestrians, motor-cyclists and car drivers. The gap is filled by associations and newspapers, which convey the wishes of different groups on particular matters to the city council.

This gives a somewhat confusing picture. The functions which on the railways are under unified direction are divided in the case of road traffic between several different authorities and offices, some of whom have other important tasks to perform. Many failures must be traced to this division of authority. A convincing solution has not yet emerged. If cities want to master their traffic problems they need to have finger-tip control of all traffic matters, ranging from density of development to the staggering of working hours. Transportation must be presented to the administration with the necessary professional, personal and political weight.

D. TOWN BUILDING ADAPTED TO TRAFFIC

I. FUNDAMENTALS

Town building is no romantic or aesthetic pastime. The town is the paramount meeting point for the intellectual and economic activities of a large area or a whole country. It is a living organism, not a museum. An ever-growing proportion of men and women earn their daily bread in towns. It is a true saying that traffic is a town's lifeblood. If industry, trade and traffic are impeded the town suffers and so does the whole country.

Passenger transport—which accounts for an average of 90 per cent of all vehicle trips in towns, and even more in the peak hours—is in the forefront of what follows. And the modes of transport which use streets deserve special attention. They pose the most serious problems and give rise to the biggest changes. Developments on the railways are much more peaceful.

1. The transport problem

In previous centuries transport problems arose when places could not be reached, loads could not be carried, mountains and rivers could not be crossed. Exchange of goods was at that time on a small scale, the growth of towns limited.

Today's transport problem is, however, not due to a shortage but to a superfluity of means of transport. The needed space is not available for traffic. The three causes of the problem are:

The increase in population.
The increase in passenger-miles per square mile.
The increase in the area required per passenger-mile.

While the traffic needs per head of population (passenger-miles performed in vehicles of all kinds) increased fifteen-fold between 1900 and 1963 in the larger cities of Central Europe, the area in transportation use *per capita* decreased sharply. According to the statistics of the Regional Planning Office of the Canton of Zürich, the area per inhabitant occupied by streets, railways and airfields decreased as follows:

$$
\begin{array}{ll}
1850 & 130 \text{ m}^2 \\
1900 & 120 \text{ m}^2 \\
1950 & 90 \text{ m}^2
\end{array}
$$

—while in the actual town of Zürich it dropped to 20 m² in 1950. The figure for the whole canton will probably drop to 60 m² by the year 2,000. The extension of the area devoted to transportation has not kept pace with the growth of population. In the cities of Zürich, Munich, Stuttgart, Cologne, Düsseldorf, Hanover and Bremen, in round terms population increased threefold, and the area devoted to transportation twofold.

Even these figures do not reveal the true situation. The new roads are motorways, long-distance roads, and local development roads. Thus they are almost all outside the inner cities. In the core areas the space devoted to transportation has remained more or less the same. Moreover the shortage of road space is considerably accentuated by the fact that a large proportion of the roadway area is taken up by parked cars and therefore not available for moving traffic.

As a result of the transition to individual vehicles about five times as much road space is needed to carry one person one mile. In Munich the proportion of private cars to total person-miles increased as follows:

1920	11%
1938	43%
1950	34%
1958	59%

On average the road space required has risen since 1900 by $15 \times 3 \times 5$, or more than 200-fold, taking account of the increases in passenger-miles, population and space required per passenger-mile. In the core areas it has increased 300-fold while the road space available in the inner cities has decreased.

The Americans have already had bitter experience with traffic problems. Traffic in the inner cities came to a standstill as a result of the overloading of streets. The resulting forced migration of shops to the outer areas led to severe economic losses. Buildings and sites in the central business districts dropped by 30 per cent, 50 per cent and even more within one or two decades.

The losses affected not only individual businessmen but also the cities themselves, because their income from taxation declined, and the economy in that the buildings were still perfectly usable. If such losses can be prevented by an improvement in traffic conditions, even high expenditures on such improvements can be justified.

The threat which in America has been felt mainly by the bigger cities hangs over certain medium- and small-sized European towns, for the load on the available road space is as a rule considerably greater in the narrow mediaeval core areas, especially as the population density in the surrounding areas is much greater than in the U.S.A.

In Europe another consideration is important: a policy of dispersion must guard against the decline which has already reached frightening proportions in the gothic old town of Regensburg, in the baroque District I of Vienna, and even in the core of several country towns. It must not allow the oldest and the historically and architecturally most valuable parts of cities to become slums as a result of inaccessibility. Thus we need to have a clear idea of the 'healthy' city and of the dangers which threaten it.

The city must be habitable. It must offer the best conditions for living, working and recreation. Transport is the link which binds all elements together: above all internal transport. The ways to work and to creation should be pleasant, comfortable and short. Goods transport should be quick and cheap. These simple basic principles are difficult to realize.

In the conurbations there is a steady increase in the number of jobs as well as in the population. Space must be found for the working population. Jobs are to a large extent more closely tied to certain places than are homes. Just as the mediaeval city had its Tailor, Shoemaker and Butcher Alleys, so the modern city has its banking, administration and shopping districts. Despite modern communication techniques, businesses and public authorities must be close to one another in order to have direct personal contacts. Except to a small extent they cannot and will not move out to suburbs and neighbouring towns.

But it is precisely these services which employ more and more people, while the number of manual workers in factories and services is decreasing. Both agriculture and manufacturing industry are continually losing labour to service industry and offices. As a result there is a very big increase in jobs in the city centre.

This process is of great significance for town building. The changes in economic life faces it with a new task. The demand for office space and shopping space in the city centre is increasing rapidly. Dwellings are continually being turned into offices, since government and business can pay much higher rents. The rooms are more densely peopled. When buildings are rebuilt, more floor area is created by reducing storey heights. Town building has no power to stop these developments. It must determine the probable scale of the changes and prepare the necessary adaptations.

Providing for the fast-growing commuter and visitor traffic is of special importance here. If the city is successful in catering for this traffic demand, the increase in jobs in the city centre will continue; and this will be a visible sign of economic health. But if traffic grinds to a halt, the result will be a decline of the city centre which cannot be halted. The core of the city will be blighted.

2. Town planning choices

The city core is and remains the centre of gravity which determines the life of a city and the traffic pattern within it. It is the magnet which exerts an economic and political pull throughout an even larger region. It is the intellectual and commercial meeting point. This heart of the city must be kept healthy.

Many city centres still have a mediaeval image with their town hall, churches, burgers' houses, town walls and towers. Even when many old buildings have disappeared, the road network has hardly altered since the time of the post-chaise, although it was originally built to serve a far smaller population. At peak hours the core areas and the important radial roads are overloaded. The ever-increasing streams of traffic demand ever more space. Saturation cannot be ruled out. Cities are thus faced with this fundamental decision:

Is traffic to break its way through urban development?
Is traffic to grind to a standstill in the narrow existing streets?
Or can an equilibrium be created between development and traffic?

No city can shy away from these questions. The die must be cast for the town-building of tomorrow.

(a) Rebuilding of towns or new towns

The traffic problem is due to the shortage of road space. Additional road space can be provided by the widening of existing roads or the provision of new ones. Either requires the taking of building land.

In many cities the central business district coincides wholly or partly with the old town. It is the most important destination for urban traffic; and thus the demand for road space is greatest there.

If new road space is to be provided, buildings which are of either historical or economic value must be demolished; buildings which have hitherto determined the appearance of the city. If the road space is to be adequate for future demands, a large part of the city centre must be broken up and rebuilt on new principles with wide streets, large parking places and less buildings.

Even if a city were to make the bold decision to embark on such far-reaching reconstruction, it would still be extremely doubtful whether it could be carried out within the foreseeable future. The new buildings would require a large labour force and large funds which would have to come chiefly out of the city's pocket. The rearrangement of sites would require lengthy negotiations. A large proportion of government departments, shops and offices would have to be evacuated for ever, and could hardly hope to find equally good locations in similar business situations. Interim solutions would have to be provided for all the remaining offices and undertakings. Since the reconstruction could only take place stage by stage, the transitional situation would last for a long time. But trade and commerce could not suffer major disturbance during the entire period of the reconstruction. Firms would not be able to interrupt their activities and would demand compensation for any disturbance.

Most jobs are in the central area and it provides the biggest tax base. Even in the cities destroyed during the war, unavoidable changes could only be carried out within very definite limits and over many years—for reasons such as these. Thus there are grave reasons against a wholesale reconstruction of cities.

Perhaps it would be more feasible to start by building a 'town adapted to traffic' in a new location in open country. This sort of thing is always being proposed. But advocates of this course overlook the fact that the existing city occupies a site dictated by nature and transport geography; and that no other location in the area can be as favourable to urban growth. Moreover they quite patently take too little account of political conditions—local authority boundaries and powers. Finally the cost must be borne in mind. The road network for a city of 200,000 inhabitants would cost about £150,000,000 to build today. This would represent an expenditure of about £30 *per capita* per annum if the network were to be built within 25 years. All these considerations rule out this course.

(b) Traffic restraint

The opposite policy is to force traffic to make do with the road space at present available. Its advocates urge that the salvation of the city centre lies in deterring motorists and 'restoring' streets and squares to the pedestrian. A complete reversal of town-building policy could and should take place. It would be unnecessary to spend so much money on providing better accessibility. Far-reaching restrictions should be imposed on vehicles—not least for aesthetic reasons.

The old towns should be barred to motor traffic and turned into pedestrian towns. Then areas of meditative peace would be created there. How much the citizens would welcome this state of affairs has, they claim, been demonstrated when important streets or whole sections of a town have been closed to traffic on festive occasions or during the pre-Christmas shopping period.

Doubtless this would be the cheapest solution at the moment. That is why the policy of traffic restraint is gaining more and more adherents. Moreover this approach takes account of feelings nourished by fear of too rapid technological progress.

The attractions of short, easily accessible pedestrian streets and links will be denied by nobody. But what is proposed by the advocates of restraint is much more, namely a sharp throttling of traffic, which would have to adapt itself to a much reduced amount of space; a deliberate step backwards to the pedestrian town, eschewing the technical achievements of several decades.

The effects of widespread traffic restraint must be examined dispassionately. If a businessman wants to stay in business he must make use of modern equipment, gadgets and aids. These include goods vehicles. If he is not allowed to use such vehicles for house-to-house deliveries from the city centre he will move his business out of the centre. If his customers do not like the long, uncomfortable walk to his shop his turnover will shrink. He must needs obey this harsh, inexorable law. He will seek a more

D

favourable situation with regard to traffic. And so the economic decline
of the old town begins.

Widespread bans on traffic lead quickly to the same end result as
traffic congestion. If a comprehensive ban were imposed throughout an
old town centre, the inhabitants of houses in the area would in the end
not be able to maintain themselves. Houses would fall into disrepair. The

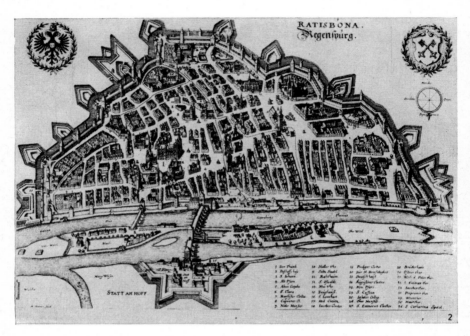

Figure 11: The narrow alleys of the mediaeval city of Regensburg on the Danube
　　are unsuited to traffic. Large parts of the gothic Old Town have already
　　suffered badly as a result. If they are to be saved the traffic circulation must
　　be improved. If more and more businesses move to newer parts of the city
　　economic eclipse will be inevitable. Traffic planning and preservation of
　　historic monuments both face a difficult task.

city could perhaps maintain certain especially beautiful houses as
museums, paying for this out of local taxation. But there would be little
point in this if the surrounding area were to become more and more
blighted.

The same result would follow if town and traffic planning favoured
the outer areas of a town too much and only made improvements there.
Too much economic strength would be drained from the city centre. It
would become an infirmary in the centre of a thriving conurbation. Many
cities are pursuing this course because they can build in the outer areas
faster, cheaper and on a bigger scale. But in the interest of self-preservation
a city should beware of artificially bringing about the decline of the old

centre. Conditions in the inaccessible parts of many historic city centres provide eloquent testimony. It is only possible to make or keep the city centre healthy if a certain amount of terminating traffic is allowed into it. Far-reaching, slashing bans on traffic will have the opposite effect (Fig. 11).

(c) Balanced planning

All lop-sided solutions are dangerous, in building as in other fields. Far too many people invoke pedestrian towns, satellite towns and sky-scrapers as slogans, without any real thought. Recently it was suggested in all seriousness that all motor vehicles should be banned from a town of 15,000 inhabitants with a lively industry and heavy commuter traffic, thus turning it into a paradise for pedestrians—'like Venice'. Cities of quite small population build satellite towns; small towns build sky-scrapers; and big cities (not only New York—Fig. 12) allow so many to be built, without any increase in the amount of road space, that the traffic engineer is confronted with quite insoluble problems.

I must warn with the utmost emphasis against exaggerations and fashionable follies. We condemn the town planning mistakes of 1880, 1900 or 1920, but we perhaps are making bigger ones.

The 'town completely adapted to traffic' and the 'town entirely free of traffic' are both impossibilities. On this basic question the 'golden mean' is not advocated as a means of evading decisions, but on the basis of a recognition that only a sensible balance between traffic and development can offer a total solution. The only acceptable solutions are those which give equal weight to the genuine needs of the men and women who earn their daily bread in the town and are therefore dependent on transportation, and also to the need to maintain the appearance of the city as we have inherited it, its peace and its dignity.

Solutions must conform to market conditions, so that the cities can preserve their role as centres of commerce. They must be on the right scale; they must not cost more than can be spent in a generation. The foremost objective must be to keep the city healthy and capable of standing on its own feet as an economic centre. Only if this condition is fulfilled can the city serve as a focus for intellectual and artistic activities throughout the surrounding region.

The structure of the city must be carefully reformed on the basis of new principles. For this purpose a comprehensive plan must be drawn up, for we are concerned with a coherent whole. The urban street network and the public transport network must be planned in a unified manner. Transportation tasks must be suitably apportioned between the various means of transport. Each must be so used that it meets the special require-ments of the town. Building regulations and ordinances for garages must be so much further developed that they are adequate in the light of the latest knowledge.

The city centre remains the most important area, with its dominating

Figure 12: The Aluminium Company of America building in New York, built
in 1955. The narrow streets in this part of Manhattan are not capable of
coping with pedestrian and vehicle traffic. People who work here reach the
nearest underground railway station by means of underground footways,
and only see daylight again after a 10 km (7 miles) trip. To traffic congestion
in the horizontal plane must be added traffic difficulties in the vertical plane.
There are 'only' 36 lifts for the 8,000 employees, so that some people on the
upper floors have to wait up to 20 minutes for one after the working day
ends.

position as the seat of public authorities, administrations, businesses and
shops. It poses the most difficult town planning and technical problems,
which must be tackled first if a plan for the sound development of the
whole town is to be worked out. The city centre is the origin and destination of the biggest traffic streams. It is there that the traffic problem is

greatest. Urban traffic planning can only work from the inside to the outside.

3. Basic types of traffic network

The size of settlements is of crucial importance. In the case of a self-contained manor set in the middle of its own fields, all planning requirements are fulfilled without exception, at any rate as regards internal traffic of men and goods. All traffic focuses on the manor. From here all ways radiate in all directions—in straight lines if the land is flat. Thus there are short and obvious ways available in all directions.

In a village there are already many connexions running this way and that across each other. If a desire line diagram were drawn it would be a fine old cats-cradle. The condition that roads and ways should follow desire lines can be only partially fulfilled. The plan of the road network and the traffic flow diagram no longer coincide exactly. Various traffic movements must already follow indirect paths. The bigger the village—and town—the more and longer are the traffic links required. Distances increase and the number of movements grows. The specific transport requirement—passenger-miles and ton-miles per head of population—increases. Already various factors are making themselves felt—type of industry, prosperity, topography, climate. Thus a mathematical formula can no longer be set up.

The cats-cradle of traffic links must be reduced to some kind of order. The traffic network must be given an economic, logical and comprehensible form. Only simple geometrical forms can be considered: in the first place the grid or the star.

(a) Grid pattern

The grid is composed of longitudinal and transverse streets crossing each other at right-angles. Usually they are at uniform spacings and have the same width. The grid was used already in ancient times. About 450 B.C. Milet was built on a grid pattern to the plans of Hippodamos. The rectangles in the older part of the town were about 55 × 60 m, while those in the newer part were 80 × 85 m. In other towns quite different dimensions have been adopted:

Pompeii	35 × 115 m	(only partial)
Carthage	180 × 330 m	(Roman reconstruction after the fire of A.D. 145)
Trier	90 × 120 m	(Imperial Roman town)
Mannheim	65 × 90 m	(baroque city centre—see fig. 13)
Stuttgart	70 × 70 m	(northern suburb)
Munich	200 × 215 m	(north-westwards extension around the Königsplatz, planned by Klenze)

Athens (Modern)

        60 × 110 m   (spacing varies owing to gradients)

La Chaux-de-Fonds

        40 × 80 m

   to 40 × 160 m   (reconstruction after the fire of 1800)

Ludwigshafen

      140 × 250 m   (city centre)

Stettin   125 × 190 m   (west town)

Figure 13: The city of Mannheim (320,000 inhabitants) was laid out on a grid pattern with its main axis oriented on the castle. The business centre of gravity has shifted south-eastwards towards the main railway station. The Rhine bridge is unfavourably located 'behind' the castle. In recent years large-scale works have been carried out to connect it with the tangential roads. Connections with the outer areas of the city are difficult.

New York 80 × 270 m   (between 14th and 59th streets and between 7th and 10th avenues)

Chicago, city centre

        65 × 110 m

Chicago, Belleville

      400 × 400 m

The grid layout leads to an economic division and use of land. It is 'statically' convenient, but not 'dynamically'. For movement in the town, for traffic, it has disadvantages. A uniform grid network has no hierarchy of major and minor streets. It has no centre. The street network has too many intersections and is monotonous and fatiguing. However, its capacity

Figure 14: The linking up of two grid pattern street networks along the line of Market Street in San Francisco has presented great traffic engineering problems. (To the south runs the urban motorway.)

can be increased without resorting to road construction by 'pairing' parallel streets as one-way streets. Inconvenient junctions arise where two grid patterns of different orientation meet each other, as on the main street of San Francisco (Fig. 14) or in Denver. In Washington (planned by L'Enfant) the rectangular grid has had diagonals superimposed on it. These facilitate certain traffic movements, but reduce the capacity of the network and make the layout of junctions more difficult. This applies also to the big arteries which, as is well known, Haussmann drove through Paris for neither architectural nor traffic engineering reasons.

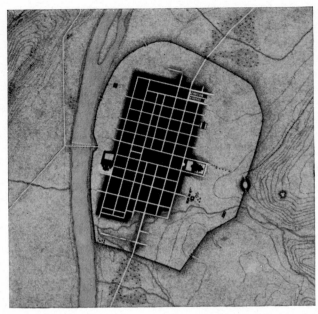

Figure 15: The Imperial Roman town of Trier on the Moselle was laid out on a
grid pattern.

Figure 16: The mediaeval town of Trier grew up with an irregular street network
radiating from the market place; the network was built on the ruins of the
old Roman town.

(b) Star pattern

The star pattern is a natural form of network which corresponds better with traffic desires. In Trier the Teutons, after the stormy period of the 'migration of nations', replaced the Roman grid pattern with a star-pattern network of 'beaten paths', providing the shortest possible connections between the Roman Bridge, the Porta Nigra and the Basilica—without regard to the ruins of the Imperial Roman town (Figs. 15, 16).

With the star pattern, roads radiate in all directions from a single point, usually the market place. Ring roads may be orbital to the same centre. Sectors of such a star pattern were chosen for the baroque city of Karlsruhe and for the New Town of Ankara. The Karlsruhe network radiates from the palace, but the Kaiserstrasse cuts across it and, because of its favourable location, became the main shopping street (Fig. 17). In Ankara the network radiates from the Atatürk Boulevard, which links the new town with the old. A new business district grew up at the centre of gravity of the new town, and this is poorly served by the streets which are semi-circular in plan offering no good cross-connexions (Fig. 18).

A star is the right form of network so long as its centre coincides with the centre of gravity of the traffic flow diagram. But in big cities the layout of the focal point, which must serve as a hub for radial movements in all directions, is extremely difficult. Its capacity determines the capacity of the entire network. This was the basic mistake made in Brasilia (Fig. 19). Here the skeleton of the traffic network is a four-pronged star—a large cross. An overloading of the central intersection must cause harm to all traffic throughout the town. The town is designed for 500,000 people. But the population growth will not stop at this level with the rapid growth of the population of Brazil—provided the site of the capital proves a good one. Thus the overloading is bound to set in one day.

Towns where public transport predominates (which formerly meant all towns) grow outwards on a star pattern if their growth is untrammelled. The rays of the star run along the traffic routes. Where there is more private traffic the star acquires more and more rays and finally grows to a full circle.

Oslo (Fig. 20) is a good example of planning following the right sequence. In the last few years large areas in the eastern part of the town have been provided with a fast tram service. The new housing areas lie on both sides of the tram routes. Between the rays of the star—which are bent on account of topography—are open spaces and areas reserved for recreation. The star has numerous rays. Each ray towards the east is to have one to balance it towards the west, so that diametrical services can be provided on the express tram routes via the city centre. The 'finger' plan in Copenhagen is a similar conception. The settlements are strung out along the five public transport fingers; recreation areas are in the wedges between them.

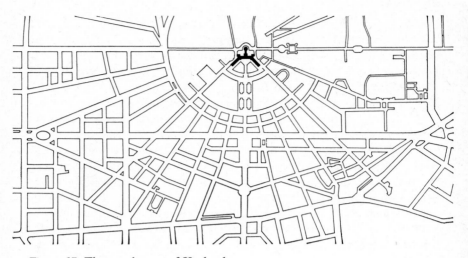

Figure 17: The star layout of Karlsruhe.

Figure 18: The new town of Ankara was laid out according to the plan prepared by Janssen in 1930. The plan reflects the town planning ideas current at the time. The street network has proved unsuitable for modern traffic.

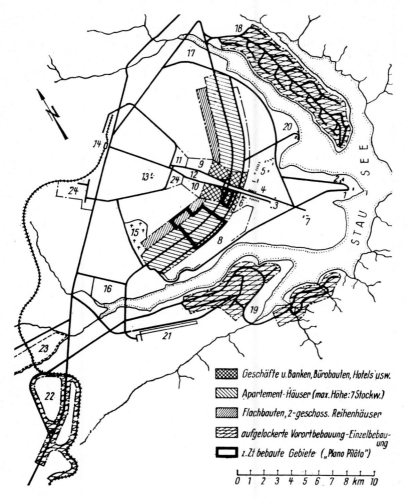

N

18
17
20
14
11 9
13 5
24 12
10 4
24 6 3
2
1
15 7
7
8
16
19
21
23
22

STAU␣SEE

▨ Geschäfte u. Banken, Bürobauten, Hotels usw.

◫ Apartement-Häuser (max. Höhe: 7 Stockw.)

▨ Flachbauten, 2-geschoss. Reihenhäuser

▨ aufgelockerte Vorortbebauung - Einzelbebau-
                                              ung

▢ z. Zt bebaute Gebiete ("Plano Pilôto")

0 1 2 3 4 5 6 7 8 km 10

Figure 19: The layout of Brasilia contradicts the fundamentals of traffic planning.
The road network is based on a central crossroads which limits the capacity
of the whole network. The other links lack clarity. The city centre is separated from the railway station by extensive playing fields, so that traffic to and
from the station must cover long distances. The railway stations and the
airport are a long way apart. Both of them will attract hotels, forwarding
agents, ware-housing and factories. The railway will hardly be able to serve
commuter traffic because it lies to one side of the city. The layout of the
road junctions will be difficult. The railway station is located at a T-junction
between the road which forms the town's main axis and a tangential road;
the former is in line with the centre of the ticket hall. It will be difficult to
build up a local public transport network.

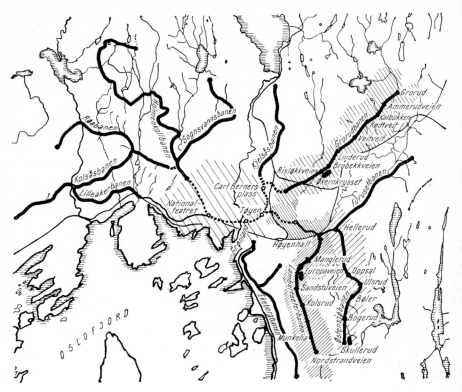

Figure 20: Oslo is developing a star-shaped public transport system to connect
the centre with the extensions of the city. There will be an express tramway
forming the spine of each ray of the star, and these lines will feed into an
underground tramway serving the city centre, being thus routed tangentially
across the centre. There will be wide green wedges between the rays.

The linear city is so to speak a star with only two rays, forming a single
axis of development. It is not suitable for it implies longer trips with more
passenger- and ton-miles as may be seen at Wuppertal or Volgograd
(Stalingrad).

The star as a proper form for the network of a healthy city must be
shaped to avoid the jamming of the core. The market place and its en-
virons was formerly the origin or destination of most trips. Carts came
from the surrounding country, bringing food into the town and carrying
goods out to the villages. Through traffic was so small that the market
place was a parking lot rather than a junction.

A star pattern, as simple as possible, is still the best type of layout for
a settlement, a suburb or a small 'new town' with little possibility of
development. But a clear separation must be made between selling areas
(groups of shops), parking areas (lots and garages) and areas for traffic

movement. The centre point at the heart of the settlement must be comprehensible and of adequate capacity. A good solution is a crossroads
with the shopping centre on one corner, laid out as a pedestrian precinct.
Next to it will be the parking areas, accessible from side streets. Public
transport boarding and alighting points will be at the crossroads. However, this arrangement is only to be recommended if the crossroads has
enough capacity to handle all traffic to be expected in the future. Also the
settlement must be kept free of through traffic, which should be re-routed
via bypasses.

In a larger town the business activity spreads itself out in the area
around the market. Thus instead of a single point of attraction, traffic
attractions are spread out over a fairly large area.

As the town grows, fairly heavy internal traffic builds up, with traffic
streams criss-crossing each other at the 'market place'. There is a close
relationship between the 'handicraft alleys' of the old towns and the industrial and business complexes of the modern large city. Moreover traffic
from the suburbs comes in to the various parts of the central area, and the
movements cross each other within that area. The superficial observer
gets the impression that the central area is overloaded with large volumes
of 'through traffic' which could be diverted away from it. This false
analysis leads laymen to suggest again and again that the solution to the
traffic problems of the central area lies in widespread bans on through
traffic and bypass routes well outside the area.

These problems will never be solved in these ways, but only shifted
to points which are as a rule less favourable from a traffic point of view
because they are located away from the centre of the road network which
has grown up over many years. One has only to think of the conditions
in Vienna, with the Mariahilfer Strasse, the commercial centre of gravity,
lying to one side of the central area. The street network is still oriented on
the old city centre, and is now 'wrongly' used: what were formerly tangential roads now serve radial traffic and vice versa. This is bad for the
city.

148193

(c) Ring roads

Detours mean additional vehicle-miles: cars must cover longer distances. But outer ring roads remain fairly empty of traffic. Direct traffic
between suburbs is not large in volume. It can usually use the existing
radial roads and the cross-connexions between them together with other
traffic. Ring roads around the periphery of a built-up area are fairly cheap
per mile to build because land is cheaper the further one goes from the
city centre and only a few buildings have to be demolished. But they are
longer and therefore more expensive in construction and maintenance
costs. A link nearer the centre of half the length may cost twice as much
per mile. If it serves three times as many vehicles it can be six times as
expensive and yet still be competitive. If the saving in vehicle-miles is also

taken into account, the economic argument shifts still further in favour of the inner ring road.

These considerations point to the correct method of building up an urban road network. In a large settlement it is neither desirable nor possible for the market place to act as the hub for the traffic of the whole

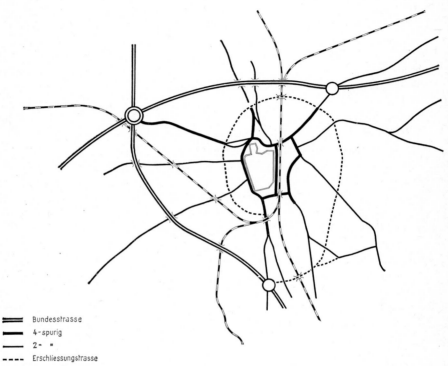

Bundesstrasse
4-spurig
2- "
Erschliessungstrasse

Figure 21: The main road network of Memmingen (35,000 inhabitants). The ring road which had been planned for many years is now to be purely a local collector street. Cross-connexions will be better provided by the tangential roads further in, which will surround the old town centre. The urban network will be connected with the trunk road network at three points. The roads from these points will have a radial alignment and then be 'bent' into the tangents.

town, which moves towards the centre from all sides. The majority of cars having destinations in the central area must be brought in close to the centre of the town. But other vehicles should not drive across it. However, the inhabitants of the western suburbs do not only want to reach the western edge of the central area, although their closest contacts will be with the nearest parts of the centre; they also want to reach the eastern, northern and southern parts of the central area. To reach these other parts without disturbing the busiest part of the central area they need cross-links. For this purpose ring roads are often suggested by laymen.

Ring roads undoubtedly provide a supplement to the star pattern of radials which is geometrically clear and impresses itself on the mind. But traffic never flows in a circular or semi-circular path around the central area. The street network of Karlsruhe or of the New Town of Ankara is a poor traffic layout since vehicles making tangential trips must turn off twice in a short space of time.

Even very wide ring roads sometimes remain minor roads as far as traffic volumes are concerned. A good road network corresponds as closely as possible with desire lines, which represent the shortest possible

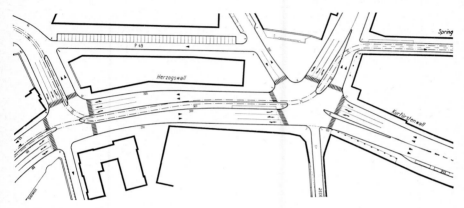

Figure 22: An example of changing a ring into a series of tangents. The Lohtor in Recklinghausen is to be converted from a ring road with T-junctions into a crossroads of two tangents, Herzogswall and Kurfürstenwall. This corresponds more closely with traffic requirements. The tramway will continue via a 'tram street' which will be closed to other traffic. To the west lies a simple crossroads which can only be used in one direction by traffic entering the old town.

links between origins and destinations of all trips—i.e. they are straight lines. There is no such thing as a bent desire line. Good cross links can only be tangential roads.

It might be argued that a series of tangent roads will finally form a ring road. But the big difference between ring and tangential networks is to be found in the layout of junctions and the links with radial streets (Figs. 21, 22).

Ring roads normally cross radial streets at right-angles. Use of the ring road is made more difficult by the sharpness of the turns in and out of it. If traffic entering the central area is in the end controlled, many incomplete junctions will remain—T-junctions the capacity of which is considerably smaller than that of normal crossroads of streets running through the centre.

Since the number of junctions must be limited in the interests of capacity, safety and speed, only complete crossroads should be laid out.

T-junctions give a false picture of the traffic network. They compel drivers to make detours, for kinks cannot be part of desire lines. It is very seldom that equal amounts of traffic turn from a radial road onto a ring road in both directions. But if the movement in one direction is greater it should be less sharply bent—i.e. it should be brought in at an obtuse angle. The cross-section of the less heavily trafficked section of the ring road will not be fully used, so that valuable road space is wasted.

(d) Tangents

On the other hand each individual tangent road can be given a different cross-section. At junctions where tangents connect with the most important radial roads and the majority of vehicles do not follow the tangential route but turn off it, appropriate junction layouts can be developed which reflect the relative volumes making each movement.

Figure 23: The natural shape for an urban road network is the star. It can be supplemented by one or more ring roads.

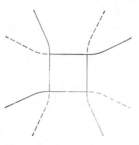

Figure 24: Radial roads should be 'bent' into tangents in the central area. In this way the town centre can be most effectively relieved and shielded from non-essential traffic. In a growing settlement a few radial streets can be added later on (broken lines).

The best solution is a layout in which the radial streets are bent before reaching the overloaded central area, and turn imperceptibly into tangents. In this way the radial roads no longer radiate from the market place but from the corners of a tangent system (Figs. 23, 24, 25).

According to the plan of the town as it has grown up the tangents may make up a triangle (Berne, Fig. 26), a quadrilateral, a pentagon, a

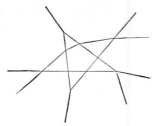

Figure 25: Radial roads can be forked before they enter the town centre. Over-complex junction layouts must be avoided; all junctions should be either four-arm crossroads or forks.

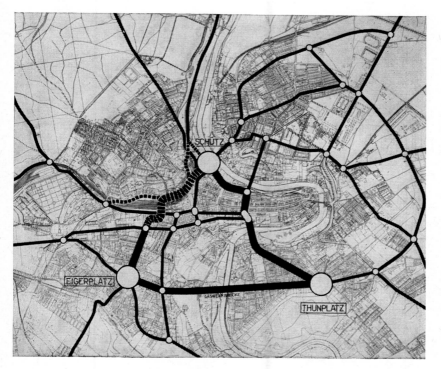

Figure 26: A 'tangent triangle' for the inner area of Berne was adopted in 1953 as the central idea of the traffic plan for the city and was confirmed once again by the city council in 1960. The south tangent was completed in 1962.

hexagon (Zürich) or some other shape. They enclose a central area of greater or lesser size, and free it from through traffic.

Sometimes the tangents can follow the mediaeval town walls. In such cases they fit happily into the urban structure. Such solutions were for example worked out in Zug (Switzerland), Zürich, Memmingen (Fig. 21) and Neuss am Rhein.

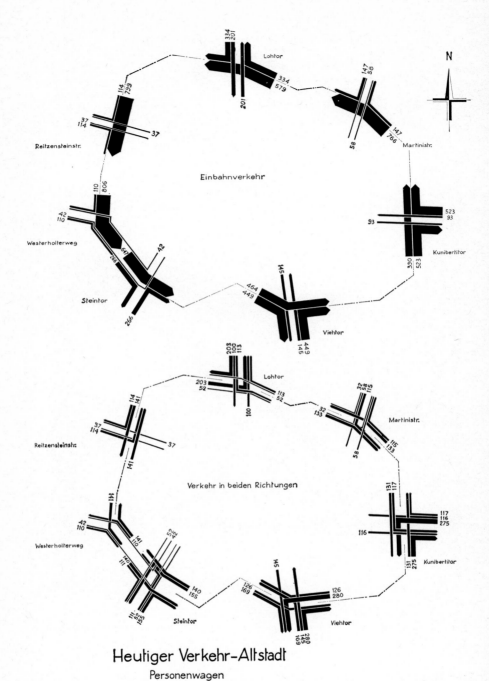

Einbahnverkehr

Verkehr in beiden Richtungen

Heutiger Verkehr–Altstadt

Personenwagen

Figure 27: In Recklinghausen (100,000 inhabitants) an investigation was made into turning the 'Wälle' into a one-way ring road around the old town, with a diameter of about 600 m (2,000 ft). The upper diagram shows the traffic loads at each intersection with such a one-way operation; the lower diagram shows the traffic loads with a two-way operation. The loads on each section of the ring road would be so much heavier with a one-way operation that a two-way operation is to be preferred, even though it complicates the layout of junctions. The figures are for 1958 peak hour traffic in p.c.u.

In some cases tangents are located alongside railway installations, where there is already a 'seam line' running through the urban fabric. In such locations it is often possible to make them at least partly free of frontage development.

In planning a new town it is best to start with a 'tangent quadrilateral' with sides 300–350 m long, or twice as long (i.e. 600–700 m) in the case of a big city. Then the traffic flow in the city will not depend on a single central intersection, but on four crossroads.

A special case is the one-way ring road around the city centre. The idea has its attractions. There would be no intersections between main traffic streams. Traffic would merge from the right on joining the ring road and diverge on the left. Traffic destined for the old town could only penetrate there after weaving with the ring road traffic. The longer routes they would have to follow would discourage through traffic from driving straight through the city centre. However, closer examination of the idea shows that the one-way ring road has great disadvantages. Vehicles would to some extent have to follow considerably longer paths, which would cost time and money. To get from North to East they would have to go round three-quarters of the circle, compared with one-quarter with two-way traffic. In Recklinghausen (Fig. 27) the traffic load on the one-way ring would have been so great that it would have required five lanes, compared with 2 × 2 lanes with two-way traffic. With five lanes, very long weaving sections would have been necessary. Moreover, the necessary road width was not available. At the junctions with the radial roads three-lane entries and exits would have been required; and such high-volume merging could hardly have taken place with sufficient safety without signal control. For these reasons the idea had to be thrown out, in this case as in several similar cases.

For big cities and for cities with important suburbs a single 'ring' of tangents is not sufficient. Additional tangents and cross-connexions are needed (Fig. 28). With increasing distance from the city centre their importance declines rapidly. Estimates for a town which has spread out evenly in all directions confirm this experience (Fig. 29). One can say in rough terms that the traffic load on tangential roads decreases with the square of the distance from the centre. Thus their spacing should be greater towards the edge of the town and their roadway widths smaller. The innermost tangents must be pushed as close as possible to the congested central area. But they must not themselves be overloaded.

(e) Motorways and bypasses

Even without traffic counts we may conclude, on the basis of these considerations, that ring motorways around big cities—such as that partially completed around Berlin and that planned for Munich, or the completed ring road around Rome—are basically wrong. The huge expense is not justified solely to cater for the very small amount of through

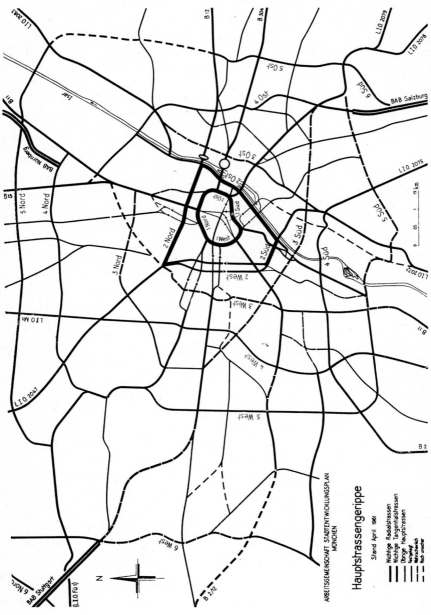

Figure 28: Network of tangential roads proposed for Munich (1·1 million inhabitants): 1961 plan with six tangential systems. The most important are the ring around the old town (1) and the inner triangle (2). Tangent 3 South would provide the connexion between the Stuttgart and Salzburg motorways.

BELASTUNG DER RADIALEN UND TANGENTEN EINER GEDACHTEN STADT

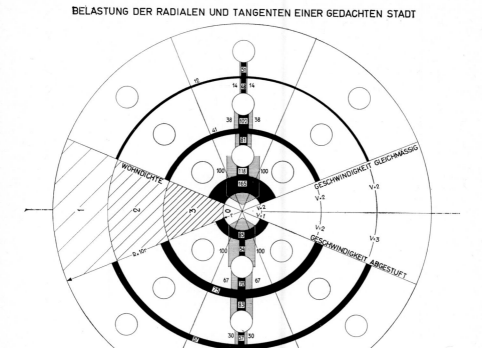

Figure 29: Traffic loads on radials and tangents in an imaginary city. A calculation of the traffic loads on the main streets of an imaginary city on the basis
of Lill's 'law of traffic gravity' shows that the innermost tangents (shown
in simplified form as a ring) carry the most traffic. This is on the assumption the residential and workplace densities increase in the proportion
1 : 2 : 3 from the outer to the inner ring.

In the upper half of the drawing a uniform speed is assumed throughout
the city; in the lower half the speed is assumed to vary from 1 on the inner
tangent to 2 on the next tangent out and likewise on the radial streets and to
3 on the outer tangent. The inner tangents carry the greatest load.

traffic. The ring is unfavourable to traffic, and leads to unsuitable forms of
junction with an emphasis on unimportant movements (Fig. 30).

In the early days of motorway building, excessive weight was placed
on long-distance connexions, which it is well known serve only a fraction
of total traffic. Thus it would have been pointless to build the motorway,
already begun, bypassing Vienna to the south and linking the Vienna
woods with the Burgenland and Hungary. This high-capacity south
tangent, at an excessive distance from Vienna and with no connexion

with the rest of the road network, would hardly have been used at all.

Whether a particular road should be built as a motorway should be decided far more on the basis of the traffic volume it will serve than on its position on the trunk road network. Today the lack of distributor motorways and urban expressways in the conurbations and in many large cities with poor road access—such as Paris, The Hague, Bremen, Frankfurt, Stuttgart or Milan—becomes more and more noticeable. Motorway

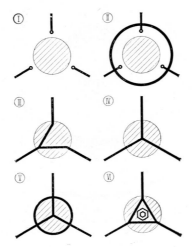

Figure 30: Motorway planning for Munich went through several stages. 1. The three motorways from Nuremberg, Stuttgart and Salzburg originally terminated well outside the city at roundabouts which were intended to slow traffic down. Between these terminals through-traffic was obliged to use urban streets. 2. It was then proposed to end this unsatisfactory situation by building an outer ring motorway. Analysis of traffic studies showed that this outer ring would carry only a fraction of the traffic from the motorways; well over 90 per cent of this traffic had destinations in the city. (The same small proportion of through-traffic is found also among railway passengers.) 3. A motorway star lying to one side of the city centre ignores one traffic stream or forces it to follow a considerable detour. 4. The shortest length of road would be that resulting from a motorway star with its centre point in the city centre. But then the motorway would become a feeder to the city centre. It would attract so much suburban traffic that it would have required 10 lanes even to handle the traffic of 1956. Long-distance traffic would be brought into the city centre, but could hardly be distributed from there. 5. The overloading of the inner sections of the motorway star could not be eliminated by the addition of a ring motorway at the edge of the city. 6. The right solution is to build up first several 'tangent quadrilaterals' of adequate capacity to serve the urban traffic and then to build a 'tangent triangle' linking the three motorways. Its size should be determined on the basis of the traffic survey; the capacity provided should be well utilized, but the roads should not be overloaded.

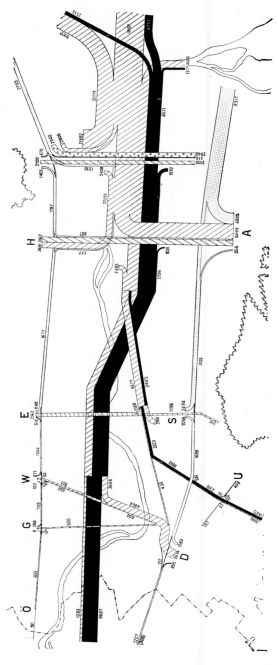

Figure 31: The Berne–Zürich motorway is to be brought via the Limmat valley into the heart of Zürich. In addition to the long-distance traffic (black) it will attract much neighbourhood traffic which will cause an overload within the city. The motorway must be 'bent' in good time away from a radial alignment onto a tangential one. In this analysis a ratio of 2 : 1 was assumed between speed on the motorway and speed on the parallel cantonal roads.

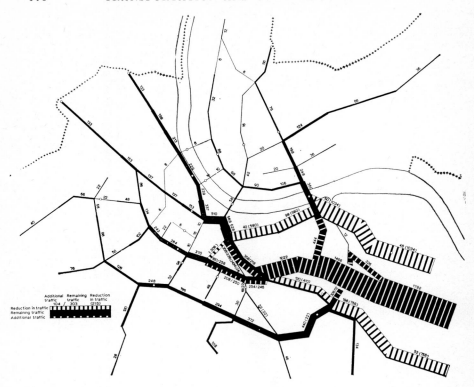

Figure 32: Building a motorway has effects inside the city as well as outside it.
The proposed motorway from Basle to central Switzerland will cause big diversions of traffic within the city centre. The above drawing shows only traffic
crossing the cantonal boundary to the south-east of the city. The survey was
carried out on a Sunday evening in summer.

traffic must be studied and catered for right up to its branching out
within the destination area (Figs. 31, 32).

In Europe and America the following distribution of vehicles approaching a city during a weekday has been observed:

Population	Destination in city centre	Destination in rest of city	Through traffic
up to 5,000	50%	50%	50%
5,000–20,000	33%	33%	33%
20,000–100,000	30%	50%	20%
100,000–500,000	25%	65%	10%
over 500,000	15%	80%	5%

Of the total vehicle-miles run within the city boundaries a still larger
proportion has destination in the city centre (Fig. 33).

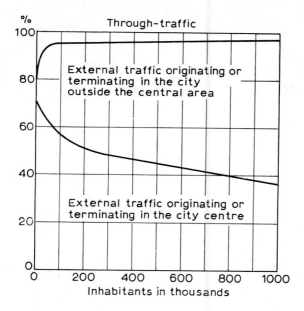

Figure 33: Distribution of traffic entering a city

The proportions vary according to the location and the type of town
—industrial town, administrative centre, harbour town, town in conurbation—as well as from one roadside interview post to another. Closer in
to the centre the proportion of urban traffic increases. Observation 'at the
city boundary' gives no sound basis of comparison because the boundaries
run completely differently in different cities. Similarly the term 'city
centre' is not unequivocal. Nevertheless the differences between towns are
surprisingly small. Traffic to and from the city centre increases in absolute
terms with increasing population, although it decreases as a proportion
of total traffic.

For these reasons bypasses are desirable for small villages and towns,
but can only provide slight relief in larger towns. Motorways must be
judged in the same way. In the larger towns traffic planning must start in
the centre and work outwards. It should not do the reverse: develop the
urban road network from the long-distance roads and motorways.

4. Overall needs for road area and parking space

Certain general statements can be made about the needs for road area
and parking space *a priori*, but these should not of course be applied
without further consideration to any particular town. They will be elabor-
ated below.

In a city of 100,000 inhabitants there may be circulating in the future:

Cars	$30,000 \times 1$	$= 30,000$ p.c.u.
Motor cycles	$2,000 \times 0.5 =$	$1,000$ p.c.u.
Heavy goods vehicles	$4,000 \times 2 =$	$8,000$ p.c.u.
Buses, special vehicles	$=$	$1,000$ p.c.u.
Total	$=$	$40,000$ p.c.u.

The average annual mileage per vehicle is 20,000 km in Denmark, the Netherlands, Western Germany and Switzerland. In France and Great Britain it is much lower. Of this mileage the greater part is run on trips outside the town. Against these must be set the trips made within the city by vehicles domiciled outside it—which however amount to fewer vehicle-miles than those run by vehicles domiciled in the city on roads outside it. Taking 8,000 km per p.c.u. as an average annual town mileage for all motor vehicles domiciled in the city, the total annual mileage run will be 320 million p.c.u./km (200 million p.c.u./miles) and the average daily mileage 0·9 million p.c.u./km (nearly 0·6 million p.c.u./miles). Of these between 9 and 12 per cent will be run during the peak hour, or 100,000 p.c.u./km (say 63,000 p.c.u./miles).

If the road space required per p.c.u. is 75 sq m (a 3-m lane width multiplied by an average headway of 25 m)—say about 800 sq ft—at an average loading on all main *and* side streets of 150 p.c.u./lane/h, or about 20 per cent of the possible capacity of lanes on urban streets, with an average speed of 25 km/h (15 mph) the road space required to carry this total traffic in the peak hour will be:

$$\frac{63,000 \text{ p.c.u./miles} \times 800 \text{ sq ft}}{15 \text{ mph} \times 20\%} = 16 \cdot 5 \text{ million sq ft}$$

or 15 million sq m or 150 hectares.

If the average residential density is 200 persons per hectare the town will have an area of 500 hectares. Thus 30 per cent of the total area of the town would be needed for roadways alone. Further areas would be required for parking areas. Such a requirement cannot be met. In central European cities roadways, footways and parking areas generally take up 24 to 28 per cent of the land in the central area: 17 to 21 per cent for roadways and 6 to 8 per cent for footways. Thus severe congestion would arise in our imaginary city.

A different method of calculation leads to the same result. In the city centre about 12 per cent of the city's cars are parked during the peak period. This parking requires an area of 250 sq ft per p.c.u. or a total of

$$40,000 \times 250 \times 12\% = 1,200,000 \text{ sq ft or } 120,000 \text{ sq m.}$$

This is an area 300 × 400 m (1,000 by 1,300 ft). This is bigger than the entire retail core and cannot be made available for car parking. Thus cars must be parked above one another on several levels.

From the parking demand we can deduce the volume of traffic which has its destination in the central area. During the hours 0700 and 2200 on average 7·5 per cent of all cars domiciled in the city are parked in the central area. If the average parking duration is 45 min, during 15 h then

$$15 \times \frac{60}{45} \times 7\cdot5\% = 150\%$$

of all p.c.u. will enter and leave the city centre. Each vehicle will of course make two trips—one in and one out of the area. A traffic survey in Stockholm showed that the average car domiciled in the city made an average of three trips daily into or out of the central area. Thus in our imaginary city 120,000 vehicle trips would be made into and out of the area.

Let us suppose the main road network of the town consists of a cross. If vehicle trip destinations are evenly spread throughout the central area half of the trips will terminate before reaching the main crossroads, the other half will pass through it. Thus the peak-hour volume passing through the crossroads would be 60,000 p.c.u./day × 11% = 7,000 p.c.u.

If the main intersection is developed on one level, then, allowing for a certain imbalance between the morning and evening flows, it would have to have six traffic lanes, plus turning lanes, on each of the intersecting streets. Adding to this roadway width parking strips and footways 4 m wide the total width of each street would have to be 36 m (120 ft). If a city of 100,000 inhabitants cannot provide so many traffic lanes through its centre—even on parallel streets—traffic jams will be unavoidable. For comparison we may note that in 1959 the Karlsplatz intersection in Munich was carrying nearly 100,000 p.c.u. per day. The grade-separated 'Stack' interchange in Los Angeles was already in 1963 carrying 400,000 cars per day; the intersecting roads are eight-lane motorways.

The values used above have been carefully chosen. Of course the round figures used must not be generalized. But they do show what sort of values determine the adequacy of a road network and how changes can work themselves out. They allow an overall judgement to be made of conditions —which must of course be followed by an exact examination.

5. Policy for accommodating population increase

(a) Planning targets

Most towns have an old centre and more or less spread-out suburbs. The problem facing town and regional planning is where to accommodate the increase in population which is expected to occur in the conurbations within the planning period. There are various possibilities:

Increased density within the city boundaries
Extension of the suburbs

Creation of satellite towns as dormitory towns
Creation of new towns with industry
Promotion of existing neighbouring towns
Uniform distribution over all municipalities
Uncontrolled development

These possibilities have been exhaustively dealt with from many angles. Here they will only be judged from the traffic point of view.

Greater concentration of population means an increase in residential density. This is not desirable since less light, air and open space would be available for each person. But even if a city council were to decide to make such a change in the planning regulations and to permit greater density, the increase in density would only take place slowly. Owners cannot be compelled to tear down existing buildings in good condition just to serve this purpose. Only over a period of many years would the old houses be gradually replaced by bigger buildings. The existing roads would carry heavier traffic volumes, especially traffic serving frontages. The trip distances between homes and jobs would remain short.

It is a simpler matter to prescribe higher densities for areas of new development. If this is done the town will spread out more slowly than it would with a lower density of new development. Vehicle mileage and trip times will increase less steeply. But only a major increase in density will have a noticeable effect on traffic.

The areas of new development for town expansion may be found on the edges of suburbs, in satellite towns with or without their own industry or in neighbouring towns. If the suburbs are expanded, short-distance transport will increase disproportionately; in the other cases travel demands on trunk roads and railways will increase more markedly. A thorough investigation for the Zürich region showed that the total of person-miles is about the same in all these cases. The differences between these alternatives have altogether very little weight in economic terms. In one case, however, the short-distance transport links must be developed faster, while in the other cases railways and motorways and their feeders must have priority.

The only objectionable course from the transport engineering point of view is the uniform development of all municipalities. In this case the economical provision of public transport services will become less and less possible.

The traffic situation in a conurbation housing a million persons will only be slightly influenced by the choice of one or other solution. Of course the creation of a 'new town' of 50,000 inhabitants will create a new centre of gravity with much local traffic; and this traffic concentration would not arise if the 50,000 were spread over several places. But despite its size, the new settlement will only generate just 5 per cent of the total conurbation traffic. The desire line diagram changes only slowly over a long period, as the comparison of old and new traffic counts proves (Fig. 8).

Unfortunately the 'overspill towns' which are being planned or built in the vicinity of various large cities in many countries are often poorly sited, as for instance in France and Germany. They are too close in to develop an economic and cultural life of their own; but too far out to permit a viable transport service.

A voluminous technical literature about 'new towns' has grown up. In reality they often owe their creation to fortuitous land ownership conditions or to political influences. The result is often an artificial, premature

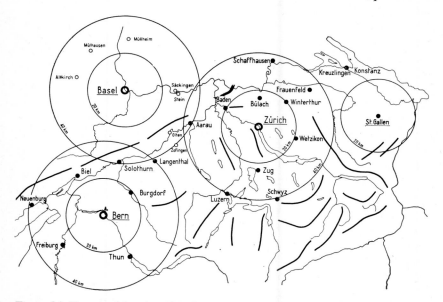

Figure 34: Towns with cultural and economic independence can only grow up at a certain distance from the 'central cities'. This 'law' is hardly affected by mountain ranges (black lines on the map) or national frontiers.

extension of the urbanized area. New traffic movements are created which run partly at right-angles to the existing roads, but are not large enough to justify the creation of new roads. Such towns demand large expenditure for new public services—schools, hospitals, traffic—and yet remain in the shadow of the central city. The 'mother town' with its bigger labour market, its manifold attractions and its short distances sucks the best forces in again.

Again and again the fact has to be recognized that it is more appropriate to promote the development of existing towns at a certain distance from the big city and guide population increase towards them. These towns will be 'correctly' sited as regards transport geography and have existing transport connexions available. In central Europe such 'natural overspill towns' are about 20 or 25 km (12 to 15 miles) from the 'central city' (Fig. 34).

(b) Reality

The big city and its immediate neighbourhood will continue to grow especially fast and call for additional areas of land for housing. Everywhere there is a big demand for building land. Sites in locations favourable from the traffic point of view are expensive. For this reason many people wanting to build move onto land which is unfavourably located or into distant villages, and later create a demand for the reconstruction of the traffic network or improved transport service.

Town planning attempts—with varying success depending on the legal possibilities—to control building development. Often property conditions are an obstacle. The land owners cannot as a rule be compelled to develop their land, to forgo without compensation the right to develop it, to sell their land or to exchange it. For this reason many settlements are located at points where by chance there is a large piece of land in one ownership. In this way town and traffic planning is upset again and again.

In reality building development in most cities is mainly uncontrolled. The laws do not permit a particular solution for the settlement of new inhabitants to be carried through.

Now that the range of the means of transport no longer sets any limit, building development can spread out almost as far as desired into the surrounding countryside. Thus planning has lost an important lever for guiding the development of settlements. Even if it were possible to declare that one of the possible courses mentioned above was to be followed, it could still be only partially realized. If for instance the authorities decided in favour of the densest possible development of the city proper, it would still not be possible to prevent the further spreading out of the suburbs. If new towns are founded, migration into the mother city could still not be interrupted.

The ban on migration into all big German cities which was introduced in 1933 had to be lifted after a few weeks. The long-standing ban on migration into Moscow is not very effective. Urban growth has proved itself more powerful than the strictest planning measures taken by the states. The building of ten satellite towns around London since 1946 has not been able to prevent the further concentration of industry or the further growth in the population of the city proper. The growth of London has been slowed down, but it has not been brought to a standstill. A really new town remains a rare exception.

One of the most important prerequisites for a true, lively town is the transport situation. In central Europe a new town of 30,000 to 40,000 inhabitants (depending on its distance from the mother city) requires rail service to supply its wants and to serve industry. Since in this part of the world the construction of new railway lines can scarcely be considered any longer, such towns should only be built around railway stations on existing lines. Equally, existing motorways and main roads must be taken into consideration.

In Europe all points which are favourable for transport have long been occupied by settlements. There are no locations left for independent new towns. Everywhere there is a dense network of roads, railways and waterways. Where villages are to be developed into towns, manifold transport connexions already exist. Therefore our attention should be directed to the existing towns, each of which has special conditions for which there is no standard treatment.

They confront us with complicated tasks. Each town must be specially 'X-rayed', each has its own unique image. But certain basic principles and general laws apply to all towns—including the rare new towns. Here we must utter a warning that town planning cannot and should not excercise a dictatorship but should merely guide development along orderly lines.

6. Town expansion

(a) Suburbs and new settlements

In the expansion of suburbs, existing roads are often extended here and there or new roads joined onto them. Sometimes the result is a mess. The roads in the centre of the suburb remain unaltered, but must serve the additional traffic of the new housing areas, for which they were not designed. Thus the conditions are created for traffic problems similar to those which exist already in the city centre. Here too a street network of limited capacity has to serve a much enlarged catchment area. Again the solution lies in tangent roads; but in the suburbs these will have a rather different location and significance. Their function will be to keep the radial traffic of the city away from the centres of settlements. The clearest but also in most cases the most expensive solution is the urban motorway, with no intersections at grade, passing clear of residential areas or even elevated or depressed.

New roads in the suburbs are often laid out without regard to the purposes they must serve, but merely to suit the property situation of the moment or the wishes of developers. Many roads may in the course of time acquire a greater significance and higher traffic loads. But by then the alignment can hardly be altered any more; all that is possible is to widen the roadway.

For this reason every development road must from the start be correctly dovetailed into a total network designed with foresight and on a big scale, even if this seems at first sight extravagant. All intersections must be located so that they may later fit in with 'green wave' signal systems.

New suburbs and settlements are often developed around a road intersection. They are usually planned for a particular population. But nobody can prevent this population from being exceeded if migration into the conurbation continues. Then the settlement must be extended. The main intersection in the centre becomes overloaded. Above a certain size of settlement it is dangerous to design an entire road network outwards from a single point. Efficient bypasses can hardly be added later. The mistake made in Brasilia has already been mentioned.

If the settlement is developed to one side of a railway station or a motorway access point, its commercial centre of gravity will not as a rule be found in the centre of the residential area but in the vicinity of the station or the motorway access point. As a result, internal trips within the settlement are longer on average than they need be, which is un-economic. Soon an attempt will be made to spread building development to the other side of the motorway, which is equally well located with regard to the shops and to the mother town. Then the railway or motorway, which was originally well located in relation to the settlement, will later cut the enlarged settlement in half. Planning must from the start take this probable development into consideration.

Building development will also continue along the connecting roads until town and suburb coalesce; for this is a considerably better location as regards traffic than the other edges of the suburb. It must be doubted whether the separation between town and suburb can be maintained. There is a danger that the intervening open space will be sacrificed as soon as the pressure of population becomes too great.

(b) Green belts and wedges

The building of settlements at a greater distance gives rise to consider-able economic costs. For instance let us assume that 20,000 people are housed in the first example at the edge of a town and in the second example behind a green belt 3 km in width. Let us assume this popula-tion owns 5,000 cars. While each car makes an average of three trips daily into the central business district in the first example, in the second example the average will be only two, the third trip per car being made to the local business centre. Thus the additional costs amount to

5,000 cars $\times$ 2 trips $\times$ 3 km = 30,000 car-km per day, or
30,000 $\times$ 250 weekdays $\times$ 0·30   DM = 2·3 million DM per annum.

These driving costs correspond to a capital of 46 million DM, assuming an interest rate of 5 per cent. If the average hourly earnings of the car occupants amount to 6 DM and the average travel speed is 30 km/h, then the extra time spent driving represents an annual waste of

1,000 h $\times$ 1·5 persons $\times$ 250 weekdays $\times$6 DM = 2·3 million DM.

But this sum will be left out of account because it is not the subject of any economic transaction.

Moreover the right-of-way of the four-lane road linking the mother town with the suburb covers an additional area of 3,000 m $\times$ 20 m = 60,000 sq m and costs about 6 million DM.

Thus the total extra expenditure on private transport could be capitalized at 50 million DM.

Even with a high degree of motorization, a purely residential town without industry will generate at least 200 transit trips *per capita* per annum. With the additional distance of 3 km and fares of 20 pfennigs per passenger-km the 20,000 inhabitants would have to pay an additional 200 × 3 × 0·20 DM × 20,000 = 2,400,000 DM per annum.

At 5 per cent interest this is equivalent to a capital sum of 48 million DM which is likely to grow if prices continue to increase.

In addition there are the losses due to increased travel time.

It will thus be economically justifiable to spend 100 million DM more in order to house the population 3 km closer in. If the total area needed to house the 20,000 people is 100 hectares, this means it is worth spending 100 DM more per sq m. It is doubtful whether building land 3 km further out is that much cheaper.

The extra cost can be reduced if jobs are created in the suburbs and the number of trips is thereby reduced, but the introduction of commerce and industry is not recommended. They lay special value on being favourably located in relation to their clients and to the main transport arteries—as they are in the mother city. Air mail and air freight, letter post and railway parcels have shorter delivery times to and from the mother city. Many enterprises cannot forgo this advantage.

(c) Residential density

Residential density also has a great influence on costs. A rough calculation for two cases gives the following picture for a settlement with 20,000 inhabitants:

Let the residential density be	100 or 200 persons per hectare
And the vehicle density	25 or 50 cars per hectare.
The new settlement will thus cover	200 or 100 hectares,
Or a square with sides of length	1·4 or 1·0 km.
Let there be a shopping centre in the middle. This will be accessible on foot from an inner square with sides of length	0·8 km,
With an area of	64 hectares.
Thus household shopping can be performed on foot by the following percentage of housewives:	31 or 64 per cent.
The remainder in each case will use the car. If 20 per cent of the total area is used for roadways and parking areas, these will occupy	40 or 20 hectares.

The roadway area will be exactly proportional to the total area,

E

because two-lane roads will suffice everywhere, since the heaviest traffic in two directions will nowhere exceed 5,000 cars $\times$ 3 trips per day $\times$ 11 per cent = 1,650 cars per h (11 per cent being the proportion of daily traffic occurring during the peak hour). Narrower streets cannot be considered.

The weekday distance run by cars in the course of shopping trips to and from the shopping centre will amount to:

$$5,000 \times 3 \times 1\cdot0 \text{ km} - 5,000 \times 3 \times 31\% \times 0\cdot56 \text{ km}$$
$$= 12,500 \text{ car/km,}$$
$$\text{or } 5,000 \times 3 \times 0\cdot7 \text{ km} - 5,000 \times 3 \times 64\% \times 0\cdot56 \text{ km}$$
$$= 4,300 \text{ car/km.}$$

If at the peak hour only one-third of cars are parked in the settlement (4 per cent of the number domiciled there) but two-thirds in the mother town (8 per cent of the number), then there will be a parking requirement in the local shopping centre of

$$5,000 \times 69\% \times 4\% = 138 \text{ car spaces}$$
$$\text{or} \qquad 5,000 \times 36\% \times 4\% = 72 \text{ car spaces}$$

Thus decreasing the residential density from 200 to 100 persons per hectare brings an additional expenditure of

200,000 sq m of road space at 100 DM/sq m	= 20 million DM
8,200 car-miles $\times$ 250 days $\times$ 0·30 DM = 615,000 DM p.a., or capitalized (at 5%)	12·3 million DM
66 parking spaces $\times$ 9,000 DM	0·6 million DM
	33 million DM

This additional cost is 1,650 DM per head of population. There are also additional costs for drains and gas, electricity and water mains, as well as running costs of street lighting and cleaning. Operating costs of public transport will also be higher with the lower residential density. About two-thirds of these additional costs must be borne by the public purse. These considerations, like those described in the previous section, show that a high residential density is essential.

The picture is somewhat different in the case of a neighbouring town which already has good public services, its own industry and good transport facilities, but lies at a large distance from the mother town. In this case the number of trips to the mother town is much smaller. Local traffic has shorter distances to cover. Transport costs are therefore lower. The transport facilities provide a greater attraction to industrialists to locate their factories in such a town.

There is much to be said for the development of neighbouring towns. But it must be stressed over and over again that industrial activity is not at the planner's command. Some new industry will grow too large for the land reserved for industry within a few years. Nobody would dream of forbidding further development. Instead, planning is adapted to provide for such development. Some branches of industry could not stand up to competition or are overtaken by new technical processes. Their production will decline, and no planner can arrest such decline.

All planning must be flexible and must be aware of its own limitations. But this by no means indicates that urban development should be uncontrolled. Many towns are surrounded by a wide belt of suburban sprawl with a confusing welter of allotments, houses and factories, which has grown up without benefit of the guiding hand of planning. It is difficult and expensive to create order in such areas after they have once been developed. This is especially true as regards transport connexions. Uncontrolled urban expansion has disadvantages which it is possible to avoid.

7. The city centre

(a) Basic data

As an example of conditions within a city centre we shall describe the inner area of Munich. This city had 1,050,000 inhabitants within its boundaries in 1961, and will grow to 1,500,000 by 1990 according to a high estimate.

The central area of a city cannot be sharply defined. The same can be said of the business core which consists of those parts of the central area with the greatest economic activity. This core is larger the bigger the population of the hinterland it serves: the city and its hinterland. In Munich it covers at present about 200 hectares, and will cover 290 hectares in 30 years' time.

Comparisons with other cities are not conclusive; but it is noteworthy that the deviations are contained within narrow limits (Fig. 35). The entire inner area of Munich covers about 880 hectares.

As in all big cities, the *residential population* of the inner area of Munich is declining. It fell from 33,000 in 1939 to 17,000 in 1961. Because of the big demand for office space dwellings are continually being converted into offices. In the future the only people who will live in the city centre will be those people who service and supervise the buildings. Their numbers and traffic needs are so small that they can be ignored. In addition there are people staying in hotels, inns and boarding houses; but these are numerically unimportant and can be left out of account.

As regards the *working population*, a far-reaching change has been taking place. With increasing automation the proportion of industrial workers is declining while the number of employees in administration and commerce is increasing. Offices of all kinds are providing an increasing number of jobs in the inner area. This phenomenon can be seen in all big cities.

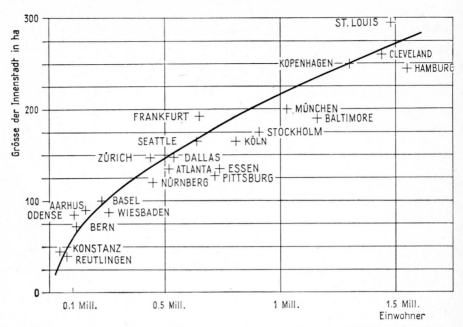

Figure 35: The relationship between the population of a city and the size of its central area varies only within narrow limits.

Town planning can hardly have any influence on this trend, but must treat it as the starting point of its considerations. The transformation has been brought about by modern forms of business and ways of living.

The business core can only be relieved to a small extent by industrial concerns moving out because the inhabitants of the entire economic region remain linked with the central services which are tied to their locations in the central area.

Thus in Munich the number of jobs in the central area will probably grow by 1990 by about 80 per cent to 450,000—of which half would be in the business core proper. The estimate cannot be considered excessive since in the decade 1950 to 1960 the number of jobs in the whole city grew by 38 per cent.

The third element which is important for traffic is *visitors*. The offices of public authorities and private firms, educational establishments, banks, shops, hotels, recreational facilities and other city-centre functions attract many visitors. Their number varies markedly from day to day, week to week and season to season. For planning purposes it is the large, regular flows of visitors which are of concern.

In Zürich the city architect's office stated in 1959 that the maximum number of visitors to the city centre was 25,900 per day. The following 'visitor densities' were found during the evening peak hours (visitors per hectare):

Big stores	700 ⎫ average
Small shops	927 ⎭ value 900
Hotels and restaurants	171
Other buildings (offices, lawyers, doctors etc.)	308

The building land in the central area is at present divided as follows:

Offices etc.	40%
Shops and stores	10%
Hotels and restaurants	10%
Other uses	40%

Sites included in this last category attract an average of only 50 visitors per hectare. Thus the average value for the whole central area is 250 visitors per hectare; and a similar visitor density may be assumed for Munich. Thus we may forecast that in 1990 there will be 250 visitors per hectare × 290 = 72,500 visitors in the business core. However, observations in Zürich show that 17 per cent of visitors are also workers in the central area, doing their shopping after they have finished work. On the other hand 'retail intensity' will increase as stores with large numbers of visitors drive shops with a small turnover out of the central core. The number of visitors present in the centre of Munich during the evening peak hours in 1990 was therefore estimated at 70,000.

Apart from this the streets in the central area have to carry public transport vehicles, goods delivery vehicles and police, postal and public cleansing vehicles having origin or destination in the central area. Even assuming thorough-going restrictions on loading and unloading, we may assume that these vehicles will in 1990 be making 6,000 trips out of the central area during the evening peak hour (i.e. in the direction of heavier flow).

It is uneconomic to design transport facilities to cope with exceptional peak loads of short duration. But the traffic peaks can only be reduced to a limited extent by the staggering of working hours. We certainly cannot assume that there will be any fundamental change in the daily traffic pattern. In the calculations which follow it is assumed that the business core is evacuated by workers within a period of 20, 30 or 60 min.

The studies in Zürich showed that the average visitor to city centre establishments stayed an average of

39·6 min in banks and offices, etc.
11·1 min in big stores
7·7 min in small shops
36·2 min in hotels and restaurants

Since shoppers often visit several shops the time spent by each visitor in the city centre may be assumed to be 40–45 min—studies in Basle,

Munich, Wiesbaden and other big cities have shown that this is the average parking duration at parking facilities in the city centre.

If all visitors to the business core of Munich came in their own cars, with an average occupancy of 1·8 persons per car and a turnover of 1·4 in the use of each parking space during the peak hour there would be a demand for

$$\frac{70,000}{1\cdot 8 \times 1\cdot 4} = 28,000 \text{ car spaces for visitors' cars.}$$

Including access aisles these would require an area of 28,000 × 25 sq m = 70 hectares. To this must be added the parking space required for other vehicles. Normally roughly 12 per cent of the cars domiciled in the city region will be parked in the business core. Since in 1990 there will probably be 525,000 cars in the metropolitan area of Munich, 12 per cent of these will require 63,000 car spaces in the centre. These would occupy 158 hectares—roughly 55 per cent of the total area of the business core. This figure is not surprising.

An employee requires a working space of 22 sq m; a car requires 25 sq m of parking space. On work trips the average car occupancy is 1·3 persons. Office buildings should have an extra 30 per cent car spaces available for visitors. Thus we arrive at a requirement, with full motorization, of 1 sq m of parking area for 1 sq m of office space. Thus every other building in the business core would have to be a parking garage if all demands are to be satisfied.

Every car makes three trips daily to or from the city centre. Thus the 525,000 cars domiciled in the Munich city region in 1990 would make 1,575,000,000 trips daily into and out of the city centre; and 11 per cent of these would be made in the peak hour, or 173,000. Of these 140,000 would be in the peak direction (outwards from the city centre in the evening peak hour). If the average lane capacity for ordinary city streets with intersections at grade is taken as 700 cars per hour, 200 lanes would be required to handle this unidirectional load smoothly; or 400 lanes of city street (assuming no reversible lanes). If the demands of motorcycles, goods vehicles and stopping lanes are added we arrive at a figure of 600 lanes. The main streets leading out of the old town would thus require a total width of roadway of 600 × 3·5 m or about 2,000 m. The existing radial streets of any importance at the edge of the central area have at present only about 30 lanes with a total roadway width of 105 m.

We must now decide how much of the area of the city centre can and should be devoted to road traffic. All other decisions depend on this basic question. We cannot provide 600 lanes; 30 lanes will not cope with full motorization. We must determine what target should be adopted in realistic and balanced planning.

(b) Theoretical calculations

The ground area of a city centre can be divided into:

1. *Areas attracting traffic:* building land and courtyards, including off-street parking areas;

2. *Areas serving traffic:* areas occupied by roadways, bus turn-out lanes, cycle tracks and footways;

3. *Neutral areas:* open spaces including churchyards, schools, theatres, museums, etc., none of which generate trips during the evening peak hour.

It is only possible to increase the area devoted to one type at the expense of the other two types. The total area for all three types always remains the same. Demands must be so regulated that there is an equilibrium between areas attracting traffic and areas serving traffic. For this purpose a watch must be kept on 'plot ratio'—the ratio between total floor space in a building and the area of the site on which it stands.

Let us take an imaginary business core area having a uniform grid-type street network; having every job and the parking space pertaining to it in the same building block; and with streets having, in addition to the lanes for moving traffic, a stopping lane on each side for loading and unloading goods and for picking up and setting down passengers. Let us suppose trucks are not allowed to enter the business core during peak hours. Motor cycles are declining in numbers and their space requirements are small. Both can therefore be ignored.

Let us calculate the requisite *plot ratio* with full motorization in the business core under consideration. The first step is to subtract the open spaces (which occupy 14 per cent of the Munich central area) from the total area. The remainder is then divided into n blocks of uniform size. Of the total working population A of the area, $\dfrac{A}{n}$ are assumed to be working on each block. With an average car occupancy of 1·3 these will use for work trips $\dfrac{A}{n \times 1\cdot3}$ cars.

Each block will attract $\dfrac{B}{n}$ visitors (B being the total number of visitors to the area), who at a car occupancy of 1·8 will use $\dfrac{B}{n \times 1\cdot8}$ cars. There will also be $\dfrac{C}{n}$ other vehicles.

With a degree of staggering of working hours Z there will be in the peak hour the following volume of traffic Q_B starting from each block in each of the four main directions:

$$Q_B = \frac{1}{4n}\left(\frac{A}{1\cdot3 \times Z} + \frac{B}{1\cdot8} + C\right)$$

The maximum volume in each direction on any street in the grid will be:

$$Q_{max} = Q_B \cdot \sqrt{n} = \frac{1}{4\sqrt{n}}\left(\frac{A}{1\cdot3 \times Z} + \frac{B}{1\cdot8} + C\right)$$

This traffic flow will be carried on f traffic lanes each 3·5 m (11 ft 6 in) wide, each of which will be loaded to its capacity L.

$$f = \frac{Q_{max}}{L}$$

Thus with a symmetrical cross-section, and adding in k for footways, stopping lanes and median islands, the total width b will amount to:

$$b = 2 \times 3\cdot5 \times f + k$$

The total area of road space that will be required is F_s.

$$F_s = 2 \times b \times \sqrt{F} \times n - b^2 \times n$$

Uneven loading and details of junction layout necessitates an addition of 30 per cent. The total area F would then be divided as follows:

Areas serving traffic	$F_s \times 1\cdot3$
Traffic-neutral open spaces	$F_{gr} = 14\%$ of F
Traffic generating areas	F_G

The total area remaining available for the latter is

$$F_G = 0\cdot86\ F - 1\cdot3\ F_s.$$

On this area must be accommodated:

Working space	$A \times 12$ m^2
Parking space for the working population	$\dfrac{A \times 25 \text{ m}^2}{1\cdot3}$
Parking space for visitors (with turnover of 1·4 within the peak hour)	$\dfrac{B \times 25 \text{ m}^2}{1\cdot8 \times 1\cdot4}$

or in total $22A + 19\cdot2A + 9\cdot9B$ sq m. The remaining traffic C requires no parking space on building sites.

The requisite plot ratio $N = \dfrac{41\cdot2A + 9\cdot9B}{F_G}$ can be calculated for different values of L and Z. For a network with intersections at grade L has a value of 700 p.c.u./lane/h, for expressways with no grade intersections a value of 2,000 p.c.u./lane/h. The resulting figures for a business core of 290 hectares are as follows:

Lane capacity L p.c.u./h	Evacuation period, Z min	Open spaces, F_{gr} hectares	Roadway area F_s hectares	Building sites F_G hectares	Requisite plot ratio N
700	20	40	>250		
700	30	40	>250		
700	60	40	227	23	45
2,000	20	40	201	49	20
2,000	30	40	158	92	11
2,000	60	40	134	116	8

If the total movement of persons into and out of the centre of a city of a million inhabitants had to be performed by private cars, for it to flow efficiently only a few sites could still be built on, and these would have to be used very intensively indeed. Moreover working times would have to be well staggered, and all the important traffic routes would have to be brought into the central area as grade-separated facilities. No existing city centre can be converted into such a pure 'traffic town'.

The same formulae can be used to estimate the requirements of the centre of a new city.

Another method of calculation shows, for the same area, how lack of parking space can limit the proportion of people using cars. Let the visitor traffic be fully motorized. The building site area F_G with a plot ratio N must accommodate working space, parking space for the work force using A_w cars and for all visitors B. The valid equation is

$$F_G \times N = 22A + 19 \cdot 2A_w + 9 \cdot 9B.$$

With all work trips being made by car $A_w = A$. In that case

$$F_G \times N = 41 \cdot 2A + 9 \cdot 9B.$$

In the business core of Munich 14 per cent of the land is open space and 28 per cent is roadway. The remaining 58 per cent consists of building sites, so that

$$F_G = 0 \cdot 58F.$$

Using the values forecast for central Munich in 1990

$$F = 2{,}900{,}000 \text{ m}^2$$
$$A = 225{,}000 \text{ workers}$$
$$B = 70{,}000 \text{ visitors}$$

the plot ratio at which the demand for parking space could be met with full motorization comes out at

$$N = \frac{41 \cdot 2 \times 225{,}000 + 9 \cdot 9 \times 70{,}000}{0 \cdot 58 \times 2{,}900{,}000} = 5 \cdot 95.$$

If not a single worker drives to work $A_w = 0$; N drops to $3 \cdot 35$. If the visitors also come in without cars, N drops to $2 \cdot 95$. At present N is $3 \cdot 6$ in the central area of Munich. The space requirements for future full motorization could only be covered if all building sites were on average developed 65 per cent more intensively and all additional ground areas were used solely for parking cars.

The next thing to be tested is whether the *street network* would be able to handle the resulting loads. The equations developed above can be solved for different values of A_w. And the number of visitors using cars B_w can also be changed; it could for instance be reduced by two-thirds. If one assumes that the additional width k for stopping lanes, footways and islands is 14 m, and the roadway width required $F_s = 0\cdot30F$, we obtain the following results:

Lane capacity L p.c.u./h	Evacuation period Z min	Visitors with cars B_w	Other cars C	Workers with cars A_w	Permissible percentage of workers with cars (A_w as % of A)
700	20			5,400	2·4
700	30	70,000	6,000	8,100	3·6
700	60			16,200	7·2
2,000	20			49,300	21·9
2,000	30	70,000	6,000	73,900	32·8
2,000	60			147,900	65·7
700	20			16,700	7·4
700	30	23,300	6,000	25,000	11·1
700	60			50,000	22·2
2,000	20			61,700	27·4
2,000	30	23,300	6,000	92,600	41·2
2,000	60			185,200	82·3

In most of the above cases the proportion of workers who can drive to work remains very limited. Even if one assumes a completely grade-separated network of urban motorways, very restricted visitor car traffic and a 60-min evacuation period, not all of the 225,000 workers in the business core would be able to drive to work. With a street network with intersections at grade such as Munich possesses, for all the workers to drive to work would require a 5-h evacuation period even with only 33 per cent of visitors coming in by car; with all visitors coming in by car a 15-h period would be required! During the peak hour the number of cars which could leave the city centre could be one of the following combinations:

70,000 visitors + 6,000 service vehicles + 16,200 workers = 38,900 cars + 6,000 cars + 12,500 cars = 57,400 cars (line 3 of the above table)

23,300 visitors + 6,000 service vehicles + 50,000 workers = 13,000 cars + 6,000 cars + 38,400 cars = 57,400 cars (line 9 of the above table).

The maximum hourly outbound flow that could be accommodated can also be determined on the basis of the total roadway area, which in Munich forms 21 per cent of the whole area of $1,700 \times 1,700$ m = 290 hectares. With the supposed grid-pattern street network, the capacity of the network in the peak direction, allowing 30 per cent above the theoretical figure on account of obstructions, comes to:

$$\tfrac{4}{2} \times 1,700 \text{ m.} \left[\frac{1 - \sqrt{1 - 21\%}}{1\cdot3} \right] \times \frac{700 \text{ p.c.u./h}}{3\cdot5 \text{ m}} = 58,500 \text{ p.c.u./h.}$$

This is approximately the same volume of traffic. It is equivalent to 20,300 p.c.u./sq km.

If the business core is only 100 hectares, the 'exit capacity' drops to 34,500 p.c.u./h, but is 70 per cent greater per sq km. If the business core is only 300×300 m $= 9$ hectares, the exit capacity is only 10,300 p.c.u./h, which is however equivalent to 115,000 p.c.u./sq km. Thus with the same intensity of development and the same level of car usage the traffic demand is far greater in big cities than in small ones. The small city with a central area of only 9 hectares can handle 5·7 times as many vehicles per sq km as Munich, or it can have a 5·7 times greater average plot ratio. For Munich to achieve the same traffic conditions, other things being equal, it would have to enlarge its roadway areas in the business core by a factor of 5·7. But in reality the opposite happens: the bigger the city the more intensively used is the land in the business core.

(c) Data for practical use

There is nowhere to be found a business core with an absolutely uniform grid network of streets and equal traffic flows towards all points of the compass.

In Munich there are 31 lanes available in the peak direction on the main radial streets, not counting turn lanes at the main intersections. Certain junctions could be grade-separated. Minor flows use side streets. But a large scale widening of the main streets is out of the question, because it would greatly alter the appearance of the city and would require an enormous expenditure. To widen a street in the inner city outside the business core costs over 40 million DM (£4 million) per km. Making full use of all possibilities an outbound flow of about 30,000 p.c.u./h can be accommodated.

This proves that the capacity of the urban street network is limited by the cross-sections of the radial streets. The average plot ratio might be increased until enough parking space was available (although this could not be filled and emptied without unacceptable delays). But the width of the radial streets sets an unalterable limit to the part which cars can play in transportation service to the city centre. The number of lanes available at the edge of the business core is the determining factor.

In all central areas the short-period parker is favoured on economic grounds. The visitor, eager to buy, has precedence over the car commuter. Of the 70,000 visitors entering the centre during the peak hour, at least a third should therefore be enabled to come by car. In addition to their 13,000 cars and the 6,000 other vehicles, it would only be possible to accommodate during the peak hour 11,000 cars carrying workers, which would serve only 14,300 or 6·4 per cent of the workers in the area.

The visitors will require, with an average occupancy of 1·8 persons and an average parking duration of 40 to 45 min,

$$\frac{70,000}{1·8 \times 1·4} \times 33\% = 9,260 \text{ parking spaces.}$$

The other vehicles require about 1,000 spaces and the workers' cars about 11,000, making a total of 21,260 spaces. Thus the total floor space requirements can be calculated as

Working space for 225,000 × 22 m² = 4,950,000 m²
Parking space   21,260 × 25 m² =   530,000 m²

$$\overline{}$$
5,480,000 m² = 548 hectares

This total floor space must be provided on the total building site area, namely 58 per cent of 290 hectares = 168 hectares. Thus the average plot ratio must amount (apart from the remaining dwellings in the area) to $\frac{548}{168} = 3\cdot26$. Thus an equilibrium would be achieved between roadway area and parking area. Any increase in, or more intensive use of, the working space would make necessary a further restriction on private car traffic. Additional business floor space would mean, besides additional workers, additional visitors and additional service vehicle traffic. The proportion of motor vehicles in the total traffic would then have to drop.

In the central areas of New York and London there is very little private car traffic. In New York 83 per cent of all short-distance person trips are made by public transport. In London 90 per cent of the work trips to the centre are made by public transport.

If the main streets in Munich cannot be widened, it would be pointless, even with far-reaching staggering of working hours, to provide more than 21,260 parking spaces in the 290-hectare business core—or more than 70 stalls per hectare. If hours were further staggered the figure could be raised slightly. But we must bear in mind that development will not stop at the end of the planning period.

The business core can grow either upwards, by raising the average plot ratio, or outwards by absorbing further sections of the city without increasing average plot ratio. If road traffic is not to be throttled by lack of road space only the second way can be considered. But even then the traffic load would increase, because vehicles would have to pass through the extensions of the business core to reach the older parts. For this reason the parking provision in the core of Munich should be limited from now on to 50 stalls per hectare. It would be a mistake to create many new parking spaces by all available means. Thus the permissible parking densities would be as follows:

Old town (present business core)   50 stalls/hectare
Rest of future business core   70 ,, / ,,
Rest of central area   80 ,, / ,,

The figures will obviously be different in every town. However, the method of calculation has been shown in detail in order to show the effect of the figures for population and for number of jobs, as well as the use of

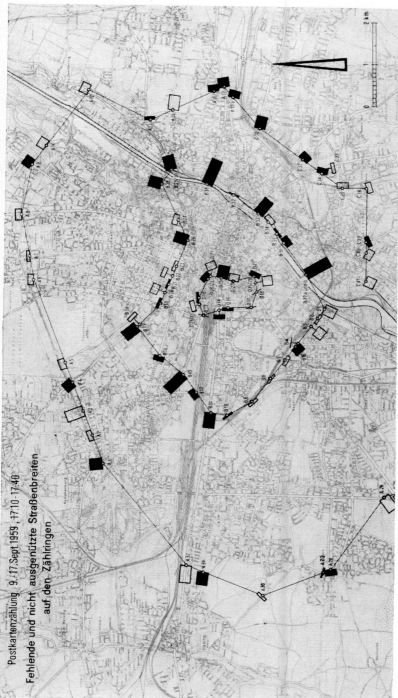

Postkartenzählung 9.17.Sept 1959 , 17.10 · 17.40

Fehlende und nicht ausgenützte Straßenbreiten
auf den Zählringen

Figure 36: In Munich the available road widths were compared with the traffic loads revealed by the postcard survey of September 1959. The results of the comparison are shown in the above drawing: the black bars indicate extra road widths needed at three cordons, the white bars indicate excess road widths. The drawing gives a clear indication of the urgency of road construction measures. Even in the city centre there are streets which are under-utilized because the network is not balanced. On the whole there is a shortage of road space in the inner areas, and an excess of road space in the outer areas. (Points A31 and A32 in the West were disrupted by a traffic diversion.)

ground area. The parking space requirement can be calculated in the same way for each individual part of the city or for a suburb. It is best done on the basis of the results of traffic counts.

Similarly we can determine where the boundaries of the area lie within which private car traffic can no longer flow without impediment. This boundary is not a circle around the centre of the town. It is irregular, and is pushed hither and thither by the population density, the terrain and the characteristics of the road network (Fig. 36). In Munich it is already well outside the centre. The wider the roads are built the nearer will the

Figure 37: High buildings in Genoa. In the top right of the photograph is the Porta Soprana at the entry to the old city. Building is so dense and as a result traffic so heavy that the old city can hardly be serviced any longer. These factors may cause part of a city to be throttled.

boundary be shifted towards the centre. Its distance from the centre of the city in various directions gives an objective yardstick for determining priorities in road works.

The city authorities must decide whether they want more open space, more intensive development or improved facilities for private traffic. They must determine whether cities shall grow upwards like New York or outwards like Washington. In most cases they will do both. More and more traffic requirements are piled onto a small land area. The traffic engineer must bring the technical and economic results of their decisions to the notice of the authorities in quantitative terms, so that they will recognize their consequences (Fig. 37). Despite all precautions and promises it is seldom that additional ground area is made available for traffic when high buildings are erected. An adequate number of parking spaces—i.e. a garage as big as the office block!—is never provided. The disequilibrium between building development and traffic becomes worse and worse.

(d) Space requirements for urban traffic

If the road network of a big city cannot be enlarged to the necessary extent and parking spaces provided in sufficient numbers, public transport, with its much smaller space requirement, must be called in aid.

The following table gives the capacities provided by various means of transport within a strip 3·5 m wide—the width of a single traffic lane—within the central area of a large city. The average speeds given are as low as they are in reality. In many places they are even lower during peak hours than those given. Speed is included because it is a measure of the quality of the transportation service provided. The average occupancies during peak hours on weekdays which have been assumed in these calculations were:

Pedal-cycle	1 person
Motor cycle	1·1 persons
Cars	1·5 persons (average of commuter and visitor traffic)
Public transport	80% of capacity

The hourly capacities calculated for the various modes are:

Mode of transport	Hourly capacity per 11 ft 6 in width (1)	Average speed km/h (2)	Product of (1) and (2) (3)	Index numbers in terms of (3) (car = 1) (4)
Pedestrian	23,500	4·7	110,000	9
Pedal cycle	5,400	12	65,000	5
Motor cycle	2,400	12	28,800	2·3
Car	1,050	12	12,600	1
Car on expressway	3,000	40	120,000	10
Bus (55 places)	7,700	10	77,000	6
Bus (150 places) Tram (150 places)	18,000	10	180,000	14
Tram (250 places)	24,000	10	240,000	19
Underground railway	40,000	25	1,000,000	80

The products of the figures in columns (1) and (2) are given in column (3). The resulting values, which are in terms of persons per hour × kilometres per hour, are a suitable yardstick for this comparison since they include both the quantity and the quality of the transportation service provided by each mode. The last column gives index numbers for the different modes in terms of these values, taking the value for a car as 1.

From these figures we can see that 23,500 pedestrians would require an area of 3·5 m × 4·7 km = 16,500 m², or 0·7 m² per person. In similar fashion we can calculate the space requirement per user for other modes. The following areas are required per person in motion at the speeds given above:

Pedestrian	0·7 m²
Pedal cycle	8 m²
Motor cycle	17·5 m²
Car occupant	40 m²
Car occupant on expressway	47 m²
Passenger on bus—55 places	4·5 m²
Passenger on bus/tram, 150 places	2 m²
Passenger on tram—250 places	1·5 m²
Passenger on underground railway	2·5 m²
Goods vehicles	75 m²

These figures do not include parking areas. Those for public transport are mostly at the edge of the city and are relatively small. Cars on the other hand require parking space at their destinations. Including access aisles the space needed per car is 20–25 m² or 13–17 m² per occupant. A boarding island 50 m² in area could handle 5,000 passengers an hour boarding and alighting. If 5,000 visitors to the city centre use their own cars, at an occupancy of 1·5, the 3,300 cars parking on an average for 40–45 min would require 2,400 parking spaces or 50,000 m². Proof of the correctness of these figures has been provided by the transport strikes in London, Paris and Rome in recent years. Where space is scarce public transport comes to the rescue of hard-pressed cities. Only public transport can give adequate transportation service to large city centres. The city authorities can do nothing to halt either the growth of population or the increase in traffic demands. They can only have an effect on the traffic problem by promoting public transport and in this way restraining the use of private transport with its big space requirements.

(e) Implications for transport economics

Economic considerations point in the same direction. In order to carry 18,000 employees in one direction in one hour, 17 traffic lanes would be needed if cars alone were used, but one lane will suffice if buses are used.

That large expenditures are involved is shown by the 1952 General Plan for Stockholm, which put the capitalized cost of transporting a single worker from suburb to city centre by bus at 27,500 Kr—or about £3,500 at 1968 prices.

The city of Philadelphia had comparative calculations carried out and drew conclusions from them for urban traffic policy. In the autumn of 1958 the city authorities began a big experiment in which they paid the savings in road building costs over six months, reckoned at $160,000, to the Pennsylvania Railroad. The railroad undertook in return to improve the frequency of service and lower the fares in suburban traffic. It was proved that this had the effect of keeping about 3,000 cars daily out of the city centre. This success so encouraged the city authorities that they converted the experiment into a permanent arrangement, and meanwhile extended it to a number of other lines. A special company was formed to administer the funds.

These indications should by no means be taken to mean that the cities should neglect their attempts to improve the street network and to provide additional parking space. Private transport remains superior to mass transport in many respects. Some outlying new settlements can only be served in this way. The purchasing power of the motorized resident ought still, at least to some extent, to benefit the city centre. But the cities should so distribute their limited resources that they get the greatest return from them and maintain the economic strength of their most valuable parts.

Public transport deserves to receive a certain priority, both in planning and in traffic flow arrangements, because it will have to perform the lion's share of the transportation tasks in the big cities during the peak hours. It must form the backbone of the city's traffic facilities. The increasing number of workers in the city centre must be carried with an acceptable expenditure of time and costs. The suggestion that is often put forward that public transport should be diverted around the most congested areas to make room for private cars is fundamentally wrong. Cities must follow the opposite course. The historical business cores can only be kept healthy and lively by good public transport.

Architects, engineers and town planners unanimously emphasized, on the occasion of the Vienna traffic inquiry of 1955, that the priceless Vienna Old Town could only be saved by thorough-going improvement of public transport. It is of course obvious that the facilities would have to be underground. Similarly the New York City Planning Commission is promoting the improvement of the underground railway network and has come out strongly against the provision of new parking facilities in the heart of Manhattan.

(f) Towns adapted to traffic

On the basis of these considerations we can now establish what should be understood by the term 'town adapted to traffic'. The term has two possible meanings:

1. A town whose design permits the unrestrained use of *all means of transport*.
2. A town whose design permits *all destinations* to be reached speedily.

With the formulae developed above we can calculate how much roadway area is needed to permit unrestrained use of private cars. It is possible in a new town to use the relationship found between building land, open space and roadways. But every healthy town grows. We are living in a time of unusually fast population increase and a heavy concentration of men in those areas where industry and service organizations press closely together.

In growing cities conditions would have to be altered more and more in favour of traffic, because vehicle-mileage grows with increasing distances. Thus even the 'New Town' would have to be altered after a certain time. If however an adequate proportion of ground area were devoted to roadways for a much larger population, then the layout of the town would be much too extensive and too expensive. Nobody can know whether the reserved roadway areas will in fact be needed later or whether quite different ways of life will arise. Thus there cannot be such a thing as a big city with private car traffic running entirely smoothly at any time (including car parking).

Only the second meaning of the term makes real sense. The 'town adapted to traffic' is one which determines and promotes that mixture of different modes of transport which best suits its circumstances. Greater density in the city centre must be resisted; but a considerably higher residential density must be achieved in the suburbs. The task has so many facets that there are no fixed rules governing it. Every place presents its special challenge—difficult perhaps but also stimulating.

II TRAFFIC COUNTS AND ESTIMATES

Transportation facilities are the biggest, the most exacting and the most expensive of supply installations. Like other kinds of supply networks, they should be carefully tailored to the demand. The more closely the supply of facilities corresponds with the demand for connexions the better is the transportation network. Thus it can only be correctly designed if present and future transport requirements are sufficiently known. The volume and direction of all important traffic streams must be determined so that we can recognize which parts of the network are already approaching capacity and how planned improvements or bypasses are likely to affect the situation.

1. Determinants of traffic demands

Trip-making *per capita* per annum is variable. In this section the factors affecting it will be examined.

(a) Population

Traffic demand per head normally increases with population. New inhabitants at the edge of the city must cover longer distances on trips for all purposes: work, shopping, recreation, etc.

In small villages there is no public transport. Most trips are walking trips. In towns the proportion of trips by some form of powered conveyance increases with size of town. Beyond a certain distance from the centre the number of trips to the centre *per capita* declines, because jobs and shops grow up in the suburbs. There is a certain relationship here which cannot, however, be expressed as a formula.

The present picture of average public transport trip-making *per capita* per annum in various sizes of town is roughly as follows:

No. of inhabitants	Trips per annum	Average length (km)
30,000	30–80	1·5 km
50,000	50–150	2·0 km
100,000	100–250	2·2 km
300,000	150–350	2·6 km
500,000	200–450	3·2 km
1,000,000	250–550	4·0 km
5,000,000	400–600	9·0 km

The average car domiciled in a big city makes 3 trips to or from the city centre every weekday, or about 850 trips per annum, and altogether 1,200 to 2,000 trips per annum throughout the metropolitan area. If in the future there is one car to every four inhabitants and the car has 1·5 occupants on average, there will be 450 to 700 car trips *per capita* per annum in cities where private traffic is not too severely restrained in the city centre. The average trip length of urban car trips is somewhat lower than that of public transport trips; in Düsseldorf (650,000 inhabitants) it is 2·7 km. It is true that the individual trip is longer because it includes those parts to and from the bus or tram stop which the public transport user must cover on foot; but on the other hand detours (interchange connexions) disappear and short trips are made by car which a non-car-owner would make on foot.

The bigger the city the bigger the proportion of trips which are made by public transport. The following figures apply to U.S. cities in 1958:

No. of inhabitants	Percentages of trips by	
	Cars	Public transport
less than 50,000	87	13
50,000–250,000	78	22
250,000–500,000	66	34
500,000–1,000,000	64	36
over 1,000,000	50	50

These figures include the low-density cities of the West where there is hardly any public transport any more. In the high-density cities of the East, which are much more comparable with European cities, the public transport proportion is considerably higher.

(b) Urban form

The more spread-out a city becomes, the longer the distances to be covered. The figures given above show for instance that in a town of 50,000 the average passenger-km *per capita* per annum by public transport amount to 200, while in a city of 1,000,000 the figure amounts to 1,600: eight times the figure for the smaller city. Mileage run per car is also considerably higher. This costs more time and money. Transport makes life in the bigger cities more expensive.

The spreading out of a city has the same effect. If the residential density is lower, or if because of mountains or water the city cannot spread out evenly on all sides, expenditure on traffic must rise. With bigger distances the proportion of walking trips goes down. A linear town, like Wuppertal, calls for many more annual person-km *per capita* than does a circular or star-shaped town. It also gives rise to a greater number of vehicles.

In flat lands more trips are made on foot or by pedal-cycle (Netherlands, Denmark); in hilly districts public transport and motor vehicles are used more. If we compare Hanover, which is flat, with Stuttgart, which is hilly (both cities have nearly the same number of inhabitants), we find that the number of public transport trips *per capita* per annum is twice as great in the hilly city. People are more inclined to travel uphill by tram or bus than downhill.

(c) Social structure

Other factors which increase the number of trips *per capita* are a decrease in average household size, a decline in the number of children, an increase in the proportion of employed persons and an increase in the average expectation of life.

The average household size in Swiss cities decreased from 4·7 to 5·0 in 1880 to 2·7 to 3·2 in 1968. Even when population remains stationary the number of households increases; and with it the number of cars. Gradually a certain state of permanence is reached and the household size declines only very slightly. There are marked differences between city and city and between city and country.

An increase in the proportion of employed persons has a similar effect. In many central European cities the proportion is very high at 45 per cent. Probably it will not go significantly higher. The number of young people not yet in employment is declining. At the same time the number of old people no longer capable of working is increasing. The proportion of people between 20 and 65 increased in Germany between 1880 and 1950 from 51 per cent to 60 per cent of the population. In the future the number of employed persons could only be increased if more women become employed, which is hardly likely to happen. Thus the number of work trips will no longer increase faster than the total of all trips. In general there will be no strong pull towards further motorization from this direction.

The well-to-do parts of a city produce more traffic *per capita* per annum than do the less well-off. They have more cars per head, and although the differences are declining, they are still so great that caution is needed in comparisons between different parts of a city.

The rapid spread of television has led to a noticeable decrease in evening recreational traffic. This does not however affect technical traffic planning because it is the peak loads produced by work trips which are decisive. The economic health of transport undertakings is however adversely affected. Such alterations in living habits cannot be foreseen; but they may arise and cause a change in the traffic picture. This provides further proof that traffic planning must always remain flexible.

(d) Working hours

In central Europe roughly half of the urban traffic on weekdays is work trips. This is true of the entire day. The proportion of work trips varies very markedly between one time of day and another. In the morning peak it may reach 95 per cent and it drops to 5 per cent in the late evening hours. Even at the same time of day it may be different in different parts of the city. Similarly the traffic peak does not occur at the same time at all points in the city. In the morning it rolls from the suburbs into the city centre, i.e. it starts earlier further out. In the evening the reverse is the case. One must watch this when making traffic counts.

With increasing motorization in big cities more car trips will be made outside the peak period, while public transport will continue to carry the bulk of the work trips. The work trip peaks will become sharper and sharper, and the utilization of public transport will become less and less economical.

The introduction of the five-day week and the elimination of long lunch-hours brought a certain reduction in trip-making. Work trips dropped by one-sixth. Public transport vehicles and installations were less intensively used. But the weekday peaks which determine the capacity required for all transport installations do not alter. Thus the shortening of working time has no significance for transport planning. Similarly the elimination of long lunch hours has mainly an economic effect. It is good for the economy as a whole, but bad for the economic health of public transport. Elimination of midday trips home to lunch and back to work has no discernible effect on technical measures, although in some cases it may facilitate the staggering of working hours.

Longer weekends and holidays give rise to an increase in excursion and recreational traffic. However, this does not counterbalance the loss of work trips within the city for the transport undertakings. Since long-distance traffic does not have such distinctive peaks it has a decisive influence on transport planning only in rare cases. In recreational areas, however, it can give rise to much heavier traffic at weekends than on weekdays.

(e) Economic situation

When economic conditions are favourable, persons and goods traffic increase rapidly. Motorization forges ahead faster and public modes of transport are used frequently. When economic conditions are bad the reverse happens. It is true that the number of cars in the U.S.A. did not decrease during the 1930–35 economic crisis, but the average car was less intensively used. During the same period public transport ridership in Zürich declined by 20 per cent. The decline was mainly in short trips and was a result of 'pedestrian competition'. At present the pedestrian in Zürich prefers to ride a tram or bus for distances in excess of 800 m. In German cities during the difficult years 1948–50 people were content to walk up to about 1·3 km.

Every variation in the economic situation generally, or in that of individual industries, is immediately noticeable in traffic. In the U.S.A. a weekly announcement is made of the number of cars registered and the number of railway wagons loaded, because the variations can be rapidly and easily seen from these figures. Predictions about the economic situation are of course subject to many uncertainties. But everything points to a further rise in the standard of living. Therefore vehicle mileages are bound to increase further. The number of private cars will increase.

When every household—including old people living alone—has its own car, there will be about one car to three people. If every adult had his or her own car, the ratio would be 1 : 1·5. At what level saturation will be reached it is hard to say. It will depend on economic, social and technical circumstances which could change in the course of time.

(f) Modes of transport

Fast, cheap and comfortable modes of transport are used frequently. No one mode of transport combines all three qualities, so that residents of a town prefer now the one, now the other. Alongside the cheap bus runs the faster and more comfortable taxi. In cities with heavy pedal-cycle traffic, traffic by other modes is lighter. An increase in public transport fares leads to an increase—often only temporary—in pedal-cycle and pedestrian traffic. Thus the boundaries swing to and fro. The authorities can influence the price structure by subsidizing either public transport or the provision of car-parking space.

Modes of transport develop differently. In many cities of central Europe a level of 250 cars per 1,000 inhabitants will soon be reached (i.e. one car to four people); but not in all of them. The conurbations of the American West, which can scarcely any longer be described as cities, have already in some cases reached a density of one car to two inhabitants. And the density is very high also in the countryside. But there is a much lower level of motorization in the high-density 'European-type' cities of the eastern U.S. There the traffic congestion is already so bad, and public transport service still so good, that many families have given up the idea of buying a car, or a second one.

Urban form sets a limit on motorization. This will probably happen in Europe also, but it cannot yet be said at what level. Then the hinterlands will forge ahead of the cities. The highest car ownership level is to be expected in the future in the areas around big cities, where public transport service is economically or technically impossible. Flat land will also have above average car ownership. The densely built-up urban areas will lag behind; here public transport will still gain riders.

Motor cycles and scooters are for many people a step towards having their own car. With the appearance of the scooter the traffic picture on city streets altered in an unexpected way which could not have been foreseen. At one counting point the number of two-wheeled motor vehicles increased sevenfold in the short period 1952–56. But the importance of these vehicles will however decline, like that of the pedal-cycle. The numbers of pedal-cycles in Basle declined as follows:

Year	Persons per pedal-cycle
1950	2·4
1955	2·6
1963	2·9

The mileage per pedal-cycle has probably also declined as a result of the overloading of streets. Even in the classical 'cycle lands' (Netherlands and Denmark) the motor cycle and the scooter are gradually ousting the pedal-cycle. They in turn will later be replaced by the car.

Goods traffic within the cities and over short distances has been fully motorized for many years. Horse-carts have become a rarity. The number of goods vehicles now increases only in proportion to the population and the increase in the standard of living. As a result the proportion of goods vehicles to total motor vehicles is continually declining. In Central and Western Europe it is still between 10 and 15 per cent. The proportion of goods vehicles during the evening peak hour is much smaller.

With the progress in vehicles and roads there has been a slow but steady increase in the annual mileage per vehicle. In many parts of Europe (Denmark, Netherlands, West Germany, Switzerland) the average car covers about 20,000 km (12,500 miles) per annum. Vehicles domiciled in high-density urban areas cover rather less. But cars domiciled in the areas surrounding big cities and conurbations cover 10 to 30 per cent more mileage. The corresponding figures are 11,000 km in Great Britain and 8,000 km in France. There are big differences between the various job categories. The lower income groups cover a smaller mileage. The second car in a two-car household covers much less mileage because the whole family goes together on expeditions and recreational trips. This is confirmed by the average car occupancies observed for different types of trip:

Work trips	1·3 persons⎫ an average of 1·5
Other weekday trips	1·8 persons⎭ in peak hours
Weekend trips	3·5 persons

As the number of cars increases, the average annual mileage per car will decrease. In the suburbs surrounding large American cities more than 25 per cent of families already possessed two cars in 1967. For this reason the average mileage per car in North America is only 16,000 km (10,000 miles). Taking account of these various factors we can assume the same average annual mileage per car in Europe in the future.

Regarding the proportions of this mileage that will be run on urban and on rural roads no reliable facts are available. An investigation in Düsseldorf in 1957 showed that the average annual mileage per car domiciled in the city run on city streets was 5,200 km (3,300 miles). The vehicle-mileage run on city streets by 'foreign' vehicles was about 50 per cent of the mileage run by 'home' vehicles. In smaller towns the mileage run inside the town itself is usually smaller because distances are shorter. In towns of 100,000 population it may reach 3,000 km (1,800 miles).

The average annual mileages covered by other vehicle types have been found in recent observations to be as follows:

Motor cycles	6,000 km
	(3,750 ml)
Taxis	60/80,000 km
	(37,500 to 50,000 ml)
Buses and goods vehicles	
delivery and charter work	30,000 km
	(19,000 ml)
local scheduled service	50/60,000 km
	(32,000 to 38,000 ml)
long-distance service	80/100,000 km
	(50,000 to 67,000 ml)

In rough calculations and in overall planning the values for private cars may be used since they form the bulk of traffic in the peak hours.

The number of public transport trips per head and per annum will probably increase only slightly in the future. But the average trip length will increase as a result of the further spreading out of cities, so that the trip-miles *per capita* will increase. Lower residential densities and the competition of cars and taxis will force the introduction of smaller units operated at higher frequencies. On certain routes with few passengers, and equally on express routes where passengers are prepared to pay extra per mile, small buses will be introduced. In many cities—e.g. in Moscow, Istanbul and in South America—taxis operate scheduled services, stopping only by request. They are very suitable for providing private, individual transport service.

Railway branch lines will be partially replaced by bus routes. Some railway stations are so located that passengers have to walk further to reach them than they do to reach a bus stop; the latter can be located in the heart of a settlement. Moreover the old railway lines are too slow in comparison with modern motorways and expressways. Another reason for the substitution of buses is the fact that, in Germany for example, the law requires that a rail bus must have a second crew member besides the driver, while a road bus may be operated by a single man, despite the more difficult task the driver has to perform.

(g) Overloading of transport routes

There is no universally valid relationship for the shift which has been observed everywhere from public to private transport. An increase of one million passenger-km per annum in travel by private car is perhaps accompanied in one city by a decrease of 100,000 passenger-km per annum in travel by public transport (this relationship was observed in recent years in Sydney), in another city by a decrease of 50,000, while in a third city there may even be an increase. This state of affairs deserves special attention since it is important in the design of future transport facilities.

Street congestion and shortage of parking space favour a return to suburban railways, trams and buses. Segregated tracks or reserved lanes become more and more valuable in ensuring fast travel times by public transport. Private traffic prefers to avoid the overloaded areas. As a result it increases at a slower rate in these areas than in neighbouring areas where it increases at a faster-than-average rate owing to traffic using detours through these areas. Vehicle-mileage is increased by these detours.

Thus there are marked differences within a big city. The traffic may for instance increase within the next two decades in the central area by a factor of 2, in outer areas and new settlements by a factor of 6 to 10, and in other areas of the city by factors between.

In converting observed traffic volumes into estimated future volumes all the influences described above should be taken into account. Despite careful basic research they cannot be accurately forecast. It is advantageous to use a range of values for the total factor which is applied on the basis of all these influences. These values should represent the possible maximum and minimum increases in traffic with normal uninterrupted development, without allowing for extreme changes. Technical planning should be based on the higher of the two values, so that facilities will be designed on a sufficiently large scale; but in economic calculations, for instance with regard to public transport, the lower value should be used, in order to avoid unnecessary or premature interest-bearing expenditures. In view of the inevitable uncertainty of the values chosen there is no point in demanding excessive accuracy in the actual capacity calculations. It is much more important to check the planning against the results of traffic counts repeated every few years, and in some cases to shift the main targets of the transport development programme.

2. Mathematical formulae

(a) Traffic volumes

As basis for the engineer's work as many statistical data as possible must be assembled. The more figures are available the more surely can the future development be judged. A sudden break in the series of figures is hardly likely. For this reason attempts are made again and again to set up mathematical formulae for further increases in traffic. It is inevitable that

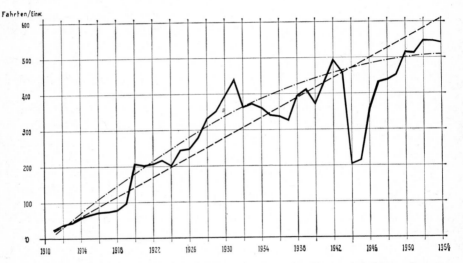

Figure 38: In Rome transport trips, in terms of annual trips per inhabitant, have increased sharply over the years (solid line). The private transport trend could be interpreted in terms of either of the broken lines. One of them gives a figure 20 per cent higher than the other even in 1954; the difference would be greater and greater in succeeding years.

they will all be wrong since traffic is not subject to any strict law of nature. The behaviour of men and women cannot be expressed in any formula.

All the factors mentioned above are subject to variations. Even the weather or big festivities play a part. If the results of the past year are somewhat lower on account of such chance factors, the mathematician will try to bend his curve downwards. The next year may by chance bring a somewhat more favourable result, so that once again a new curve would have to be drawn (Fig. 38). Both would be chancy and inaccurate.

Traffic is part of the economy and of human life. Changes in the economic situation and in living habits can never be accurately predicted. Since 1950 the estimates of the future number of vehicles have several times had to be raised sharply. Also the population figures for the cities have increased beyond all expectations. This was the result of an economic upswing, the rate of which no one had foreseen. It led to heavy migration into the cities. In recent years a reverse trend began here and there.

We must therefore beware of purely mathematical calculations. It is correct and necessary, however, to observe every influence continually and thoroughly, and to evaluate all available statistical data. In this way more reliable approximate values can be found.

On the other hand attempts have been made to estimate traffic volumes directly on the basis of population, distribution of jobs and other data. This is certainly appropriate for rough calculations. The numbers of trips *per capita* per annum by public and private transport are well known, and so are the average trip lengths. But exact studies of traffic, which should serve as the basis for capacity and rate-of-return calculations, always show wide deviations from the results of the 'comparative' calculations. While the mathematician might be surprised to learn that 1,000 inhabitants of the northern suburbs of a city behave differently from 1,000 inhabitants of a southern or western suburb, the engineer trained in town planning will know this is so. Similarly it is not possible to determine rates of traffic increase for different parts of a city with the help of mathematical formulae. Various formulae which have been published in recent years have proved unusable.

Per contra the results of a survey of trip-making by public transport in a certain area, which reflects the effects of all local factors, can on certain conditions be applied to the prediction of private traffic and vice versa. The survey is close to life; the formula is not.

It is more than eighty years since the Viennese engineer Lill worked out his famous 'travel law' for predicting the characteristics of person trips. This states that the number of trips between two areas decreases with increasing distance between the areas. The law is expressed in the formula:

$$V = K \frac{P_A \times P_B}{E^x}$$

where

V is the number of trips between A and B,
K is a constant to be determined from the local conditions,
P_A and P_B are the populations of A and B,
E is the distance between them and x is an exponent which usually varies between 1 and 2·5.

Recently attempts have been made to determine this 'law of traffic gravity' even more precisely. According to Swedish investigations road traffic decreases with increasing distance in the ratio $1 : E^{1.5}$. For passenger traffic on the Netherlands Railways the ratio is between $1 : E^2$ and $1 : E^{2.2}$. Other observations show a much sharper decrease, with a ratio in some cases of $1 : E^{2.7}$.

A decrease in the ratio $1 : E^{1.5}$ means that for

1 person travelling 100 miles there are
30 persons travelling 10 miles and
1,000 persons travelling 1 mile.

The 'travel law' is not however a law of nature. There are big variations in reality. Observations never produce smooth, simple curves. For this reason

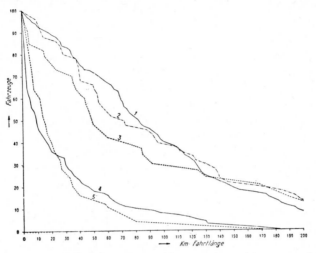

Figure 39: Cumulative trip length curves for cars whose drivers were interviewed at five different interview stations:

1. In Biel, Switzerland, on the western boundary of the town, where there is little local traffic, on a Sunday;
2. Amt Marl in the Ruhr region: heavy regional traffic in a conurbation, weekday;
3. Biel, on the southern edge of the town, where there is heavy local traffic, Sunday;
4. Biel, on the Neuchâtel road, with little local traffic, weekday;
5. Biel, on the Berne road, with heavy local traffic, weekday.

attempts have already been made to use changing exponents. The trip length distribution curve also looks different on Sundays and weekdays because on Sundays long excursion trips are made while on weekdays short work trips are made (Fig. 39). Lill himself did not want his formula to be understood as a rigid law, and did his best to investigate the various influences more closely. He considered, for instance, the passenger traffic on the Vienna–Brunn–Prague railway line, and demonstrated that there was much more traffic between one German-speaking area and another, and between one Czech-speaking area and another, than there was between areas the same distance apart but on opposite sides of the language boundary. Human relationships are the determining factor, and these cannot be mathematically determined.

Certainly Lill had recognized a basic fact: that there are far fewer long trips than short ones. Thus in Zürich in 1959 the following numbers of trips *per capita* per annum were made:

> 450 tram and bus trips average length 3·0 km
> 65 railway trips average length 31 km
> 0·3 trips by air average length 1,050 km

For the entire population of Switzerland there were 43 rail trips and 0·08 air trips *per capita* per annum.

(b) Capacity calculations

In the field of capacity calculations we find once again that pure mathematical formulae, such as Poisson distribution, headway distribution, Monte Carlo method, queueing theory, or for that matter electronic simulation of traffic flow, can only occasionally give usable results. Vehicles do not move in accordance with purely physical laws. Drivers again and again take new, unforeseeable decisions.

Poisson assumes that there is a purely chance distribution of vehicles on a roadway. This is only possible as long as queues do not form as a result of speed differences. But this does in fact happen even on rural roads carrying little traffic. On heavily travelled roads it is the normal case. When traffic is approaching the capacity of a road the assumption underlying the Poisson distribution is certainly no longer true. Generally this assumption is never fulfilled. On heavily travelled urban streets chance distribution is deliberately got rid of and driving in 'green waves' substituted. Here the traffic streams do not flow freely.

Operations research procedures also start from the same assumption. They do not for instance take account of any timetable or lights, although obviously this puts an end to uniform flow. A while ago the number of check-in points at an airport was determined with the aid of queueing theory. The result cannot be correct, since the arrival rate of passengers depends on the flight timetable, and this is continually changing. So long as chance no longer has free play, such methods of calculation lose their value. One should also not carry out, without good cause, calculations which are complicated or not easy to check.

On the other hand it is not sufficient simply to translate observed values for the present situation into plans for new facilities. Moreover the American values for the capacities of lanes and intersections are about 25 per cent too low for Europe with its smaller cars. Observation and calculation must interact on each other, in the way which will be described below.

3. Traffic flow patterns

(a) Traffic desires

It is not enough to determine the approximate order of magnitude of the volumes of person and goods movements in an area and their distribution between the different modes of transport. Only when the strength and direction of the most important traffic streams are known can it be determined which parts of the network are already approaching capacity and what effect planned changes in the network—reconstruction, relief roads or bypasses—will probably have.

Road planning must start from actual traffic desires. The present-day traffic picture at many points is already disturbed in that many drivers are

Figure 40: Residential density in Basle (220,000 inhabitants); the white areas have less than 50 inhabitants per hectare, the areas with horizontal shading between 50 and 200, those with cross-patching between 200 and 400, and those shown in solid black over 400. The areas of highest residential density form a wreath, as it were, around the city centre, mainly in the north and west.

already avoiding the overloaded areas. They make considerable detours in order to travel faster. Thus traffic loads arise at points where they should not properly speaking be. Different routes may be chosen for the same trip according to the time of day. Thus the proportion of total traffic carried by the bypass streets varies sharply. Because of the increasing congestion in the most important destination areas longer and longer detours are used. But traffic planning should not perpetuate such a picture of illness, but should satisfy real needs as well as possible.

The first and very important indication of traffic desires is the distribution of homes and jobs (Figs. 40, 41). From this we can estimate with some certainty the main directions of work trips (Fig. 42). The biggest volumes of work trips will be between the areas with the highest residential density and those with the highest employment density.

Such a 'static' calculation is however not enough. Work trips are mixed up with other types of trip. It is not possible to estimate exactly what proportion of total traffic they constitute since they are often linked

Figure 41: Job density in Basle. The highest densities are in the city centre and where the chemical industry and other plants are located. The white areas have less than 50 jobs per hectare; the areas with horizontal shading between 50 and 100; the areas with cross-patching between 100 and 150; and those shown in solid black over 150.

with other trips (Fig. 43). The proportion is quite different at different times of day. It varies from one part of a town to another, and even within the length of the same route.

It is the same with the various types of non-work trips, for which only a small amount of statistical data is available. For this reason volume counts are inevitable; they give a different picture from the values which can be deduced from the population and job data, and a better one (Fig. 44).

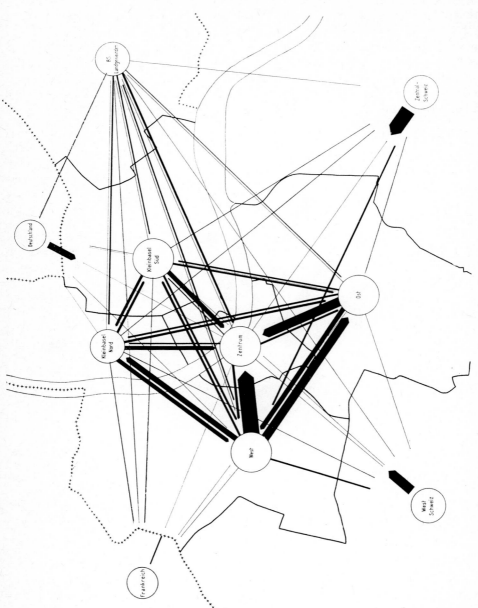

Figure 42: The pattern of trips between homes and workplaces was determined by the statistical office of the city of Basle. The road network should be adapted as far as possible to meet these desire lines. (Further study showed

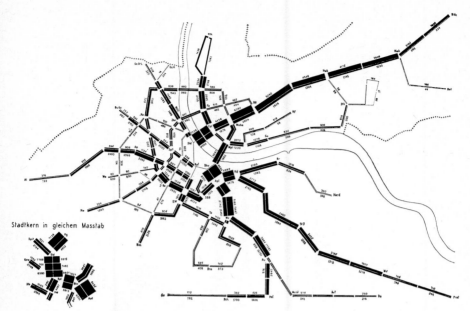

Stadtkern in gleichem Masstab

Figure 43: Overall picture of work trip loadings on each section of the public transport network of Basle (*Inset left:* the city centre with loadings drawn to the same scale.)

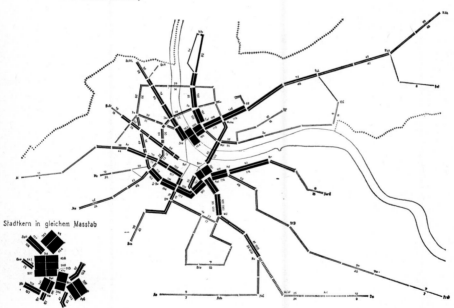

Stadtkern in gleichem Masstab

Figure 44: Overall picture of non-work trip loadings on each section of the Basle public transport network. The difference between work and non-work trips is especially noteworthy on the Rhine bridges. The ratios between the loadings on the Central Bridge and on the Wettsteinbrücke to the east are 2·2 : 1 for work trips, and 4·4 : 1 for non-work trips. (*Inset left:* is the city centre with loadings drawn to the same scale.)

F

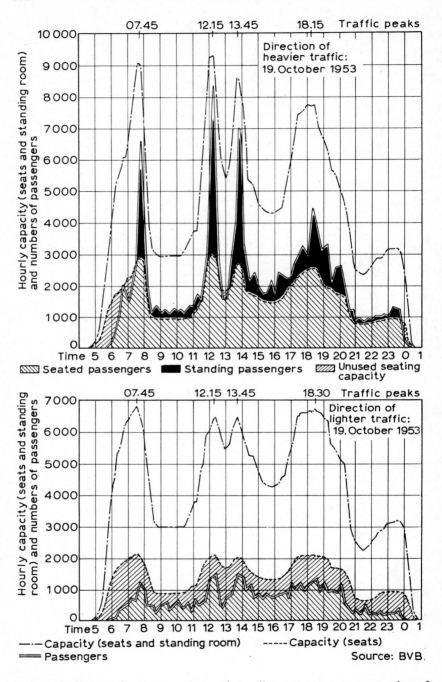

Figure 45: Curves of seat occupancy and standing passengers as proportion of capacity for the Basle public transport system. These curves are an important basis for the planning of schedules and for economy of operation.

(b) Traffic peaks

For purposes of traffic planning and structural design we are concerned only with the greatest loads which are regularly repeated. Hourly variations are also very important with regard to public transport (Fig. 45), because

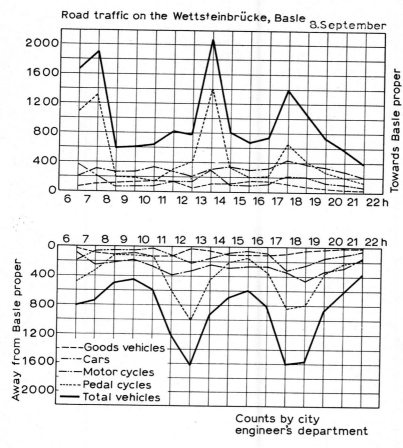

Figure 46: Hourly distribution of traffic on the Wettsteinbrücke, Basle, in autumn 1955. The traffic peaks occur at different times and in different directions for different vehicle types.

they affect the economic situation of the transport undertaking. The flow of private traffic during the quiet hours of the day is fairly unimportant since at these times it can usually move without friction. It is otherwise when it is a matter of designing a signal system, since in a case where there is considerable hourly variation in the composition and size of the various traffic streams, several signal control programmes must be worked out. The peak traffic is however always the most important. Its size can never be quite precisely established.

It is overdoing things to take as the design volume—as is done in the U.S.A.—that volume which is exceeded during 30 hours of the year or alternatively on 7 days of the year. There is even a certain contradiction

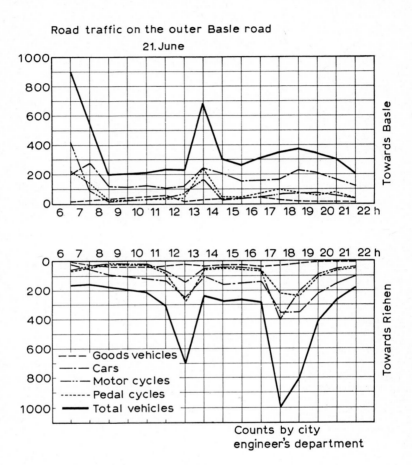

Figure 47: Road traffic on the outer Basle Road.
    The hourly pattern of traffic on the outer Basle Road shows quite a different picture. Further out from the city centre work trips, with their marked peaks, form a smaller proportion of traffic, so that the fluctuations in hourly volumes are smaller, and as the distance from the city centre decreases so do the fluctuations.

between these two standards, since the 30 highest hourly volumes might be spread over 30 days or they could all occur within 3 days, so that the 7-day value might be higher or lower. There is nothing to be said against this criterion as a general guide, but there is much to be said against making it a hard and fast rule.

The hourly pattern of traffic (the expression may be used in connection with hydraulic engineering) and the distribution of the traffic peaks over the whole year differs from place to place and from year to year. It makes a great difference whether the traffic load during the 30 highest hours is a great deal or only slightly higher than it is during the rest of the year and whether it occurs regularly—perhaps every weekend during the summer. If in a recreational area a road is overloaded every day during the short season of peak travel, then the road must be widened or otherwise improved.

Similarly the 30th highest hour criterion leads to inadequate road widths in the vicinity of large factories, if much higher 10 and 20 min peaks occur after the works close on every workday in the year, and these cannot be got rid of by staggering working hours. Regular delays of 30 min and more in order to spread short traffic peaks over a whole hour would not be acceptable.

Here again a warning must be uttered against standards and formulae; the peculiarities of each individual case must be carefully considered.

The traffic peak occurs at different times for different types of vehicle and in different parts of a town (Figures 46, 47). In the town of Baden near Zürich, for example, the following peak times were observed:

0630–0700 Motor cycles before the start of work in factories
1100–1130 Goods vehicles
1200–1230 Pedal cycles (lunch hour in factories and end of school)
1700–1730 All vehicles
1730–1800 Pedestrian, commuter and shopping traffic
1900–1930 Cars (heavy through traffic from nearby Zürich)

So long as no special facilities are to be provided for certain types of vehicle—e.g. cycle tracks—the overall peak for all vehicles, which usually occurs in the evening, determines the design volume. This peak contains a large proportion of work trips; and it usually moves outwards at a certain speed from the city centre and from big factories, gradually flattening out owing to speed differences and the queues which are characteristic of the peak. It also happens that peak 'waves' starting from different origins overlap with each other. In Zürich the midday peak at the Paradeplatz in the city centre is from 1158 till 1209 h, but at the south-west boundary of the city 3 km from the centre it is from 1209 to 1226 h. For this reason it is sometimes necessary to choose different counting periods for different parts of a city. But in the cities the evening peak is generally so long and the traffic in the non-peak direction so heavy that it is better—perhaps with the exception of distant suburbs—to make simultaneous observations throughout the city. But for certain processes a staggering is essential. For instance traffic counts made in Switzerland, in connection with the planning of the Swiss main road network and its links with the cities, of peak excursion traffic returning from the Alps on a Sunday evening in summer were carried out in Chur between 1500 and 1600 h, in Lucerne between 1700 and 1800 h, in Zürich between 1800 and 1900 h and in Winterthur between 1900 and 2000 h.

The transportation planner must decide the time, place and division of a traffic count. He must choose the most suitable method of counting. The best results are obtained when he has already worked out a tentative solution for the problem under study and can design the survey to answer the most important questions. Then he can locate the counting stations at the decisive points and limit their number to that which is absolutely necessary. Similarly he can determine the shortest counting period which is sufficiently long in the particular case. In this manner much time and money can be saved.

The count should cover the shortest possible period in order to find out the characteristic conditions in the peak hour. Any lengthening of the counting period dilutes the result. Times with less traffic and no work trips yield lower average values, and these will be too low for planning purposes. The more carefully a count is prepared the better the result will be.

In general there are still not nearly enough counts made, not least because the authorities shy away from the costs involved. But often a large proportion of the results obtained at considerable expense disappear unseen into the wastepaper basket, or are only evaluated statistically without having any impact on planning.

4. Methods of gathering data

In designing traffic surveys several considerations must be borne in mind. In the light of the figures quoted above, we might expect the following approximate numbers of trips to be made on an average weekday in a town of 100,000 not forming part of a conurbation:

Trips within the city	
by public transport	60,000
by car	140,000
by motor cycle, goods vehicles etc.	30,000
External trips by inhabitants of the city	
by public transport	20,000
by car	80,000
by motor cycle, goods vehicle etc.	20,000
External trips by persons not living in city	50,000
Total	400,000

It is inconceivable that so many trips will ever again form exactly the same pattern, in terms of numbers, direction and distribution in time, as they did on the day of the survey. An exaggerated accuracy is therefore of no value. Even with the most careful counting of public transport trips in a big city on two successive weekdays, with 180,000 observations made there were local variations of 15 per cent, while the total load varied by almost 10 per cent. Unfortunately the second day was a Wednesday, which is early closing day for certain trades.

On the other hand a quite small number of observations can give a surprisingly true picture. When the results of an 'exact' count of about 450,000 passengers on a tram network were compared with the evaluation of 1,000 tickets picked at random, the biggest difference at any one point was only ±15 per cent. This is not to say that the big count is quite reliable, because observations during the peak period were difficult.

If the results of a small count are to be grossed up to a large total, the word 'random' must be strongly emphasized. Very particular attention must be paid to ensuring that the sample chosen is truly random. In this case we were dealing with an attempt to get by with very few assistants. Otherwise a considerably larger number of tickets would have been used.

In another case where the results of a 1-h survey of peak traffic were compared with the results of a 16-h survey there was only a 1·6 per cent difference in the results. Indeed the agreement was so good that it must be regarded as having been due to chance. For the transportation planner 1-h counts on 16 different days would be a much better basis than a single 16-h count which costs just as much and which ignores conditions during the peak hour.

Naturally the survey period must be long enough for the 'law of large numbers' to operate. In other words we must ensure that the picture given by the survey is not appreciably affected by mistakes in observation or by two or three 'chance' trips. The heavier the traffic the shorter the survey period can be. Thus the special conditions prevailing during the short, critical peak periods can be investigated.

In no event should more or longer counts be made than are absolutely necessary. It is better to devote increased care to small observations. In the results there is usually a margin of error of only ±10 per cent. The future increase in traffic volumes cannot be so accurately predicted.

Geometric design also sets a limit to accuracy. Roads can only have an integer number of lanes; in towns usually an even number. Railways have only a full complement of tracks. Thus small increments of capacity cannot be provided. If the capacity of a traffic lane is once exceeded, an entire additional lane must be provided.

Nevertheless meticulous precision is called for in the preparation, execution and evaluation of traffic surveys. Arbitrary elimination of ostensible mistakes from the results is not good enough. In this way important details may be lost. The quality of the planning depends on the reliability of the survey data.

(a) Ordinary traffic counts

Traffic counts in towns are best made on an ordinary weekday outside the school holiday periods, and not immediately before or after a public holiday, between March and June or between September and mid-November so that the volumes recorded will be close to the annual average. Then the very important work trips, with their characteristic peaking, will be fully covered. The 30th highest hourly volume or another suitable design hourly volume will generally occur at these times of year. The highest load the road must carry can be determined from the graph showing the seasonal variation in traffic at the counting station. From the graph of hourly variation we can see the time of day when the traffic load is heaviest. We can then select the most suitable time of day and duration for the count.

In special cases, e.g. a road carrying heavy excursion traffic, a Sunday afternoon in midsummer may be the best time to do a survey.

Two types of survey must be distinguished: ordinary traffic counts and origin-destination surveys.

The first is simply a matter of counting the numbers of vehicles or pedestrians passing a particular point. The process needs no further explanation. The vehicles passing the point are usually recorded by drawing bars on a form which is sub-divided into sections for different vehicle types. Where traffic is heavy this requires intelligent and alert observers.

Such ordinary counts do not give any insight into the flow of traffic. We cannot learn from them the probable results of alterations in the road network, bypasses or road closures. At the most they serve merely to prepare the way for other surveys, or to supplement them, and for the observation of a quite simple situation. A number of automatic counters which were installed some years ago to make continuous counts on main roads are now very seldom used.

Origin-destination surveys, on the other hand, record trip ends. They are much more difficult to carry out, but provide much better data about traffic conditions.

There are many techniques for carrying out O-D surveys. The simplest consists of observing separately the different traffic movements through an intersection using straight and turning lanes. In cases where traffic is heavy, one observer is required for each traffic stream. Such surveys are really extended traffic counts. They only provide data on the traffic pattern at a single location; they do not provide data on vehicle trip ends or the pattern of movements over a wider area. When an intersection has to be studied in isolation such surveys may give good service. But they are not sufficient to meet wider needs.

(b) Registration plate surveys

Traffic movements through a wider area can be studied by recording the registration numbers of all vehicles passing certain observation points during the survey period. By comparing the records made at each point the routes followed between them can be deduced.

This sounds simple, but is in reality very difficult as soon as a large area has to be covered. The observation posts must be closely spaced, so that many assistants are needed both for observing and for analysing the results. And the method does not provide data about trip ends, but only about those parts of trips between observation points. Whether a vehicle has gone a short or a long distance before reaching the first post remains unknown; and so does its final destination after it has passed the last post. No data can be gained about bypasses and detours either outside or between the observation posts.

If a vehicle passes only one observation post, no more is learned about its route than could be learned from an ordinary traffic count. Vehicles which pass an observation post before the start of or after the end of the survey period are no longer recorded as through trips; they will appear in the evaluation as having started or finished their trips within the survey area. Thus the result of the survey is defective if the survey period is a short one. Part of the through traffic is 'transformed' into terminating or originating traffic. In and out trips, round trips and triangular trips can only be detected with difficulty. If the survey period is long there are many such trips. They can only be determined with certainty if the average through travel time is recorded. But this makes the evaluation even more difficult. And with heavy traffic numbers often get confused. If this happens a through trip will appear as two short trips. Because of the expense and the difficulties the method is normally used only in simple conditions on rural roads, or for the study of single intersections where no vantage point is available from which to observe through movements.

Sometimes the origin of a trip is determined on the basis of a registration number. This has the effect of exaggerating the amount of long-distance traffic, since some drivers reside for a long time in a new place without changing their number plates, and of course make many local trips there.

(c) The label method

As an alternative to observing number plates use may be made of labels: a label is stuck on a car as it passes the first observation post and is read as it passes other posts. Sticking the label on causes a certain delay; and therefore the method is ruled out where traffic is heavy. Confusion between numbers is at least largely eliminated since simple symbols can be used. But to the possible mistakes described above must be added the possibility of a label being torn off or lost. The survey can be conducted more easily and quickly than a survey using the number plate method.

The label method has proved useful in the study of pedestrian movements. At the entrance to particular streets or squares, pedestrians are given labels of different colours which they throw into the wastepaper baskets provided at the exit points from the areas under study. Pedestrians will participate almost 100 per cent in a survey of this kind.

(d) Roadside interviews

In this type of survey all road users are stopped at particular points on the road network—or, to speed things up, only a predetermined proportion of them—and questioned about the origin and destination of their trips. A similar technique may be used for surveys of trips made by public transport. Each interview with a driver of a vehicle takes at least 8 to 10 sec even where conditions are simple. Thus interviewing may give rise to irritating queues on heavily loaded roadways where vehicle headways are about 2 sec. In such conditions drivers will attempt to bypass the interview station or will give information only reluctantly. The answers are not always reliable because there is no time for further questions. For the interviewing many intelligent interviewers are needed. The expense of the survey is great, the results often disappointing. This type of survey is impossible in dense urban traffic.

In surveys of public transport, however, with trips made between a limited number of origins and destinations (railway stations, bus and tram stops and fare stages), good results can be obtained with this method if the survey is carefully prepared. The number of interviewers can be greatly reduced by questioning only a certain proportion of riders. The choice must be free of any bias—e.g. it must not be confined to riders in non-smoking cars on trains and trams. And the law of large numbers must be allowed to operate. Interviews will give data about entire journeys from origin to final destination, with stops on the way, changes and detours. Double counting can easily be eliminated.

(e) Home interviews

The disturbance of traffic flow can be avoided by interviewing road users at their homes or at their jobs instead of at the roadside. With this method only a certain number of people are of course questioned. Home interviewers will not cover the movements of vehicles coming into the survey area from outside; and employees of small firms are often neglected when the interviewing is done at workplaces. The result is thus distorted. In Düsseldorf it was shown that a third of the vehicle-mileage run within the city was run by vehicles coming in from outside. Home interviews would not cover this third, with its special conditions. On certain roads more than half of all trips would not be covered.

Experience also shows that the answers given by those interviewed are not reliable. A large proportion of the non-work trips and the detours get forgotten. Some answers are not given entirely frankly, or else they follow a certain point of view. The resulting traffic volumes of cars and public transit calculated on the basis of the survey are generally smaller than the true volumes. The differences can be considerable. Also the times at which trips are made—whether inside or outside the peak hour—cannot always be definitely determined.

Home interview surveys usually produce far too many facts which either are not evaluated or else are of no real value since all trips made outside the peak period are of no significance for traffic planning. There are a lot of objections to this type of survey even when a great deal of money is spent gathering the data. In most cases, however, not enough money or not enough manpower is available to interview an adequate, representative sample of the population within an acceptable period of time—even when no personal visits are made and all the interviewing is done by telephone.

If only a small proportion of the population can be interviewed, then—as is the case with opinion polls—care must be taken to obtain an evenly distributed sample. The persons chosen must be distributed over the whole survey area, and the surrounding area as well.

Interviewing at home or at workplaces is however useful for particular purposes, for instance for studying commuter traffic in some places or to and from big industrial works. Certain valuable data about work trips can be obtained by this method.

(f) Postcard questionnaires

From the foregoing considerations we can see which conditions must be fulfilled by a truly useful method of studying road traffic. The conditions are these:

1. All trips, including non-work trips and trips by vehicles coming from outside the survey area, must be covered, together with the routes used, in order to build up a complete picture.
2. Traffic must not be impeded, so that even the most heavily-loaded intersections can be studied.
3. The real peak traffic, which is of crucial importance for road planning and which lasts only a short time, must be studied.
4. Economy of manpower and money must be achieved, both in data-gathering and evaluation—it is more useful to carry out a 'cheap' survey every two years than a very detailed, expensive and comprehensive survey every ten years, which is probably no more reliable and in any case can only give the chance picture of a single day.

The postcard questionnaire fulfils all these conditions. With this method all private vehicles are momentarily stopped at the survey stations, which are chosen in relation to the project which is being studied. The postcard questionnaire is handed to the drivers. No explanations are needed. The vehicle is stopped for less than 2 sec, which is the minimum vehicle headway. Even in the densest big city traffic, e.g. the Karlsplatz in Munich between 1715 and 1745h, the handing out of postcards went very smoothly and there were no delays or queues.

The cards are completed at the end of the trip, and posted unstamped

Zählstelle: Mozartstraße
Bahnunterführung
(Richtung Osten)

23

1. Ausgangspunkt Ihrer Fahrt (Ort, Straße)

....

2. Letzter Zwischenhalt für eine Besorgung **vor**
   Erhalt der Karte (Ort, Straße)

....

3. Nächster Zwischenhalt für eine Besorgung **nach**
   Erhalt dieser Karte (Ort, Straße)

....

4. Ziel Ihrer Fahrt (Ort, Straße)

....

5. Fahrzeug (durch ✕ bezeichnen)

............Personenwagen oder Lieferwagen bis 1 t

............Lastwagen

............Autobus

............Motorrad/Roller/Moped

............Fahrrad

Figure 48: The front side of a postcard used in a traffic survey. At the top are the name and number of the counting station. The questions asked depend on the object of the survey.

1. Origin of your trip (place, street)
2. Last intermediate stop before receiving this card (place, street)
3. Next intermediate stop after receiving this card (place, street)
4. Destination of your trip (place, street)
5. Vehicle type (mark with an X)
   Car or goods vehicle up to 1 ton
   Goods vehicle of over 1 ton
   Bus or coach
   Motorcycle/scooter/moped
   Pedal cycle

to the authority concerned (City Engineer, City Planner or statistical office). Special cards are printed for each survey station, with the exact description of the location. If different colours are used for different stations the evaluation is made easier.

As a general rule the questions listed in Fig. 48 are asked. For certain purposes the questions are somewhat different. Thus information is obtained about up to five characteristics of the trip, the fifth being the checkpoint. The questions can be altered if required, or questions added concerning the type of vehicle, the trip purpose, the number of occupants, parking habits, special wishes and remarks.

It is best to carry out the survey as a surprise move, without any previous publicity through motoring organizations, newspapers, radio or television. Otherwise it may happen that the advance warning reaches only inhabitants of the place or a limited circle of road users, and these send in more answers than other drivers. Such mistakes can to a large extent be compensated for by special adjustment of the figures; but this requires a considerable amount of work.

For the preparation of the survey, the briefing of policemen and enumerators and the printing of postcards one to two weeks is generally sufficient. Students, apprentices or senior schoolchildren are suitable as enumerators. The stopping of vehicles must be left to the police. The stations at which the cards are to be given out must be strikingly signed. Where traffic is heavy, there should be three men to each lane; a policeman to stop the traffic, a man to hand out the cards and a man who counts the number of cards handed out to drivers of each type of vehicle. Where traffic is light each man can take care of several lanes.

At every station a count is made of the number of postcards handed out to drivers of each type of vehicle. In this way an ordinary traffic count is carried out. It is necessary to determine the number of cards handed out so that the figures resulting from the cards which are returned can be grossed up to the total of drivers who received cards at each station.

In cities the cards are usually handed out for a period of exactly 60 min during the peak period on a normal weekday. When traffic is light they are handed out for a longer period, so that the 'law of large numbers' can operate; when traffic is especially heavy a shorter period is sufficient. If the counting periods are not purposely staggered in order to follow the shifting traffic peaks, the counts at all stations throughout the area must start and end at precisely the same time so that differences due to hourly variations will not creep in. If the count at one station goes over the hour chosen for the survey by one minute there is already a mistake of 1·6 per cent. The count should be made in the peak hour, some time between 1600 and 1800 hr or later, but if possible by daylight. The most suitable weekdays in most cases are Tuesdays, Thursdays and Fridays.

The counting stations must be so chosen that all major traffic streams are covered. Ideally they should be located at the busiest intersections, which are the most important for planning purposes. In the dense street network of a town, many counting points are needed. An excessive number of points should however be avoided since traffic is unnecessarily disrupted.

It is often a help if counts are made only for one direction of traffic, e.g. outbound traffic only in the case of a ring of counting stations around the central area of a city (Fig. 49). In this case the through traffic is completely covered. If traffic in both directions is counted, conclusions about destinating traffic can be drawn on the basis of the originating traffic.

But it often cannot be helped that important traffic streams are disturbed by two, three or even more counting stations. Where this happens

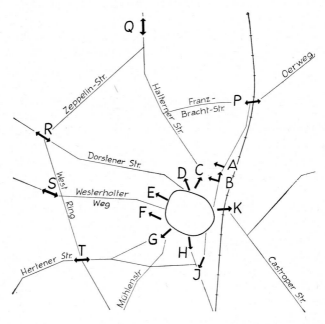

Figure 49: Counting stations in Recklinghausen: study for the general traffic plan (excerpt).

the driver can either fill in all the cards handed to him or only one of them. If he drove through the first station before cards were being handed out, or drove through the last one after it had stopped giving them out, he would not have received cards at all stations. For this reason it is unlikely that similar traffic volumes will be observed at all stations on the same road. In such cases the arithmetic mean of the various results should be used, or in some cases the highest figure obtained. Alternatively with some surveys the individual volumes obtained from each counting station can be regarded as valid for a certain section of road on both sides of the station.

The results of a postcard survey are incomplete in that short trips which do not pass through a counting station are not covered. The stations must not be too far apart so that the number of such short trips remains small. Such short trips are however of even lesser importance to road planning since they cannot in any case be diverted onto other roads.

If there are so many counting stations that there are not enough policemen and enumerators to man them, groups are formed which are counted either on successive days or on the same day in alternative weeks. When this is done counts must be made at one station on all of the days, for comparative purposes. The number of stations depends also on the process of evaluation—by hand or by computer.

Already on the day after the count a large proportion of the postcards come back duly completed, so that the evaluation can begin. After two or three weeks only a few answers trickle in and the count is closed. The proportion of cards which are returned reaches similar levels under quite different conditions—industrial area, rural area, big city, foreign countries —the response rates being as follows:

Cars	30/40%	Motor cycles	25/30%
Goods vehicles	25/35%	Pedal cycles	20/25%

According to both German and American standards a 20 per cent response rate is considered adequate for good results. This rate is regularly exceeded by a large margin. The proportion of cards which are unusable is generally 0·4 per cent.

Public transport surveys can also be carried out by the postcard method. Special cards must be printed for each case. Rail and air traffic can also be surveyed by means of questionnaires. For bus and rail traffic applications season tickets or passes, on which origin and destination can be written in, may be used. In the case of local public transport undertakings it can usually be deduced from the accounts how many trips are made using single tickets and how many using season tickets. They may be analysed separately, since non-work trips using single tickets often occur in different relationships and at different times from the work and school trips using season tickets. The counting points may be fare stages or individual stopping places. It is a matter of building a reliable, representative picture, yielding the right order of magnitude everywhere, on the basis of few facts; this calls for careful selection of the counting points. Such surveys have been carried out with great success in many cities. Since the fare structure, the type of network and the type of season ticket play a big part, and differ very much from one place to another, no general standards can be quoted.

5. Evaluation

(a) Calculations

With postcard surveys the cards from each counting station must first be handled by themselves, and the figures grossed up by the appropriate

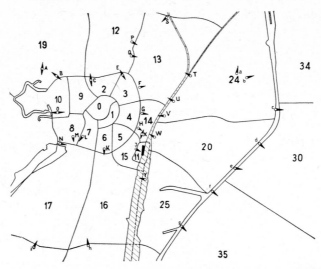

Figure 50: Counting stations and traffic zones in Münster in Westfalen (extract). The city centre was divided into especially small zones. Traffic in both directions was counted on the north and west sides of the city centre; traffic leaving the city centre was counted on the east and south sides; and traffic towards the city centre was counted at the railway underpasses. Most of the counting stations are on zone boundaries.

		1	2	3	4	5	6	7	8	9
Stadtkern Bregenz	1	■								
Nördlicher Stadtteil	2		■							
Südl Stadtt.m.Rieden	3	5	1	■						
Lochau	4	9	6	6	■	.			1	
Hörbranz,Hohenw	5	6		4		■	7		8	
Hard.Fussach.Höchst	6	33	4	32			■			
Lauterach	7	14		10	1			■		
Wolfurt	8	15	12	13	5				■	
Langen	9	1		1	4			8		■
Bregenzerwald	10	9		3	3	3				
Schwarzach	11	2		2	3					
Dornbirn	12	21	1	29				7		7
Hohenems-Rankw	13	7	10	3	5	3				7
Feldkirch	14	8	2	6	8	3				
Vorarlb östl Feldk.	15	7		5						
Übriges Österreich	16	9	2	9			2			
Liechtenstein	17	3		2					3	

Figure 51: Extract from a trip matrix for the city of Bregenz, Austria.

factor to the number of cards handed out. The index numbers of origin and destination zones are marked on the cards. A suitable division and numeration of the zones makes the task of coding easier and quicker (Fig. 50). Then the cards are sorted and counted. In this process it is usually possible to group two-way movements between zones from the beginning. The sorting and counting goes so quickly that it is not worth using punched cards. This applies also to the analysis of registration plate, label and roadside interview surveys.

The results for individual counting stations and different vehicle types are summarized in tables which show the traffic volume from each origin

Figure 52: Car traffic in Basle in 1955. The city centre is the most important destination.

zone to each destination zone (Fig. 51). The individual tables are grouped together into an overall table. This reunites traffic streams which, having started from the same zone, reach another zone by different routes. Where there is no special reason for studying different vehicle types separately (Fig. 52, 53) all vehicles are converted into passenger car units (p.c.u.). The values normally used are:

1 pedestrian	= 0·1 p.c.u.
1 pedal cycle	= 0·25 p.c.u.
1 motor cycle	= 0·5 p.c.u.
1 goods vehicle or bus	= 2 p.c.u.
1 tractor-trailer combination	= 2·5 p.c.u.
1 tram-train	= 2–3·5 p.c.u.

These round figures facilitate the calculation, but are only average values. In reality there is a very wide variation in the relative road capacity required for each type of vehicle, depending mainly on speed. It can happen that a pedal cycle requires the entire width of a traffic lane. In this case it is 'worth' 0·6 p.c.u. If on the other hand it stays at the edge of a traffic lane and does not impede motor traffic it is 'worth' 0 p.c.u.

Figure 53: Goods vehicle traffic in Basle in 1955. There is comparatively little traffic over the borders into Alsace and Baden, and also in the city centre; and comparatively heavy traffic on the tangential links in the industry and harbour areas and in the direction of central Switzerland. Thus the proportion of goods vehicles in total traffic varies a great deal.

When traffic is stationary, pedal cycles press close together. But experience shows that it is not worth using different values in capacity calculations. The result of such a calculation is very seldom affected appreciably by the adoption of different p.c.u. equivalents. In cases where it does make a difference, the solutions being compared are rather similar from the traffic engineering viewpoint, so that other factors, such as construction cost or appearance, will determine the choice.

Public transport is usually handled separately. Usually passengers are studied, not vehicles. For the capacity calculations concerning streets and intersections everything must, however, be brought to a common denominator.

The overall table forms the basis of traffic planning. The existing and the planned traffic networks are loaded with the flows determined from the overall table or possibly with flows taken from the individual tables. If there are 50 origin and destination zones there will be 49 × 50 = 2,450 possible zone-to-zone movements. The various traffic streams must be loaded onto a large number of roads and intersections. Because of this a

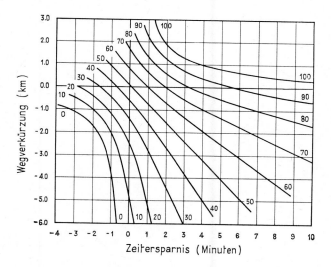

Figure 54: The American diversion curves for assignment of traffic from parallel routes to urban motorways shows the percentage of traffic which will divert according to the percentage gain or loss in trip time and in travel distance. The shape of the curves is valid only for certain roads and must not be used indiscriminately.

tremendous number of additions must be carried out, even if the network is very much simplified by the eliminating of all side streets. This work is best carried out using computers. The loading of each section and the number of straight ahead, left-turn and right-turn movements at each intersection is done mechanically. In this way much work and time are saved. However, the direct connection between survey and design is interrupted.

If several routes are available for a given zone-to-zone movement, the choice of the best route is difficult. In many cases a traffic stream must be split. The usual assumption made is that if two routes are of the same length in terms of time and distance, half the traffic will use each of them. If one route is quicker by 1 min or shorter by 1 km it will attract more than half the traffic but certainly not all. If the difference is 2 min or 2 km the proportion attracted by the more favourable route will be even greater. This approach is certainly correct even if certain deviations, resulting from other influences, cannot be ruled out.

Diversion curves can be drawn on the basis of which the traffic between two zones can be divided between the two routes. Such curves have been drawn in the U.S.A. for assigning road traffic to alternative routes (Fig. 54), and by Bendtsen in Copenhagen for assigning public transport trips. The following are the percentages of trips which will use the suburban railway there rather than the parallel tram service when the time saving

Figure 55: Flow diagram of future traffic in the city of Neuss am Rhein (90,000 inhabitants) after completion of the ring road. It was assumed that average speed on the ring road would be 50 per cent above that on urban streets.

obtained by using the former is a given number of minutes (the fares being equal):

Time saving (min)	Percentage of travellers using faster mode of transport
0	50
1	60
2	68
3	74
4	78
5	80
7	84
9	88
10 or over	95

With the aid of such facts computers can undertake the assignment of trips.

The curves should not be indiscriminately applied to different cities. The time or distance advantage should be related, in the case of road traffic, to the total trip length. It has a different effect where the latter is 10 min than it does where the trip length is 2 h. Thus there is a different

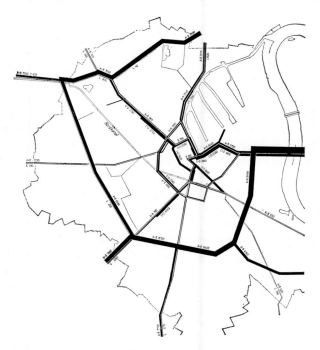

Figure 56: If it is assumed that the average speed on the ring road would be twice as high as on the urban streets the volumes assigned to it are much greater.

curve for every stretch of road. Moreover the time savings are not always equal. They depend on the vehicle, the method of driving and the amount of traffic on the roads. Speed differences have a marked effect on the traffic picture (Fig. 55, 56). If the shorter links have no spare capacity the longer

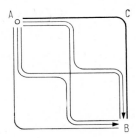

Figure 57: Even on this small grid network there are six possible routes between A and B, all equal in length. The driver will prefer that on which he can keep moving fastest and has to make the fewest turns. With right-hand traffic the route via C is the most favourable in terms of turning movements. But the future loadings on streets will only be known at the end of the evaluation. Drivers will choose different routes at different times of day; their behaviour during the peak hour is the most important.

ones will be used. Often more than two routes are available (Fig. 57). Moreover drivers may prefer a longer route for one of several reasons:

1. It has fewer signal-controlled crossroads.
2. It has fewer turns.
3. It has a better road surface.
4. It is more varied or more beautiful.

All of these elements can only be built into an evaluation programme with difficulty. For this reason it is often best to let the computer assign trips purely on the basis of desire lines (Fig. 58)—the shortest-distance links between origin and destination—and then re-assign some trips manually where necessary, using judgement to determine the likely distribution of trips between two parallel roads in each particular case.

Prädel developed an apparatus in which each link in a road network was represented by an electrical resistance. A high-capacity road was given a low resistance. An electric current would then seek out the 'way of least resistance' between origin and destination and would light it up. The idea is good. But the process has two drawbacks: it does not automatically draw out the routes selected, and it works with resistances which cannot be altered, although road capacity is gradually absorbed by increasing traffic volumes. These drawbacks could be overcome. But then the apparatus would become very expensive.

Traffic surveys on road networks in towns of up to about 25,000 inhabitants are best done entirely manually. In 1967 very cheap computer

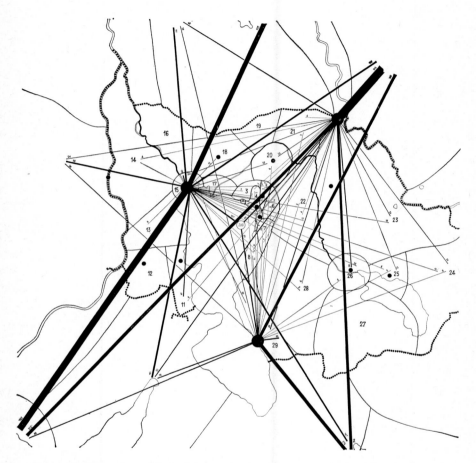

Figure 58: Summer traffic desire lines in the Canton of Zug, Switzerland.

programmes have been prepared by French engineers bringing down the cost of the evaluation for the entire network of a city with 200,000 inhabitants, inclusive of prediction, to less than 10,000 DM (£1,000).

For comparing different road routes relative time contours can be drawn. All points within a given zone can be reached faster by one route than the other. The best line will give the biggest time savings to the total population. Such studies can be made for all means of transport inside and outside cities (Figs. 59, 60).

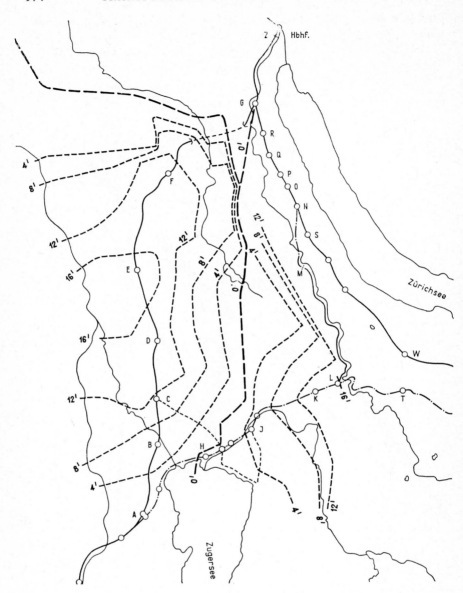

Figure 59: Comparison of two alternatives routes for the Zürich–Lucerne
motorway. The zero line in the middle (heavy dashes) links those points
which would be reached in the same time by either motorway. Both alternatives bring time gains of up to 16 minutes to certain areas. Assumed speeds:
40 km/h on rural roads.

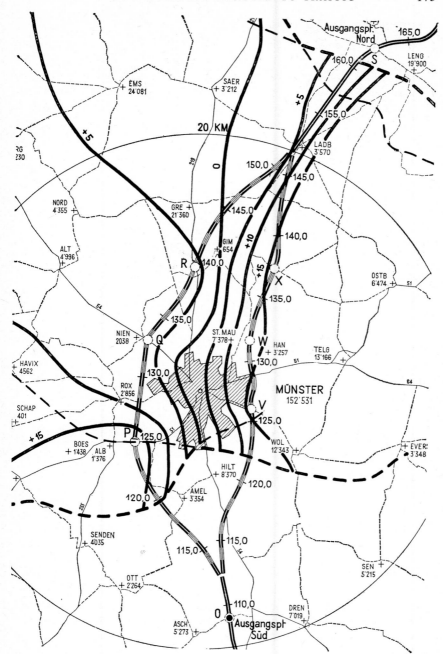

Figure 60: The Bremen–Ruhr motorway could be taken either west or east of the city of Münster. For traffic from the south the zero-line runs through the middle of the city. There are differences only between the dashed lines. For both alternatives the products inhabitants × time saving was calculated. They provide an impartial yardstick for comparison.

(b) Traffic flow diagrams

The results of the assignment of trips are drawn out, or else projected directly by the computer onto a television screen. Each drawing will show either the flows through a particular counting station (Fig. 61) or the flows in a part of the network (Fig. 62) or the flows on an entire network. These drawings are called in German 'traffic spiders' because the flow diagram

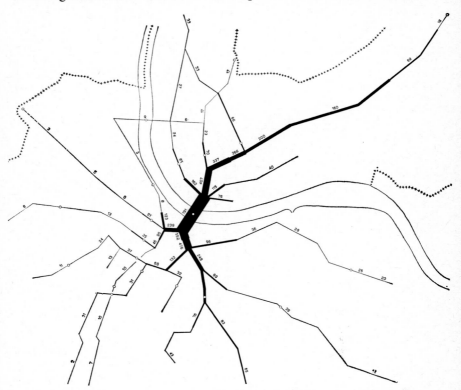

Figure 61: Flow diagram of car traffic using the Wettsteinbrücke in Basle during the peak hour (1730–1830) on the 7 July 1955. The branching out of the stream can be clearly seen.

for a town generally consists of a large blob in the middle with long, thin legs. The thickness of the legs represents the number of vehicles or passengers. Such 'spiders' can be drawn for existing or planned networks and for present or future traffic volumes. They give a clear picture of conditions. Deficiencies in the traffic network can with their help be rapidly detected (Fig. 63).

Flow diagrams of future volumes cannot be built up simply by multiplying the survey results by a certain factor. In new settlements around a city traffic will grow faster than in the old parts of the city, so that there are considerable differences even in the desire lines. The more traffic grows, the

more will desire lines and actual loadings deviate from each other, because
the congested area will get larger and larger and drivers will make longer
and longer detours.

Traffic surveys show that Lill's traffic law generally does not apply to
inner-urban traffic (Fig. 64). It is basically right in its approach and therefore it remains a useful aid. But it can only be used to a limited extent inside
cities or conurbations. If in the neighbourhood of city *A* a satellite town *B*

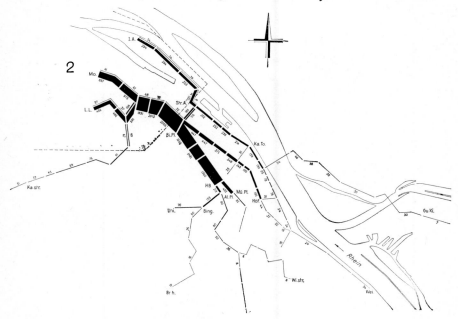

Figure 62: Public transport in part of a network. The non-work trips originating
  in the north-west part (zone 2) of the city of Mainz (130,000 inhabitants)
  mostly terminate in the central area, especially at the main railway station
  (HB on the plan). The amount of through traffic to other suburbs is extremely small.

grows up, the number of work trips made by the inhabitants of *A* will not
alter. If no jobs are provided in *B*, there will be no work trips from *A* to
B. If new factories grow up in *B*, workers will travel there from *A*. But then
they will no longer make work trips to jobs in *A*. The number of work
trips per head of population in *A* remains the same.

Much the same applies as regards non-work trips. The inhabitants of *A*
will hardly make any more trips however large *B* grows. Otherwise the
desire to travel would grow with every new suburb added. Only a few
changes in trip-making habits will be made. The new inhabitants of *B* are
interested almost exclusively in the link with the town centre of *A*. This is
the only place where they will have much contact with the inhabitants of
A and of other suburbs. They will have very little direct contact with the
other suburbs.

Thus the population of *A* should not be given full weight in estimating the traffic volume that will arise between *A* and *B*. The inhabitants of *B* will make a similar number of trips *per capita* per annum as other inhabitants at a similar distance from the city centre, provided traffic conditions are comparable. Vehicle-mileages *per capita* do not grow proportionally to the

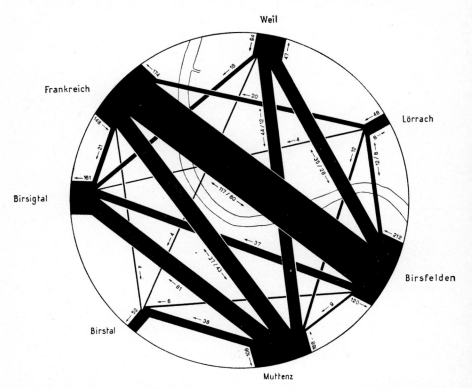

Figure 63: Through-traffic in Basle on a summer Sunday evening. Diagrams of this type are dangerous. A false impression can result from shifting the centre of the circle and the schematic distribution of radial roads. Flow diagrams should not be too stylized; geography must still be apparent.

population of a city, as one would expect from the 'law of traffic gravity'. As soon as *B* comes within the catchment area of *C*, only a portion of its traffic will still go to *A*. Then the population of *B* should not be given full weight in estimating the *A* to *B* traffic. In conurbations trips are made to a whole series of traffic-attracting points which are quite close together.

Such complex conditions can only be clarified by the evaluation of surveys. All probable changes in the various influences must be taken into account in drawing the flow diagram of future traffic. The results of possible or planned constructional or operational measures affecting a net-work must be investigated in detail. Shifts in traffic due to turn prohibi-tions, one-way streets, parking restrictions, widening of roads, new roads,

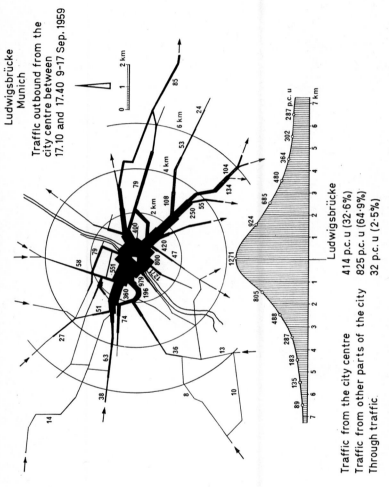

Ludwigsbrücke
Munich

Traffic outbound from the
city centre between
17.10 and 17.40 9-17 Sep. 1959

Ludwigsbrücke

Traffic from the city centre   414 p.c. u (32·6%)
Traffic from other parts of the city   825 p.c. u (64·9%)
Through traffic.   32 p.c. u (2·5%)

Figure 64: Traffic flow diagram and distribution of trip distances for outbound traffic using the Ludwigsbrücke in Munich. The distribution curve is very different on the two sides of the interview station. It cannot be mathematically determined. Short-distance trips are by far the most numerous.

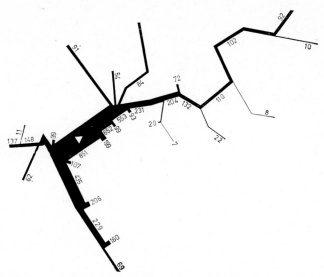

Figure 65: The intersection in front of the railway station in Freiburg, Switzerland, must be relieved by a bypass. An interview station was set up at the critical point (white triangle).

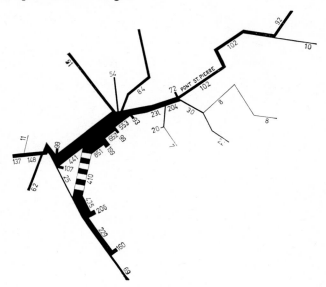

Figure 66: Evaluation of the results showed that an east tangent would divert 48 per cent of all vehicles from the station.

the reconstruction of intersections or even the opening of a new public transport line can be checked on, and can be shown very clearly in special flow diagrams (Figs. 65 to 70). The traffic loadings on individual road sections form the basis for capacity calculations.

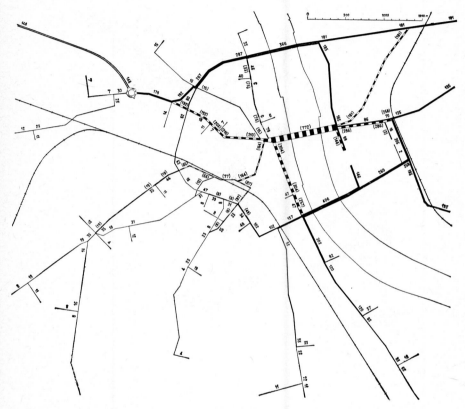

Figure 67: For the city of Bonn (140,000 inhabitants) it was calculated that a north and a south bridge could reduce the load on the existing Rhine bridge by nearly 50 per cent. The flow diagram also shows the changes on all feeder roads (increases in black, reductions in black-and-white).

Figure 68: In Basle it is planned to build a series of tangents, including a new Rhine bridge, to protect the city centre on the west side. This diagram shows the flows assigned to the urban network with the tangential route carried across the radial street which follows the south bank of the Rhine.

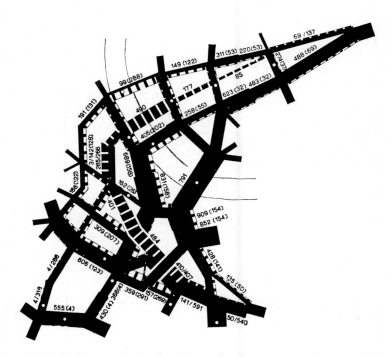

Figure 69: This diagram shows the effect of providing a connection between the tangential route and the street which follows the south bank of the Rhine. This solution would cost more to construct, but the new bridge would attract 75 per cent more traffic. The cost and utility of individual measures can be compared on the basis of such investigations.

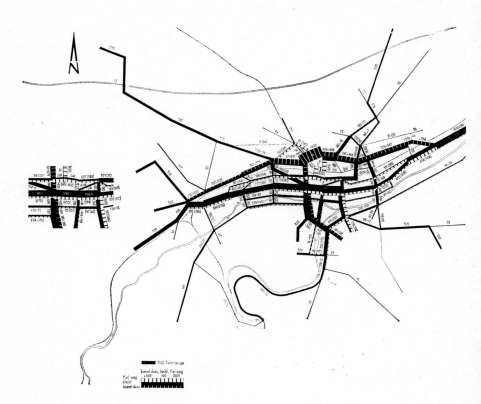

Figure 70: The north tangent proposed for Pforzheim affects not only the streets parallel to it but also, via the access points to it, the streets at right-angles to it. The traffic loads at all important junctions are altered. In cases of such thorough-going diversions of traffic new surveys should be made after each section is opened. (*Inset left:* the town centre, drawn to a larger scale.)

III. PUBLIC TRANSPORT

1. Scope

Public transport was introduced to give every man in the growing towns, with their increasing distances, a means of getting about. With increasing motorization this necessity is gradually falling away. It cannot therefore come as a surprise that in many cities in the U.S.A. public transport closed down. If big efforts are now being made to revive public transport in the U.S.A., the reason for it is the congestion of city streets with private vehicles and the serious consequences of this congestion for the commercial life of the city centres.

Where the shortage of space cannot be done away with, the 'private production' of person-miles in private cars must be restrained in favour of the 'mass production' by means of public transport. The relationship between the two has already been explained above. But it must be pointed out that there is no fixed boundary, e.g. a certain city population, above which public transport must be introduced. The shortage of space may be more or less serious, depending on the previous development of the city.

Public transport should be introduced, even with the highest degree of motorization, wherever delays exceed the level which is tolerable. But its operation must not be confined to the congested areas since otherwise interchange points with big garages would have to be set up at the edges of these areas. If the city or its traffic grew these interchange points would have to be pushed further and further out. And all travellers would have to change mode shortly before arriving at their destinations. Riding with transfer is bad riding, as Lehner has rightly warned.

Thus the public transport routes must extend well beyond the congested area and serve the residential areas directly, in so far as this is economically feasible. These areas must have a sufficiently high residential density to justify a fairly frequent bus service—or rail bus service on any railway there may be.

2. Form of network

(a) Radial lines

The biggest traffic flows from various parts of a city and from the suburbs are oriented towards the city centre. All important transport routes must lead there: in Berne to the Bubenbergplatz, in Stuttgart to the Schlossplatz, in Frankfurt to the Hauptwache, in Berlin formerly to the Potsdamer Platz, in Hanover to the Kröpcke-Ecke, in Brussels to the Bourse, in Copenhagen to the Radhusplatz. Routes are then added in other directions. In the course of time the inner-urban transport networks became in part quite difficult to comprehend. They should be built up and organized on the basis of certain definite principles. The various elements—traffic,

operation, construction, engines and vehicles, and, not least of all, economy
—must be brought to a common denominator.

The usual form of urban transport network is a star, whose rays
radiate from the central area. The star is like the 'traffic spider'. The individual rays can be laid out as radial lines beginning from the city centre
and leading to the outskirts. Such an arrangement is found for the most
part in Vienna, Berne, Bonn, Maastricht (formerly), and also—with the
railway stations as the hub—in Potsdam and Bruges, as well as on many
suburban railway routes.

Individual radial lines can be justified when the town has developed
entirely to one side. Basle, for instance, cannot expand in the Alsace and
Baden directions, so that there is nothing to balance the suburban rail
service to the east and south. Cologne forms a semi-circle on the left bank
of the Rhine, which can never be expanded into a full, evenly developed
circle embracing Deutz and Mülheim. In other cities the main railway
stations are so far away or so much to one side that no counter-balance
can be provided—e.g. Graz, Linz, Biel, Karlsruhe, Darmstadt, Düsseldorf, Trier, Münster, Brunswick, Bremen and The Hague.

But radial routes have considerable disadvantages. Even a town of only
10,000 inhabitants usually no longer has a single central *point*, but a whole
business *district*. With radial lines a trip from a suburb to the opposite side
of the central area entails either a change in the centre or a long walk. Both
are unsatisfactory and lead to unnecessary loads on bus and tram stops
and footways. Traffic piles up at the terminal stopping places in the town
centre, where long waits must sometimes be faced. Trams with facing-one-
way stock and buses needed terminal loops. Turning out of heavily loaded
streets in the city centre disrupts other traffic. To provide recovery time in
the schedules to make up for delays, long waits at the turn-round point are
necessary. This necessitates the use of valuable ground in the central area
as 'parking space'. Waiting and turning times cost money.

Attempts are sometimes made to compensate for the operational drawbacks of radial lines by giving them extended terminal loops taking in a
large part of the central area. The best-known example is the 'Loop' on the
elevated railway in Chicago. Such solutions are sometimes seen on bus and
tram networks too (e.g. Mainz). In no city do the main shopping streets
form such a loop; this would be at variance with the law of urban growth.
Thus the loops provided the same service to streets of greater and lesser
economic strength, which cannot be right. Many passengers are obliged to
make unnecessary detours either coming or going. And sometimes there is
an additional loss of time at the terminal stop. The building and operating
costs are higher than with a reversing terminal. Finding one's way about is
made more difficult. It is much better to have a terminal station or at least
tram and bus lines with small terminal loops and movement in both directions on the same streets.

Splitting up of public transport lines, so that the stops in the two directions are in different streets, especially one-way streets, is not on the whole to be recommended. The two streets will very seldom have the same traffic potential. People who are strangers to the town will not find the stops. If splitting up cannot be avoided, the two directions should not be further apart than is absolutely necessary.

(b) Diametrical lines

Wherever possible, radial lines lying on opposite sides of the city centre, and carrying similar volumes of traffic, should be joined together to form diametrical lines. Well-known examples of this treatment are the main-line rail link-ups across the centres of Berlin (north-south S-Bahn) and Brussels (the Jonction). The advantages are operational economy and better traffic service.

It is true that at the stopping places in the central area an almost complete change of passengers takes place, for the amount of through traffic between the suburbs on opposite sides of the city is extremely small; but nevertheless the diametrical line has its advantages. If traffic on such a line is very one-sided, a certain proportion of cars should still run through.

If the two spokes of the diametrical line do not lie directly opposite each other; if for example such a line runs from the north via the city centre to the east, there will be heavy interchange of passengers at the 'kink' onto lines running west and south. The short-distance traffic between the northern and eastern edges of the central area will not be well served, and will try to cut out the detour. As soon as a tangential line is available this traffic will divert. The bent line is still operationally better than two radial lines; but on traffic service grounds the diametrical line should still be routed as directly as possible.

In many cases diametrical lines are routed around the city centre on a semicircular alignment. Such decongesting measures have operating advantages; but they increase the number of passengers changing at the edge of the city centre very considerably. The usage of the line drops. Therefore solutions of this type are unsuitable from the traffic point of view. The planner must not do violence to the traffic flow pattern.

It is also not very suitable if for local reasons radial or diametrical lines branch before reaching the city centre. If this is done, each branch will operate at twice the minimum possible headway in the city centre, which is the origin or destination of most trips; and the line is thereby devalued and the service to the public suffers. The eastern part of the tram network of Zürich had to be developed in this way, since owing to big differences in height trams from the east can only reach the city centre by indirect routes via either the Quaibrücke to the south or the Bahnhofbrücke to the north (Fig. 71). This disadvantage was mitigated by providing a high frequency of service, which of course entails heavy operating cost. In the context of the studies for the General Transport Plan for this city an attempt was made to create a new crossing in the centre between these two bridges, and to divert all tram routes to it. But apart from the big obstacles offered by terrain and buildings, such a far-reaching recasting of an existing network is no longer possible since traffic has adapted itself over decades to the existing crossings of the Limmat river, so that these have become centres of economic activity.

One must proceed carefully with the recasting of transport networks, taking into account the long-acquired traffic habits of the inhabitants. In suburbs short-distance public transport must not be diverted to bypasses but must pass through the hearts of the new settlements. Even seemingly

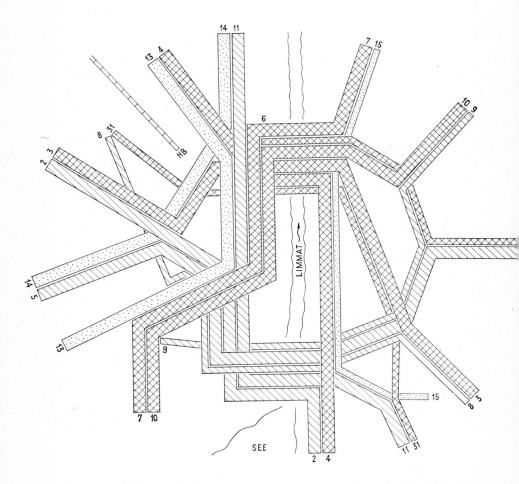

Figure 71: The public transport network in the central area of Zürich (450,000 inhabitants) suffers from the fact that it is not possible to provide an east–west route in the centre. But the system has been correctly developed. East of the Limmat river are six branches, each served by two routes of which one crosses by the Quaibrücke and the other by the Bahnhofbrücke.

unimportant new facilities must be developed in strict accordance with the
basic principles of traffic planning.

(c) Ring lines

The star pattern formed by radial and diametrical lines is sometimes
supplemented by one or more ring lines, e.g. in Berlin, Vienna and Rome.
The ring or circle is of course an intelligible shape and therefore gains

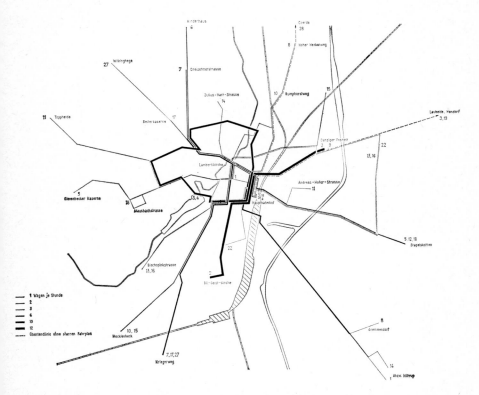

Figure 72: The existing public transport network of Münster in Westfalen
(180,000 inhabitants) with a high-frequency ring service (trolley bus) the
north–west part of which is little used, and with individual radial and loop
lines. The thickness of the lines is related to the frequency of service.

public support; but it is basically wrong from the traffic point of view
(Figs. 72, 73). Traffic always aims at the centre. For this reason the trains
on the Berlin ring railway which turned inwards onto the diametrical line
carried many more passengers than those which ran right round the ring.
The alignment of the Vienna Stadtbahn is not satisfactory. No one will
make a semi-circular journey if a good diametrical link is available. It
would mean unnecessary expenditure of time and money. It is hardly

possible for the different sections of the ring route to be equally loaded. Thus it is uneconomical to provide equally good service on all of them.

What are really needed, however, are transverse and tangential links between important parts of the city. It may happen that several such links together form a semi-circle. In that case much interchange and long delays

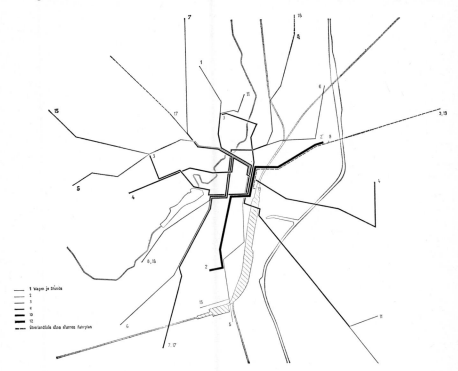

Figure 73: The new bus network for Münster, planned in 1962 after a traffic survey. Parts of the ring route would disappear; the tangential routes would be more closely knit together. The thickness of the lines is related to the frequency of the service.

to passengers are to be expected. In various towns, for instance in Stuttgart, ring lines have been abandoned in recent years because the traffic on them was too small (Fig. 74). Moreover where interchange takes place between the ring line and other lines, the relationship between waiting time and onward travel time is unfavourable.

A public transport system based on the principles laid down above was prepared for Ankara (Figs. 75, 76, 77). All the important lines link the centres of the old city in the north and the new city in the south. From these two points they fan out in all directions to the suburbs. The main station in the west and a big market in the east are also of importance. The network certainly provides a large number of tangential links, but no ring line. The schedules were drawn up carefully on the basis of traffic counts.

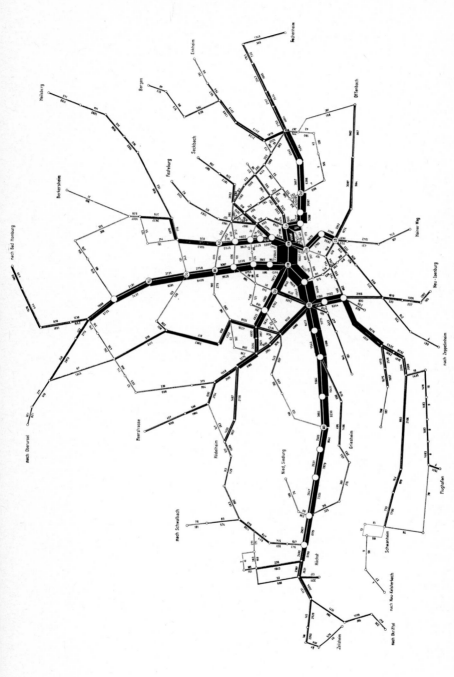

Figure 74: 'Spider' diagram of the public transport network of Frankfurt am Main (660,000 inhabitants), taking account of the planning proposal for a underground tramway. The tangential routes carry very little traffic.

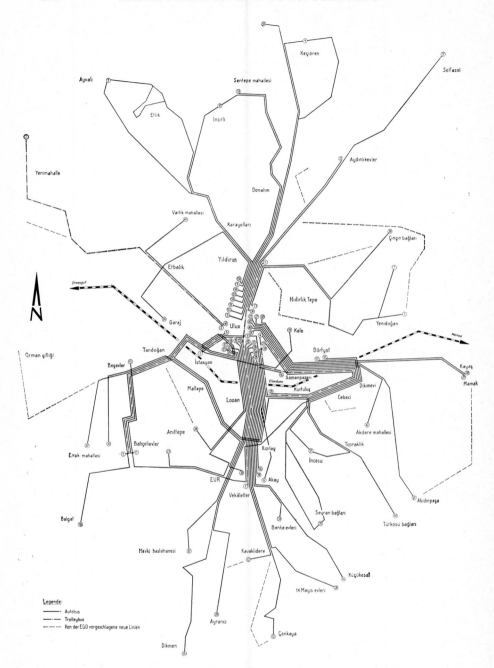

Figure 75: The bus network of Ankara (800,000 inhabitants) is composed predominantly of radial routes. The central point Ulus carried an additional
load in the form of numerous loop workings of buses and heavy interchange
traffic.

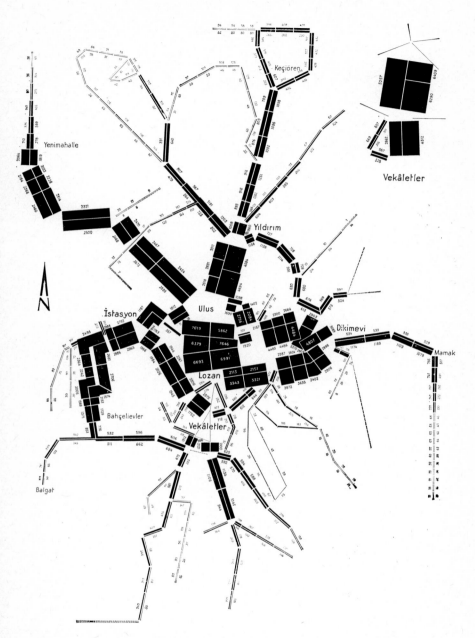

Figure 76: The public transport 'spider' of Ankara. Long, thin legs stretch out in all directions from the centre. The heaviest passenger traffic is on the north–south axis linking Ulus, centre of the old town, and Lozan, centre of the new town. The east–west traffic forks at the main station (Istasyon) and at the Dikimevi junction into streams heading for these two main destinations. (*Inset top right:* part of the new town.)

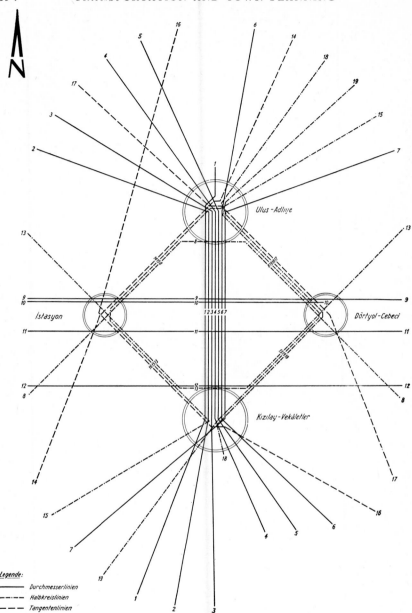

Figure 77: The planned bus network for Ankara. The diametrical lines 1–7 link
the two most important centres of gravity in the north and south, the diametrical lines 9 to 12 run east–west, with three of them (9–11) linking the two
centres of gravity Istasyon and Dörtyol. The semi-circular lines 8, 13, 15, 18
and 19 all serve three of the main centres of gravity, and each of the tangential lines 14, 16 and 17 serves two of the four centres. In designing the
network and the timetable special weight was laid on economic utilization of
buses.

It is possible to try out bus routes on a temporary basis so that the traffic demands can be sampled. But a later re-routing will encounter resistance because people will claim that they have 'established rights'. The same applies to express services, which are only advantageous economically, and bring about worthwhile time-savings, where traffic is very heavy indeed; in other cases they lead to a splintering of service.

(d) Density of network

The public transport network must branch out towards the edge of the city. Thinly-populated outer areas are served by feeder buses, which collect passengers and bring them to the trains or trams. The bus services should not run parallel to the rail lines, in order to avoid an uneconomic splitting and a double requirement for traffic space (for instance by having bus and tram stops next to one another). Only in the very largest cities is the passenger traffic so large that in addition to the inner-urban rail network a complementary bus network for fine distribution can be operated without heavy losses. This permits wider spacing of stations on the rail network and thus a higher average speed. For many big cities such a double service is too expensive; and they must retain the normal spacing of stops on their rail network.

The number of lines must be limited, so that passengers can understand the system and find their way about on it. For the same total of seat-miles offered, a few lines with frequent service are better than many lines with infrequent service. The urban lines should be so arranged that only one change is necessary on any link of importance. If two changes are necessary, the waiting time becomes an excessive proportion of the overall travel on short trips. This is so inconvenient that passengers will switch to private transport. For the same reason the only lines that can be considered for 'park-and-ride' service are those which provide direct links between parking place and destination (usually the city centre). 'Park-and-ride' on tangential routes would not work.

Limitation of the number of lines often leads to a loosening up of the network. Public transport should use only a few streets. The minimum spacing of routes is dictated by the distance between stopping places, since there will be interchange between routes at all crossroads where they intersect. Interchange should not be discouraged by higher fares or other regulations, since otherwise more direct lines will be demanded and the network will be further splintered. Ideally the spacing between routes in the central area should be the distance between alternate stopping places. In the city centre the distance between stopping places should not be less than 250 m (800 ft). In the outer areas and on long routes it will be considerably greater, so as to raise the average speed. The following are the average distances between stopping places in certain cities:

Basle	Tram	320 m
	Bus	368 m

Zürich	Tram	323 m
	Motor bus	374 m
	Trolley bus	461 m
Munich	Tram	429 m
Cologne	whole system	520 m
Düsseldorf	whole system	479 m
Hanover	Tram	590 m
	Bus	720 m
Hamburg	Tram	525 m
	Bus	702 m
	Underground	1,220 m
Berlin	Underground	820 m
London	Underground	1,200 m
Madrid	Underground	580 m
Moscow	Underground	1,500 m
Paris	Underground	510 m
Stockholm	Underground	780 m
Buenos Aires	Underground	600 m
New York	Underground	750 m
Tokyo	Underground	950 m

The walking distance to the nearest stopping place ought not to exceed 250 m (800 ft) in the town centre, and may increase to 600 m (2000 ft) or more in the outer areas. No point of the city centre and no major settlement should be more distant from a stopping place (Fig. 78).

In the planning of a network operating costs play an important role. If a bus line with a 5-min frequency is extended by 100 m, then, assuming the service operates for 15 h a day, the extra bus-miles run in a year in both directions will be:

$$2 \times 100 \text{ m} \times 12 \text{ trips/h} \times 15 \times 365 \text{ days} = 13,200 \text{ bus-km}$$

If one bus-km costs 2·00 DM, the additional cost would amount to 26,400 DM per annum. This is equivalent at 5 per cent interest, to a capital of over half a million DM. Thus it is worth spending up to this amount in construction costs in order to shorten the bus route by 100 m. When alternative network proposals for a town are being compared it is quite usual to find differences of several millions of DM. Unfortunately too little attention is paid to this viewpoint.

(e) Travel speed

If stopping places are eliminated the travel speed increases. Traffic at neighbouring stopping places increases. This may in some cases increase the stopped time of trains and buses so sharply that the capacity of the route drops.

A change in the travel speed has an especially marked effect on econ-

Figure 78: Area coverage of the public transport system of Dortmund (excluding railways). The cross-hatched areas are areas in the inner parts of the city not within 5 minutes' walk of a bus or tram route; and areas in the outer parts of the city not within 10 minutes' walk. The solid lines are tram routes; the broken lines are bus routes.

omy. If the speed drops from 11 to 10 km/h every driver and conductor produces 10 per cent less. Moreover the receipts will drop since the saving of time will be smaller. A speeding up of public transport is therefore also needed for reasons of operating economy. The tax-payer does not really gain anything if the city engineer's department saves several millions but annual subsidies have to be paid to the transport undertaking to cover its operating loss.

An important means of speeding up public transport is to give it priority over other traffic. Trams enjoy such priority in for example the Netherlands, Austria and Switzerland; and it should be extended to buses. In a number of cities, e.g. Chicago, special lanes are reserved for buses and

forbidden to other vehicles. At signal-controlled junctions public transport should also be given preferential treatment.

3. Choice of transport mode

The choice of public transport mode depends on traffic, operational, technical, economic and town-planning considerations. There are, therefore, no fixed norms. Even with similar conditions from the one or other point of view quite different solutions may be equally suitable.

(a) Motor bus and trolley bus

From the traffic engineering point of view it is immaterial whether motor buses or trolley buses are used since both types of bus behave similarly in the traffic stream. Arguments for the trolley bus are its greater attractiveness, freedom from fumes, low noise level and, in some countries, the use of indigenous fuel. The higher installation costs for the overhead wire indicate use only on heavily loaded routes. The motor bus is not tied to a route or network and can be used for excursions and similar work. The economic boundary between motor bus and trolley bus varies with the relative prices of diesel fuel and electric current, as well as with the interest rate on capital investment.

(b) Tram and bus

Much more important is the boundary between bus and tram. As long as only a single route is concerned conditions can still be easily judged. But with a whole network the operational integrity must not be destroyed by partial replacements. The rail connexions to the tram depots must be preserved. Traffic links must not be arbitrarily broken since passengers will then be compelled to make more changes.

Traffic congestion cannot be overcome by substituting buses for tram lines. Since the largest articulated buses cannot be as large as a streetcar train, with its reliable and exact tracking, more vehicles or at least the same number must be used, each of which must maintain the necessary headway. The road space requirement must therefore increase. On curves, buses occupy more road space than trams because their rear wheels track differently from their front wheels.

Trams being larger than buses also have the economic advantage that for the same labour cost they can provide more capacity in terms of passenger-miles. But there must of course be sufficient demand to fill the larger units. Where small units are wanted the bus is preferable because the capital investment to provide a given number of seats is much smaller.

The prime costs of tram and bus operation must be calculated as accurately as possible. The following should be taken into account:

Fixed installations: foundations, rails, supply of current, depots for trams; depots and refuelling stations for buses

Vehicles: annual operating and maintenance costs
Labour costs
Material costs
Interest and amortization for fixed installations and vehicles
Depreciation on tram tracks, difference between book value and resale value of vehicles

The comparison may be made for individual lines or for the whole network, depending on the particular task in hand. Often an old system in its present state is compared with a new system. This favours the older system. From a wider point of view it is more correct to compare two new systems. Amortization should then be based on the technical and economic expectation of life since once this has run out the equipment will in any case have to be replaced. There would still however be a considerable financial difference in that, if the old system is retained, replacement of worn-out equipment can be spread over a long period, whereas if it is replaced with a new system big expenditures are needed all at once.

Doubts are sometimes cast over the results of the comparative calculations. But the following items can be easily checked:

Mileage run per worker per hour
Capacity offered
Relation of labour costs to capacity offered

However, comparative figures for other undertakings should not be quoted uncritically, because conditions vary considerably.

Operating costs alone cannot be decisive. The traffic engineering aspect must also be considered. This involves setting a definite cash value on getting rid of a difficult rail layout or of a stopping place which disrupts traffic, so that the advantage to be gained from such things can be weighed against consideration of profitability alone. This is of course a problem of measurement. The replacement of trams by buses which, being smaller, are run at higher frequencies will lead to an increase in receipts which must be allowed for in the profitability calculations. In a Dutch town of 60,000 inhabitants where buses replaced trams, and the frequency of service was doubled, receipts increased by 8 per cent in the first year of bus operation.

(c) Size of unit

Only adequate traffic demand can justify the introduction of large units. Ideally, waiting times should not be lengthened in order to assemble more passengers. A sufficiently frequent service must be provided to meet the competition of private vehicles and of walking. A good rule of thumb is that the scheduled headway of bus, tram or train should never exceed the travel time to the most important destinations. In a town where the average travel time is 10 min there should be at least a 10 min headway service on all important lines. This applies to railways as well as trams and buses. The right size of vehicle can be decided in the light of this rule. Increasing competition gradually compels public transport undertakings to operate more frequent services.

Small buses with 8 to 10 seats are used in thinly populated suburban areas (e.g. in Lausanne) with a one-man crew; and higher fares per mile are charged because traffic is so thin. With higher population density, larger vehicles are introduced. There is no sharp boundary between the smaller one-man bus and the larger bus with driver and conductor: in this question too economic, operational and local influences all play a part. The trend is towards one-man operation even with the largest vehicles. In cities of 50,000 inhabitants and over, buses with the largest permitted dimensions should be considered; while in cities of about 100,000 inhabitants, articulated buses should be considered. In most countries carrying passengers in trailers is forbidden.

Modern buses 2·50 m wide, and with seats for 20 to 25 per cent of their passenger capacity, can carry 9 to 10 passengers per metre length of the vehicle, allowing 0·15 to 0·17 sq m per standing passenger. In Austria 0·2 sq m per standing passenger is insisted upon, so that only 6 passengers per metre length is possible. It should be noted that generally speaking an increase in the proportion of seated passengers is sought after.

In a city with a big catchment area, or in the peak period, more and more buses must be used, with the result that they form queues in the central area which cannot get through and the schedule cannot be maintained. Loading at single or double stopping places becomes more and more difficult. If each bus route has its own stopping place, the stopping places become difficult to find; and buses must overtake each other, thus requiring more lanes. On main streets in big cities therefore big units and reserved lanes are needed.

As soon as two buses are coupled together to form a train, one vehicle headway disappears and the traffic lane can carry more. Trains can however only be formed when all axles are guided by a 'rail' of some kind. The 'rail' may take the form of the classical railway or tram rail, the concrete guidance flange of the Paris 'Metro sur pneus', the overhead steel rail of the Wuppertal monorail, the concrete beam of the Alweg monorail, a mechanical guidance device (the invention of Kuch, Nuremberg, or the 'route guidée', being experimented with in Italy and France), or a high-frequency cable in the centre of the lane (American and British experiments).

With low-density development of outer suburbs such as is common today, big cities are best served by buses, which require no special equipment and no installation costs in the suburbs, and which can be joined together, before reaching the central area, to form trains, requiring little road space per passenger. However, mechanical or electrical guidance systems are needed. In this way most settlements could be given direct connections with the city centre.

The following difficulties stand in the way of this type of operation:

1. The transition from ordinary roadway to rail track takes time.
2. The buses must be coupled together to form trains, and must await the arrival of the last bus.
3. The drivers of all buses must remain aboard the train, to avoid excessive dependence on schedules and transference of delays, so that costs can hardly be lowered.

As long as no satisfactory solution is found for these problems, changes of vehicle must be accepted.

(d) Rail transit

The largest volumes of traffic can only be carried by means of rail vehicles of large capacity running at least for part of their routes on segregated tracks. The routes should be extended as far outside the city as is economically feasible so that many inhabitants will have a direct service to the central area. The longer the trains the harder it is to fulfil this wish. Therefore careful consideration must be given in every case to the question whether a proper rail rapid transit line is the best solution. In this context the word 'rapid' must be used with care. Inside a city an average speed of 25 km/h (16 mph) must be regarded as 'rapid'.

In cases where rapid rail transit is the best answer, two alternatives are possible:

1. Use, with modifications, of existing railway installations.
2. Building of new tracks.

In the first case there is already an experienced operator with a large network available. If settlements spread further out the suburban rapid transit services can be extended without any large expenditure.

From the viewpoint of the national economy, as much as possible of the traffic of a conurbation should be channelled onto the railways. The future of the railways does not lie only in long-distance expresses but also in mass transport over short distances. Plans for bringing suburban rail services further into the cities, such as have been evolved for Zürich, Munich, Stuttgart and Frankfurt, are basically right. As long ago as 1938 the Netherlands Railways deliberately introduced throughout their system a rigid 'tram-type' schedule. Given frequent, fast services railways are fully capable of competing. With increasing congestion on the roads the advantage of a segregated track, making it possible to maintain a high average speed, is more and more evident. But in many places interchange with road transport, bus and car, remains a problem. Uncomfortable mixed-mode travel, with long waiting times and tiresome methods of payment, frightens away some travellers.

If cities alongside a railway want to have a special rail network then they should devote it to other tasks. It would be wrong to develop a means of transport of similar type, suitable for regional traffic. Cities must think first and foremost of serving their own territories. City-owned rail systems should serve short-distance traffic. They form the backbone of the inner-urban traffic network, which must have many branches in order to serve the largest possible areas.

A large number of big cities are now faced with the question whether they should build new rail systems similar to the state railways, or develop their tram networks into rapid transit systems. Competition between the state railways and urban transport systems, both financed out of the public purse, is undesirable. They should complement each other. But unfortunately the fact that their fare structures are different leads to parallel services in some cases. The fundamentally different characters of the two systems make it impossible, as a general rule, to introduce a common fare structure, even with the best will on both sides. And transfer fares exist in only a few cities, e.g. in Berlin before 1939. East Berlin and Hamburg now have common fare structures for suburban railways and the urban transport system.

There are two possible types of rail rapid transit system:

1. Networks with self-contained lines with no switching of trains from one to the other, possibly with connexions solely to allow trains to reach the repair workshops (the Paris Metro, Barcelona).

2. Networks with branches and connexions (S-Bahn and U-Bahn in Berlin, Hamburg, Stockholm, London, New York, Chicago).

From the operating viewpoint, the first has advantages. Operating dangers which arise at junctions are eliminated. This point of view is strongly stressed, and reference is made in this connexion to the serious accident which occurred over half a century ago at the rail triangle at the Berlin Elevated Station.

But from the traffic point of view the 'separate lines' system means for many passengers bad, broken journeys with inconvenient changes and waiting times which can be ignored only where the frequency of service is very high.

In view of the justified demand for convenient services, and of the progress achieved in rail safety technique, we should not be afraid to opt for the second type of system. Independent lines can hardly all be routed into the town centre. Therefore they are of lesser traffic value. Even considerable expenditure on the creation of regularly travelled interchanges is justified. It was a good solution that, in Berlin before 1939, in addition to the diametrical and circular services operated on the S-Bahn, some trains used to run from the diametrical line onto part of the ring rail route, passing through junctions and crossings at grade. Here it is relevant to quote the last sentence of Potthoff's *Verkehrsströmungslehre* (Theory of Traffic Flows):

The gains in capacity to be obtained by the elimination of flat junctions are—as has been quantitatively proved—smaller than many people have been inclined to assume from a superficial consideration of the relationships involved.

(e) Underground tramway

So long as there was little road traffic the speed of the tram was adequate. With increasing traffic congestion, however, it is continually dropping. In this situation the case for a reserved lane for buses or trams becomes ever stronger. But such lanes can only be introduced on wide streets; for trams they should ideally be in the form of a special median.

Reserved lanes however only increase speed and safety between intersections. Difficulties still arise at intersections. A cure for these difficulties is only possible by means of grade separation. Trams or buses can cross the intersection via underpasses or flyovers. In most cases considerations of townscape mean that only underpasses are possible.

With such underpasses the tram becomes an underground tramway, the bus lane a bus tunnel.

Whether it is better to have a special median for trams combined with underpasses or a continuous tunnel is first of all a question of costs. If a tunnel is chosen, then for an expenditure of about 20,000–30,000 DM per metre (including stopping places) an entirely new, additional traffic channel is created. For the same channel to be created above ground, the streets along the route would have to be widened by two lane widths, or 7 m (23 ft). The building line must be set back this amount on one side. The building of a tram tunnel is therefore worthwhile if the widening of the existing streets by 7 m would be more expensive, i.e. if it would cost more than 3,000 to 4,000 DM per sq m, including the value of buildings which in the city centre are usually of four or more storeys. The demolition will affect the street facades of the buildings, which are the most valuable parts of them. One cannot simply cut away a strip 7 m deep. A complete demolition and rebuilding is generally necessary. The city will also be responsible for maintenance of the additional road surface area, which is no longer bringing in taxes.

The tramway tunnel is therefore to be preferred wherever the basic cost of land exceeds 400 to 600 DM per sq m. It exceeds this value today in the business districts of all big cities.

Similar considerations apply to underground busways—in which, on account of ventilation problems, operation with electric trolley buses is to be preferred. If the buses are not guided by steel or concrete rails or high frequency cables, but are steered in the normal way, the tunnel cross-section must be larger, especially on curves. Calculations to date show that the widening is cheaper. Sight distances are better so that no signals are needed on curves. A mixed service of trams and trolleybuses can use the same tunnel.

In the first stage of construction the underground tramway will carry ordinary trams which outside the central area will run at surface level and on the streets. It must therefore be equipped with overhead wires and not rails for current supply. This means that the tunnel cross-section must be higher. Moreover it must be possible to board the trams from rail or roadway level. On a proper undergound railway, on the other hand, the platforms are on the same level as the floors of the cars, so that boarding and alighting can take place more quickly and comfortably.

If the trams are of the facing-one-way type, terminal loops must be provided at both ends of a route, even with an underground tramway.

As a general rule tickets are sold in the cars on trams, but in ticket offices on an underground railway. However, tickets could equally well be sold at ticket offices on an underground tramway or by conductors on board underground railway trains, or automatically in both cases. But sufficient space must be provided at the platform barriers. If car conductors are to collect fares, the platform must be on the right so that he can keep a watch on the doors: the fitting of doors on the left-hand side of the car must be rejected on grounds of inadequate vision for the conductor and safety. With automatic control of doors and television surveillance, platforms on both sides of a track are admissible to shorten boarding times and train stops.

The length, width and height of the cars can be the same for underground railways and tramways. So can speed, acceleration and deceleration. Both of the latter are limited on all public transport vehicles to between 1.0 and 1.2 m/sec^2, because standing passengers might be hurt by excessive acceleration or braking. The maximum speed depends on all railways and tramways on the type of vehicle, the curve radii, the gradients and the station spacing. The average speed of underground railways is very slightly higher because of faster boarding and alighting, with high platforms, but drops with long trains on account of the time needed for train despatching. The ratio of the number of doors to the number of passengers that can be carried plays a part. With heavy passenger traffic the flow of passengers through the car, as on trams, is an advantage not possessed by underground railways, if they do not have platforms on both sides as in Athens (Omonia), Barcelona or Osaka. The average speeds of underground railways in several cities are:

Berlin	24·0 km/h
Hamburg	24·0 km/h
Paris	22·0 km/h
London	26·4 km/h
Stockholm	33·0 km/h
New York (I.R.T. system)	26·0 km/h

The safety installations on an underground tramway can be kept simpler than those on an underground railway operated completely on railway lines. Intersections and merge points as well as tight curves with restricted sight distance can be made safe by means of local signals. But block signalling is not necessary because with close spacing of stopping places, no great speed can be attained. Incidentally in the U.S.A. certain underground railways still operate without block signalling.

By not adopting block signalling it is possible to have double-length stopping places below ground as well as above, and to raise the number of trips on the intervening sections of line because the distance headway between trains can be shortened. This is the system adopted on the section between the National Theatre and the Majorstua in Oslo and on the underground tramway in Philadelphia. The surface section only needs signals if considerably higher speeds are to be attained on special tram rights-of-way than hitherto.

Merging and crossing manoeuvres should be eliminated from tunnels as far as possible by the arrangement of the rail network. But this principle should not be taken so far that the traffic value of a network suffers appreciably.

On railways, the danger of merging manoeuvres is minimized by running tracks alongside opposite sides of a platform so that they come together only at the end of the platform. On trams, above and below ground, where fares are taken by conductors and the trams keep to the right, each platform has only one edge. If all trains having the same destination have to stop on the same platform edge—conforming to the wishes of the users —the track will have to be brought together before the entrance to the station. In the immediate neighbourhood of the stopping place this can be accepted, as in above-ground tram operation. The shorter tram-trains are running slow there. One possible way out is left-hand traffic for trams, but this usually causes higher expenditure.

An underground railway is only an advantage for traffic if a continuous stretch several kilometres in length is open. On the other hand the underground tramway enables short stretches of tramway to be taken out of the congested streets while the rest of the above-ground network remains as it is. This is its decisive economic advantage. It is only necessary to build as much underground line as is absolutely essential. The existing rolling stock can continue to be used until each unit is replaced in the framework of planned replacement.

Each construction stage must be viable since the intermediate stage may last many years. Since ramps cannot be built everywhere, and their number must be restricted, changes in the network or in individual lines may be necessary.

Following the building of an underground tramway through the city centre, the operation of the entire network will become more punctual because the worst congestion spots will have been bypassed. On the outer stretches all tram systems still reach quite satisfactory average speeds, in many cities over 20 km/h (12½ mph). The networks are *sick* only in the city centre, where the average speed falls in many instances below 10 km/h (7 mph) (Fig. 79). It is only there that costly construction is justified. On the outer stretches traffic congestion is only slightly felt, so that trams still run almost on schedule, except where delays suffered in the

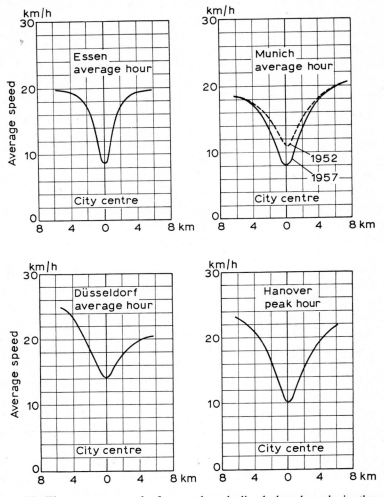

Figure 79: The average speed of trams has declined sharply only in the city centre. All cities show the same picture. In the outer areas the trams are still quite fast enough.

central area are transferred to trams in the other direction. On many stretches the much cheaper tram right-of-way at ground level can be retained.

The underground tramway usually uses smaller units than an underground railway, and can branch out above ground into many tram routes. In this way far better area coverage is possible than it is with the underground or suburban railway. Thus the underground tramway is a transportation engineering solution which corresponds particularly well with the modern type of urban expansion with low residential density and wide sprawl. A means of transport must not be judged solely by its technical performance. Its role in urban development is more important.

The fears in some quarters that a small underground tramway network will soon be overtaken, and that the congested area will soon spread out, are unfounded. If the population of a city doubles, the area of the central business district does not double; it grows much more slowly. If the city centre is enlarged its diameter increases only as the square root of the increase in area. But with the increase in area the number and width of the radial streets increase. The outer areas are more spaciously laid out. Should congestion set in on streets further out from the centre the underground tramway can always be extended later. For certain intersections on main streets an underpass or a flyover to carry other traffic above or below the tram median may be considered.

In Milan the authorities are intending, for the reasons stated above, to build further tunnel facilities not as 'classical' underground railways (the policy followed hitherto) but as underground tramways. In this way the rail transport network can be suited to the changes in the type of urban development and the resulting changes in traffic needs.

Unfortunately the opinion has been advanced by outsiders that the underground railway is the only really adequate means of urban transport. But if an underground tramway is built to take them, and is segregated from road traffic, it too can take long trains. And they can attain just the same speeds as underground trains since they can be given the same power to weight ratio. Whether the line is equipped with overhead current supply or 'third rail' is a technical question which does not affect the passengers. The same applies to block signalling, which in any case can be added later, but which (a) cannot result in higher speed in the central area owing to the close spacing of stopping places, and (b) lets fewer trains through. It is also possible, as once happened on the S-Bahn in Hamburg, to switch from one kind of current supply to another. Similarly it is possible to replace the conductor on the car by a ticket inspector at a barrier, if the former system is not more economical with short trains and many stopping places. The modern solution will be automated ticket control in any case. The existence of ticket barriers is not a true distinguishing feature since in many countries the railways do without them.

Thus there remains, as the only true difference between an underground railway proper and an underground tramway, the height and the position of the platforms. When electric traction was introduced on the Berlin S-Bahn all the platforms were raised one at a time by 24 cm (10 in). In Oslo also the present low platforms will be replaced later on with higher ones.

Thus there is no very sharp distinction to be drawn between the underground tramway and the underground railway (which is certainly no faster).

There are half-way houses which combine certain characteristics of both types of rail system.

It is deplorable that slogans like 'railway-type operation' or 'rapid transit operation' should be bandied about in argument. The engineer should be given the task of moving so many people in such-and-such a time to such-and-such a place. How it should be done is his problem, which he must solve in a manner which is suited to the city in question and its surroundings, and is economical.

4. Capacity

The capacity of a means of transport depends on the capacity of the line between stations and the capacity of the stopping places. The stopping times according to schedule will be as follows:

| Suburban trains | 15–60 sec |
| Trams and buses | 10–40 sec |

The actual stopping times on the Berlin S-Bahn in 1939 were:

| At main stations | 50 sec |
| At all other stations | 25 sec |

On the Paris Metro they are up to 57 sec, and on the London Underground they are at least 20 sec.

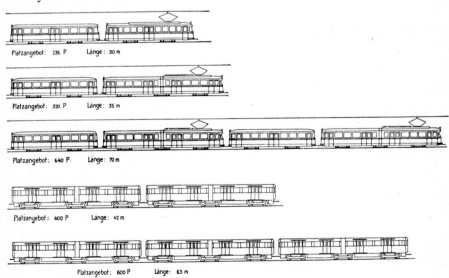

Platzangebot: 236 P   Länge: 30 m

Platzangebot: 320 P   Länge: 35 m

Platzangebot: 640 P   Länge: 70 m

Platzangebot: 400 P   Länge: 42 m

Platzangebot: 600 P   Länge: 63 m

Figure 80: Possible composition of trains on street or underground tramways and on underground railways. In big cities 8–car trains 160–180 m long (480–540 ft) are normally used (in London, however, the trains are 375–420 ft long). The figures given for capacity (seats and standing room) and length were used in the public transport planning for Frankfurt am Main, 1961.

On rail systems with automatic block signalling trains run at a minimum scheduled headway of 90 sec, which can be dropped temporarily to 70 sec where the flow of trains is irregular. Thus the headway is considerably longer than the stopping time. Capacity is limited by the line between stations. At station platforms only one train at a time can stop.

Buses and trains operated without block signalling can operate on heavily loaded sections of line at much closer headways. The headway is sometimes shorter than the stopping time. Then the capacity is limited by the stopping place. A stopping place which can only accommodate one train or bus can become the bottleneck. In this case two-unit stopping places are an advantage.

The capacity depends also on the size of units used. On tramways, above ground and underground, trains 40 m (135 ft) long can be used, consisting of one articulated motor-car and one articulated trailer-car; and these can be coupled together, on sections of line where road traffic is not affected, into double trains or even longer units. On underground railways trains 160 m (540 ft) long are normal (Fig. 80). On the London Underground, however, the trains are only about 400 ft long. With 75 per cent occupancy the following peak capacities can be attained:

Mode	Length	1-unit stopping places		2-unit stopping places	
		Headway	Capacity	Headway	Capacity
Articulated bus	16·5 m (60 ft)	24 sec	150 units × 160 persons × 75% = 18,000 persons/h	20 sec	180 × 160P × 75% = 21,600 persons/h
Tram	25 m (83 ft)	30 sec	120 trains × 220 persons × 75% = 19,800 persons/h	25 sec	144t × 220P × 75% = 23,800 persons/h
Tram or underground tramway with articulated units	40 m (135 ft)	37·5 sec	96 trains × 350 persons × 75% = 25,200 persons/h	33 sec	110t × 350P × 75% = 28,900 persons/h
Underground tramway with double trains	80 m (270 ft)	45 sec	80 trains × 700 persons × 75% = 42,000 persons/h	Not possible	
Underground railway	160 m (540 ft)	90 sec	40 trains × 1500 persons × 75% = 45,000 persons/h	Not possible	

The figures given for bus and tram are valid only on roads with uninterrupted operation. On inner-urban streets with heavy cross traffic the capacity drops to 50 per cent of the values given, i.e. with two-unit stopping places it falls to the following:

Bus: 48 sec headway; 75 units × 160 persons × 75% = 9,000 persons/h

Tram: 60 sec headway; 60 trains × 220 persons × 75% = 9,900 persons/h

As soon as a line of underground tramway is segregated from street traffic over its entire length the values appropriate to the underground railway can be used for it. But then the question should be asked whether the traffic is best served by a few long trains or by many short trains.

The underground tramway in Philadelphia, which operates without block signalling and with only warning signals ahead of danger points, regularly carries 118 P.C.C cars operated as separate units per hour, and the rate of flow rises to 180 units/h for short periods. With such heavy traffic the capacity is not limited by the stopping places but by the merging points.

At flat junctions of two-track sections of line there are interactions between merging points, intersections and diverging points. The capacity depends on:

> Total number of trains
> Proportion of trains on each branch
> Order of trains
> Time headway
> Length of safety section controlled by warning signal.

The capacity of such points cannot be accurately determined mathematically. Probability techniques (queueing theory, Monte Carlo method) are not suitable because the trains do not arrive in random order but almost always in the order they are scheduled to follow. The best method of calculation is by approximation with the help of time-distance diagrams in important cases, taking into account the necessary margin for unavoidable irregularities. Dilli did much research work on necessary allowances in railway operation.

5. Design of facilities

(a) Lines

A segregated track for public transport is undoubtedly the best solution. Where it can only be achieved with great constructional difficulties or high costs, trams and buses should be given priority over other traffic by means of measures such as the following:

> Priority over all private traffic
> Priority at important intersections, in countries where there is no general priority for trams and line buses. Exceptional regulations for trams at rotary intersections. Priority at signal-controlled junctions by means of special phases or 'pre-phases' which are either part of the regular cycle or can be actuated by special detectors
> Reservation of special lanes by means of roadway markings in the approaches to intersections or on longer stretches
> Turn prohibitions for other traffic
> Parking prohibitions, at stopping places and elsewhere

'No stopping' regulations for other traffic
Partial or complete barring of other traffic from certain streets
Introduction of one-way system for other traffic
Creation of purely tram and bus streets

In general public transport should use the main streets. Only thus can
it be given a clear run both between and at intersections. High speeds call
for big curve radii. Trams are slower in rounding curves than are road
vehicles. Therefore tram tracks must be straighter than lanes.

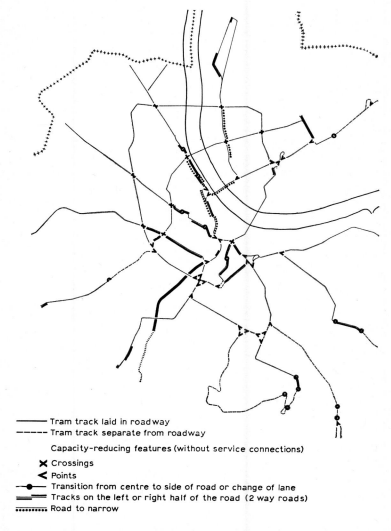

------ Tram track laid in roadway
------ Tram track separate from roadway

    Capacity-reducing features (without service connections)

  ✕ Crossings
  ◁ Points
—●— Transition from centre to side of road or change of lane
══ Tracks on the left or right half of the road (2 way roads)
·········· Road to narrow

Figure 81: Capacity-reducing features of the Basle tram system. Crossings and
    points are among the hindrances.

Tram tracks should only be laid in streets with at least four lanes, because in narrower streets a single obstructive vehicle can, despite 'No stopping' regulations, bring the tram service to a standstill: unless of course the 'tram street' is barred to other traffic in one or both directions.

The distance between the axes of the two tracks depends on the dimensions of the trams being used; on straight sections of a route it is usually between 2·40 and 3·00 m (8–10 ft). In a few cases tram tracks still lie at the edge of the street, e.g. in Vienna and Berne. This is not a good arrangement. It is true that tram loading islands can be dispensed with, but the trams cannot move fast. They hinder 'neighbourhood traffic' and endanger the pedestrian. On streets with traffic in both directions the tracks should on principle be in the centre, preferably on a special median. This requirement is still not met everywhere by a long way (Fig. 81).

To be consistent, tram tracks should be in the middle even in squares. Solutions where they are placed to one side of the roadways, as they are in front of the main railway stations of Stuttgart and Frankfurt, lead to a criss-crossing of movements which is not easy to accommodate, thus reducing the capacity.

A special tram median must be large enough to accommodate the tracks, barriers or safety strips and—in wide streets—also the supports for the overhead wire and sufficient clearance on either side of these supports. The minimum width without stopping places and supports is usually 6·80 m (22 ft 4 in).

The tram tracks can diverge at the approach to important intersections, so as to sort out the trains by the directions they are taking. While with right-hand traffic the left-turning vehicle is the most disturbing with ordinary road vehicles, with trams it is the right-turning train which is the most

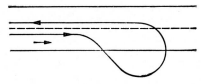

Figure 82: A terminal loop for trams on the right-hand side of a street cuts the roadway at an acute angle and blocks it completely.

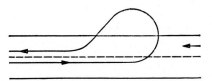

Figure 83: A terminal loop on the left-hand side is better. The tram driver turning out of the street has a clear view of the oncoming traffic whose path he must cross; when rejoining the street he enters the traffic stream from the right. With such layouts there is no symmetry!

nuisance because it cannot place itself in the right lane, and therefore interrupts all the straight-ahead traffic as it turns.

Terminal loops should, for safety reasons, be laid out to the left of the street. If they are on the right the trams completely cut the path of other traffic as they turn into them (Figs. 82, 83).

(b) Stopping places

In countries with right-hand traffic, stopping places for trams and buses should always be to the right of the track or lane used by these vehicles. They should be just on the near side or the far side of crossroads, so that they can be easily reached from cross streets. If they are on the near side of the intersection the loss of time caused by a second stop is avoided. This is the best arrangement with trams and also with buses stopping in the middle of a street (Figs. 84, 85). On the other hand, near-side bus stops along the kerb take up one reservoir lane and block vision of pedestrians and of the side street; and left-turning buses are incorrectly positioned. In

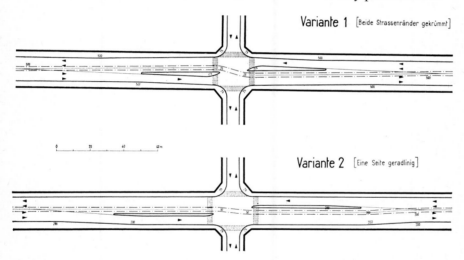

Figure 84: Insertion of tram loading islands in a street built up on both sides. The asymmetrical solution (Variant 2) is preferable; it entails widening the street on one side only.

the interests of higher capacity and safety kerbside bus stops must be placed on the far side of the intersection, even though the average speed of buses drops owing to the double stopping.

Tram and bus loading islands should be at least 1·50 m (5 ft) wide. Where traffic is heavy they should be wider. An area of 0·3 sq m (3 sq ft) should be provided for each waiting passenger, so that fairly rapid boarding and alighting is possible. Where people are pressed together 1 sq m (10 sq ft) can accommodate up to six people.

Protective posts should be erected at the ends of the islands to protect

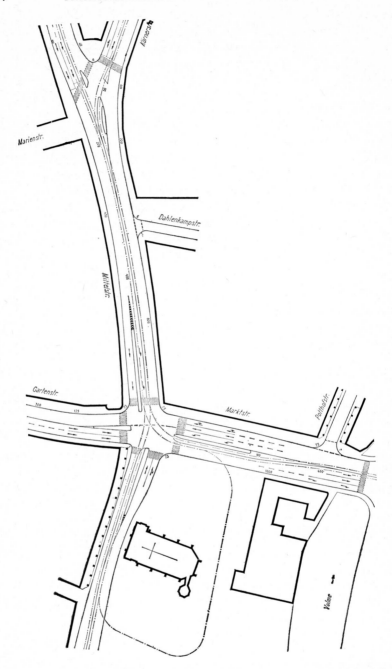

Figure 85: Crossroads with tram loading islands and tram terminal loop. Because of shortage of space left-turning motor traffic from Mittelstrasse into Marktstrasse has to be allowed to use the same strip of roadway as the tram track.

waiting passengers. The islands must not suddenly appear in the cross-section of the street. The driver must be able to recognize them in good time. The lanes should be smoothly diverted to one side. Their width should not be reduced alongside the island.

All this applies to bus loading islands in the middle of the street, too. Such islands are as yet seldom seen in Europe, but have been in use for a long time in American cities in streets with heavy traffic. If buses are to get a clear run unimpeded by parked cars they must be given the best lanes: those in the middle of the streets.

With kerbside bus stops the footway must have enough room for waiting passengers and should be correspondingly wider. Bus turnout lanes (Fig. 86) are advisable only at terminal bus stops where buses must

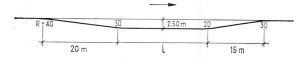

Figure 86: Bus stopping bay. l = length of the longest bus, or the length of two buses plus 1·50 m (5 ft) if two buses have to be accommodated.

wait a long time, and on two-lane roads and streets. The acceleration lane can be shorter than the deceleration lane because the speed of the bus is lower when moving off after stopping.

The length of loading islands is determined by the length of the largest vehicles used. They should be longer than the longest bus or tram-train. Where headways are close two-unit stopping places are used. The second unit does not stop a second time where the first has stopped, but resumes its journey as soon as all passengers have got in and out. In this way the capacity can be increased by about 20 per cent. With long tram-trains two-unit stopping places are no longer possible because passengers would have too far to walk. For the same reason three-unit stopping places cannot be used with buses. They would in any case not bring any further advantages.

A two-unit stopping place is double the length of a single, plus 1·50 m for the gap between the trams or buses.

(c) Depots

Multi-track stopping places or stations for inner urban transport are rare. With short stopping times the capacity of a loading island or platform edge is so large that they are only needed in a few places. On suburban and underground railways they occur almost solely at junctions. As regards tramways the track triangles of Zürich (Paradeplatz, Central and Bellevue) may be mentioned; likewise the four-track layouts in Berne (Bubenbergplatz), Basle (Zentralbahnplatz), Stuttgart (Bahnhofplatz), Essen (Hauptbahnhof) (Figs. 87, 88). In many cases these layouts have not

H

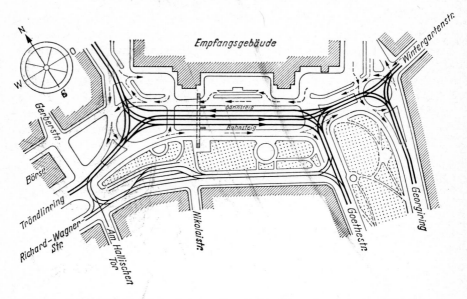

Figure 87: Street and tramway layout outside the railway station in Leipzig. Note the generously-proportioned four-track tramway layout, with parallel operation.

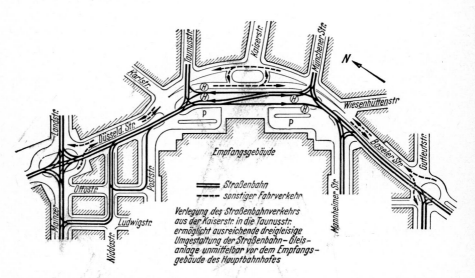

Figure 88: Street and tram layout outside the railway station in Frankfurt am Main. The four tram stopping places are so far apart that a saving can be made in width. Pedestrians never have to cross more than three tram tracks. The way the tram tracks swing across from the centre of the street to the side of it in front of the ticket hall disrupts traffic flow in the Düsseldorfer and the Baseler Strasse. The Düsseldorfer Strasse was subsequently improved by a flyover.

been provided to increase capacity but because of the form of network, to ease interchange and speed up the operation. They are also needed where radial lines of different undertakings or with different types of technical equipment (track width, type of electric current) cannot be linked together to form cross-town lines, e.g. the interchange points in Berne between the trams, the Solothurn–Zollikofen–Berne railway and the two branches of the Berne–Worb railway; and those in Bonn between the trams and the Cologne–Bonn railway, the Siebengebirgsbahn and the Godesberg railway. Such a splintering brings many disadvantages.

With suburban bus routes it is often not possible to have cross-town links. Many such lines have an infrequent service. They serve mainly commuter and shopping traffic. In the morning the buses come into the city from all directions, in the evening they return home. But the traffic

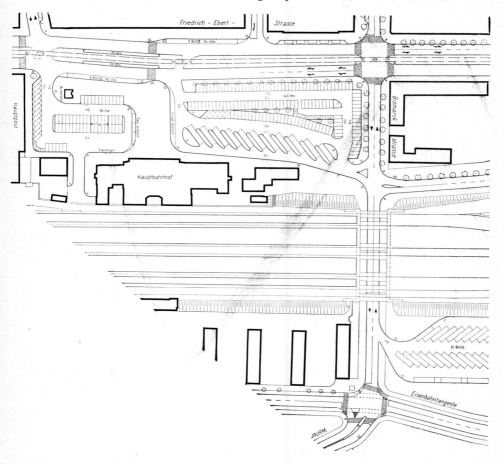

Figure 89: Plan for the station forecourt at Bremerhaven. The pedestrian peninsula is asymmetrical. The bus boarding station is supplemented by a bus parking area on the other side of the railway viaduct.

demand in the opposite direction is very small at these times. The buses must start their run at the hub of the town's traffic, usually at the main railway station, often in order to facilitate interchange. Sometimes the buses remain standing at their terminal stop during the whole day until the working day ends. Thus some big bus stations have been built the platforms of which are very poorly utilized.

Most such installations are too big. Valuable space in prime locations is squandered on them. For the bus operator the arrangement is advantageous because it eliminates 'empty legs' to and from a parking place some distance out. But from the urban development point of view it is otherwise. In the course of a few decades the railways have had to separate their train storage from their passenger stations. They have often done it under compulsion, in that they cannot acquire sites for the extension of

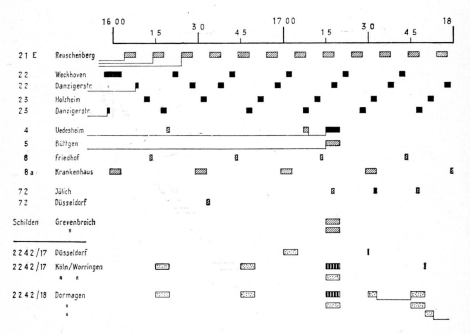

Figure 90: A diagram showing the type of analysis of bus timetables and waiting times which should be used as a basis for deciding on the number of bus standing spaces and loading islands. Long-distance routes present different problems from urban routes, since they do not normally run through and require longer stopping times. Buses waiting for longer periods should be on a parking area.

their installations, and must use their storage areas for other purposes. Traffic planning for buses must also see the need for separation of bus station and parking area (Fig. 89). As with the railways the following basic rules are true:

The smallest station is the best
Operational installations out of the centre, traffic installations into the centre

The size of bus stations is determined on the basis of the schedules of existing and planned bus lines (Fig. 90). The stopped time must of course

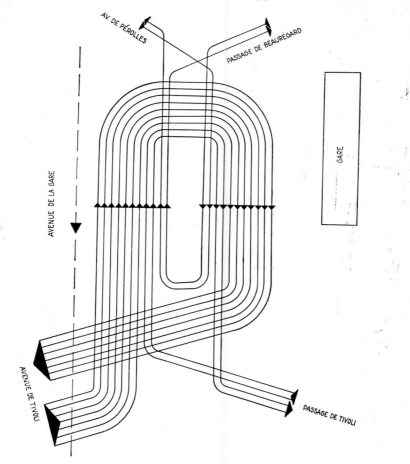

Figure 91: Diagram of motorcoach and bus movements in a station forecourt. For local reasons the terminal loop must be operated anticlockwise.

be assumed to be longer than that at intermediate stopping places in urban traffic. In designing the layout the exact paths followed by vehicles and the frequency of their use must be given close attention (Fig. 91). According to the space available the stopping places will be laid out parallel, at an oblique angle or at a right angle. The most useful are those at an oblique angle (Fig. 92). With the parallel layout the buses must be able to arrive and depart independently of each other. Therefore the roadway between

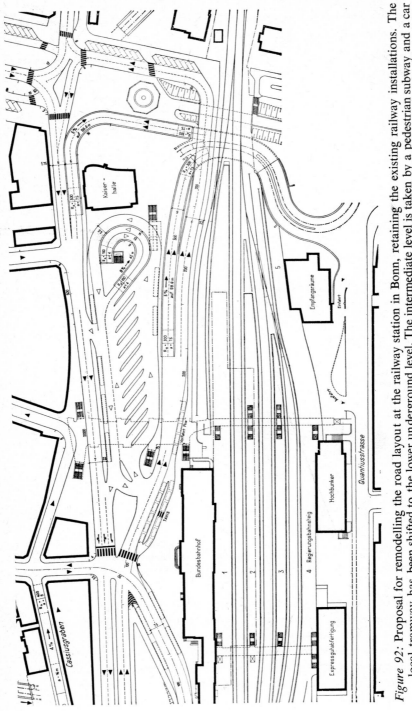

Figure 92: Proposal for remodelling the road layout at the railway station in Bonn, retaining the existing railway installations. The local tramway has been shifted to the lower underground level. The intermediate level is taken by a pedestrian subway and a car park for 200 cars; the entrance to the latter is via a curved ramp placed inside the terminal loop for buses. The bus station has 11 diagonal islands, and kerbside stops along both sides. The local buses stop along the left side of the pedestrian peninsula in front of the ticket hall.

the islands must be widened from 3·50 m to 6·00 m (20 ft). Islands must be 1·50 m (5 ft) wide with the usual moderate traffic, and 2·50 m (8 ft) wide with heavier parallel traffic or if trees are planted on them (Fig. 93).

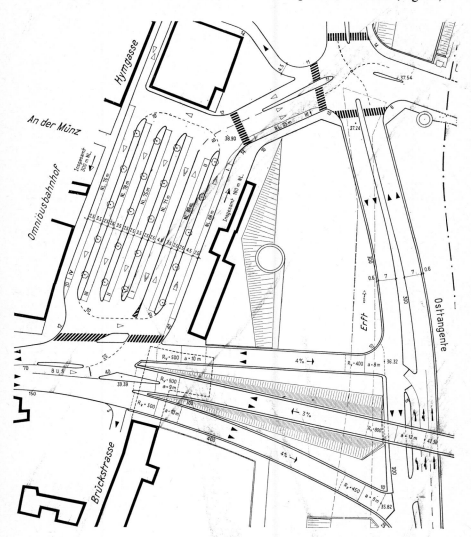

Figure 93: The bus station in Neuss, with longitudinal loading islands. The asymmetry of the layout is a result of the situation. The bus station lies close to the market where the east Tangent crosses the new east–west radial. This radial is carried on a flyover over the tangent route and the harbour railway tracks. No buses run in this direction.

6. Underground installations

(a) Lines

The rules and standards of railway construction and operation apply also to suburban and underground railway lines. They need not be described here.

When tramways are placed underground, the kinds of layout of junctions and forks used above ground should not simply be reproduced underground, as was done at the Midi station in Brussels, because sight lines are restricted by the tunnel walls and it is harder to put things right in the event of an accident. On the other hand the driver no longer has to worry about road traffic. The number of points and intersections should be kept as small as possible but still providing the right conditions for an efficient service.

Whenever possible a fairly straight alignment should be provided in the interest of good visibility. In the immediate proximity of stopping places, at which all trams will in any case have to stop, the same radii as are used on the surface can however be safely used. This will not reduce the average speed. With a rate of acceleration of 0·8 m/sec² a tram will reach a speed of 40 km/h (25 mph) only after it has travelled 80 m (270 ft). This calls for a minimum radius of 80 m if superelevation is provided on curves and the trams have a low centre of gravity, and of 130 m where neither of these conditions is met.

Use of these small radii makes it possible to lay out underground junctions even where buildings are close together without tunnelling under buildings. The network will thus take the form of a polygon with sharp bends immediately before and after the stopping places, and straight or only slightly curved stretches of line in between.

Even on suburban and underground railways smaller radii can be used than on long-distance railways. For instance the following minimum radii are found on underground railways in various cities:

Paris Metro, old lines	40 m (135 ft)
Paris Metro, new lines	75 m (255 ft)
Berlin, U-Bahn	100 m (340 ft)
Berlin, north–south S-Bahn	150 m (500 ft)
Toronto	120 m (400 ft)
Buenos Aires	80 m (270 ft)

The easiest possible radii are of course desirable in order to minimize wear on wheels and rails.

On all of these rail systems fairly steep gradients can be permitted because only light trains with powerful motors are used: up to 4 per cent on suburban railways (e.g. Berlin) and 5·5 per cent on underground tramways in hilly cities (e.g. Oslo). Ramps ought not to be steeper than this, even with bus tunnels, because they are exposed to rain and snow.

(b) Stopping places

For safety reasons stopping places should be on straight sections of line so that the driver and conductor can watch all doors. Platform edges which are slightly concave in plan are good; but platform edges which are convex in plan are dangerous because they cannot be supervised either by the tram conductor or by supervisors or close-circuit television monitors on the platform.

With straight tracks the gap between the platform edge and the tram-cars remains small.

Tracks can have the same gradient at stopping places as they can between them; but acceleration and braking is easier on a moderate gradient or none at all.

The stopping places should be as shallow as possible under the street level, so that they are easy to get to. A sawtooth profile, with the stopping places at the summits and the running tunnels forming sags in between, has operational and fuel consumption advantages. Power can be cut down as the train enters the station, and less power is needed to accelerate on the downgrade beyond the station. Braking and acceleration will be faster. However, steep gradients ought not to begin immediately before or after stations because this makes acceleration and braking more difficult. Merging or diverging points ought not to occur at the foot of ramps or on steep gradients.

Where fares are taken by a conductor, which is still mostly the case on underground tramways, the platform must be to the right of the track. Island platforms are in that case only possible with an 'inside-out' layout on one of the lines (Figs. 94–96). This can be achieved either by having unidirectional ramps placed one after the other at the transition point from above-ground to underground operation, or by 'roll-overs' underground. In cases where platform supervisors are used the island platform has the advantage that one man can supervise two lines if the traffic is not too heavy. But this advantage has ceased to be important since the introduction of close-circuit television monitors on the second platform (on the Hamburg Hochbahn).

Stations are usually placed under streets. With platforms on either side of the tracks access can be provided from both footways, and no intermediate level is needed; whereas with platforms between the tracks an intermediate pedestrian level is usually necessary to provide access. This means the platform level must be about 3 m (10 ft) deeper. The intermediate level can be made available for general pedestrian traffic which cannot be taken across the roadways at heavily-loaded intersections.

The width of the platform should be generous since later widenings are expensive. A platform should have to hold at most 3 persons per square metre, half as many as in fully loaded trams and buses. If more are squeezed on the boarding and alighting is too slow. Moreover a safety strip should remain free at the edge of the platform. When service is irregular the stations must accommodate a large number of waiting passengers. Where there are no platform barriers they cannot be held back and press forward onto the platform. At stations in the neighbourhood of sports stadia and the like, where there are big surge demands, it must be possible to instal barriers quite easily. The usable width between platform edge and wall should be 3·50 m in the case of single platforms. A width of 10·00 m (33 ft) is sufficient even for the most heavily used island platforms. With such a

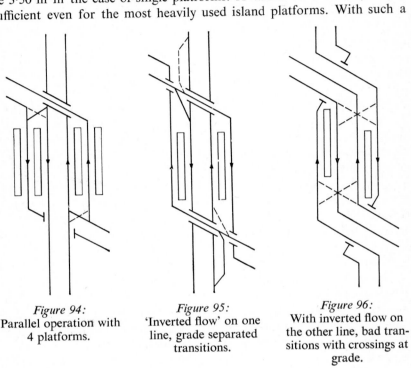

Figure 94:
Parallel operation with
4 platforms.

Figure 95:
'Inverted flow' on one
line, grade separated
transitions.

Figure 96:
With inverted flow on
the other line, bad tran-
sitions with crossings at
grade.

There are three possible layouts for interchange stations on two underground tramway lines with some through running from one to the other. Tramcars have doors only on the right. There is no symmetry.

width there is room for centre supports and such items as telephone kiosks and benches. No such 'furniture' should however be allowed, on safety grounds, within a strip 1·50 m wide and 3·00 m high alongside the edge of the platform (with railways the strip should be 3·00 m wide and 3·05 m high, measured from the top of the rails).

On suburban and underground railways the platform should preferably be at the same height as the floor of the cars. Underground tramways must have low platforms as long as they still have to serve above-ground stopping places (as in Brussels). On average each passenger boarding takes 1·2 to 1·5 sec, and each alighting passenger 1·0 to 1·2 sec. The lower figures apply to systems with high platforms, the higher figures to tramways, including underground tramways. When the cars are overloaded the times are considerably longer. Sale of a ticket by a tram conductor takes 3 to 5 sec, inspection of a season ticket takes 1·2 to 1·5 sec. The average time in any particular system depends on the tariff, the type of ticket and the proportions of single-trip tickets and multi-trip tickets. Use of the latter speeds up service. But the desire for simplification should not be taken so far that a flat fare is charged throughout the system, regardless of length of trip. When this is done the flat fare has to be so high that short-distance traffic switches to private transport. This is wrong from the standpoint of transportation planning and of the economy of the transport undertaking. The fare structure is an important element in planning.

(c) Entrances and steps

Stairs to platforms should be carefully located so that they provide comfortable access from a large catchment area. Use of platform barriers leads to a reduction in the number of access points in order to keep down staffing costs. This is a big disadvantage for passengers.

The entry and exit points must have so much capacity that no delays arise at peak times. All passengers must be able to get clear of the platform before the arrival of the next train, i.e. within 90 sec at peak times on suburban railways, and within an even shorter time on underground tramways. And departing passengers must be able to reach the platform at the same time.

The exits are usually most heavily loaded after arrival of a fully-loaded train, because all arriving passengers will want to leave the station almost simultaneously. Departing passengers are better distributed in time. Stations serving sports stadia and meeting halls should not be located too close to them so that the surge demand is already spread out.

On fixed stairs people in urban traffic move upwards at 0·8 m/sec and downwards at 1·0 m/sec. On a width of stair wide enough for one man, i.e. 0·60 m (2 ft) wide, with each person 1 m behind the other 40–50 people can move upwards in 1 min and 50–60 people can move downwards in 1 min. Widths of stairs are calculated in units of 0·60 m (2 ft), with an allowance for handrails. On tram loading islands the width of the stairs must sometimes be suited to the islands. Such stairs have been built 1·50 m (5 ft) wide, but this is unpleasantly narrow. A desirable minimum width is 2·50 m (8 ft). A width of 4·00 m (13 ft) is common; a width of 8·00 m (26 ft) is rare even with heavy surge demands.

Stairs should not be steeper than 15/33 cm. With heavy traffic an inclination of 13/37 cm is to be recommended. The formula $2b + h = 63$ cm should be used. After each 8 or 10 steps a landing 1·50 m (5 ft) long should be introduced.

Climbing stairs is found to be wearisome. For old people, mothers with prams and the lame, stairs are a great obstacle. Therefore the height of the stairs must be kept to a minimum. A headroom of 2·20 to 2·50 m (7 to 8 ft) is normally provided in pedestrian tunnels. Where sufficient length is available stairs are replaced with ramps, which are more comfortable. Pedestrian ramps should never be steeper than 16 per cent (1 in 6); at stations and stopping places they should not be steeper than 10 per cent (1 in 10). Pedestrians walk up ramps at about 0·9 m/sec and down them at about 1·2 m/sec. Unfortunately ramps are difficult to fit into cramped street corners, and they lengthen pedestrian paths.

Ordinary stairs are often placed alongside escalators because some people are wary of using them. In such cases the fixed stairs are used mainly in peak hours, which cannot be catered for adequately by escalators because of costs.

Escalators are usually single-width or double-width with an inclination of 30 or 35 degrees (Fig. 97). They run at a speed of 0·4 to 0·6 m/sec. Recently experiments have been made with escalators running at 0·7 to 0·75 m/sec. A single-width escalator can carry 60 persons per min, a double-width one can carry 120 persons per min. Descending escalators must not be too steep, and it must be possible for users to stop them at any time in case of danger. Severe falls and accidents have occurred on descending escalators which were feeding more and more people onto overcrowded platforms. There must be adequate reservoir space at both ends of all stairs and escalators. A platform barrier, if one is provided, must be at least 4 m (13 ft) from the foot of an escalator.

Moving walkways (sometimes called travelators) can have an inclination of up to 15 per cent.

The passage at a barrier must be 65 cm (2 ft 2 in) wide. A width of 80 cm. (2 ft 8 in) must be allowed for a ticket inspector's seat. Inspection of tickets at the exit is usually dispensed with. Where a flat fare is charged, as in many American cities, passengers enter through automatic barriers actuated by a coin box, and the inspector can be dispensed with. It is however estimated that with such a system about 6 per cent of passengers do not pay their fares.

An entry barrier can handle up to 25 passengers per min with single-trip tickets or 50 with multi-trip tickets; an exit barrier can handle 50 to 60 per min.

The above-ground exits, whether stairs or ramps, must be correctly sited from the traffic standpoint. Where there is a shortage of space they are sometimes placed inside buildings. This requires expensive basement space. In many cases neighbouring shops will pay for the construction of access points within their buildings because they can thereby improve their business situation.

Underground spaces must always be easily comprehensible. Direction signs do not make a good layout out of a bad one. All paths followed by passengers should be as straight as possible and without sharp corners. Conflicts between heavy streams of pedestrians and unnecessary losses of height should be avoided. A 'keep to the right' rule for pedestrians is very desirable. It cannot always be followed, however, without making the installation too complex.

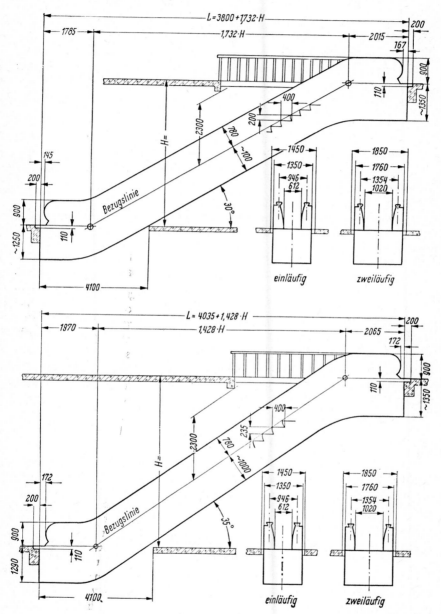

Figure 97: Longitudinal and cross sections of escalators inclined at 30° and 35°.

IV. ROAD NETWORKS

1. Form of network

(a) Classification of roads and streets

In cities and conurbations the road network forms a dense spider's web with manifold links. The roads have different tasks, loadings and traffic importance, and must be classified according to these attributes. Roads can be classified:

1. By function into trunk roads, local roads.
2. By use into primary distributors, secondary distributors, district distributors, local distributors, residential roads and frontage roads.
3. By traffic volume into high-capacity roads, main traffic arteries and side roads.
4. By design features into motorways, expressways, roads and ways.
5. By administrative responsibility into national roads, provincial roads, cantonal roads, county, city and municipal roads.

There are further possible sub-divisions. A further gradation or splintering is however not desirable because it makes overall comprehension difficult. The boundaries cannot be sharply drawn. The transition from local to long-distance traffic is fluid. Many roads serve several purposes. Municipal roads can become county roads, provincial roads can become national roads. But for planning purposes they all form one unified network. Basically the only valid distinction is between main roads and side roads. And it may be pointed out that as a general rule too much money is spent on side roads to the detriment of the main roads. Roads should be sharply distinguished by their traffic importance and graded accordingly as regards reconstruction.

(b) Inventory of existing streets

The existing road network of a city mirrors the history of its growth. In the city centre the irregular network of the mediaeval alleys has been completely or partially retained. Around it lies the ring of the 19th century urban extensions, laid out on a grid pattern. Further out are the additions of the last few decades. In these the 'practical' but monotonous and boring grid pattern has been deliberately replaced by an irregular pattern which to some extent follows the contours and reflects the shape of the landscape. The moods and impressions of that time have left us a confused street network with irregular junctions and poor alignment, with many links missing (Figs. 98, 99).

A large-scale recasting of the network is out of the question. An attempt must be made to develop a master plan under which the important road arteries will be gradually remodelled and made uniform, and here and there

Figure 98: The street network of Basle. In the mediaeval city centre the streets are at odd angles; the new parts of the city are laid out on geometrical patterns. New settlements need a street network adapted to traffic. The only large-scale street lies in the western part of the city. It uses the right-of-way of the former Alsace Railway, but has poor connexions at both ends.

supplemented. In framing this master plan the planner must not stake his ambition on doing everything bigger and better than his predecessors and differently. Existing plans and designs should be followed as far as possible. Theoretically right suggestions can only be partially carried through. Careful and thorough working out of the details is not less important than the basic idea. Only this can show whether the plan can be carried out in practice. It involves exact knowledge of the location and condition of buildings and infrastructures (Fig. 100).

(c) Main road network

The detailed redesign of the street network involves several stages. The first stage is the design of the main road network. All roads of importance, including important side streets, are drawn on white paper or on a base map of the city. The network must fit naturally into the urban fabric. It must be clear and comprehensible and contain all the links that are needed.

The nodes of the network—the junctions—must be so laid out as

Figure 99: The street network of Munich (1·1 million inhabitants) shows the same stages of development as Basle. In the outer areas the network is very fragmented. In between lie large areas with no road connexions. How should the many small networks each serving one settlement be arranged and be co-ordinated?

Figure 100: Street widths in Basle. Here as in most other cities the streets are in general narrowest where the traffic is heaviest.

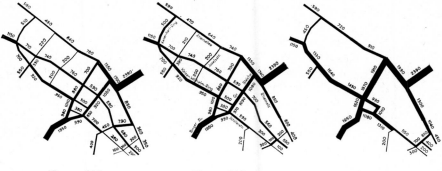

Figure 101:	Figure 102:	Figure 103:
Close-mesh grid network.	Network with no cross link through the old city.	Network with few main streets.

In Mainz the most suitable 'mesh' for the main street network was determined by assigning observed traffic flows to different network designs. The network with the coarsest mesh proved the best. It also enabled resources to be concentrated on only a few streets.

regards shape, location and spacing that a high capacity can reasonably be expected (Figs. 101–106). The building up of the network is a purely creative activity for which a 'feeling for town building' is just as essential as the mastery of the totality of technical data. The task cannot be done under pressure of time. Numerous solutions must be sketched out and compared. And they must be thought about in peace and quiet.

The main road network should consist of radials and tangentials which serve the whole urban area, and here and there in the outer suburbs these are supplemented by diagonals. The number of main roads should be kept small in order to facilitate route-finding and to avoid excessive construction and maintenance costs. With an existing network one must test how closely one can approximate to this favourable type of network.

(d) Traffic lane plans

The dimensions of roads must depend on the traffic volumes to be carried. The traffic streams which have been determined from the traffic survey must be assigned to the planned road network. Excessive traffic loads can be reduced by widening the streets or shifting their location. Bypass roads can also be introduced or interchanges altered. Construction possibilities and traffic routings must be carefully weighed against each other.

From this process there emerges gradually the traffic lane plan, which says how many lanes each section of main road should have in order to cope with the traffic load (Figs. 107–109). The number of lanes which is mathematically necessary must be increased in certain places on structural grounds to avoid bottlenecks and create the possibility of detours.

Within an urban area we must assume many detours will be made on account of building work, festivities and accidents.

A good traffic lane plan is similar to the 'traffic spider'. On the basis of the capacity calculation, the scale designs and the individual studies it is continually improved as the planning progresses. From the traffic lane plan the form of the network and the functions of the various parts of it can be exactly seen. If it has been well thought out the designs for each element can be prepared much more quickly.

The capacity calculations must be made at the same time as the design of the individual junctions and sections of road is going ahead. They lead one to consider designs not merely in plan, but dynamically in relation to the large and small traffic streams flowing in all directions.

An engineer who is trained only in civil engineering sometimes has difficulty in understanding the pattern of traffic streams and the methodology of designing traffic installations. This is the root cause of much misunderstanding. Civil engineering knows only the three dimensions of space and the calculation of static loads in kg/cm^2 or lb/sq ft. The traffic engineer, on the other hand, must think in four dimensions, the fourth being time. The dynamic capacity calculation must be in terms of

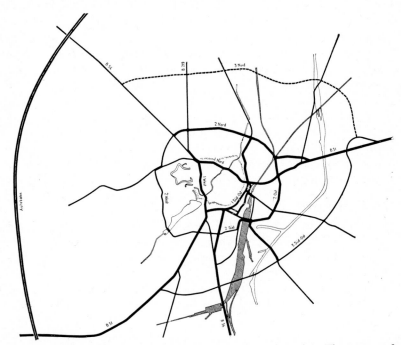

Figure 104: The main road network of Münster in Westfalen. The centre of the city is to be girdled by a 'tangent triangle' which would deflect all traffic having no business in the centre. A small distance out there will be a second tangent 'ring' most of which already exists. Much further out are the third external tangents.

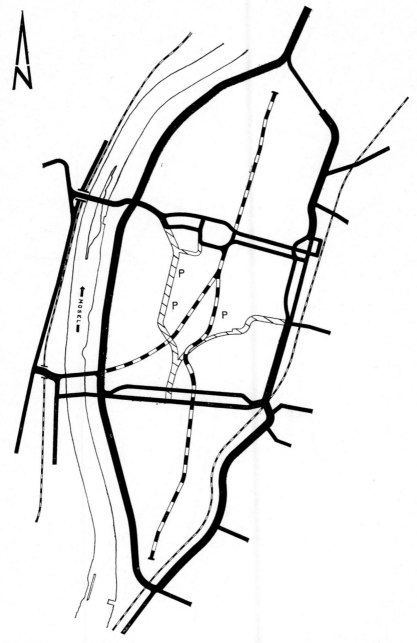

Figure 105: In the main road network proposed for Trier (90,000 inhabitants) there is sharp segregation of public transport, local car traffic, which is routed to park places, and through traffic. Through traffic on the north-south axis would have to go out of its way to use the public transport routes.

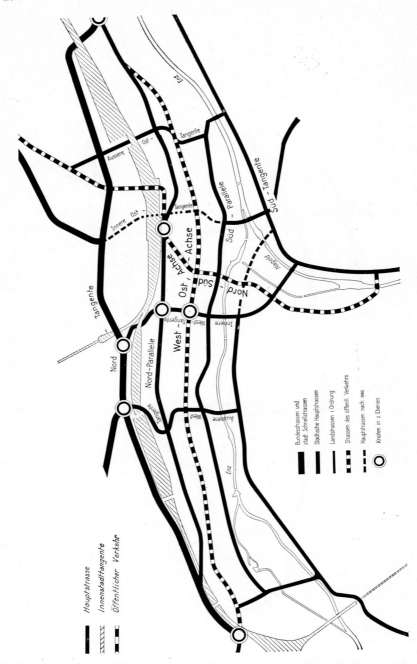

Figure 106: The main road network proposed for Pforzheim (80,000 inhabitants). The two main public transport axes (served mainly by trolleybuses) intersect in the business centre of the city. On each side of these there are two tangents, an inner and an outer.

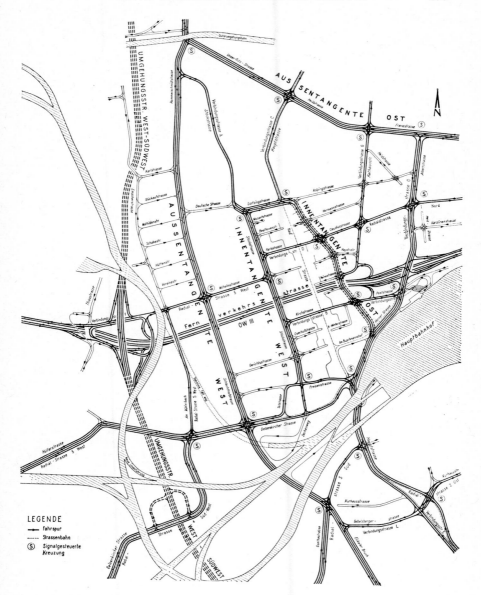

Figure 107: Traffic lane plan for Wanne-Eickel (100,000 inhabitants) in the Ruhr region. The main north–south street, which has hitherto carried very heavy through-traffic is to be turned into a shopping street used only by pedestrians and public transport. The shops and other buildings will be serviced from the rear via cul-de-sac streets and courtyards. The elongated city centre between the two inner tangents will be traversed by two connecting streets. Space will also be reserved for a depressed highway running east–west across the centre.

Figure 108: Traffic lane plan for Neuss. The design for this city with its mediaeval
centre is very similar to that for the young industrial city of Wanne-Eickel.
On the present main north–south street only trams, buses and frontage
traffic are permitted. The west and east tangents follow the old city walls.
Using such 'seam lines' for tangents is very good from the town planning
point of view. There will be two east–west connexions across the old town so
that traffic in this direction will not be subjected to an excessive detour,
causing new overloads. The two-lane flyover at the northern end of the city,
alongside the railway viaduct, is noteworthy. Another flyover is proposed
on the eastern radial (Figure 93).

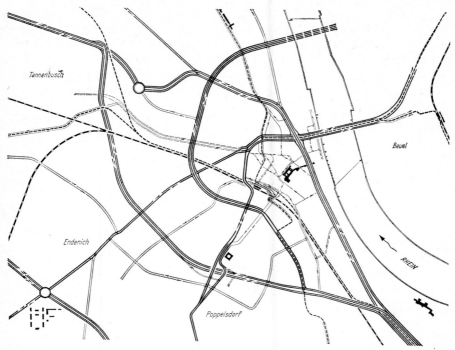

Figure 109: Traffic lane plan for Bonn, with the railway station retained in its old position. The city centre would be protected by leading the main roads past it as tangents. The city centre around the university (drawn in black) would be served predominantly by one-way streets. The number of lanes proposed is based on traffic survey data; note the two-lane flyover on the east tangent. The width of all important streets can be determined on the basis of the traffic lane plan.

vehicles per unit of time (cars/min, trains/hr, etc.). The time-distance relationship applies to the whole network. Usually it is a matter of a big area with manifold, interacting dependencies, so that the traffic planner must think in terms of big relationships.

(e) Spacing between main roads

The capacity of every traffic network depends on the three elements: lines, junctions and vehicle storage areas. The size and location of the junctions and parking facilities must therefore be brought into the planning of the main road network from the beginning. Every network is as strong as its weakest link. And the weakest links are the junctions, where these are not grade-separated.

Intersections at grade must be so laid out that they fit into the green wave signal systems. Intersections between main streets are usually sited 300–350 m (1,000–1,150 ft) apart in the city centre; further out, where speeds are higher, they are usually sited 400–550 m (1,300–1,800 ft) apart, or a multiple thereof (Fig. 110). Where construction would be difficult or expensive the distance between main streets is usually doubled.

In cities which are divided by railway embankments or cuttings the over and underpasses should never be more than 700 m (2,300 ft) apart, or the separation will be too strongly felt. The same applies to river crossings. The average distances between river bridges in the central areas of certain cities are as follows:

City	River	Number of bridges	Average spacing
London	Thames	11	825 m (2,580 ft)
Paris	Seine	15	360 m (1,180 ft)
Rome	Tiber	13	400 m (1,300 ft)
Geneva	Rhone	5	180 m (600 ft)
Berne	Aare	5	780 m (2,450 ft)
Basle	Rhine	5	800 m (2,500 ft)
Zürich	Limmat	5	270 m (900 ft)
Munich	Isar	8	550 m (1,800 ft)
Budapest	Danube	5	900 m (3,000 ft)
Breslau	Oder	6	350 m (1,150 ft)
Berlin	Spree	15	350 m (1,150 ft)
Frankfurt	Main	6	860 m (2,700 ft)

The most important roads in a network should have partial or complete grade separation. A sharp distinction between fully grade-separated urban motorways, expressways with few intersections at grade and other main roads is not necessary. As the traffic load decreases, a motorway may be continued as an expressway and an expressway as an ordinary main road. All the roads together form a unified network. It would be wrong to develop a motorway network independently of the other roads. The urban road network can certainly consist of roads of different types. Even the side streets fulfil a vital role.

(f) Local streets

The side streets—generally local distributors and residential streets— should be laid out in relation to junctions with the main roads whose location is determined by the need to fit them into the green wave signal system. In the old parts of a city it is often difficult to comply with this requirement, and unequal spacing must be taken into account. Unfortunately this golden rule of junction spacing is frequently broken even in newly-built areas. Since a road once built can hardly be shifted over, such mislocation often permanently reduces the service given by otherwise high-capacity stretches of road. Even in the layout of unimportant side streets in new settlements the traffic engineering ground-rules must be observed from the very beginning if permanent drawbacks are to be avoided.

A host of suggestions are made for new suburbs and settlements.

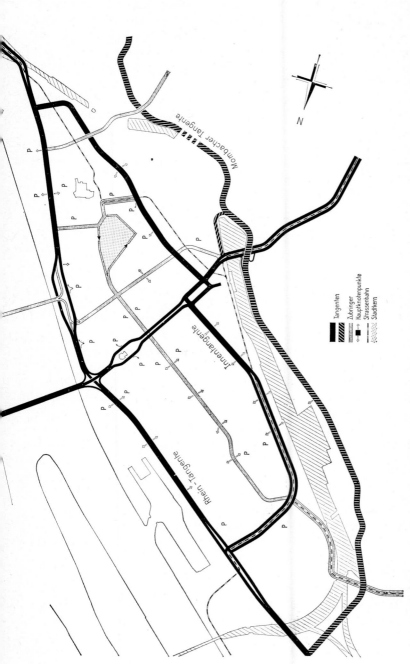

Figure 110: Outline plan of main road network proposed for Mainz with Rhine Tangent, Inner Tangent, Mombach Tangent and Rhine Bridge Axis running diagonally across to it. The existing Rhine bridge would serve only neighbourhood traffic. The heart of the old town would be developed as a pedestrian precinct, with a one-way triangle of streets around it; the one-way street on the same side as the Rhine would however carry buses in both directions. Special care was taken to ensure fairly even spacing between main junctions without doing violence to the old urban framework. The new network creates order out of the confusion of the mediaeval alleys of the old town and the uniform grid network of streets in the new town to the north of it, and joins them together on a uniform traffic engineering basis.

Often the residential groups are laid out first and the roads fitted in afterwards. This cannot produce satisfactory results. Roads are not an ornamental feature for a plan which has already been painted, but the most important and expensive type of supply installation which must be laid out according to the recognized rules of traffic engineering.

What happens most frequently is that old-fashioned types of layout are chosen. The grid network, with the land area divided up into squares or rectangles of equal size, leads to a favourable utilization of the building land. But it also leads to the creation of numerous intersections between streets of equal importance, which are dangerous. The monotony of the streets has been rightly criticized—a monotony which also favours accidents. For this reason sometimes certain links in the grid are interrupted for vehicular traffic (Fig. 111).

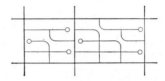

Figure 111: In a residential area with a grid-pattern street network accident frequency was reduced by the subsequent interruption of certain links. But such a network is inefficient and unsuitable for new settlements.

An irregular street pattern can give residential roads an attractive appearance, but a larger proportion of the total area is occupied by roadways, so that costs rise. With uneven and short spacing of the junctions of residential roads with local distributor roads the capacity of the network drops—and with urban expansion and rising motorization the capacity of the network becomes more and more important. The arbitrary layout of the streets in most cases leads to unusual blind and dangerous junctions. On the edges of cities there is a plethora of very recent examples to be seen.

Recently the roads in various new settlements have been developed fanning out from a single point into a large number of cul-de-sacs (Fig. 112). In this way any nuisance from through traffic is to be eliminated. But the thinking is misguided, since through traffic in any case moves almost solely on the main roads. The inhabitants do not usually have one single traffic objective, such as the city centre—unless the settlement lies on a peninsula or in a closed valley. If they wish to drive in other directions they are compelled to make big detours.

An earnest warning against cul-de-sacs is called for; they are just as mistaken as one-ended sidings on railways; they are detrimental to traffic; their areas will be poorly utilized. A traffic lane which could serve 2,000 cars an hour will perhaps be used only two or three times in a day. All service traffic—post, refuse collection, food delivery—must drive uselessly back out of the cul-de-sac before they can serve the next street, which gives rise to unnecessary and continuing costs. Tractor-trailer combinations carrying fuel oil or furniture can hardly serve the houses because there is not sufficient room for them to turn round. For these reasons the city of Philadelphia has forbidden the building of cul-de-sacs more than 150 m (500 ft) in length.

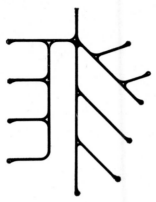

Figure 112: A street layout in which all the streets branch out from a single point. Such a layout is oriented towards a single destination, usually the city centre. Road users wanting to get to anywhere else are subjected to long detours. Serving such a settlement—delivering mail and food, collecting refuse, etc.—is time-consuming and uneconomical, because the cul-de-sacs give rise to many 'empty legs'. Peaceful residential areas can be created without such extreme treatment.

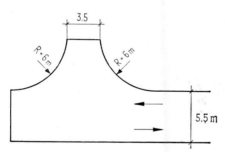

Figure 113: A 'turning hammer' at the end of a cul-de-sac (residential street).

At the far ends of cul-de-sacs circular turning areas, or alternatively 'turning hammers', are provided. If they are of sufficient size they take up much space.

The same result can be achieved, in terms of peace and quiet for the inhabitants, without these disadvantages, by joining both ends of a residential street onto the local distributor. This can be done in the form of bows or loops (Fig. 114).

For larger areas the recommended form of street system is one with a definite hierarchy of roads, with the main roads sharply emphasized, a small number of junctions on them at the correct spacing and no frontage development (Figs. 115, 116). They need not run in straight lines and can be adapted to the landscape. The local distributor and residential streets are fitted into the grid of main roads. Certain links are provided only for pedestrians in order to reduce the number of crossroads. But the traffic on side streets is so small that no segregation between types of traffic is necessary. Special footway and cycleway networks within the quiet residential

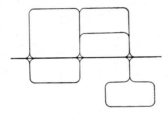

Figure 114: Residential streets laid out as loops or bows are better than cul-de-sacs even in small settlements.

areas would be a waste of money. On many streets sidewalks can be dispensed with without any worries, so that a total width of 5·50 m (18 ft)—which in any case is the minimum width of roadway that should be provided—will be sufficient.

Residential streets can enter local distributors either opposite one another or in a staggered fashion. With the staggered layout the number of danger points on the local distributor is doubled and its capacity is reduced. The small amount of cross traffic between residential streets will be compelled to merge with traffic on the local distributor and then almost immediately diverge again. In this way it disturbs the traffic on the local distributor unnecessarily. Simple crossroads without staggering undoubtedly have the advantage. Staggered crossroads should only be provided at junctions between residential streets.

The number of junctions should be kept small. The more important the road the fewer junctions it should have. A motorway must be entirely free of intersections, the main road must have very few (Fig. 117). The side streets, however, must have so many crossroads and connections that the necessary links are provided in the network and the traffic can be distributed in all directions without excessive detours.

Emphasis on peace and quiet should not be taken so far that houses can only be reached by covering long distances on foot. Each house requires vehicular access. With a single family house the siting of a garage directly next to or inside the house is taken for granted. The inhabitants of a multi-family dwelling have the same requirement. The work of housewives must be facilitated. A long walk between the door of the building and one's own car or a delivery van is intolerable in bad weather. Ambulances and fire appliances must be able to drive right up to a building. Often

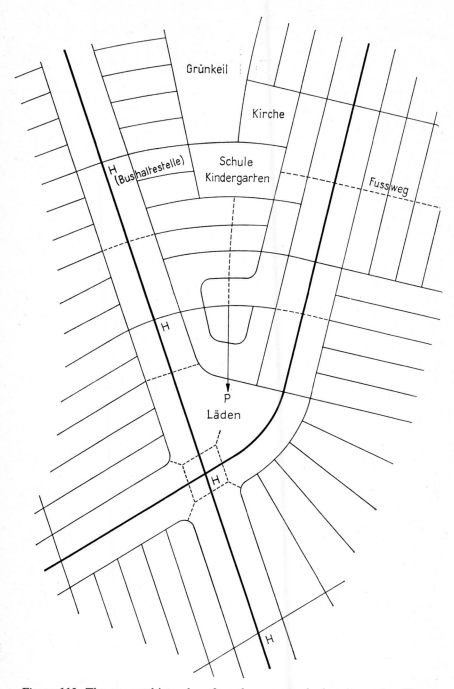

Figure 115: The correct hierarchy of roads, composed of main roads with no frontage development, collector roads and residential roads, still leaves plenty of scope for architectonic treatment and can be adapted to any residential density.

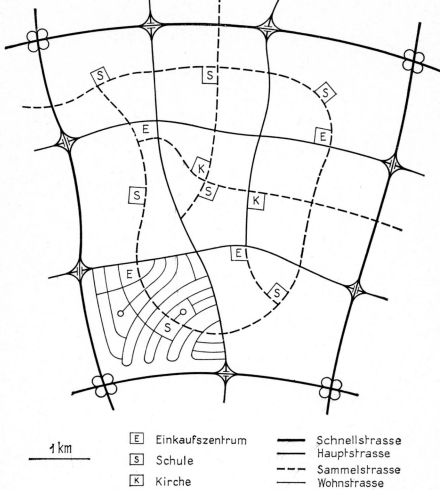

E	Einkaufszentrum	▬▬▬▬	Schnellstrasse
		▬▬▬▬	Hauptstrasse
S	Schule	▬ ▬ ▬	Sammelstrasse
K	Kirche	▬▬▬▬	Wohnstrasse

1 km

Figure 116: A similar layout is proposed for large settlements in the U.S.A.; but it will hardly be possible to give these public transport service.

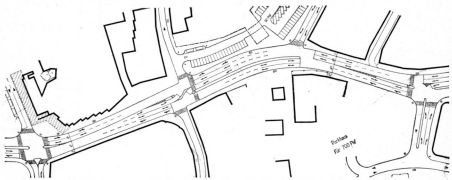

Figure 117: One-way streets branching off from an inner tangent road, which cannot be widened. With few crossroads the tangent has a high capacity. The indoor car park (*lower right*) is reached via a T-junction on the tangent road.

the inhabitants of pedestrian paradises have no hesitation in using the footways as vehicular accesses. Dwellings without vehicular access will only find tenants as long as the housing shortage leaves people with no choice.

2. Traffic segregation

The task of designing a coherent road network for a whole new settlement or town is an exceptional one for the traffic engineer. Much more often he is called upon to adapt to modern traffic needs old parts of a town which have road networks designed over the years on a great variety of principles.

Because of high costs or the difficulty of getting a road through such areas, structural alterations are only possible in most cases within a limited framework. For this reason measures aimed at better utilization of the existing roadway areas are of great importance. The capacity of a road network can be increased by separating:

Trafficways
Different types of vehicle
Traffic levels
Traffic in different directions
Through traffic and terminating traffic
Moving and stationary traffic

(a) Separation of trafficways

Any trafficway carries the most traffic if all vehicles move at the same speed. The greater the speed differences between vehicles the bigger the reduction in capacity. Even a single vehicle moving somewhat faster or slower causes a noticeable reduction in capacity. In the extreme case a single stopped vehicle causes the loss of the capacity of a whole lane.

For this reason it is right that maximum and minimum speed limits should be imposed on heavily loaded streets. The smaller the difference between the limits the greater the rate at which cars can be pushed through. A fast and a slow lane can carry more traffic than two lanes with any speed allowed on either. On railways a four-track line can for this reason carry three times as many trains as a two-track line. Naturally speed is important in itself. Since vehicle headways increase at higher speeds, the highest lane capacity is achieved with traffic moving at between 25 and 40 km/h (15 and 25 mph).

There are big differences in the traffic behaviour of public and private transport. Public service vehicles must serve many stopping places. They have therefore a lower average speed. Thus one or other class of vehicle will not be able to keep up with the 'green wave', which can only be set for a particular speed. As a result there is much overtaking, which reduces the capacity of the roadways and is dangerous. If each type of traffic can be given its own right-of-way the friction disappears. This can lead to the provision in a fairly big city of two different main road networks, one for public and the other for private transport.

Because of the great importance of public transport and because of the number of trips, every link used by public transport must be regarded as a main street. In network planning it must be included in the traffic lane plan and given priority in the layout of junctions.

Similarly pedal-cycle traffic is best separated from motor traffic and given its own right-of-way. Unfortunately usable parallel links are very seldom available and cyclists find detours especially objectionable.

Separate routes for pedal cycles are better than the provision of special cycle tracks. On a cycle track the cyclist's behaviour is to some extent undesirable. He impedes people boarding and alighting from buses, people getting out of cars and the loading and unloading of goods. And he cannot get into the correct lane to make a left turn (right-hand traffic).

On a long stretch of road without frontage development traffic safety is certainly increased by cycle tracks; but at intersections, where the greatest danger arises, cycle tracks diminish traffic safety. Street capacity is decreased by the segregation of cycle tracks. Peaks in cycle and motor traffic occur in many towns at different times. If the roadway is not subdivided each type of traffic can use more of the available street space as needed. With rigid separation this is no longer possible.

There is no uniform approach to the question whether pedal cycles with auxiliary motors should use cycle tracks. Pedal cycle traffic is declining—certainly as a proportion of total traffic—and therefore cities are not justified in spending money, and cutting down roadway areas which are in any case smaller than they should be, in order to provide cycle tracks in the city centre. Cycle tracks should only be provided in recreational areas, in the vicinity of schools and on long stretches of road on the outskirts of a city.

(b) Separation of lanes

If separate ways cannot be provided for different types of vehicle, separate traffic lanes should be allocated to them within the same roadway, namely:

Driving lanes for fast traffic
Crawling lane for slow traffic
Bus lane
Separate lane or special median for trams
Frontage and parking lanes
Cycle tracks
Footways

Providing separate lanes for different types of vehicles enhances safety and capacity. If the individual lanes are to be separated off by dividing strips the road will have to be very wide. The necessary areas can only be provided on cheap land, and not in the city centre. The total capacity of such roads is only seldom utilized because the biggest permissible loading can hardly occur simultaneously on all the various traffic lanes. In the event of unusually heavy peak loads of one vehicle type, or of reconstruction or accidents, the other lanes cannot be brought into use. A tram median cannot for instance be used as overflow capacity for a peak flow of goods vehicles. In the inner areas of a city the existing high-density development and high land values usually compel the provision of a single roadway for all types of vehicle. If reserved lanes for buses or trams are demarcated by painted lines on the road surface they can take over the traffic of the adjoining lanes in case of emergency.

With a single roadway dividing strips are dispensed with, so that extra roadway width is won. Capacity is thus increased at the expense of safety.

Regarding frontage roadways there is also a contradiction between the requirements of safety and capacity. Where a frontage roadway is separated by a green strip from the main roadway there is no risk of frontage traffic either obstructing or colliding with moving traffic. But only a fraction of the capacity of a frontage roadway is ever utilized. In every case it must be decided whether greater safety or greater capacity is to be preferred. Shortage of road space swings the choice more and more in favour of the latter.

(c) Vertical segregation

In densely-developed areas vertical segregation may be introduced to achieve segregation of traffic streams. Planning must run well ahead of demand in order to secure the necessary areas and to adapt the underground network of services in good time. But here again we must warn against exaggerations. All possible solutions at ground level should first be tested.

Traffic running straight through can be diverted to elevated or depressed roads free of intersections—as has been done in Berlin, Duisburg, Düsseldorf, Rotterdam and Brussels. Similarly the tram system could be put underground or up on viaduct level. Elevated structures are much cheaper than tunnels, but are unacceptable in parts of the town with historical buildings or which are architecturally valuable and where frontage development leaves little space. Similarly elevated roads must be approached with caution, although they are better from the traffic engineering point of view than depressed roads and more pleasant to drive on.

Everybody wants the 'place in the sun' where lighting and ventilation presents no special problem. There ought to be no objection to elevated roads in recently built, spaciously laid out parts of a city. At the same time American solutions such as the elevated motorways of San Francisco, which cut right across the grid of the street system without regard to building, must serve as an awful warning (Fig. 118).

I

When grade separation is applied at individual junctions, it is usually private transport which is shifted to the new level. Flyovers or underpasses can be provided, either at once or later, at heavily loaded junctions (Figs. 119–28). Where however a choice must be made between an underground tramway and a depressed highway over a long bottleneck section or obstacle, it is as a rule best to shift the tram or even the bus to the new

Figure 118: Multi-level elevated roads in the heart of San Francisco. No account was taken of the old grid pattern of streets. Construction work is to be continued.

level. Public transport vehicles require no overtaking or parking lanes, and two lanes are sufficient for them even with heavy volumes. They serve only a comparatively small number of stopping places. Ventilation and lighting require only a modest expenditure. If on the other hand motor traffic is taken underground, frontage roads will still be required at ground level because every house requires vehicular access. Thus the former street cannot be entirely dispensed with. At junctions the possibility of turning left or right must be retained, so that much space must be made available for on and off ramps.

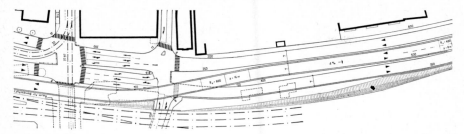

Figure 119: An elevated road next to a railway embankment does not disrupt the townscape. The area reserved for the ramps will be used temporarily as open space. An anti-dazzle screen is to be provided between the rail tracks and the elevated road.

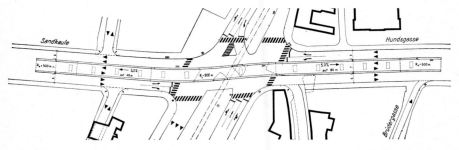

Figure 120: At the Berta-von-Suttner-Platz in Bonn a two-lane flyover can be built later to carry the heavy north–south traffic at the approach to the Rhine bridge. An elevated structure is acceptable where the width between buildings is very great.

It is increasingly common practice to have vertical segregation of pedestrian traffic (Fig. 129). Pedestrian overbridges are seldom provided because it involves too much climbing for pedestrians. With an overbridge pedestrians must climb the minimum headroom required over the road (16 ft 6 in in Britain, 14 ft 8 in or 4·50 m in European countries), plus the construction depth of the bridge. With a pedestrian subway they need only descend about 7 to 8 ft or 2·20 m to 2·50 m plus the thickness of the span supporting the road above. Overbridges are moreover aesthetically objectionable; and in winter there is a danger of icing. Escalators should preferably be protected from the weather and placed in roofed-over spaces.

For these reasons subways are usually preferred, despite higher costs. A well-known, large-scale example of a pedestrian subway is to be found at the Opera House intersection in Vienna. Subways are found above all outside main railway stations, e.g. in Geneva (hardly used), Lucerne, Basle, Munich, Augsburg, Tübingen, Stuttgart, Frankfurt/Main, Hagen/ Westfalen and Mönchen Gladbach. But pedestrians, especially old people, are not keen on climbing, even with the aid of escalators. At the Potsdamer Platz in Berlin (pre-1945) and at Piccadilly Circus in London people prefer

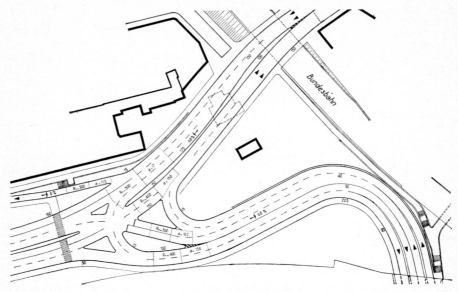

Figure 121: T-junction on restricted, steeply-sloping site: first stage, one-level layout. With the steep gradient (nearly 7 per cent) a curve which 'tightens up' is permissible in this special case.

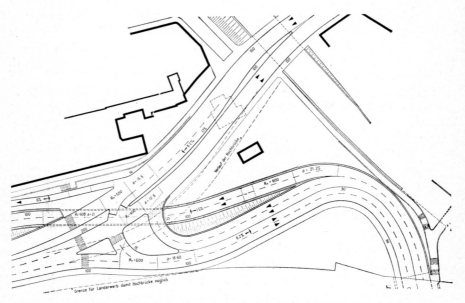

Figure 122: The same junction after conversion in State 2 to a two-level layout. The design is such that the minimum of alteration is needed to the other roadways. The last conflict could be eliminated later by adding a flyover. A three-level junction would be perfectly acceptable on such a steeply-sloping site.

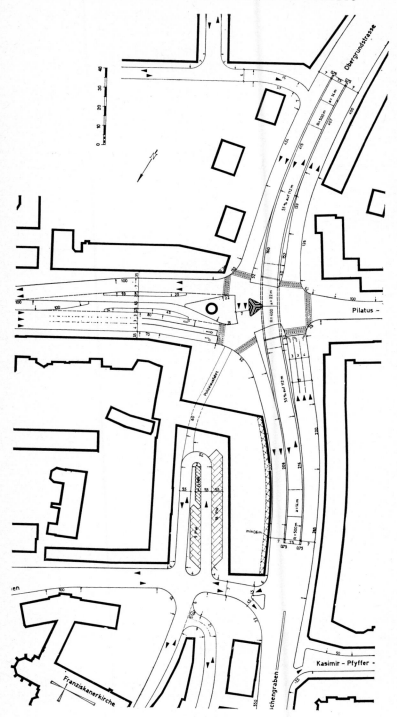

Figure 123: The Pilatusplatz in Lucerne. The two-lane underpass is designed to be used by traffic in both directions, except on Sundays in summer when it would be used by traffic in the peak direction only. In the Pilatusstrasse (top centre) the bus stops are placed in the centre of the street because there is much interchange between routes, one of which turns onto the Obergrundstrasse and the other into the Hirschengraben.

to wait at signals on the surface rather than use the subway connexions via the entrance halls of the underground railway stations.

Even with the best design pedestrian subways remain an emergency solution. Pedestrians should only be directed into underground passages where there is no other possible way out.

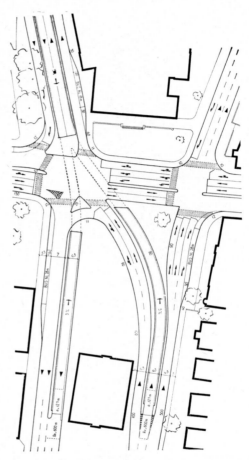

Figure 124: 'Forked' underpass connecting a two-way main street with a pair of one-way streets. A flyover would cover exactly the same area in plan, but was considered unacceptable owing to townscape considerations.

The building of subways in outer areas and where there is little pedestrian traffic is inadvisable, because they are not easy to police and keep clean. Often they are not used at all. Some local authorities are too eager to do good in this respect.

At ordinary crossroads it is possible in most cases to get pedestrians across the street with signal protection simultaneously with main vehicular streams. In exceptional cases a pedestrian phase can be introduced into the

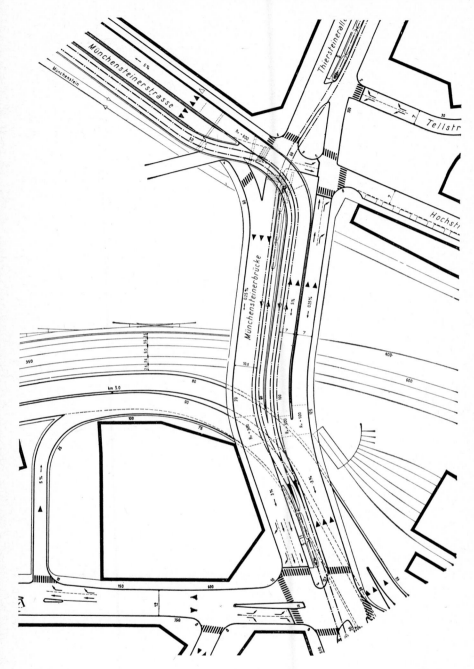

Figure 125: Plan for the Münchensteiner Bridge in Basle. A flyover carries a left-turn movement plus tram tracks—which would swing immediately sideways to run on a reserved right of way.

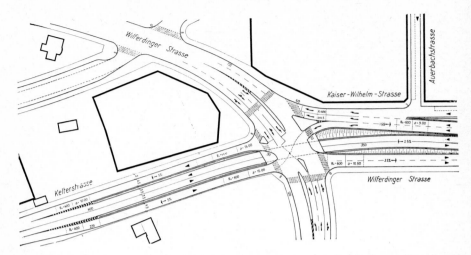

Figure 126: Two-lane underpass at a junction in Pforzheim. The depressed road-way is at the same level as the railway goods station. The parallel ramps take up little room. The main north–south connexion is led around in a wide curve. The only heavy turning movements are between the two arms of the Wilferdinger Strasse (north and east). The Kaiser-Wilhelm-Strasse is a one-way residential road carrying little traffic. Left-turning drivers in one direction must negotiate an S-curve; but a short straight section has been inserted between the curves.

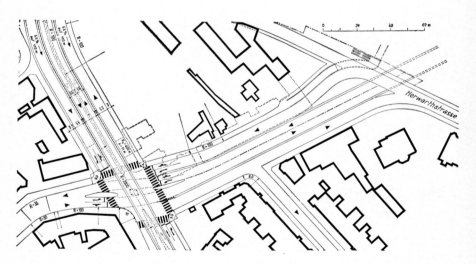

Figure 127: In Bonn a former railway level crossing (on the right) is to be the site of an underpass, giving a grade-separated Y-junction with the Herwarth-strasse. The ramps are so short that weaving is not possible between the ramp nose and the junction on the left. The cross traffic is therefore carried over on a flyover.

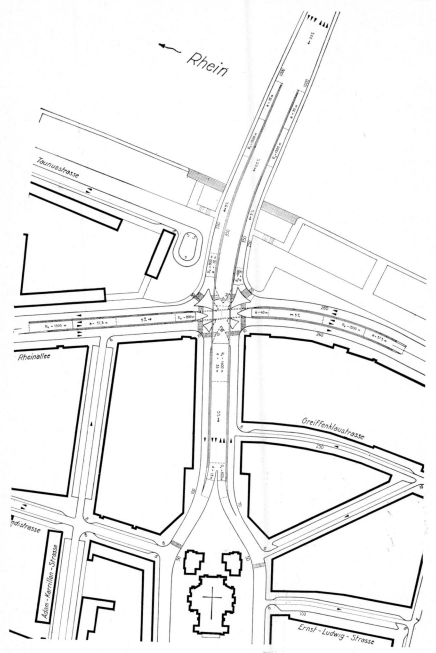

Figure 128: Design proposed for the junction between the Kaiserstrasse, the proposed Rhine Bridge and the Rheinallee in Mainz. The traffic to and from the
bridge would be carried across on a four-lane flyover, the cross traffic on the
Rheinallee would be taken through a two-lane underpass, and all the turning
movements would be at street level.

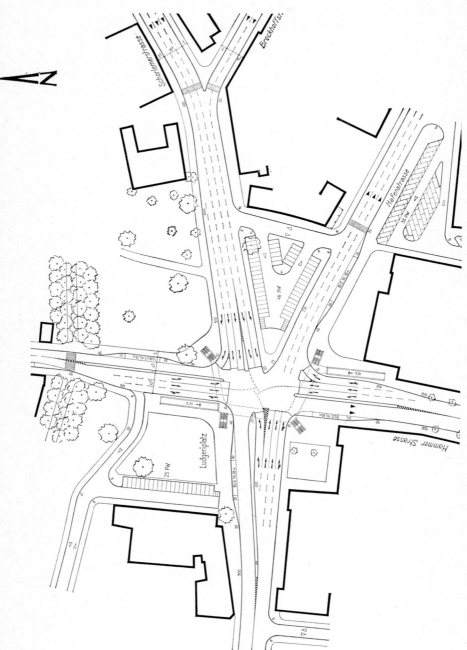

Figure 129: Proposed layout for the Lugeriplatz in Münster (hitherto a roundabout, cf. Figure 162). The pedestrian underpass can be reached via four staircases and two ramps. Since pedestrians need no longer cross on the surface, special right-turn lanes can be provided. The four bus stops are 'far-side' stops. To the east of the junction a one-way street couplet begins. Open spaces

signal cycle, during which pedestrians can cross over the intersection in all directions, including diagonally. It is rarely that the capacity of the signal cycle is so fully utilized by traffic that there is no time available for pedestrians.

(d) Pedestrian areas

It is right and proper that special provision is everywhere being made for the pedestrian. On all urban roads of any importance footways are provided on both sides. On certain rural roads they are an urgent necessity. But on residential streets with only small volumes of frontage traffic they are not needed. Segregated pedestrian links are provided only where motor traffic really disturbs pedestrians, but never in settlements with little traffic.

In this respect exaggerated treatments are found in some low-density outer areas. Separate footways cost additional space, cleansing, snow clearance and lighting. One can only speak of an exhaust fumes and noise nuisance on heavily-travelled streets. Wide footways and promenades are of assistance in such cases. Promenades between the roadways, as in the Hohenzollerndamm in Berlin and the Ramblas in Barcelona, are also popular.

Pedestrian traffic increases more and more in the central areas of cities, and requires more area for which it must compete with vehicles. For purposes of traffic segregation it can be useful to reserve a particular street entirely for pedestrians and to take pedestrians out of another street. But pedestrian-only streets are only provided in the busiest areas with exceptionally heavy traffic, because they break up the coherent traffic network and can bring considerable disadvantages with them.

The 'pedestrian town' which is spoken about so much can only flourish in the immediate vicinity of a 'main station'—a station for long-distance and suburban rail lines, a stopping place for trams and buses, or a large parking garage. These conditions are fulfilled just as well in the Kalverstraat in Amsterdam, the Westenhellweg in Dortmund, the pedestrian street at the main station in Gelsenkirchen and the Kettwiger Strasse in Essen as they are in the undergound shopping streets which have already been mentioned. The traffic lane plans of which illustrations have been shown provide examples, and so do Figs. 130 and 131. The well-known Coolsingel in Rotterdam is already rather too wide and less favourably laid out. The middle section of the Hohe Strasse in Cologne lacks a connexion with the public transport network. It suffers economically from this lack. Groups of shops and shopping centres in the outer areas of cities are also built around such 'main stations'. They grow up at stopping places or in the middle of extensive parking areas.

Distances from stations must not be increased; rather the reverse. The longer the travel time from the residential areas, the less time is available for continuing shopping trips to their destinations. It is no secret that as people get accustomed to having cars they get lazier. Today the walking distance from parking place to destination must not exceed 250 m (800 ft) in America, or 300 m (1,000 ft) in Europe if people are not to find it excessive. An uninterrupted pedestrian street ought therefore not to be more than 300 m (1,000 ft) long. A good arrangement is to have short arcades and passages such as are found in many cities, e.g. the 'Unter den Linden' in Berlin, the Galleria in Milan and the Corso in Rome.

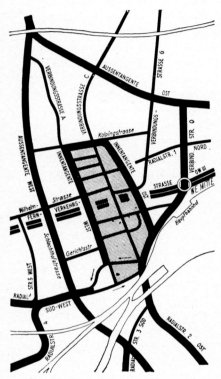 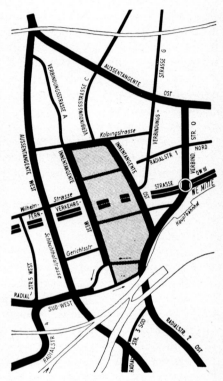

Figure 130: Outside of the busy traffic hours the city centre of Wanne-Eickel would remain open for vehicles servicing the buildings.

Figure 131: During the busy hours only pedestrians and public transport would be allowed into the area (cf. Figure 107).

The area prohibited to motor traffic ought not to be made too large or put in the wrong place, or the part of the town concerned will suffer in its economic development. The term 'pedestrian town' is in fact a contradiction in terms, since a town cannot exist without traffic. Good accessibility and a good business location are inseparable. Delivery vehicles must serve the shops either via nearby parallel streets or, at slack times of day, via the pedestrian streets. This question is of great importance. It is solved differently according to local conditions. We may refer once again to the traffic lane plans. Many exceptions have been made to the ban on road traffic in the Old Town in Zürich and in the prohibited zone in the spa area of Badenweiler, in order to avoid economic loss.

For the pedestrian a careful and painstaking 'traffic plan in miniature' is required, which maintains the right scale and avoids any one-sidedness or exaggeration.

(e) One-way streets

An effective means of increasing street capacity and reducing accident risks is one-way operation of streets. A pair of one-way streets has greater capacity than two two-way streets of the same total width. Between intersections there is, it is true, little difference in capacity; but at intersections there is a big difference. Left-turners have no oncoming traffic to cut across and have the entire length of the block between the two streets as reservoir space. Green wave signal systems can be more easily installed because the progression has to be provided in only one direction on each street. On the other hand frontage traffic is compelled to make detours; and for this reason a certain hesitation about the introduction of one-way operation is in order.

One-way streets should not be seen as a temporary emergency measure. They are in many cases a very useful permanent measure which costs very little to adopt.

One-way streets should as far as possible be arranged in pairs. A pair of one-way streets is, from the traffic engineering viewpoint, like a divided highway with a built-up median strip. Intersections between pairs of one-way streets are 'extended crossroads'. The distance between the paired one-way streets should be small, and should preferably be such that green waves can be provided for the cross traffic. With one-way couplets a sufficient number of cross-connections is necessary. If they are too far apart there is a danger of overloading; and there is also too much hindrance to local traffic.

One-way systems can most easily be introduced where there is a grid pattern street network. Thus in many American cities there are one-way systems covering whole areas of the city. But the American networks have the disadvantage that they have altogether too many crossroads of equal importance, and the distances between crossroads is often so great that green waves are only possible in one direction (e.g. Manhattan).

The direction in which each street should run should not be arbitrarily chosen. The results of traffic surveys make it possible to calculate which arrangement will be most serviceable. In one old town centre with an irregular street system the reversal of a single 'supernumerary' one-way street increased the peak-hour capacity of the whole network by over 10 per cent; and this gain was achieved without any expense for structural works. This is an example of the way in which road space in many places can be better utilized without any need for expensive remodelling of roads and streets.

(f) Segregation of through traffic

Segregation of through traffic from terminating traffic is achieved by the tangential streets described above. They should offer such uncongested detours that drivers will prefer to use them. If they do not, then signposting and police regulations will be necessary to direct the traffic streams. It is difficult to tell to what extent signposts are being followed. Visitors to a city may follow them more readily than the inhabitants, who are far more numerous and who know their way about exactly. The inhabitants will select now the short route through the city centre, now the detour, depending on the traffic loads at different times of day. The two routes complement each other like communicating pipes. Thus the distribution between the two routes of the trips determined from the survey is fraught with a good deal of uncertainty.

The most severe measure that can be taken against through traffic in the city centre is the erection of barriers. Coherent routes are interrupted by kerbs, hedges or walls. Public transport may be excepted.

As an example it was proposed in 1948 to turn the Schlossplatz in Stuttgart and its immediate surroundings into a pedestrian area, and to prevent private traffic using the Königstrasse as a through route. The city unfortunately decided to do the opposite.

A plan was worked out for Berne in 1953 whereby the main axis of the Spitalgasse and Marktgasse was to be reserved for public transport, pedestrians and frontage traffic; and access for through traffic made deliberately difficult by means of traffic islands.

Following this line of thought a stage further, an old town can be divided up into cells having no vehicular links with one another and accessible only from the outside—as was done in Bremen. The pedestrian obtains in this way the use of long, coherent pedestrian ways free of cross streets. Drivers have a harder time finding their way about. They can get into cells only from tangents or from a ring. They can get from one cell to another, for instance for the purpose of servicing several shops, only by driving out onto the tangent. A car coming from a radial street must in most cases turn onto the tangent and follow it as far as the entrance to the cell the driver wishes to visit. The high proportion of turning movements imposes a heavy strain on the junctions. Between the junctions the tangents will have to carry an additional load while streets in the city centre will be much less used. Thus the first condition for such partition is the provision of tangents of adequate capacity. A benefit/cost calculation must decide to what extent the advantages of such a compulsory shifting of traffic outweighs the disadvantages (Fig. 132). This method, like others, should only be applied after careful investigations and capacity calculations.

Figure 132: It was proposed to relieve the main crossroads in the centre of Bochum (350,000 inhabitants) by means of a ring road. But the majority of vehicles would still come straight through the city centre to avoid the two turns involved in using the ring road. Only traffic coming from the west would be led easily onto the southern detour. If, however, the city centre were barred and traffic compulsorily detoured round the city centre, then the crossroads on the ring road would become T-junctions at which all vehicles on a radial road would have to turn left or right. The capacity of the network would then be considerably smaller.

(g) Segregation of parking areas

With the big shortage of road space the parking and even the stopping of cars on important or narrow streets can no longer be tolerated. This is not just a question of parking space but of entrances and exits. If a car slows down prior to stopping or to parking it reduces the capacity of its lane considerably. The same applies, perhaps even more strongly, to vehicles entering and leaving the traffic stream. Such disturbances of traffic flow—apart from those caused by accidents and breakdowns—can be eliminated by providing parking off the street. Special parking lots are therefore better than parking lanes at the edge of the street. Side streets are also suitable for parking, serving in this way like frontage roadways along a main road.

3. Roads between junctions

(a) Cross-section

In designing a road network a high degree of uniformity should be aimed at. The traffic lanes on all streets should be 3·50 m (11 ft 6 in) wide. This basic dimension is suitable for fast lanes on trunk roads as well as for urban streets with a large proportion of motor cycles, scooters and pedal cycles. In cramped conditions the dimension can be reduced in towns to 3·00 m (10 ft). But then a single pedal-cycle will be able to hold up a whole column of cars. Unusual lane widths of less than 3·00 m or more than 3·50 m are dangerous because they entice drivers to behave dangerously (overtaking, straddling two lanes or cutting in). On a roadway with three lanes each 3·75 m (12 ft 3 in) wide, i.e. altogether 11·25 m (36 ft 9 in), drivers can even make four lanes. Apart from this, excessive width is a pointless extravagance.

As a general rule then, a two-lane road is 7·00 m (23 ft) wide. A four-lane road should be 14·00 m (46 ft) wide. Parking lanes for stopping or parking of cars are normally 2·50 m (8 ft) wide, or occasionally 2·00 m (6 ft 6 in) in narrow places. It is inadvisable to provide a total width of 12·00 m (39 ft) or even only 11·00 m (36 ft)—the minimum width—for a two-lane road flanked by parking lanes unless it is out of the question that the outer lanes will ever have to be used later as moving lanes. Single-lane links at junctions and likewise ramps should have a width of 4·50 m (14 ft 6 in) if they are bounded by kerbs on both sides, so that even the widest tractor-trailer combination can negotiate them easily. If a car breaks down and is pushed hard against the kerb, other vehicles can still get past it slowly. A width of 5·50 m (18 ft) is desirable on long single-lane sections—composed of 3·50 m (11 ft 6 in) for the traffic lane and 2·00 m (6 ft 6 in) for an emergency parking lane. This same width of 5·50 m is the minimum width for all roadways in residential and side streets.

On four-lane roads a median strip is desirable; on roads with six or more lanes it is essential. The median can be in the form of a continuous island at least 1·00 m (3 ft 3 in) wide. A 'greater width is desirable, and should be provided when a new road is built on vacant ground. Unfortunately the presence of buildings often compels the road engineer to be content with the smallest dimensions.

Where the median is to serve as a pedestrian island it should if at all possible be widened to 1·50 m (5 ft); a desirable width is 2·00 m (6 ft), for this is the minimum width which will (a) give sufficient lateral clearance where traffic signs or protective bollards are placed on the island and (b) make the people who are most endangered by road traffic (old people and mothers with prams) feel really safe.

On urban streets continuous medians should be capable of being driven on, so that in the event of reconstruction, detours or disturbances, vehicles can be diverted onto the other roadway. They are, therefore, only 6–8 cm (about 3 in) high. Safety islands should be 12–20 cm (5–8 in) above the road surface.

At the edge of all roadways a lateral clearance of at least 60 cm (2 ft) and preferably 80 cm (2 ft 8 in) should be provided, within which no fixed objects or handrails should be placed. Here pedestrians can find safety and drivers can leave broken-down cars.

The cross-section of a road should, once it has been chosen, be carried through without variation to the next big junction, even alongside traffic islands. An increasing width is uneconomic and brings only small advantages; a decreasing width in the form of a funnel or a bottleneck is dangerous.

(b) Symmetry

An important requirement in the layout of urban trafficways is symmetry. Traffic is seldom equally heavy in both directions. Outside the city centre there is at most times a heavily loaded and a lightly loaded direction. In the mornings private transport towards the city centre predominates, and in the evening the reverse flow to the suburbs. But over twenty-four hours the numbers of people and vehicles (laden and empty) usually balances out. The symmetry of traffic movements corresponds to the symmetry of trafficways.

On certain specially heavily-loaded streets and railways which, carry heavy tidal traffic flows reversible lane allocation is practised—e.g. on the three-track Ludwigsburg-Bietigheim railway near Stuttgart and the eight-lane Lake Shore Drive in Chicago, which has six lanes for inbound traffic in the morning peak and six lanes for outbound traffic in the evening peak. Such arrangements are very economical. Usually, however, all trafficways are symmetrical in cross-section, especially in the central areas of cities. There are exceptions at the approaches to intersections (Figs. 133, 134), although even here symmetry of opposite approaches is common; and also where crawling lanes are provided for goods vehicles on steep hills.

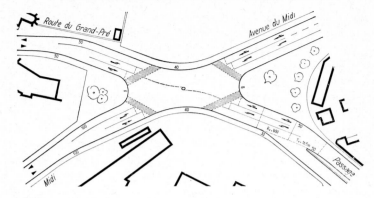

Figure 133: Acute-angled crossroads between two two-lane roads. All four approaches are two-lane, all exits are one-lane. The marked approach lanes are straight. Such symmetrical junctions are not common on main roads and in city centres.

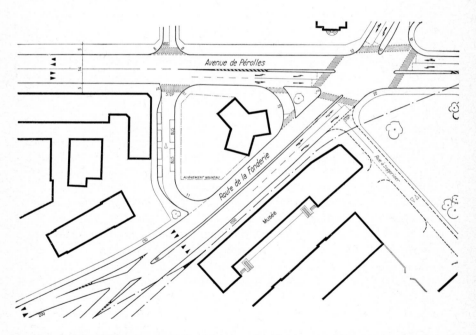

Figure 134: Oblique crossroads which is symmetrical in layout but not in traffic loads. There is no left-turning traffic from the Route de la Fonderie; thus right-turners can use both lanes in this approach. The bus terminal loop introduces another irregularity owing to the need for a wide right-turn lane. (Buses using the Avenue de Pérolles turn round without entering the junction.) At the bottom of the plan there is a very acute-angled fork next to a connecting track.

Three-lane roads, with the centre lane available for overtaking in both directions, are dangerous and should not be used where traffic is heavy— which means in all towns. They are still unsafe even when—as on the elevated road in Brussels and elsewhere—the use of the centre lane is controlled by means of signals.

With an asymmetrical layout the narrowest side determines the capacity. On a three-lane street with two tram tracks, the third lane, which is free of tram tracks, is not much use. The street has to be widened as soon as the capacity of the single lane in one direction is absorbed.

On four-lane streets permitted parking or stopping on one side only, which cannot sometimes be avoided, upsets the equilibrium. Transitions from an asymmetrical to a symmetrical cross-section often do not give satisfaction; transitions of the opposite kind often cannot be seen by drivers and give rise to accidents.

Symmetry also simplifies the layout of junctions. Unfavourable siting or layout of the junction can give rise to unequal traffic loads in the two directions on the roads that intersect there. The roadway areas provided will then be uneconomically used.

(c) Cycle tracks and footways

Where cycle tracks are still required they should be placed at the edge of the roadway 1·50 m (5 ft) wide and either flush with it or raised by 6–8 cm (about 3 in). Where they are flush with the roadway they must be clearly distinguished by the colour of the surface. The danger that cyclists will be hurt by doors of parked cars being opened can only be eliminated by a dividing strip or lateral clearance. A similar division can also be used to prevent pedestrians wandering carelessly onto the cycle track. But a cycle track with dividing strips both sides of it is about as wide as a traffic lane. So much space can hardly be devoted to a cycle track in city centres. Cycle tracks are a disturbing influence at bus stops even when they are led around a segregated waiting area for bus passengers. Two-way cycle tracks placed to one side of a road are dangerous because other road users will not be looking out for traffic in the opposite direction. And they are difficult to deal with at an intersection (Fig. 135).

The width of a footway depends on the amount of pedestrian traffic to be expected. A width of 60 cm (2 ft) must be provided for each person. And to this must be added a small supplement at the edge of the roadway or in front of buildings or along a garden fence. The minimum width of footway which will allow two people walking side-by-side to pass two other people also walking side-by-side is about 2·50 m (8 ft); and this width should be kept clear of buildings, trees and parking meters. On important shopping streets the footways are often too narrow, e.g. on the Bahnhofstrasse in Zürich where the footway is nominally 4·50 m (14 ft 6 in) wide but only 3·50 m (11 ft 6 in) between the buildings and the trees.

Trees on footways should be planted 1·00 m (3 ft) from the edge of the roadway and 8–10 m (26–33 ft) apart.

Footways are usually 8–15 cm (3–6 in) higher than the roadway. At pedestrian islands the 'travelled way' for pedestrians should be flush with the roadway to avoid steps.

On unimportant side streets in purely residential areas footways can safely be dispensed with. For such roads the already-mentioned total

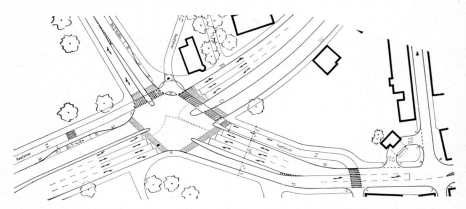

Figure 135: Two-way cycle tracks to one side of a road at a big junction. There are dangerous cuts at the ends of the cycle tracks. At the neighbouring junction with a one-way street is a small filling station.

width of 5·50 m (18 ft) is sufficient. But a protective strip should be reserved on one side of the roadway for underground services.

Minimum headroom over roadways must be 4·50 m (14 ft 6 in) in most countries and 16 ft 6 in in Great Britain. Reduced headroom is dangerous, but sometimes cannot be avoided on minor roads. A headroom of 2·20 m (7 ft) is sufficient for pedestrians and one of 2·50 m (8 ft) for cyclists, so that at underpasses footways and cycle tracks need not drop as deep as roadways (Fig. 136).

Pedestrians normally move, even in shopping streets, at 1·3 m (4 ft)/ sec, or 4·7 km/h (3 mph). Allowing a headway of 1 m (3 ft) 4,700 people can pass in one hour on a strip of footway 60 cm (2 ft) wide. But to allow adequate freedom of movement the flow should not exceed 1,500. A higher figure should be used in capacity calculations only in rare cases— the entrances to and exits from mass festivities and at stopping places.

(d) Gradients

Gradients on main roads and on ramp connections at interchanges should not exceed 4 per cent in flat terrain, 5·5 per cent as a general rule in hilly country and 6·5 per cent in extreme cases. Even with a 5 per cent gradient, ice may cause loss of traction on upgrades and skidding on down-grades. On main roads carrying fast traffic crawling lanes are desirable on long gradients in excess of 4 per cent. Reservoirs at the approaches to junctions should not have a gradient in excess of 3 per cent, so that vehicles can stop safely and move off easily. On side roads steeper gradients can be permitted. But gradients must be moderate in the interest of safety. No road should however be completely horizontal. Even with adequate

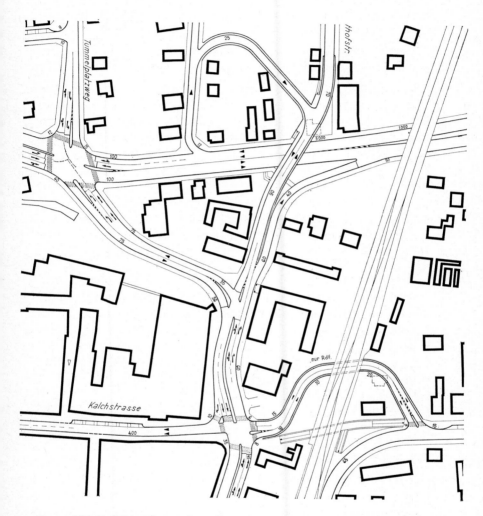

Figure 136: In Memmingen the railway level crossing at the north end of the station is to be eliminated. The motor traffic will be shifted to a new tangent to the North. This will keep through traffic away from the old town. The left-turn movement from the new underpass to the old city will follow a cloverleaf routing, taking advantage of differences in level. At the site of the present level crossing there will be a pedestrian underpass with ramps on a 10% gradient and a slightly less direct pedal-cycle underpass with 4% gradient and somewhat greater headroom.

crossfall a longitudinal gradient of 0·3 per cent or more is of advantage to assist drainage,

For pedestrian connections the gradients recommended for underground installations should be used. The gradient should not exceed 16 per cent.

Changes of gradient on roadways must be rounded out. The bigger the curve radius the more comfortable is the ride in a vehicle and the better the sight distance. On urban roads the following vertical radii are sufficient:

> On summit curves   600 m (2,000 ft)
> In sag curves   400 m (1,300 ft)

In the Manesse underpass, built in Zürich in 1960, the minimum radii were respectively 400 m and 250 m; and these should be regarded as absolute minima. The bigger radius on summit curves is necessary because the roadway cuts short the view of the driver who is seated low. Transition curves are unnecessary with vertical curves.

(e) Curve radii

The minimum radius needed on a curve depends on the design speed. With adequate superelevation the design speed v in km/h can be calculated as follows in relation to the curve radius R of the vehicle path in metres:

> Cars with low centre of gravity $v = 8\sqrt{R}$
> Goods vehicles $v = 6·5\sqrt{R}$
> Suburban trains, light express trains $v = 4·5\sqrt{R}$
> Railways $v = 4\sqrt{R}$
> Trams on the street $v = 3·5\sqrt{R}$

Thus a curve of $R = 100$ m can be negotiated by a car in dry weather at 80 km/h (50 mph), and by a tram at 35 km/h (22 mph). Thus trams cannot keep pace with motor traffic on curves. But the values for motor traffic drop sharply when the road is wet or icy. Trams are not dependent on the weather because they are guided by rails.

The minimum kerb radii that should be used are as follows:

> Road with heavy goods vehicle and bus traffic   15 m (50 ft)
> Other main roads and streets   10 m (33 ft)
> Side streets   6 m (20 ft)
> Residential streets   3 m (10 ft)

These radii must be observed for all turning lanes at junctions. Tight curves for turning vehicles increase pedestrian safety since drivers are forced to drive slowly. Thus radii for turning lanes should not greatly exceed these values where vehicles must cross pedestrian movements.

A road alignment is a combination of tangents and curves. Curves which 'tighten up' are dangerous, as the driver is enticed into entering the curve too fast. S-curves should be avoided on urban streets. A tangent of adequate length should be inserted between a right-hand and a left-hand curve, so that drivers will keep to their lane and not cut the corner. The tangent should if possible be 30–60 m (100–200 ft) long, but local circumstances and the permitted speed play a great part. For the same reason approaches to junctions should as far as possible be straight.

For transition curves between tangents and curves clothoids are mathematically the right solution. With railways, which are exactly guided by their rails almost to the millimetre, second or third degree parabolae are in use. No transition curves at all are provided at junctions and with certain curves. With roads the excessive use of clothoids is inadvisable. Drivers never follow them exactly, so that an approximation to the clothoid is sufficient. On right-hand curves clothoids lengthen the distance over which overtaking is dangerous (with right-hand traffic). Long clothoids have the same disadvantage as curves which tighten up. Curves where a tightening and a widening clothoid follow each other immediately should be avoided altogether. With sharp curves a transition curve double the radius of the main curve may be used. With wide-radius curves transition curves are often dispensed with. Transition curves are generally not used in towns with the low speeds which are usual. And it is in any case usually impossible to provide them for right-turn lanes at crossroads because buildings on the corner do not leave sufficient room. Left-turners (with right-hand traffic) generally have sufficient freedom of movement. As long as the turner is led round in a single lane, a width of 4·50 m will give him enough room.

The widening of traffic lanes on curves depends on the dimensions of the vehicles used. Articulated buses and tractor-trailer combinations require generous dimensions. For example the latest type of articulated bus 16.50 m (54 ft) long and 2.50 m (8 ft 2 in) wide when rounding the tightest curve has an inner turning circle of 8.70 m (29 ft) radius and an outer turning circle of 13.50 m (44 ft). The tracking of large vehicles must be considered when designing turning lanes at junctions. Similarly the clearance between tram tracks must be increased on tight curves.

4. Junctions

Road junctions are the nodes of a road network. It is here that the vehicle paths intersect. Only here can vehicles turn off in another direction.

Every junction has a more or less large number of traffic cuts, merging points and diverging points, and sometimes weaving sections (Fig. 137).

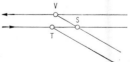

Figure 137: Road fork with 1 cut S, 1 merge V and 1 diverge T.

Junctions should be at least so far apart that between them enough length is available for reservoir space and weaving sections.

Formerly very little attention was paid to traffic engineering considerations in the design of urban focal points. The modern principles were

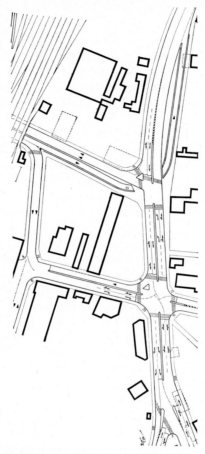

Figure 138: At a T-junction too close to a crossroads, left-turning traffic from a railway underpass is to be taken under the junction via a one-way underpass; while right-turning traffic is to be given a new link with the main junction.

unknown. These focal points must now be remodelled in order to increase safety and capacity.

The most common road layouts at these places are forks, T-junctions, rectangular and oblique crossroads, rotary intersections and stars. Besides these there are complex layouts consisting of various elements of these basic layouts.

The simplest junctions are the best. The art of the engineer lies in designing obvious solutions which hardly give a hint of the trouble and work which went into finding them. Leonardo da Vinci said this a long time ago. Complex, over-elaborate and incomprehensible junction layouts should be avoided. Junctions should be 'foolproof'. A stranger should be able to understand one immediately he first sees it, otherwise road safety suffers. If he cannot drive smoothly through the junction but hesitates, capacity will be reduced.

(a) Forks

An age-old, natural and correct form of junction is the fork. Where a road forks but there is no traffic turning between the two branches the junction has only one conflict point (Fig. 139). This is the simplest junction imaginable. It can be controlled by two-phase signals (Figs. 140, 141). As soon as there is an appreciable amount of traffic between the two branches there are three conflict points between vehicle paths, and three movements

Figure 139: Fork with one cut.

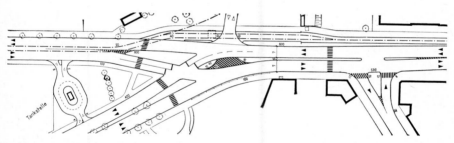

Figure 140: Simple fork with no traffic 'doubling back'. The filling station and the access road (white arrows) had to be retained. Opposite the access road the median island was lowered and specially marked. The tram line swings over to run alongside the main road. Two tracks are provided over a sufficient distance for two trams to pass each other outside the intersection area.

which must alternate (Fig. 142). This calls for three-phase signal control. Heavy turning traffic indicates a defect in the street network, a missing tangential link.

A three-way junction can take the form of a Y, a 'Mercedes star' with angles of 120° between the branches, or a T. It can also be a branch at an oblique angle from a straight road. In the latter case it makes a difference whether the road branches off to the left or the right. If the traffic on the main road has priority then at a right-hand fork with right-hand traffic the traffic entering from the side road waits in the side road to enter the junction, while at a left-hand fork vehicles waiting to turn into the side road wait in the main road. They may block up the main road if a left-turn lane is not provided between the two through lanes. Forking left is more dangerous and more expensive. Here there is no symmetry—for a certain layout can be considerably better or worse than its mirror image with regard to capacity and safety.

The bigger the angle between the two arms of a fork the heavier as a rule is the turning traffic. With a 'Mercedes-star' layout it is to be expected

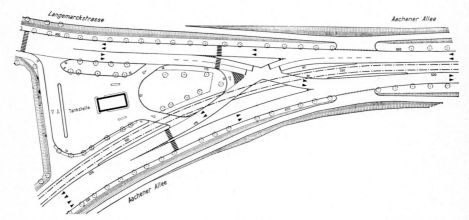

Figure 141: Forking of the Aachener Allee from Düsseldorf at the entry to Neuss, with no 'doubling back' traffic. The tram lines switch from a median (right) to a reserved right-of-way to the side of the road. The tram tracks cross over the roadways close to the cut between conflicting traffic directions, the cut being controlled by signals. The filling station was not to be shifted.

Figure 142: Fork with three-way conflict.

that the three conflicting left-turning movements (with right-hand traffic) will be of equal volume (Fig. 143). Then the capacity will be lowest. If all three streams must be led through the same point then, even ignoring lost time during the amber phases, the three left turn lanes will together have only the same capacity as one uninterrupted traffic lane. And each approach lane will be loaded to only two-thirds of its capacity—one-third for the left-turning traffic and one-third for the right-turning. The full capacity of the road can only be utilized if additional turning lanes are provided so that two left-turners can drive through the junction simultaneously.

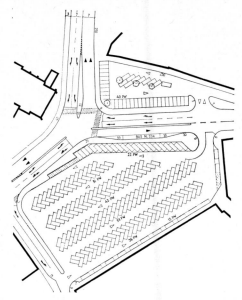

Figure 143: A 'Mercedes star' junction with almost equal loading of the three directions, with nearby bus turnout. The entries to the car parks are well away from the junction.

(b) T-junctions

The worst form of three-way junction is the T-junction. A second road pushes into another road, which continues straight ahead, at a right-angle (Fig. 144). It seldom happens that the volumes of traffic turning in each direction along the main road are equal. Where they are not equal the main road to one side of the junction will be underused (Figs. 145, 146). All traffic to and from the side road must make a turn. This is a sign on

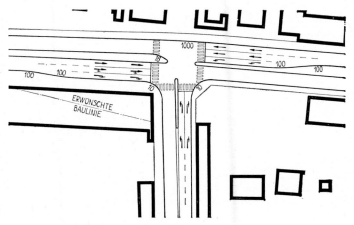

Figure 144: T-junction in a large city.

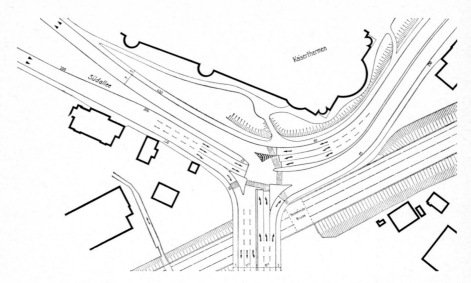

Figure 145: Proposed T-junction layout for the Kaiserthermen in Trier. The main road winds its way through between the Roman ruins and the railway cutting. Note the straight kerbs inserted between curves in opposite directions.

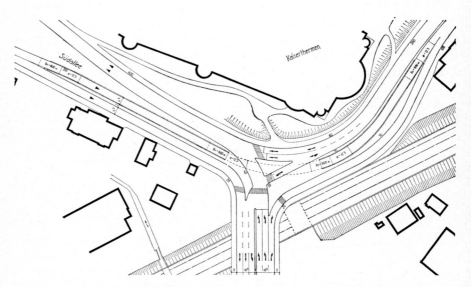

Figure 146: The same junction with a single-lane underpass for traffic in one direction along the main road. With the resulting increase in capacity one lane will be adequate for the left turn movement onto the bridge.

arterial streets that the layout of the network is not good. Both of the left-turning movements, into and out of the side road, conflict with the main road traffic going straight ahead on the same side as the side road, so that the three must be alternated. If the side road were continued on the opposite side of the main road and the bulk of its traffic flowed straight across, there would then be a simple crossroads with only two conflicting main movements. Thus the T-junction is a truncated crossroads, which must cope with an additional conflicting traffic stream and therefore needs an additional signal phase.

The same applies to the Y-junction, although here vehicles can turn in and out more easily because of the more favourable angles of intersection, and can therefore clear the junction more swiftly (Fig. 147).

The T-junction should only be used where residential streets intersect with each other or with local distributors. At such minor junctions the traffic load is so small that safety has priority over capacity; and safety is increased because all drivers must drive slowly along the side street.

At three-way junctions the three conflicting movements should inter-sect at a single point in order to avoid unnecessary time losses on clearance periods; and also in order to provide a layout with maximum visibility and favourable angles of intersection. Where this principle is not followed the three conflicting vehicle paths form triangles with three conflict points, oblique-angled cuts and short reservoirs. Such triangular junctions are only advantageous where they offer sufficient length for reservoirs or permit the use of green wave signals. This requires triangles with a minimum length of side of 50 m (170 ft). In urban areas there is seldom enough space available for such treatment (Figs. 148–51).

A special type of layout that must be mentioned is the staggered cross-roads, consisting of two T-junctions close together, often replacing a normal crossroads. Staggered crossroads are often found in residential areas. They are designed to slow down cross traffic, which however is usually very small in volume. But in fact the safety, traffic value and visibility of the local distributor are reduced because twice the number of danger points will occur along it.

Staggered crossroads are also found on arterial streets. They must always be considered as a unit because each of the two T-junctions is strongly influenced by the other. If the amount of stagger is small the cross traffic must make an S-movement; and drivers will try to cut the corners. Strict lane discipline is especially necessary in this case (Fig. 152). If the amount of stagger is larger the crossing vehicles join the lanes on the main road correctly. But the reservoir space between the two T-junctions is so small that mutual interference between vehicles turning into the inter-vening section of main road from both side roads is to be expected. This section of road carries more traffic than the main road to either side of it and must in some cases be provided with more lanes (Fig. 153). Only where

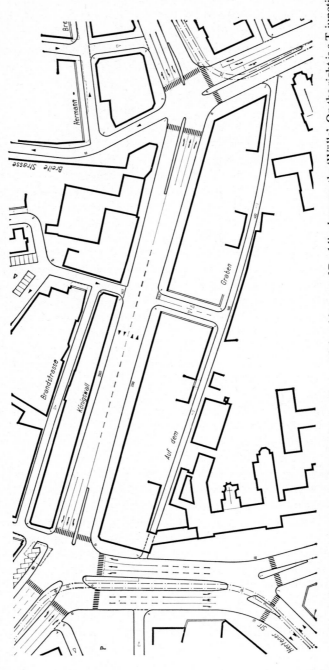

Figure 147: Two radial roads intersect with the ring road around the old town of Recklinghausen, the 'Wälle'. On the right is a T-junction where the tram lines cross over to the side of the ring road; on the left a mixture between a T-junction and a 'Mercedes star'. At both junctions the traffic having destination in the old town is led straight ahead via one-way streets, while the traffic originating from the old town enters the 'Wälle' between the junctions. (See Figure 222.)

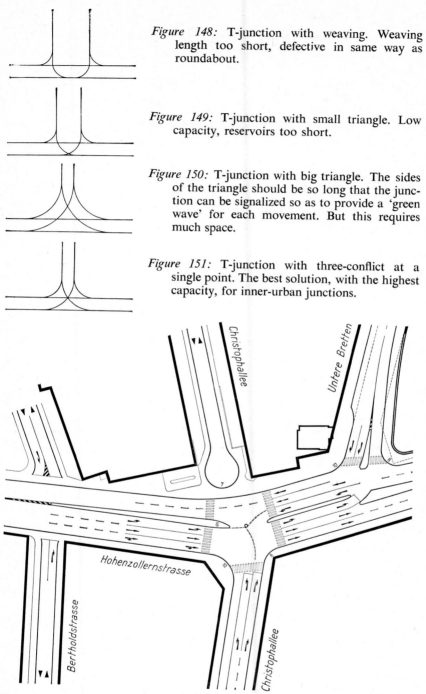

Figure 148: T-junction with weaving. Weaving length too short, defective in same way as roundabout.

Figure 149: T-junction with small triangle. Low capacity, reservoirs too short.

Figure 150: T-junction with big triangle. The sides of the triangle should be so long that the junction can be signalized so as to provide a 'green wave' for each movement. But this requires much space.

Figure 151: T-junction with three-conflict at a single point. The best solution, with the highest capacity, for inner-urban junctions.

Figure 152: Staggered crossroads in Pforzheim. The northern arm of the Christophallee is severed to prevent the conjunction of two many traffic streams. Where the Bertholdstrasse enters the Hohenzollernstrasse the footway alongside the latter is continued, but dropped down, so that pedestrians can only enter and exit at walking pace. At the corner of Untere Brettenstrasse a building (dashed line) would have to be demolished and the building line set back to the double line.

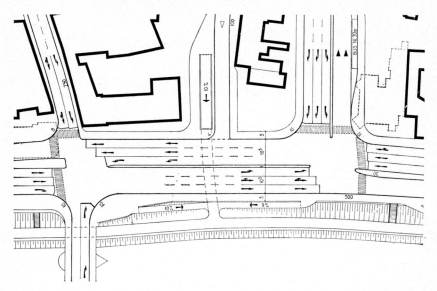

Figure 153: Staggered crossroads at a bridgehead. The reservoir length is so short that both must be widened to three-lane to give enough capacity. Pedestrians can reach the riverside walk via a subway. At the right-hand corner a building (dashed line) would have to be demolished.

there is a large distance between the two T-junctions is the capacity higher than that of a simple crossroads. Whether more capacity will be provided in a particular case can only be reliably decided on the basis of a capacity calculation.

(c) Simple crossroads

The ordinary crossroads, right-angled or at least oblique-angled, is by far the best solution for the intersection of main streets (Fig. 154). The simple crossroads is clear and easily comprehensible. It has therefore been used since time immemorial in all planned urban developments or extensions based on a grid pattern of streets. So long as the proportion of turning vehicles does not exceed the usual number, two-phase signal control is sufficient. The capacity of the junction can be increased as required by adding to the number of traffic lanes. However, there are limits to this process on several grounds. As a general rule main streets in urban areas cannot be widened to the necessary extent as traffic flows increase. The sections between the junctions are, therefore, under-utilized. Time losses due to the increasing number of signal-controlled junctions become more and more objectionable.

Difficulties arise chiefly through heavy turning movements. These may be due to deficiencies in the street network, but often cannot be routed away from a junction. At crossroads there is often insufficient reservoir

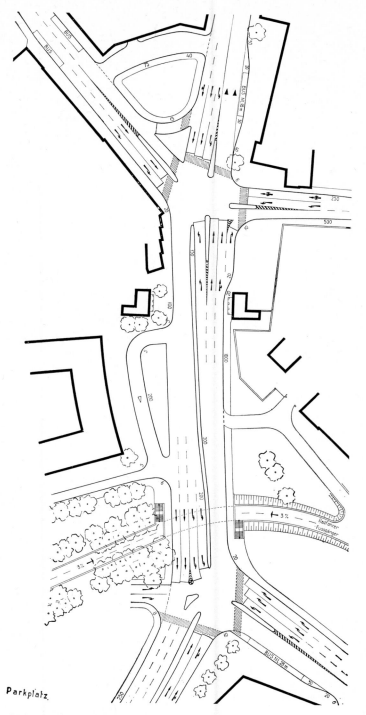

Parkplatz

Figure 154: Crossroads and fork, the two 'classical' forms of junction. The number of lanes and the lengths of the reservoirs were determined on the basis of the capacity calculation.

K

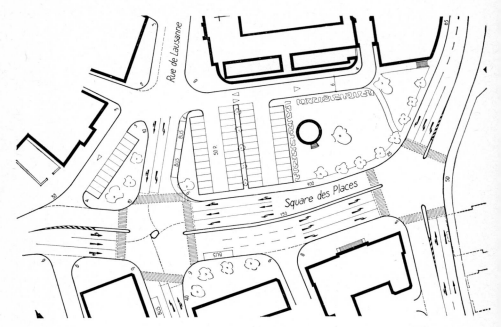

Figure 155: Simple crossroads and T-junction too close together and therefore with greatly widened reservoir lengths.

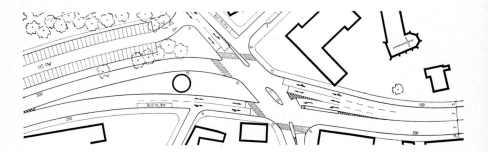

Figure 156: A crossroads at an old tower widened out on architectural grounds. A certain loss of capacity was taken into account in the elongated, acute-angled crossroads.

space for left-turners (Fig. 155). It can be provided by widening the cross-roads: by pulling the two main streams of traffic on one or both streets so far apart that there is room for left-turners between them (Figs. 156, 157). A circular island can be provided in the centre of the junction. This will not create a rotary intersection because the traffic proceeding straight ahead will be led straight across the junction, crossing the paths of cross traffic at a right-angle or an oblique angle. The junction of two pairs of one-way

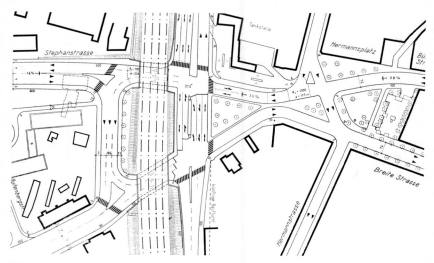

Figure 157: 'Expanded' crossroads on the important tangent parallel to the rail-way embankment in Neuss (Hermannsplatz). To the east the east–west traffic is carried by two one-way streets, to the west by two two-way streets. The filling station could not be eliminated.

streets is really such an 'expanded' crossroads. This form of junction has very high capacity and is safe in operation (Fig. 158).

At a simple crossroads the left-turners can be led to pass to the left of the centre of the crossroads. In this way conflict between left-turners from opposite directions is eliminated, and the capacity increased (Figs. 159, 160, 161). Where this sensible method of making a left turn is not generally laid down it can only be used if the non-conflicting vehicle paths are indicated clearly by islands or roadway markings.

(d) Rotaries

A rotary intersection is one where traffic must follow a circular path around a central island. Vehicles must usually make a sharp right-angle turn to enter the rotary, and then a wide turn in the opposite direction, followed by a fairly sharp turn where they leave the rotary.

The rotary has undoubted aesthetic advantages. It has the advantage of uninterrupted traffic flow, while a simple crossroads requires regulation

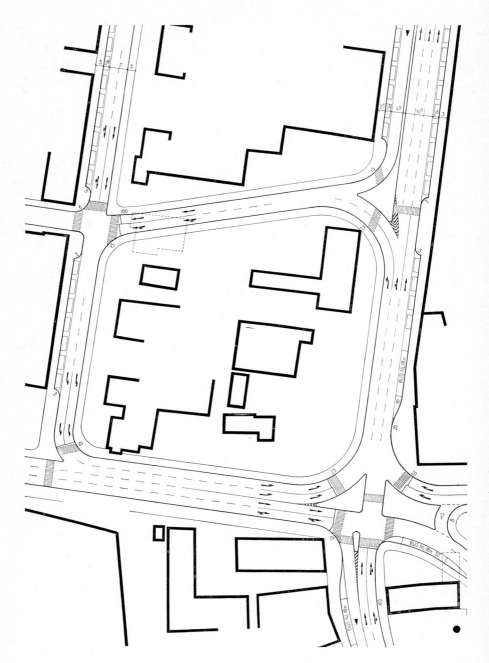

Figure 158: Part of inner-urban network of one-way streets, with big reservoirs for left-turners.

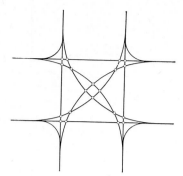 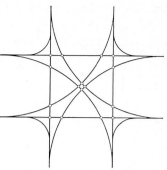

Figure 159: A simple cross-roads with left-turners led to the right of the centre point has 20 cuts.

Figure 160: A simple cross-roads with left-turners led to the left of the centre point has only 16 cuts and therefore has greater capacity.

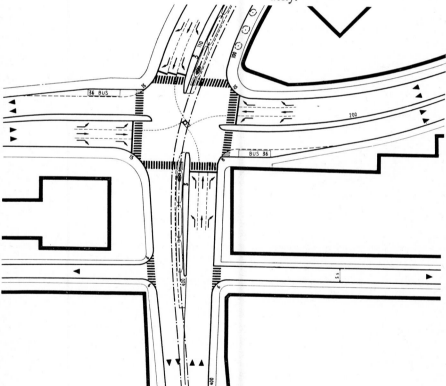

Figure 161: Simple, regular crossroads between two four-lane streets. All four approaches are widened out to three lanes. Left-turners pass to the left of the signpost in the centre of the junction. The tram stops are ahead of the junction; but the bus stops on the other street are 'far side' stops. Either side of the junction the tram tracks are laid in the roadway.

either by 'Give Way' signs, 'Stop' signs, police or signals. Many drivers find a rotary less of an obstacle than a crossroads because they are less often stopped. The sharp turns at the entries to the rotary slow traffic down so much that serious accidents are rare. However, vehicle paths still cross each other at a sharp, dangerous angle, and the exact position of the intersection point and the speed of other vehicles cannot easily be judged. The

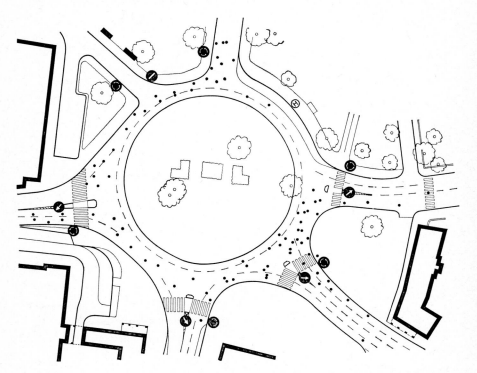

Figure 162: A rotary junction in a big city (Ludgeriplatz in Münster, see Figure 129) at which 86 accidents occurred in 1966, at the points marked with a dot.

number of accidents is thus considerable compared with that at a signal-controlled crossroads carrying the same traffic volume (Fig. 162).

With a large-diameter central island the traffic cuts become weaves. Vehicle paths are less bent. The sides of the rotary can even become straight lines if the rotary is laid out in the form of a quadrilateral with rounded corners. This form of rotary is common in England, where rotaries are called roundabouts (Fig. 163). But the vehicle paths must still cut across each other. At any one point vehicles whose paths cross must goose-step behind each other. There is little sense in increasing the number of traffic lanes, as has been done at the Prater in Vienna (six lanes), the Grosser Stern in Berlin and the Place de l'Etoile in Paris, which can hardly be controlled (Fig. 164).

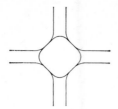

Figure 163: Rotary junction with straight weaving sections.

Multiple weaving manoeuvres, with several vehicles weaving two or more abreast, cannot be carried out with adequate safety without an impossibly complex signal system. No rotary in which several traffic streams must cross each other can dependably carry more traffic than two traffic lanes with uninterrupted traffic, i.e. 4,000 vehicles/h. This cannot be improved on even if the rotary is greatly enlarged (which requires a large area of land).

As soon as a rotary intersection has to be controlled by signals—as at the Gedächtniskirche in Berlin or the new 'Hochkreisel' at the approach to the Rhine bridge in Mainz-Kastel—the last advantage of this type of lay-out, uninterrupted traffic flow, is lost (Fig. 165). But the disadvantages remain, namely poor routing of traffic movements and the need for a very large area. Moreover it is impossible for motor cyclists and pedal-cyclists to weave their way in and out of the traffic on the rotary, and thus traffic

Figure 164: Traffic on a rotary junction in Paris (Place de l'Etoile). Signalization has been improved in the meantime.

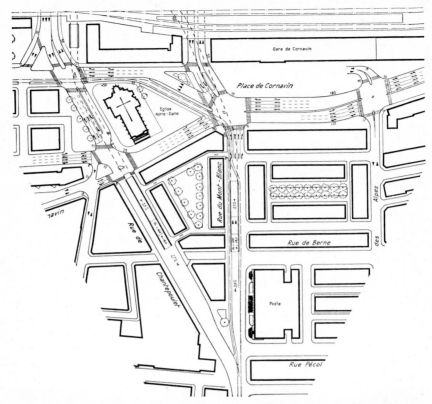

Figure 165: Proposed crossroads replacing a rotary junction outside the Cornavin
station in Geneva. The streets from the west are brought together as a one-
way couplet. The entrance to the station forecourt is pushed so far to the east
that a simple crossroads is left. The heavy north–south traffic is to be carried
initially on a partial one-way system; later it will be transferred to two one-
way underpasses. The tram tracks must be taken directly past the station.
The Southbound track in the one-way northbound Rue du Mont-Blanc is
on a reserved right-of-way.

cuts occur at the entries to and exits from the rotary where these vehicles
intersect the paths of other traffic. An example can be seen at the Hofplein
in Rotterdam.

It is particularly difficult to route tram tracks through a rotary. As a
rule they are led directly across the central island as at the Ägidientorplatz
in Hanover. They thus cut across the paths of other traffic at a right-angle,
turning the rotary into a series of intersections too close together. But even
where the tracks are led around the rotary they must still hinder other
traffic (Fig. 166).

Despite their well-known disadvantages, rotaries are still being provided even today at complex intersections where more than four roads

meet. In this way star-shaped junctions are avoided; junctions which are considered unsatisfactory because of lack of clarity concerning priority, incomprehensibility and low capacity. But these disadvantages are not eliminated by substituting rotaries. The solution of the traffic engineering problem is merely passed on to the drivers, who are left to fend for themselves in the maelstrom of the rotary. An intersection can only be said to be satisfactory when all vehicle paths and the points at which they intersect are made absolutely clear. Moreover a capacity calculation must be

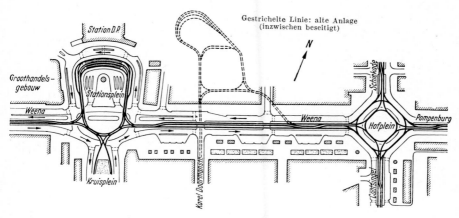

Figure 166: Layout of tram tracks in the area of the new Rotterdam D.P. station. Conflict with road traffic was eliminated by providing an underpass for westbound traffic opposite the ticket hall (see also Figure 236). At the Hofplein junction, a straight-sided rotary, two alternative routes are provided for trams. Normally they use the outer track in the centre of the annular roadway, thus mixing with the weaving traffic. In emergency they can cut across the rotary via the inner loop track on the central island.

carried out to determine the number of lanes needed and the amounts of green time to be allocated to each traffic stream (Figs. 167, 168).

At multi-level junctions turning traffic should also not be led through a rotary, but clearly led as right-turners and left-turners. Then they will not have to make any S-movements (Figs. 169, 170).

Rotaries serving to reduce the speed of vehicles—as in Bonn at the end of the motorway from Cologne, and also where the motorways enter Lausanne, Mannheim and Munich (motorway from Stuttgart)—are not satisfactory because the transition from the straight trunk road to the rotary is too sudden. Speed can and should be reduced by the choice of suitable curve radii. But in such cases several curves of smaller and smaller radius are more suitable than a rotary.

Figure 167: Five-way rotary junction in New Orleans. The dark bands on the road surface prove that vehicles do not weave, but cut across each other's paths at an acute angle.

Figure 168: The same junction after it had been rebuilt in 1957 as a five-way crossroads. The new layout brought—as expected—a considerably higher capacity and a big reduction in accidents. The picture is taken from a different viewpoint from that in Figure 167.

Figure 169: A rotary serving turning movements at an intermediate level between the two main roads. Here too the circle gives bad, acute-angled cuts. The rotary permits speeds which are excessive in view of the conflicts. The structural cost is too great.

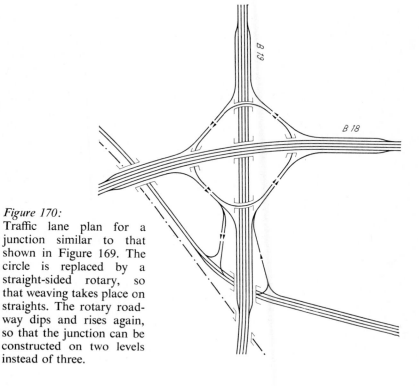

Figure 170:
Traffic lane plan for a junction similar to that shown in Figure 169. The circle is replaced by a straight-sided rotary, so that weaving takes place on straights. The rotary roadway dips and rises again, so that the junction can be constructed on two levels instead of three.

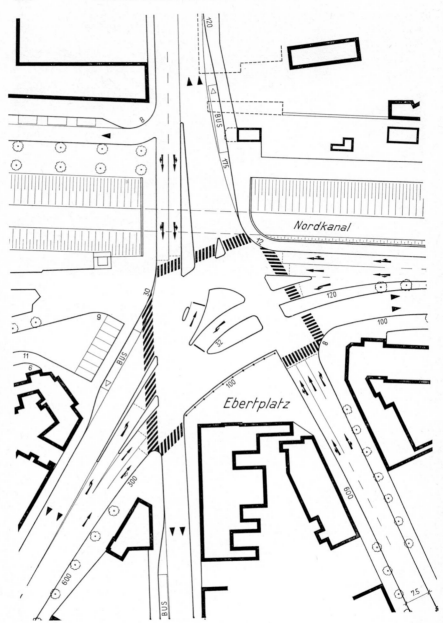

Figure 171: A six-armed junction was simplified by making a one-way couplet out of two streets and blocking the entry from a third. In the simple cross-roads thus created left-turners from the two main approaches are led to the left of each other. The three bus stops are 'far side' stops. The pedestrian crossings are very direct. The one on the West side of the junction is certainly very long; but it is not hidden by stopped buses and is subdivided by an additional island.

(e) Stars

Junctions from which five or more roads radiate are called stars. If two or more roads lying opposite each other are linked there are three or more main traffic streams to cope with and as many main phases to be included in the signal cycle. We can at first leave open the question what kind of traffic control should be installed. With every additional phase the capacity of the junction is reduced; and more and more time is lost on clearance periods.

At star junctions there are a great many possible turning movements. At a normal crossroads with four arms, traffic from each direction can go straight ahead, to right or to left, so that there are $4 \times 3 = 12$ possible movements. At a five-way junction there are $5 \times 4 = 20$ possible movements; at a six-way junction there are thirty. It is difficult to pass such a large number of movements through the junction in an understandable

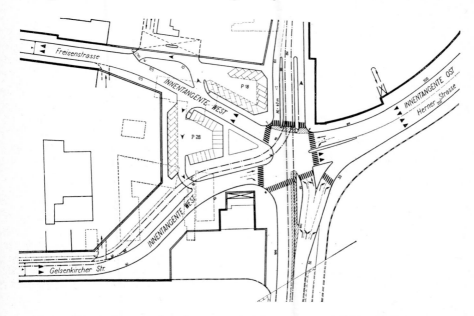

Figure 172: A five-way junction converted into a crossroads by introducing a one-way couplet. The trams run in both directions through one of the one-way streets, but in traffic engineering terms they are in the middle of the one-way couplet. The track carrying trams in the 'wrong' direction is on a reserved right-of-way. Private traffic entering the city centre from the south is deliberately throttled. For this reason drivers from the south are encouraged to turn left or right, partly by providing, as an exception to the general rule, separate right-turn lanes to the east—which means that pedestrians on the south-east side have an extra roadway to cross. The filling station on the north-west side has to remain. Existing buildings due for demolition are shown by dashed lines, and proposed new building lines by double lines.

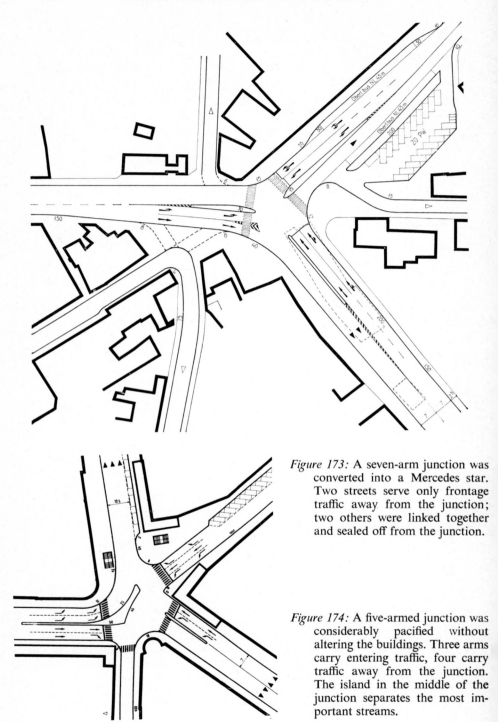

Figure 173: A seven-arm junction was converted into a Mercedes star. Two streets serve only frontage traffic away from the junction; two others were linked together and sealed off from the junction.

Figure 174: A five-armed junction was considerably pacified without altering the buildings. Three arms carry entering traffic, four carry traffic away from the junction. The island in the middle of the junction separates the most important streams.

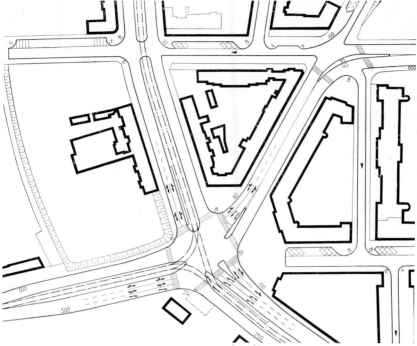

Figure 175: Simplification of an existing street network. The fifth arm of the junction is sealed off. At the other junction to the north–east a curved island prevents any conflicts; drivers can only weave and merge.

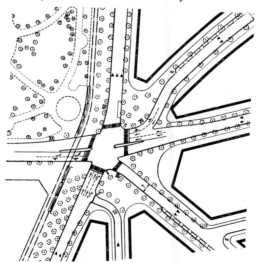

Figure 176: A seven-armed junction is converted into a simple crossroads. Two streets are bent so that they join other streets before the junction; and one is made one-way away from the junction. Moreover one of the main streets is made one-way.

and safe way, and it cannot be done without a long signal cycle. If space is limited it is almost impossible. Signalling becomes very intricate. At the Piazza Venezia in Rome, for instance, the traffic can only be regulated by very skilful police control. Star junctions must therefore be eliminated if possible. This can be done in various ways.

One method is to create a pair of one-way streets, so that two streets are in effect combined into one from the traffic engineering point of view. In this way the number of possible movements at the junction is considerably reduced (Figs. 171, 172). Another method is to make supernumerary streets one-way away from the star junction, so that they serve

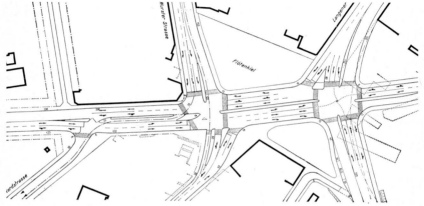

Figure 177: At the Flötenkiel in Bremerhaven a six-armed junction was converted into two crossroads, forming an 'H'. A seventh street from the south was 'bent away'. The short reservoir space between the junctions is six-lane. The south–west arm consists of a one-way street couplet. In the Wurster Strasse there is a left-turn lane to the left of a tram track.

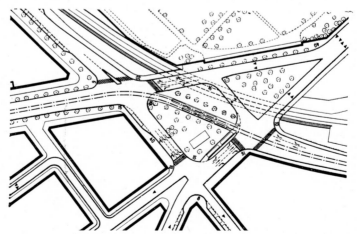

Figure 178: Eight streets linked together to form a one-way quadrilateral. The trams and a terminating bus route stop on the centre island.

only as exits from the junction and require no special control (Figs. 173, 174). An old example of such treatment was the Bellevueallee in Berlin; by making this street one-way the Potsdamer Platz was converted from a five-star junction into a simple crossroads.

Another method is to divert supernumerary streets before entering the star junction so that they join other streets away from the junction—which is thus in effect broken up into a number of junctions (Fig. 175). The resulting forks or T-junctions must be taken into account in the capacity calculation for the main junction (Figs. 176, 177).

Yet another method is to replace the star junction with a one-way street circuit, thus creating a one-way quadrilateral connecting the intersecting streets (Figs. 178, 179). This one-way circuit may surround blocks

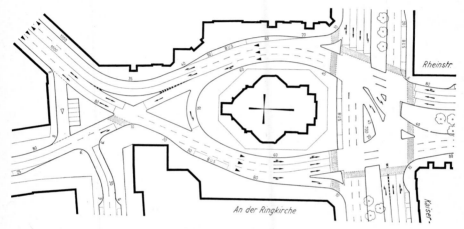

Figure 179: Traffic engineering layout for a place of architectural value in Wiesbaden without altering the buildings. The main junction is simplified by leading left-turners from the Rheinstrasse around the Ringkirche. At the junction to the west of the church main and secondary streets are handled quite differently.

of buildings, as in the case of the Stureplan in Stockholm. The area inside it is also available for stopping places for public transport.

The weaving sections thus created must be of adequate length and should be straight. In this way the star will, as with the previous method, be replaced by a number of junctions. These should be so arranged that smooth traffic interplay is achieved and green waves provided for vehicles which must pass through several junctions. There are a fairly large number of examples of such one-way circuit solutions, which bear some relation to the straight-sided roundabout. The following may be mentioned:

Piazza del Duomo, Milan.
Bellevue Platz, Zürich.
Plärrer Platz, Nuremberg.

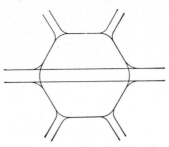

Figure 180: 'Expanded' crossroads on a main road with a one-way hexagon providing links with side roads.

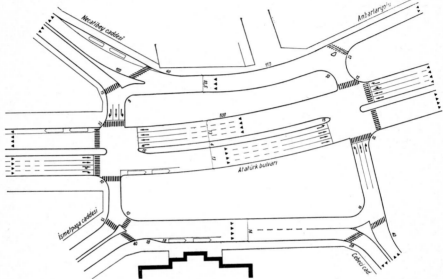

Figure 181: A one-way quadrilateral in Ankara, with the main street of the city cutting across it.

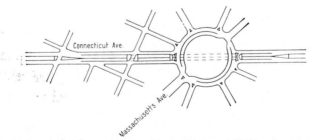

Figure 182: At the Dupont Circle in Washington, D.C., the most important traffic streams were taken out of the rotary, by taking motor traffic and tram traffic on Connecticut Avenue under the junction in two separate tunnels. The trams stopped running in 1962. Traffic on Massachusetts Avenue uses the inner of two annular roadways—signals regulate the cuts at both sides of the rotary. The central island was not to be cut across.

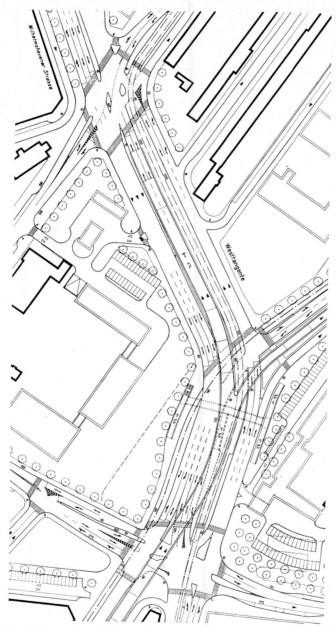

Figure 183: The proposed West Tangent in Bremerhaven will cut across the Platz an der Plesse-Ecke, running from south-west to north-west. The north-bound roadway must be taken across the twin junctions on a flyover. The tram stop will be under the flyover. Further north the tracks are to one side of the downramp, so that turning trams do not interfere with main traffic movements. The junction complex also has a single railway track running across it. Several side roads are sealed off or made one way. The double lines indicate planned buildings.

Heumarkt, Cologne.
Bahnhofsplatz-Raschplatz, Hanover.
Lützowplatz, Berlin.
Gustav Adolfs Torg, Stockholm.

A variation of this type of treatment consists of taking a main road across the centre of the one-way circuit. This produces a 'stretched' crossroads on the main road. An example is the Johanna-Platz in Berlin-Grunewald, where the Bismarckallee is taken straight through while the four other debouching streets are connected up by a one-way hexagon (Figs. 180, 181). A similar solution for a star junction is the Dupont Circle in Washington, where one main artery cuts across the rotary traffic (Fig. 182).

(f) Grade-separated junctions

All forms of junction can be developed on several levels. The simplest solution is the building of a flyover for traffic in one main direction (Figs. 183, 184). When traffic cuts are eliminated lane capacity is increased, including the capacity of adjoining stretches of road. However, high construction costs mean that the number of grade-separated junctions will always be small. They can only be considered where traffic is very heavy or the topography is very favourable. The structures also reduce the number of possible turning movements, and those that are 'lost' must be catered for by means of ramps or other connexions (Fig. 185). This requires additional areas and expenditures.

All the forms of interchange used on rural motorways—cloverleaf,

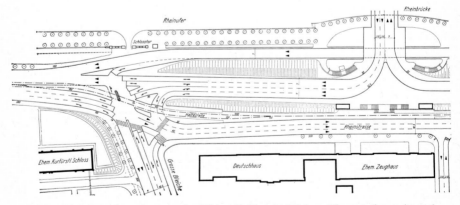

Figure 184: Junction close to the Rhine Bridge in Mainz. The westbound roadway of the Rheinstrasse passes under the bridgehead. The tram tracks are taken out of the ramps, and combined into a single track over a short distance. The single-track section remained in operation for a few years only because trams were replaced by buses recently. Traffic from the other side of the Rhine comes off the bridge on two lanes, which are widened first to four and then to six lanes in the approach to the junction.

trumpet, diamond and rotary—may also find applications in cities. Their dimensions can be adapted to the lower speeds (Fig. 186). For example, the cloverleaf interchange at Slussen in Stockholm was designed with a minimum inner radius of 10·5 m (35 ft). However, in densely-built-up areas

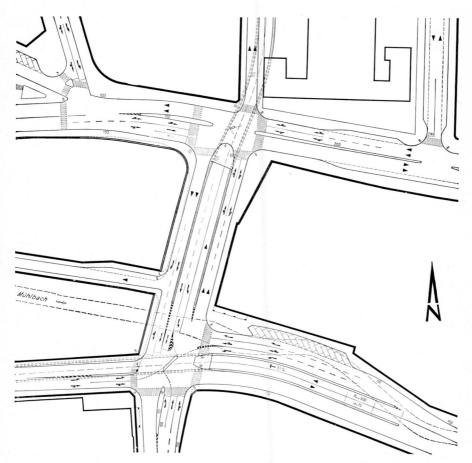

Figure 185: A crossroads at the mouth of a two-way road tunnel. Turning right from the tunnel is prohibited, and so is turning left from the parallel southbound roadway, so as to avoid the need for an additional phase. The cross traffic is to be taken underneath in a later stage of construction.

and in the constricted street network with its poor visibility, special care must be taken to ensure sensible routing of traffic streams; otherwise drivers will easily make mistakes. A cloverleaf has the disadvantage that a left-turner must turn first to the right; and in urban traffic that is bad. For this reason the Americans have given preference, in Detroit and Los Angeles, to the development of three- and four-level junctions with directional turn connections (Figs. 187, 188). Four-level junctions require long

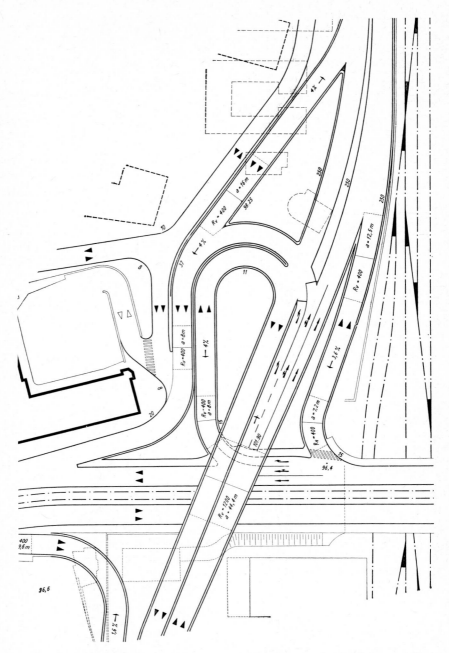

Figure 186: A clover-leaf connection on a very cramped site. A conflict between a modest left-turn movement off the flyover and the straight-ahead movement onto the flyover could not be avoided. The frontage roadway serving a building contractor and the works entry (white arrows) could not be got rid of.

Figure 187: The 'Stack' in Los Angeles. A four-level directional interchange between two urban motorways. It carries over 400,000 vehicles per day.

ramps and are aesthetically objectionable. It should always be possible to get by with only three levels (Fig. 189).

Trumpet interchanges are also bad in urban traffic. Similarly arrangements requiring 'Q-movements' (Fig. 190), which are sometimes resorted to in order to eliminate left turns, should be regarded as an emergency measure. The traffic engineer must prove that the extra loading on the side-streets used for the Q-movement is outweighed by the improvement in traffic flow at the junction.

Figure 188: The four levels of the 'Stack' at night.

At complex junctions a solution can only be found by means of a very systematic, step-by-step analysis (Figs. 191–94). Construction stages must be thought about from the beginning, since in many cases the reconstruction must be carried out without interrupting traffic.

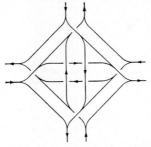

Figure 189: Substitute for a cloverleaf interchange: a three-level directional interchange.

Figure 190: A 'Q' movement: a driver must make three right turns instead of one left turn.

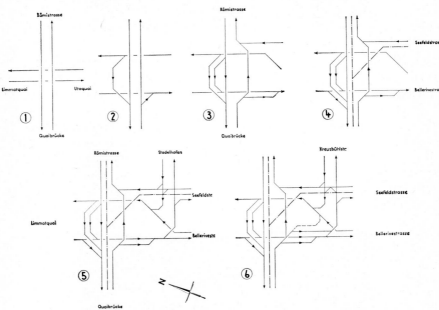

Figure 191: Building up the outline plan for the Bellevue junction in Zürich.

1. The grade-separated crossroads.
2. Fitting in the turning movements between the Quaibrücke and the Utoquai, and therefore separation of the roadways linking Limmatquai and Utoquai.
3. Fitting in of turning movements between the Rämistrasse and the Utoquai. Left-turners from the Rämistrasse must branch off right before making the turn.
4. Fitting in tram tracks, with no intersections at grade.
5 and 6. Additional connections on the south side of the junction.

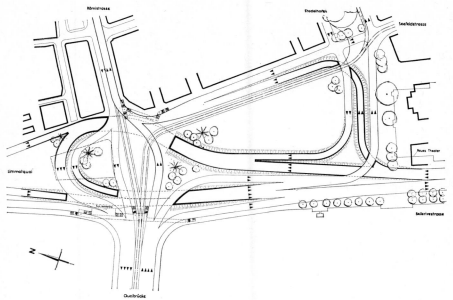

Figure 192: Design for the Bellevue junction in Zürich, which can be carried out in six construction stages.

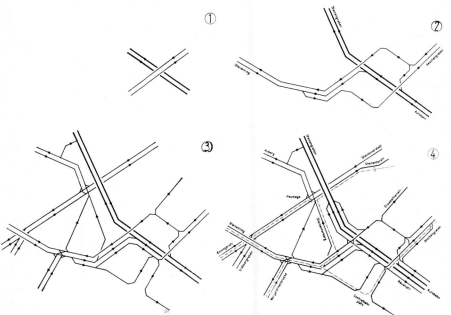

Figure 193: Development of the outline plan for the Elizabethenanlage junction in Basle.
1. Grade-separated cross.
2. Separation of the cross-street into two roadways and fitting in of the left-turners from the Autobahn to the Steinenring.
3. Fitting in of the other streets, some of them one-way.
4. Addition of tram lines.

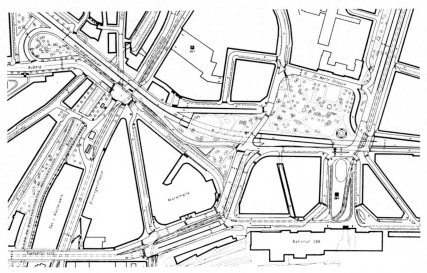

Figure 194: Scaled design for the big Elizabethenanlage junction in Basle. The amount of building land and park land taken for roads is very small.

(g) Details of layout

Designs of junctions and interchanges calls for certain talents: a feel for traffic movement patterns, a capacity for creative design, a power of spatial imagination and aesthetic sensibility. These are talents which the born engineer possesses.

Despite design standardization, every designer will develop a certain technical style. This one will place more emphasis on clarity, comprehensibility and breadth of scale; another designer will produce designs which are economical of both land and construction costs. But differences will also be found in many details: in the handling of pedestrians or of public transport, in the choice of particular dimensions and in the structural design. Many of these things remain questions of measurement.

The simplest solution is the best. The 'Columbus egg' is usually, however, the result of thorough consideration and serious work. Chance seldom gets one any further.

All junctions along a stretch of road should be developed in a similar manner, so that visitors will easily find their way about. Uniformity in the design of traffic facilities throughout the town, throughout the country and indeed throughout the world is very desirable. For this reason unusual arrangements must be regarded with suspicion. In Amsterdam, for example, left-turn lanes in narrow streets are placed on the right of the street, so that right and left turners can make wider-radius turns. This arrangement confuses visiting drivers, who expect a left-turn lane to be on the left. Traffic safety can only be achieved if certain rules are observed.

In designing road layouts the installation of signals, including green wave systems, should always be assumed, because all junctions should, within the framework of existing possibilities, be developed as maximum capacity installations. It should always be possible to instal signal systems later on without any additional expenditure on construction.

The most useful scale for road design work is 1 : 500. The junctions should first be sketched freehand. This saves much time and sharpens the designer's appreciation of the geometrical interplay of straights and curves. Only later does the precise design work begin.

Firstly, all the traffic lanes running through in the various directions, as shown on the traffic lane plan for the town, are drawn on the plan. The lanes for turning traffic are then added. The minimum number of lanes required is given by the capacity calculation. Since in an urban area many detours on account of constructional work, festivities, accidents or other causes are to be expected, it is advisable in many cases to provide additional traffic lanes within the intersection complex, if the cost of doing so is small. This can sometimes be done by substituting roadway markings for islands, so that the areas concerned can be used by traffic in exceptional cases. In many places it should also be possible for a driver to turn right around and go back along the same street.

In the approaches to junctions the lanes should be clearly allocated to straight ahead, left-turn and right-turn movements so that each can be taken through independently of the others thus increasing the capacity; and so that they can flow during different signal phases. Where only two approach lanes are available, the nearside lane usually serves both straight-ahead and right-turn traffic, and the offside lane only left-turners who are harder to get through the junction and often require a separate signal phase. Where there are three approach lanes, the nearside lane is generally used by straight-ahead as well as right-turn traffic to give better utilisation. Variations can be determined from the capacity calculation.

The lanes for straight-ahead traffic should have an easy alignment, preferably a straight one. Turn lanes should be so designed that drivers are not encouraged to cut corners. Where an S-movement is required within a junction, a straight section of sufficient length should be inserted— usually 30 m (100 ft) or more (Fig. 195). At a junction on a right-hand curve, for instance, the left-turn lane should be straight for a few yards, as in the layout shown in Figure 126. Figure 196 shows a layout with no such straight section.

At the approach to a junction a driver must wait until the path he wishes to follow is clear. With very heavy traffic a vehicle can enter every two seconds on each lane. The length of lane occupied per passenger car unit by traffic waiting at signals averages 7 m (23 ft). Thus every second of red time requires a reservoir length of 3·50 m. (11 ft 6 in). In cramped conditions the reservoir space can be so short that it is just large enough to hold the number of vehicles actually arriving during the red phase at the peak hour. If the length is not sufficient even for this number, then additional lanes must be provided.

Although with a proper green wave signal system no vehicle should ever be stopped at signals, reservoir space still cannot be entirely dispensed with.

Between junctions the offside lane is the fast lane. At a signal-controlled junction straight-ahead traffic often has the green light while left-turners must wait. There is thus a danger that fast vehicles will remain in the offside lane and collide with waiting left-turners. This can be prevented by

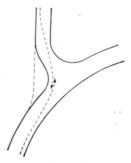

Figure 195: The bending of a side street which formerly entered the main street tangentially is correct; it creates a better angle of intersection. But because of the lack of a straight section between curves in the side street drivers making S-movements cut the corners. The danger can only be eliminated by inserting either a sufficiently long straight or—in wide streets—a centre island.

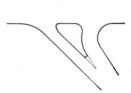

Figure 196: No straight section for drivers turning left from the side street. The concave piece of road next to the island is not used. Drivers cut the corners.

providing a 'shadowing lane' for left-turners notched into the median, which makes the left-turn lane very obvious (Figs. 197, 198). Left-turning vehicles can only enter the shadowing lane at reduced speed. But this is not a drawback since they can only make the turn at low speed.

With a suitable layout two left-turn lanes can be provided alongside one another. A greater number is hardly ever needed. If such a need manifests itself it would be a sign of a defect in the network.

If a road or roadway has to fan out in three directions the forks should be staggered as much as possible, so that the traffic routing remains comprehensible.

Not more than two roadways should merge at the same point. In tunnels or long underpasses two roadways should be brought together only if there is permanent signal control or if each lane is continued independently of the others. There is no particular objection to forks in tunnels, but they too would be better transferred to the surface.

Weaving sections should as a general rule be over 60 m (200 ft) long, and in exceptional cases at least 30 m (100 ft). Longer ones are preferable. Weaving manoeuvres occur where turning vehicles weave in and out

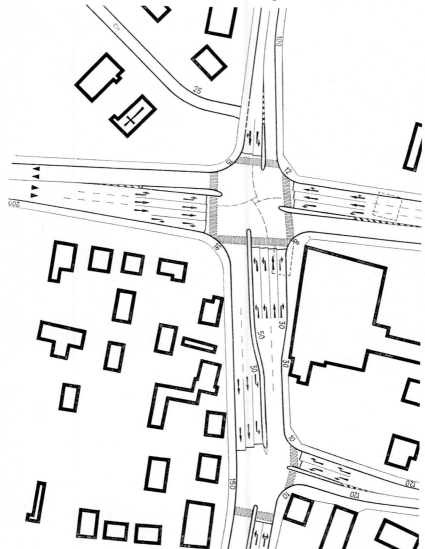

Figure 197: Markings lead the left-turner to the left of the centre of the junction. Left-turning lanes are shifted distinctly to the left.

of a main stream; between intersection points within a complex junction; and between independent junctions. There should be no entering roads within weaving sections and junction approaches.

Traffic streams ought not to cut across each other at too fine an angle, otherwise long, ill-defined conflict points arise which reduce capacity and are dangerous. Vehicle paths and the points where they intersect should be clearly defined by channelization, and easily recognizable. In the unoccupied areas between the lanes islands are inserted to guide vehicles and

Figure 198: Left-turn lanes protected by indicative painted islands with concrete ribs on a road in California.

also to some extent to provide a safe refuge for pedestrians. A few big islands are better than many small ones (Fig. 199).

Pedestrian islands are unnecessary on two-lane roads (7 m or 23 ft); possibly desirable on three-lane roads (10.5 m or 34 ft 6 in); desirable on four-lane roads (14 m or 46 ft); and necessary on wider roads.

Channelizing islands for guiding vehicles may be considered with other widths of road. They should be at least 1·50 m (5 ft) long, or cover an area of 4 sq m (40 sq ft) so that they will not be overlooked. Traffic signs can be placed on the islands. These can be supplemented not only by roadway markings painted on the road surface but also by what the Dutch call 'traffic mushrooms'—small internally illuminated bollards which a vehicle can drive across if need be.

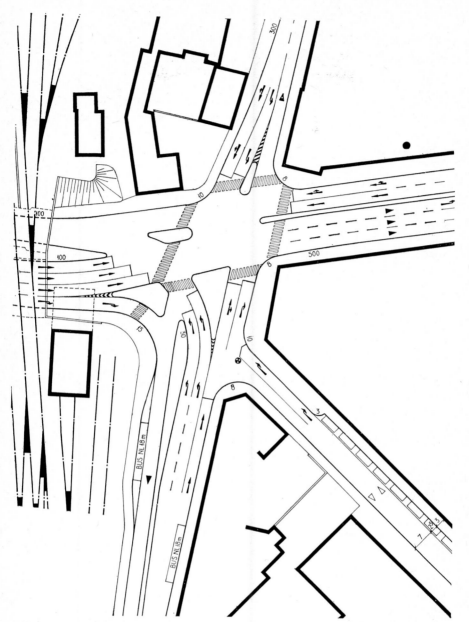

Figure 199: Layout for a junction at the exit from a rather long underpass under a railway. The junction is clearly divided up by a few large islands. The pedestrian crossings are right next to the main intersection area. A special right-turn lane had to be provided for buses. The stop lines in each lane are staggered so that vehicles stopped at the signals are close to the conflict point. The roadway markings are embedded in the road surface: directional arrows, solid and unbroken lane lines, and two different kinds of markings at the approach ends of islands, indicating either 'keep right' (in the north approach) or 'pass either side' (in the south and west approaches).

Each traffic lane should have good optical guidance. This can be tested by looking at the drawing with one's eye only 2 mm ($\frac{1}{10}$ in) above the paper—corresponding, at the 1 : 500 scale, to a driver's eye 1m (3 ft) above the road surface—and following each vehicle path individually. Then one can see details as the driver will see them (Figs. 200, 201).

Optical guidance does not mean only traffic engineering construction.

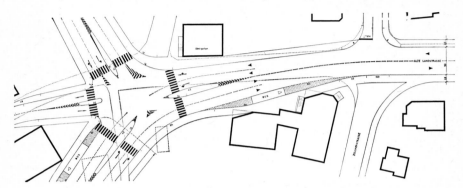

Figure 200: The main road runs from east to south-west. The centre of a small town lies to the west. There is a secondary bypass route running north westwards. In this scheme the bend in the main road is shifted westwards, and the three-way fork is laid out as a crossroads. Owing to inadequate optical guidance drivers unfamiliar with the junction would be misled into proceeding straight ahead into the centre of the small town.

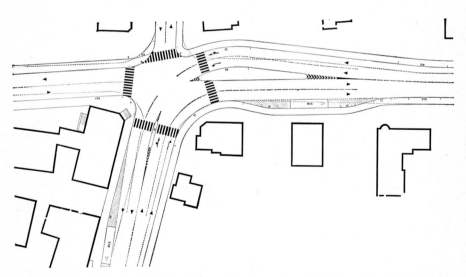

Figure 201: It is better to leave the bend in the main road at the old location, and to swing the westbound roadway round in such a way that at the entry to the intersection it is pointing at the corner building. Apart from the better optical guidance the junction with the side road and gradients both favoured this solution.

Conspicuous buildings indicate junctions and main traffic directions better than signposts. Trees and hedges can show the line of a curve. They ensure that at night the headlight beam will not simply be lost in emptiness. On the other hand visibility at junctions must not be spoilt by bushes. At the approaches to intersections and other danger points no vegetation should be higher than 50 cm (20 in). And street lighting should likewise contribute to optical guidance.

A vehicle path is only partially marked off by kerbs. Between kerbs there is a lack of clear guidance so that the vehicle may deviate from the proper path. Moreover curve widenings are necessary. These principles are recognized by making single-lane roadways between kerbs 4·50 m (14 ft

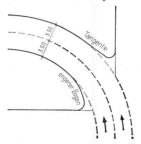

Figure 202: The line of the kerbs departs from the edges of the traffic lanes to make driving easier. The funnel starts off 30 cm (1 ft) to 1 m (3 ft) wider than the travelled way.

Figure 203: The point of the island is cut back by 30 cm (1 ft) or more. If this is not done some drivers are 'kerb shy' and swing slightly to the left.

6 in) wide. Driving is also facilitated if, following a long gap without kerbs, the lanes begin with a greater width than usual (usually 30 cm to 1 m—1 to 3 ft), and then fine down to the normal width after a short funnel-shaped stretch. For this purpose kerbs are laid out as in Fig. 202— with a tighter radius of curve one side and a line drawn tangentially to the curve on the other.

The ends of islands should be slightly set back from the edge of the travelled way as in Fig. 203. The ends of islands which vehicles might run into should be rounded off with radii of 0·50 to 2·00 m (1 ft 8 in to 6 ft 6 in); the other ends should be cut off without rounding (Fig. 204). Further details may be deduced from the illustrations of whole junctions.

Junctions often have to be provided on gradients. In such cases it sometimes happens that the road surface is banked the wrong way for certain turning movements, so that vehicles making these movements are so to

L

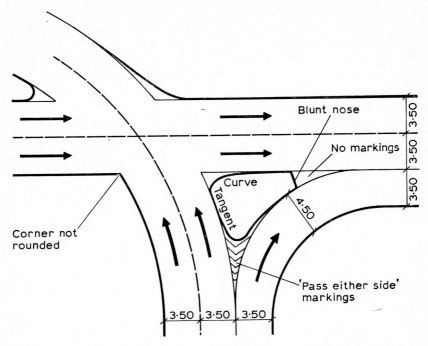

Figure 204: Detailed design of a traffic island between traffic lanes. The single
lane for right-turners, which is bounded by kerbs on both sides, is widened
out from 3·50 to 4·50 m (14 ft 9 in). Long single-lane ramps are widened
to as much as 5·50 m (18 ft) so that if a vehicle breaks down on the ramp
other vehicles can still get past.

speak pushed outwards. Gradients should therefore be made as moderate
as possible at junctions. For difficult junctions test designs should be
worked out with contours at levels differing by 10 or 20 cm (4 or 8 in),
like a very large-scale relief map. In this way vertical curves, gradients and
drainage etc. can best be appreciated.

Where high-speed roads join and leave urban roads, drivers must be
prevented from overtaking just where some vehicles are merging or
diverging. A dangerous situation arises where a driver in Lane 2 wishes
to turn right into another road and a driver in Lane 1 wishes to go straight-
ahead. For this reason the entries and exits should be single-lane, as in
Fig. 205. Within an urban area it is best to build the connections as two-
lane roadways, and to seal off the second lane by means of roadway markings and signals. It is then immediately available for use in the event of dis-
ruption or detours. This means that at a merging point the maximum flow
that can enter is the capacity of a single lane, i.e. 2,000 p.c.u./h; and the
same applies to a diverging point. As a general rule the entering or leaving
flow ought not to exceed 800 p.c.u./h.

The distance between a merge and a diverge ought not to be less than 400 m (1,300 ft). If possible the number of such points should be limited, because every entering flow hampers the through traffic.

Where an unimportant side street enters a main street, the footway alongside the latter should be continued without kerbs, so to speak. Drivers will then safely recognize that they are on a minor road and must

Figure 205: Grade-separated junction not yet completed between a bypass and a radial road with tram tracks down the middle. Left-turners swing off to the left. The outbound roadway of the radial road is throttled down to one lane before the merge point.

give way to pedestrians and vehicles on the major road. As a general rule the road layout should be so clear that special signs and markings can to a large extent be dispensed with.

Cyclists should in general mix in with the rest of the traffic. However, where there is heavy cycle traffic a special lane at least 1 m (3 ft) wide should be provided for them alongside the other lanes at the approach to a signal-controlled junction. Where there are cycle tracks cyclists can be led around to the right, even if they are turning left, and fed through the junction during the two phases for the intersecting main streams of traffic.

Such an arrangement requires more area and offers rather more safety. But it is not popular with cyclists, who are delayed by the double waiting. There is increased danger where left-turning cyclists cannot 'get into lane' with other vehicles and have to turn left immediately at the junction.

Pedestrians should cross over roadways by a short route. Uncontrolled pedestrian crossings should be marked with zebra markings, i.e. stripes parallel to the roadway, which can be seen better than other kinds of marking. The British procedure whereby pedestrians using a zebra crossing have priority over traffic, but the number of such crossings is drastically fewer than on the Continent, is to be strongly recommended.

So that pedestrian crossings will be easily seen they should be at an obtuse angle to the roadway, but not necessarily at a right-angle. Pedestrians want the shortest route and will cut out detours. Crossings on either side of an island should therefore be more or less in line with each other.

Where a pedestrian crossing is at an oblique angle, there should be staggered stop-lines for the individual traffic lanes in advance of the crossing. Stop lines must be close to the junction so that drivers will be able to see the whole layout clearly while waiting at the signals, and moreover will not lose any time when the green phase begins. For the same reason the pedestrian crossings must be narrow, e.g. between 2·5 and 4 m (8 and 13 ft). As a general rule they need not be wider than the footways which they connect. The stop lines for vehicles should be 50 cm back from the crossing.

In residential and shopping areas separate right-turn lanes should not be provided, because pedestrians will then have to cross over several crossings, some of them not easy for drivers to see, and will be compelled to make detours. At acute-angled crossroads such lanes cannot always, however, be avoided. In such cases the right-turn lane should not have too big a radius; otherwise the danger zone for the pedestrian will be too long and turning vehicles will go too fast. Curve radius is the most important means of regulating speed.

At danger points pedestrians should be prevented from walking on the roadway by railings. Unfortunately railings, which must be 1 m (3 ft) high and 60 cm (2 ft) back from the edge of the roadway, cause a waste of space. And they do not look well.

Where more space is needed for roads and junctions, trees must be cut down, land acquired and sometimes buildings knocked down. Sometimes arcaded footways are provided under buildings, but these are unusually expensive because they take away valuable sales floor space on the ground floor of shops. Such measures, necessary as they may be for the improvement of traffic, arouse resistance from the inhabitants of a town and push the cost up sky-high. But the opponents of such measures should bear in mind that all traffic engineering improvements must be seen in the framework of the town as a whole. It is illogical to approve of the design of a whole network and then later insist on preserving local bottlenecks. But the design engineer will make progress much more easily if he tests all sensitive points in his scheme with special care, and if he lays down building lines for later changes as soon as possible. In difficult cases it is also worth preparing alternative schemes, if necessary with cost estimates, which will show that the recommended solution is the least of the evils.

5. Capacity

The capacity calculation has the same decisive importance in designing a traffic facility as the calculation of static loads has in the design of a structure. As a general rule junctions set the capacity limit because they have to handle different streams of traffic on the same area of roadway. It is generally not enough to select individual junctions and improve these. It may happen that, as a result of detours, turn prohibitions and similar changes, the difficulties will be transferred to another junction. As a rule a large, coherent sub-network must be studied at the same time, with a view to achieving a higher capacity for this sub-network as a whole. The weakest junction determines the capacity of the whole system.

(a) Signalization

During off-peak hours traffic can still flow satisfactorily in many places with only 'Give Way' or 'Stop' sign control. But this is irrelevant for planning purposes, for which peak traffic is the starting point.

In congested areas of towns, where land is valuable, traffic facilities must be designed to work close to their capacity. All important traffic intersections should be designed for signal control. Signal control is necessary at a junction as soon as the traffic flow in both directions on each intersecting street exceeds 400 p.c.u./h. Signals are needed even with lower flows if there are not adequate sight distance triangles at the junction. Signal control enhances safety and improves the utilization of a junction; but it causes time losses. For this reason signals should be replaced in off-peak hours by flashing amber indications, or be switched off altogether.

Traffic signals can be either fixed-time or vehicle-actuated. The latter, making use of mechanical or electrical detectors, give higher capacity and shorter waiting time, but are considerably more expensive to install. The best form of traffic-dependent control is still police control, for the policeman can observe all movements continually and act accordingly, but it can only be considered for exceptionally difficult junctions because manpower is too valuable.

For traffic planning purposes fixed-time control can be assumed because in peak hours at a busy junction vehicle-actuated signals operate exactly like fixed-time signals, with a fixed cycle time and cycle split.

By separate signalization of individual lanes, the operation of signals can be closely adapted to demand (Fig. 206). Where traffic demands are substantially different at different times of day, different programmes must

Figure 206: Junction between the north and west tangents in Memmingen. The
land falls away to the east, which facilitates a two-level treatment. It was
difficult to fit in a left-turn lane from south to west, which had to be usable
by a few vehicles from the old town to the south. Only two houses would
need to be demolished. The plan shows, in addition to the layout, the
positions of signals and direction signs, the signal indications and the word-
ing on the signs.

be introduced, so that different phases will be of different duration, and will even occur in a different order, according to the time of day. Traffic flow can also be monitored by means of television apparatus so that the signal programmes for whole sub-networks can be continually adapted to demand.

The design of streets and junctions must be based on the volumes during the heaviest peak hour. With a given distribution of the total flow between the various movements, the capacity is determined in terms of saturation flow per hour of green time. The traffic volumes in the design year are deduced from the survey results.

(b) Free traffic lanes

The capacity of free-flowing traffic lanes depends on local conditions. Much research has been done recently, especially in Chicago, on the relationships between rates of flow, speeds, characteristic headways and density (vehicles per lane-mile). It has been found that, so long as traffic flow remains smooth—i.e. as long as a critical density is not exceeded—the characteristic headway of vehicles moving in platoons (if a platoon is defined as a column of vehicles following each other at headways not exceeding 2·1 sec) is 1·3 sec, which corresponds with a rate of flow of nearly 2,800 vehicles/h; and these high rates of flow are achieved at a speed of around 80 km/h (50 mph). When 'speed inversion' occurs (owing to excessive density) the speed drops to around 40 km/h (25 mph), and the characteristic headway lengthens to 1·7 sec, but the rate of flow is still maintained at around 2,000 vph.

Thus it seems that, while maximum hourly flow is attained at quite a range of speeds (40 up to 80 km/h, or 25 up to 50 mph), flow could in theory be maximized, with drivers as experienced as those of Chicago, at around 50 mph and a rate of at least 2,500 vph, provided that stable flow could be maintained. Flows of 2,800 cars over a whole hour have regularly been observed on the fast lane of the M.4 motorway in England, with traffic moving at around 80 km/h (50 mph). However, flows in the adjoining slow lane at the same times were around 1,400 vph, so that the average for the two lanes was 2,100 per lane.

Thus an hourly flow of 2,000 cars/h can be safely taken as the capacity of each lane of a well-designed free-flowing facility in Europe. The reduction in maximum flow on a level road caused by buses and other large vehicles depends on the speed at which traffic is moving: in Chicago vehicles over 8 m (24 ft) long have the same headways as cars under free-flow conditions, i.e. at around 80 km/h (50 mph); but in the New York tunnels, where speeds are much lower (around 40 km/h or 25 mph), a bus was found to be equivalent to about 1·5 cars. Large vehicles are of course steadily declining as a proportion of the traffic stream.

The general relationship between speed, density and flow has been represented by Chicago researchers in the form shown in Fig. 207. The

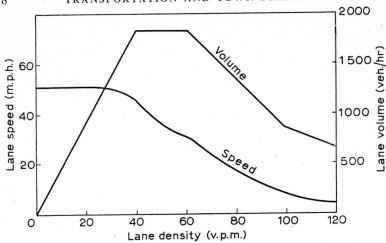

Figure 207: The above curves, based on observations of congested flow on
Chicago urban motorways, show the relationship between density (vehicles
per lane-mile) and (a) speed and (b) volume or flow. Volume is maximized
at speeds between 30 and 45 mph (48 and 82 km/h) with a density of
between 40 and 60 vehicles per lane-mile. This relationship holds only
for motorways.

speed/flow curve is much more 'blunt-nosed' than it is often represented
to be.

(c) Static calculation

Simple crossroads can initially be the subject of static calculations.
Where two equally heavily-loaded lanes intersect, each one can carry only
900 p.c.u./h, less lost time. Light signals should operate with a cycle time
of 40 to 140 sec, and preferably of 60 to 80 sec. A clearance period
(amber time) of 3 to 4 sec must be inserted between the green phases for
conflicting traffic streams. Where there are two conflicting streams and the
cycle time is 80 sec, the lost time in every cycle is 8 sec, or 10 per cent of
the cycle. Both lanes will then have a capacity of 810 p.c.u./h.

The capacity can be slightly increased if the cycle is lengthened, since
the proportion of amber time is reduced. With a cycle time of 140 sec,
132 sec are usable; and the lane capacity is increased to 850 p.c.u./h.

There are some signal systems where the proportional split of green
time between the conflicting traffic streams remains constant, but the cycle
time is lengthened automatically when detectors at certain points register
heavy traffic volumes. For the purposes of capacity calculations it is
enough to know that the sum of the flows on two conflicting lanes can
never exceed 1,700 p.c.u./h.

With a 140-sec cycle the red and amber phases on each of two equally-
loaded approaches will together last 78 sec. Thus if each lane feeding the
approach were working at capacity, with vehicles at 2-sec headways, a
queue of 39 cars would form in each approach lane. This would require a

reservoir $39 \times 7 = 273$ m (about 900 ft) long; but this is still less than the most favourable junction spacing.

This calculation takes no account of turning movements. Right-turners can be ignored because they can make their turn at any time provided pedestrian traffic is light. Left-turners can only be ignored at 'expanded' crossroads with adequate reservoir space, e.g. the intersection of two pairs of one-way streets. At intersections of two-way streets, a few left-turners can slip through during the amber period. But when there are many left-turners they require a special phase because they ought not to cross over oncoming traffic.

With the normal proportion of left-turners we get the familiar figure of 700 p.c.u./h. as the average capacity of an inner-urban traffic lane. This is only about a third of the capacity of an uninterrupted traffic lane.

This would suggest that three times as many lanes are needed at intersections as between them. However, it is not advisable to narrow down the width of the roadway between junctions; to do so would produce dangerous funnels, and would oblige drivers to make many lane changes. Only the kerb lane is 'taken away' from moving traffic beyond the junction and used as a parking lane or as a bus stop.

At certain junctions the straight-ahead traffic does in fact have fewer lanes available to it beyond the junction than it does entering it (this was formerly the case at the Rudolfsplatz in Cologne). As a result of different acceleration rates the vehicles starting from a standstill do rapidly sort themselves out and the individual columns dovetail into each other. But such an arrangement is not sufficiently safe. And as a general rule it is not worthwhile because the distance to the beginning of the next junction approach is usually short.

If the junction does not have adequate capacity, additional lanes must be added. Whether it is worth having special left-turn and right-turn lanes cannot be safely determined on the basis of the static calculation.

A considerable drawback of the static study lies in the fact that it takes no account of the form of the junction or its position in the network; and yet these are of decisive importance in the irregular street networks of the older cities. Such a study reveals no difference between a simple and an 'expanded' junction, although there most certainly is a difference. If further lanes are added the intersection area becomes larger and the clearance period for cross traffic therefore becomes longer. And at a major junction it cannot be decided automatically whether vehicles using parallel lanes, e.g. traffic entering from opposite directions and proceeding straight ahead, should move at the same time or whether the green phases for the two movements should be staggered. If they are staggered this will affect capacity; but the static study method will not take this into account. Thus the method can be used to determine capacity only in simple cases.

An important operational point must also be borne in mind. The result of the static calculation is the same whether the conflicting lanes, *A* and *B*, are each carrying 800 cars/h or lane *A* is carrying 1,590 and lane *B* only 10. But in reality there is a big difference between these two cases, since if *B* is only carrying 10 cars/h, signals are entirely unnecessary—a 'Stop' sign would suffice. Lane *A* would then have almost the same capacity as a lane with no intersections at grade.

In a complex junction there are cuts adjacent to each other with quite different traffic loads. At one the flows are of about the same volume; at the other they are quite different. There is an interaction between the individual cuts which must have an effect on the capacity of the whole junction. A static calculation, which ignores the passage of time, does not clarify this interaction. At complex junctions nonsensical results can arise if the traffic loads at several cuts are totalled in an unsuitable way. If each of two conflicting lanes *A* and *B*, is carrying 800 cars/h, the cut would be carrying 1,600 cars/h. If two lanes are substituted for *A*, each of them carrying 400 cars/h, then the load at each of the cuts is 1,200 cars/h. But it is not correct to say that the loading of the whole junction is now 2,400 cars compared with 1,600 before, as is sometimes done. In difficult cases such a 'summing process' should not be used.

(d) The value method

In a simple grid network with two north–south and two east–west streets (Fig. 208) there are two possible routes for a driver proceeding from junction *P* to the diagonally-opposite junction *S*. If the traffic stream

Figure 208: The possible routes through a grid network P-Q-S and P-R-S.

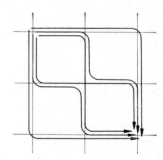

Figure 209: In a grid network with 3 East–West and 3 North–South roads a driver proceeding diagonally from one corner to another has a choice of 6 possible routes.

P–Q–S is shifted over to *P–R–S*, the loadings at all four junctions will be altered. The same applies to a diversion of traffic between *Q* and *R*.

If further streets are added, the number of junctions and the number of possible routes increases rapidly. For every three parallel streets in both directions there are nine junctions; and for traffic between diagonally-opposite corners there are already six possible routes (Fig. 209). With four parallel streets in both directions there are sixteen junctions and twenty-four possible routes, and so on.

However, most networks are irregular (Fig. 210). From the multiplicity of possible routings (Fig. 211) the most favourable solution, or a small number of favourable solutions, must be found quickly and at moderate expense. For this purpose a simple and labour-saving method is necessary which will permit an overall study of networks or sub-networks.

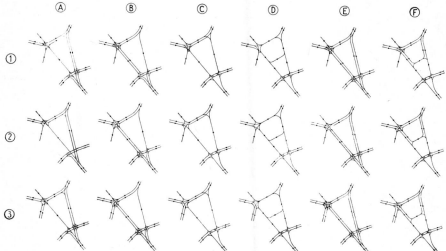

Figure 210: Possible traffic patterns in a triangular network. Only a selection of the possible alternatives is shown. The letters indicate different methods of operation of the triangle with one-way or two-way traffic. The figures indicate three alternatives for the street entering the north-west junction (top left in each diagram) from the south: one-way northbound, one-way southbound and two-way operation. These alternatives exist for each of the other six streets radiating from the complex. In all the examples chosen the road running north–west from the complex is assumed to be one-way away from the junction. A study using the value method showed that D1 and F1 were the most promising alternatives; and only these were tested using time/distance diagrams. This further test showed D1 was the best solution.

The summing process is obviously not suitable for this purpose. Even if a computer could make the selection and calculate flows simultaneously at all junctions in an urban network, it should not be used for this purpose at an early stage, because the direct mental link between planning and capacity check would be broken. Suitable machines cannot design! Also questions of townscape, road layout and economics must be taken into account from the beginning; and these cannot be fed into the computer programme. The structural designer must feel the interplay of forces in his structure; the traffic engineer must grasp the interplay of traffic streams.

For this task a method of approximation, the value method, can be evolved from probability calculation. In the case of the two lanes *A* and *B*

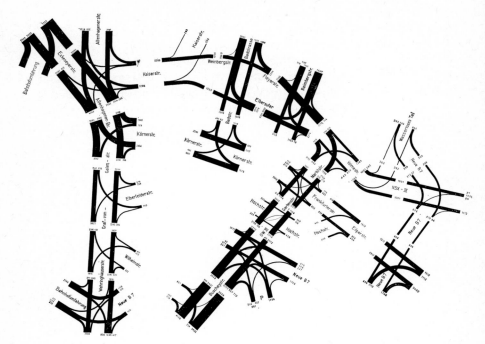

Figure 211: Future loadings of the 21 most important junctions in the main road network proposed for Hagen in Westfalen (180,000 inhabitants). All the junctions will have approximately the same capacity.

each carrying 800 cars/h, in the most unfavourable case all 800 cars from *A* will arrive at the conflict point simultaneously with one of the 800 cars from *B*. Thus the probability of mutual interference is $800 \times 800 = 640,000$. If however *A* carries 1,590 cars/h and *B* carries ten the probability of interference between the 1,600 cars involved is only 15,900. Traffic does not flow forty times better, but still it flows with less friction.

If *A* becomes a two-lane road, each cut will have the value $400 \times 800 = 320,000$. The value for the whole junction remains as high as ever at 640,000. The multiplication does not lead—as does the summing process—to contradictions. It is true it gives only the most unfavourable case. But with increasing traffic loads junctions are approaching this state.

If two parallel lanes are available, at least a proportion of the vehicles in both columns, if not (thanks to signals) all of them, will pass through the junction simultaneously. The value method does not reflect this improvement. Dr. Rapp dealt with this question for uncontrolled junctions in his dissertation, and arrived at precise but very difficult mathematical formulae which are valid only for a few particular cases and are not suitable for a quick overall check.

Experience has shown that the desired number of advantageous solutions can be quickly selected by using the value method. The effects of a

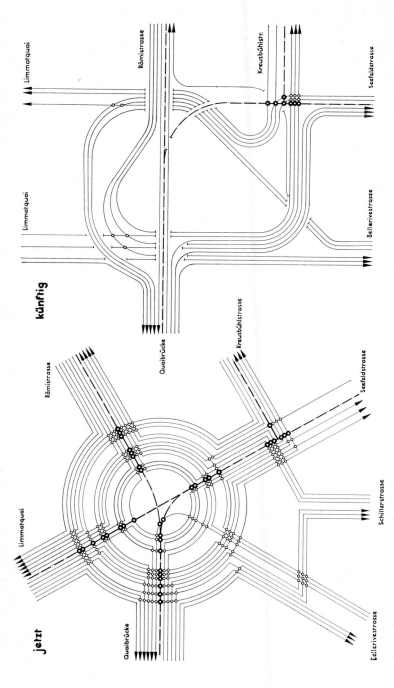

Figure 212: The traffic streams in the Bellevue complex in Zürich in its existing form (left) and in its planned form (right). Of the present 227 conflicts 18 would remain. In value method calculations the product of the conflicting traffic flows at each conflict point is calculated (cf. Figures 191 and 192).

diversion of a traffic stream can be quickly read off. The streams which are the biggest nuisance, or cause overloadings, can be seen at once, and also which cuts are the most sensitive.

The value method does not, however, give a reliable order of magnitude because it is based on the probability of mutual interference between traffic streams; and with signalization these will not occur. In the event of

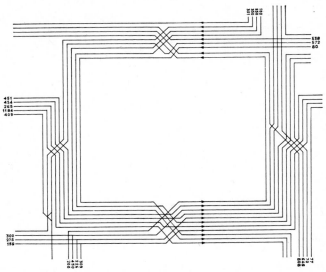

Figure 213: A difficult junction complex with 9 cuts and 67 weaves. All 76 conflicts must be brought into the value method calculation.

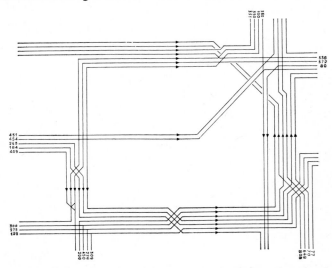

Figure 214: The same complex with 33 cuts and 29 weaves. The most favourable solution was to be selected by the value method from a large number of such sketches.

different solutions reaching approximately the same values, then each of them must be investigated in detail. However, only a few calculations will have to be carried out. Usually one solution very quickly emerges as the best.

The method is used also in connexion with trams. All tram movements through an area are drawn diagrammatically (Fig. 212, 213, 214); and the product of the movements through each conflict point is worked out. The products for all conflict points are then added together; and the solution with the lowest total is selected.

Products of car/car, car/pedal cycle and car/pedestrian conflicts can also be added together.

Weaving sections can be evaluated in a similar manner; for a weaving section is a conflict point, even if it is a somewhat elongated one. Sometimes merging points are evaluated, since they influence capacity. But this is pointless. Diverging points should never be taken into account since they cause no loss in capacity.

(e) Other methods

Other probability methods and methods based on field observations are sometimes used. The starting point for many of these methods is the Poisson distribution of vehicles. But the distribution of vehicles can only be a purely chance one if they are all moving completely unhampered by each other and can overtake at will at any point on the road. This condition is no longer fulfilled even when the traffic volume is moderate, and 'bunching' begins to take place behind the slower vehicles. At the higher volumes found in urban areas, and especially at the peak times which alone are important for traffic planning, a Poisson distribution is inconceivable. It would in any case be broken up by signals, which marshal vehicles into platoons and 'schedule' their movements.

All methods based on the calculation of probabilities—including the value method—have the disadvantage that changes in the geometrical layout of the junctions or in the shape of the network are not taken into account. There are for instance big differences between a right-angled and an oblique-angled crossroads, and between staggered crossroads with big and small distances between the two T-junctions. Observations of general validity are only available for simple crossroads, but not for the numerous other forms of junction and for their interactions.

(f) The time/distance method

A reliable capacity calculation must be based on the exact position of all traffic lanes and stop lines. Movements must be studied dynamically, i.e. taking into account the passage of time and the phase sequence. It is this requirement which has so far defeated the attempts to calculate capacity using an electronic computer. For these attempts to succeed all details of the road layout must be included in the programme and must be interchangeable. It was only in 1964 that a computer programme for the calculation of junction capacity was successfully developed: a programme which could select the best phase sequence and the correct length for the green, amber and red periods at each signal for every type of intersection (patents pending in many European countries, U.S.A., Australia, and New Zealand).

In exact capacity calculations schedules must be worked out for all important traffic streams. Traffic movement takes place in three dimensions: the two space dimensions of the roadway and the time dimension. On the drawing board only two dimensions can be shown at a time:

Length/width (plan of the junction)
Length/time (time/distance diagram, pictorial schedule)
Width/time (time/distance diagram for the cross-movement)

First of all the plan of the junction or of the sub-network must be drawn out to a suitable scale; 1:500 for roads. Then the time/distance diagrams must be drawn. The time axis is usually vertical, the distance axis (longitudinal or cross-street) usually horizontal. The various traffic streams are drawn in one after the other. At a simple crossroads with straight-ahead, left-turning and right-turning traffic from all four directions there are twelve traffic streams, and many more at a complex junction. The volume of each in p.c.u. is taken from the survey results. If the survey covered sixteen hours on a weekday, between 9 and 12 per cent should be taken as the peak hour flow. But it is far better to make a count at the peak hour, because the distribution of traffic is often different from the average for the day. If the count was made in a quiet month the result must be factored up to the level of the peak month. Data about seasonal variations in traffic flow are usually obtainable.

The calculation procedure may be illustrated by the following example —the actual values would be different in each case:

Flow in one direction in the peak hour, according to survey results (in p.c.u. 200 cars
Apply seasonal factor 1·25 250 cars
Convert to design year, factor of 2·0 500 cars
Of the peak hourly flow the flow during the peak minute, allowing for unavoidable fluctuations, will be 1/50 (not 1/60) 10 cars
If each car requires 2 sec, the lane will require during the peak minute 20 sec of green time.
The equivalent of 200 p.c.u. is 20 sec in this case.

If the same flow were to be carried on two lanes it would require 10 sec of green time; on three lanes 7 sec; on four lanes 5 sec. It is obvious that simple methods of calculation facilitate the work. All the traffic streams are converted in the same way into 'lane-seconds'.

In this example a peak minute was chosen as the basis of calculation.

If a different cycle time is to be used, all details should be calculated for that time. The most usual cycle length is 80 sec.

On the time-distance diagram the traffic streams are drawn as curved bands of varying width. The first driver sees the signal turn to green. On average his vehicle moves off 0·8 sec later. He accelerates more and more, so that the nose of his vehicle describes a curve on the time/distance diagram which gradually flattens out. The following vehicles follow at shorter and shorter time headways. Depending on their length the first pair of vehicles have a headway of 2·3 to 2·4 sec as they cross the stop line; the last pair in a long platoon have a headway of about 1·5 to 1·8 sec. The average headway of 2 sec corresponds to an hourly flow of 1,800 vehicles per hour, the lowest, 1·5 sec, to an hourly flow of 2,400 vph. The rear end of the last vehicle passing through the junction describes a fairly flat curve. The two curves—nose of the first vehicle and rear end of the last one—embrace the whole traffic stream. The second curve is more or less steep depending on whether the platoon is long or short. It must be constructed afresh for every traffic volume. Consequently the drawing of a suitable time/distance diagram is tiresome and time-consuming. But little is to be gained by an exact calculation since the phase length is only changed by fractions of a second if the end curve is somewhat flatter or steeper. And it will also hardly alter if instead of the two slightly curved lines representing the beginning and end of the vehicle platoon straight lines are drawn in. This will considerably reduce the amount of work. It will then only be a question of giving the straight lines the correct position and slope.

For this purpose we can rely on the results of an extensive series of observations at junctions on the level and on gradients of up to 5 per cent, with small and large volumes of turning traffic, and with no goods vehicles, motorcycles and pedal-cycles or with moderate amounts of these vehicles. The average speed of traffic moving through urban junctions was established, on the basis of numerous observations and films, at 5 m/sec (16 ft/sec), or slightly less with heavy pedal-cycle traffic.

Curves representing the actual movements of all vehicles, shown very precisely, were drawn alongside simplified 'artificial' curves composed of two-second wide bands for each vehicle at a slope corresponding to a speed of 5 m/sec, the lost time at the beginning of the green phase being ignored. In the most unfavourable case the differences between the two curves for particular directions and for entire cycles amounted to only 4 per cent. The simplified method is therefore permissible and useful.

Turning vehicles move more slowly. They are represented on the time/distance diagram by tangents to the two curves drawn as far as the conflict point, showing a longer path as basis. With a right-angle the speed of turning traffic is thus reduced from 5 m/sec to 3·9 m/sec. This too is near enough to the true situation.

The traffic streams are now drawn in phase sequence, beginning usually with the main stream in the longitudinal direction. Because of lost time and clearance periods each green phase should normally last at least 10 sec (6 sec in extreme cases). And there must be a 3-sec gap between conflicting traffic streams at the point where they intersect. A gap of 2 sec is enough between streams which follow one behind the other in the same direction. Streams from different directions should only be allowed to enter the same roadway simultaneously if separate lanes are available for them beyond the junction. Otherwise a dangerous jostling will result.

When all conflicting traffic streams have been pushed through the junction the signal cycle is complete. It is a question of so choosing the phase sequence that the shortest possible cycle time results; that the streams dovetail nicely into one another (Fig. 215). At difficult junctions the capacity can vary by more than 20 per cent according to the phase sequence selected. The computer programme mentioned above chooses the best sequence at once.

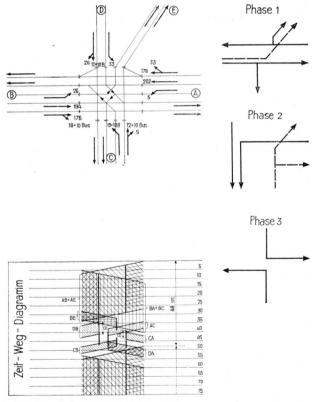

Figure 215: Capacity calculation for a simple crossroads. The traffic flows entering in 144 seconds could be handled in 48 seconds. Thus the junction could handle three times the present flows. Calculations are usually carried out only for cycle lengths between 60 and 100 seconds. Bottom: the time/distance diagram.

Capacity must now be unequivocally determined. The traffic volume arriving at the junction during the selected time period must be able to clear the junction in the same or less time. If the cycle time is the same duration the junction is loaded to capacity. If on the other hand the selected time was 80 sec and the requisite cycle time is only 40 sec, then the

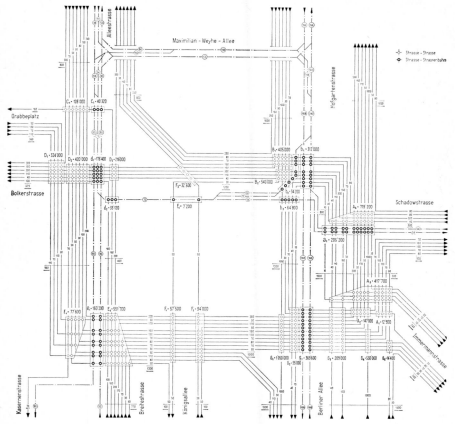

Figure 216: Value method calculation for the Jan-Wellem-Platz in Düsseldorf. Value method calculations should always precede any complicated or difficult calculations using the time/distance method. For each movement the number of vehicles per hour is given. (The thick rings indicate cuts involving tram tracks.)

junction could handle 200 per cent of demand. And if the requisite cycle time is 60 sec then it could handle 133 per cent of demand. In a balanced network all junctions have capacity reserves of similar size.

Time/distance diagrams for the two directions of a crossroads are drawn alongside each other. Turning movements appear on both—as far as the conflict point on one, and beyond it on the other. In most cases the two diagrams can be placed one above the other. At difficult junctions it may be necessary to select suitable axes, which may be curved in plan, e.g.

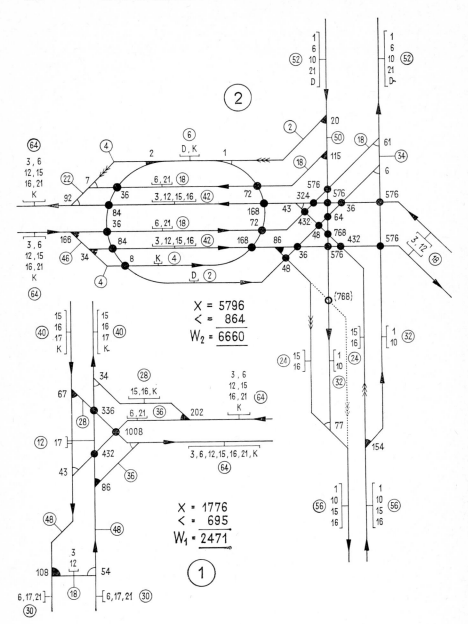

Figure 217: The value method calculation for the tram track layout at the Jan-Wellem-Platz. The number of tram movements per hour is shown by the figures in rings. At each conflict point the product of the conflicting movements is written in. The route numbers are also shown.

(2) (top and right) = western side

(1) (bottom left) = eastern part.

following an especially important turning movement (Fig. 218). The green phase lengths for each signal can be read off directly from the diagrams.

Pedestrian streams are also drawn onto the time-distance diagrams. Pedestrians can cross the roadway so long as no conflicting traffic stream is flowing. It must be noted here that the minimum green phase for pedestrians is 5 sec, and that a pedestrian who starts crossing right at the end of the pedestrian green phase must be given sufficient 'running out' time to reach the next island safely at a speed of 1·3 m/sec (4 ft/sec) or better 1 m/sec.

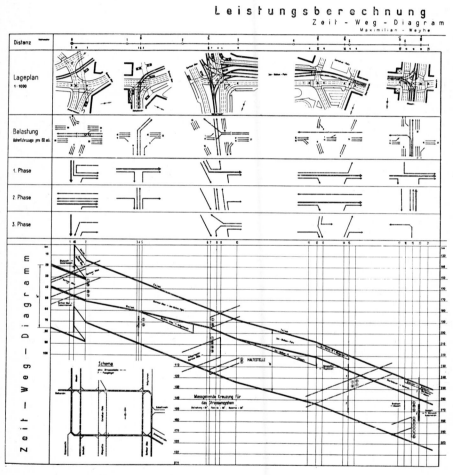

Figure 218: Part of the time/distance study for the Jan-Wellem-Platz. The distance axis of the diagram is a large rectangle and includes the Alleestrasse to the west and the Berliner Allee to the south (as shown in the diagram bottom left). This capacity calculation showed that the southbound link from the Hofgartenstrasse to the Berliner Allee must be diverted via a one-way underpass.

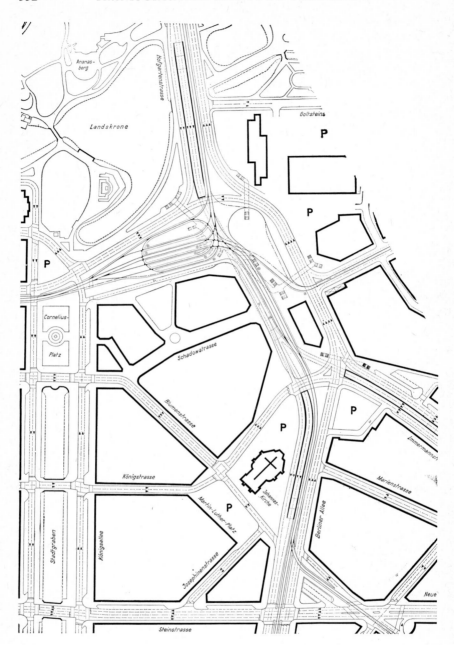

Figure 219: Scale drawing of the design for the Jan-Wellem-Platz with terminal loops and interchange for the local and long-distance trams. The grade separation for the north-to-south movement was originally proposed as an underpass, but was carried out in 1961 as a flyover.

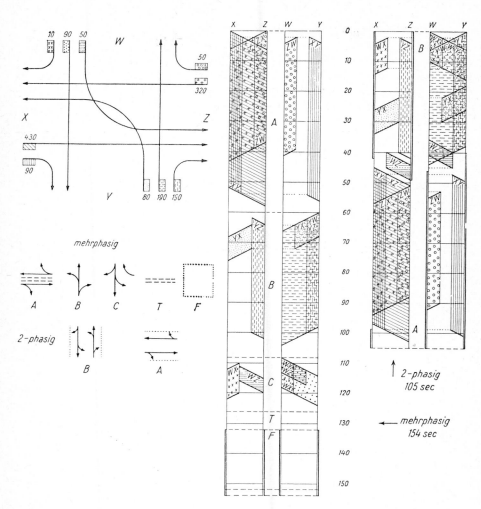

Figure 220: Two different signal programmes for the same crossroads. With an all-red phase for pedestrians, plus three phases for motor traffic and one for trams, a 154-second cycle was needed. The capacity of the junction can be increased by 46 per cent without reconstruction if turning movements are permitted in the same phase as pedestrian movements. On this basis and with two main phases the same traffic volume can be handled in a 105-second cycle. The pedestrian phases are indicated by thick vertical lines on the time/distance diagram. With the old signal programme it was observed that, because of the excessive cycle length, 85 per cent of pedestrians crossed the street outside the pedestrian phase. Thus the old system was no safer in any real sense.

There are often differences of opinion as to whether turning movements should be allowed at the same time as pedestrian movements or not. If both are allowed to share a phase the capacity is greater; if they are segregated safety is increased. If the cycle time and the waiting time have to be increased too much in the interest of safety, many pedestrians will ignore the signals or will cross the streets some distance from the signals. This creates new hazards. Traffic congestion and the high cost of reconstruction generally means that one is compelled to give capacity priority over safety. Turning vehicles must yield right of way to pedestrians crossing parallel with the straight-ahead movement in any phase (Fig. 220).

The most important field of application of the time/distance method is in the irregular sub-networks and complex junctions of the central area. In planning only the peak loads are usually studied, since the road layouts must be capable of coping with the biggest traffic volumes which occur regularly. Different signal programmes can be introduced for other times of day if required. All programmes should be checked from time to time and adapted to changes in the traffic pattern.

(g) Green wave signal systems

Capacity calculations must be extended from individual junctions to the whole main road network (Fig. 221). With simple networks—only one main road or a grid—this can be done by calculating junctions individually and then linking them together with a green wave signal system. All junctions in a network must operate with the same cycle time. Between junctions traffic on urban streets in the core area flows at 7 to 12·5 m/sec or 25–45 km/h (16–28 mph). All junctions in a coherent network are controlled from a single point. The signal programme can be changed simultaneously at all junctions. But in exceptional circumstances an individual or local signal control should be possible.

With a 'green wave' system vehicles which maintain a certain speed, which can be indicated to drivers, arrive at each successive crossroads during the green phase. The green wave should work in both directions; but where junction spacing is not favourable it has to work in the direction of tidal flow—inbound to the city in the morning, outbound in the evening. It not only serves to speed up trips but also saves reservoir space and roadway areas (Fig. 222).

Linked signal systems are sometimes divided into three types: simultaneous, alternate and progressive. With a simultaneous system all the signals along a street are green at the same time. With a cycle time of 80 sec and a junction spacing of 400 m (1,300 ft) drivers would have to drive at 5 m/sec (12 mph). With the alternate system one signal is green while the next is red and vice versa. The progression speed would then be 10 m/sec (23 mph) (Fig. 223). The progressive system is suitable on streets with varying spacing of junctions.

This division into types is only of theoretical significance, since on all

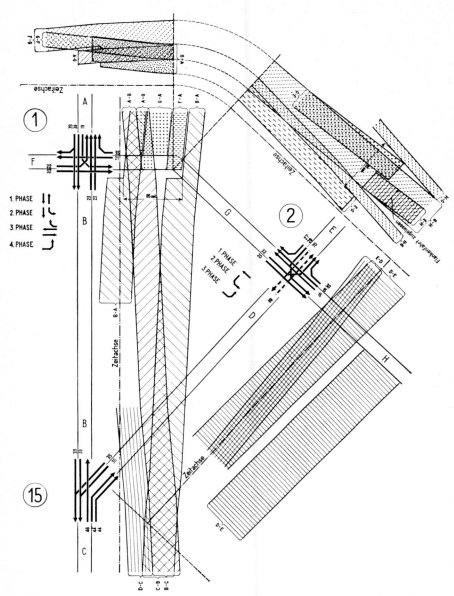

Figure 221: Time/distance study for a triangle of two-way streets. After 'green waves' had been provided for movements (1) to (15) and (1) to (2)—both of which form parts of green wave routes through a series of junctions—the movement (2) to (15) had to be fitted into the cycle. A green wave could be provided at 3, 28 or 72 km/h; but in practice only 28 km/h ($17\frac{1}{2}$ mph) can be considered.

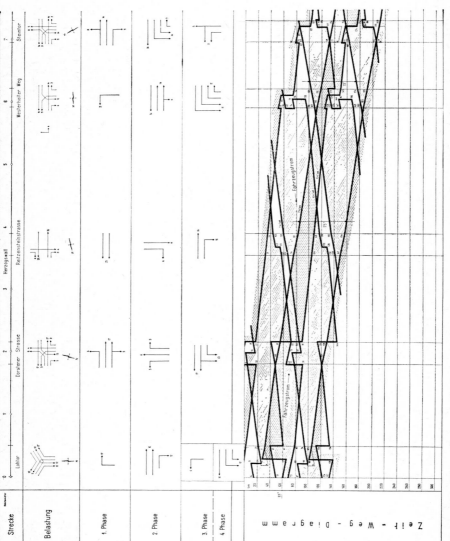

Figure 222: Time/distance diagram of green wave system for the 'Wälle' in Recklinghausen. The relevant section of this street forms the horizontal axis (see top of diagram). The progression speed should be roughly the same on all sections despite the unequal spacing of the junctions. Turning movements at certain junctions are heavy.

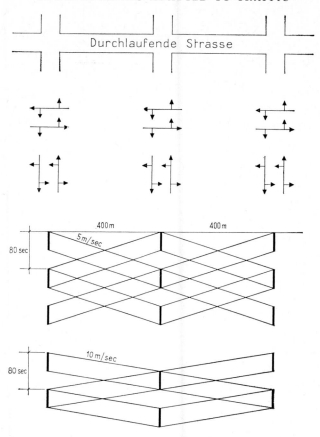

Figure 223: Green waves with different types of linked signal control. With the simultaneous system (*above*) the progression speed is only half that provided, with the same cycle length, with the alternate system (*below*).

irregular networks the phasing must in any case be calculated by means of the time/distance method, and not only for a single axis but for all main roads.

If the traffic in a grid street network is of equal volume in the north–south and east–west directions and flows at 8 m/sec = 28·8 km/h (18 mph), then the junction spacing with a cycle length of 80 sec may be calculated as $\frac{1}{2}$ × 8 m/sec × 80 sec = 320 m (1,070 ft). If the speed drops at peak times, the phases must be lengthened in order to maintain the green wave. Thus for example a speed of 5 m/sec and a cycle time of 130 sec gives about the same spacing: 325 m. In outer areas of cities most vehicles move at 12·5 m/sec = 45 km/h (28 mph). In these areas the junction spacing should therefore be $\frac{1}{2}$ × 12·5 × 80 = 500 m (1,660 ft) or a multiple thereof. All important junctions should be at these fixed spacings, increasing steadily from 300 m in the central area to 550 m in

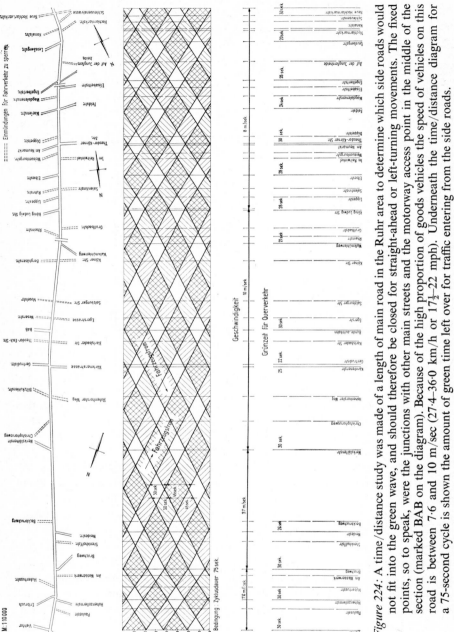

Figure 224: A time/distance study was made of a length of main road in the Ruhr area to determine which side roads would not fit into the green wave, and should therefore be closed for straight-ahead or left-turning movements. The fixed points, so to speak, were the junctions with other main streets and the motorway access point in the middle of the section (marked **BAB** on the diagram). Because of the high proportion of goods vehicles the speed of vehicles on this road is between 7·6 and 10 m/sec (27·4–36·0 km/h or 17½–22 mph). Underneath the time/distance diagram for a 75-second cycle is shown the amount of green time left over for traffic entering from the side roads.

the outskirts. Every crossroads which does not correspond with these conditions has a lower capacity. In the middle of stretches intersections should not be permitted at all if a big loss of capacity on the main street is to be avoided. Forks and T-junctions are an exception since these can be fitted in at any point since they conflict with main street traffic in only one direction. The worst junction spacing in the inner area is 150 m (500 ft) (Fig. 224). Crossroads can of course be left out so that double or multiple spacing results.

With the advent of green wave systems a new rule of network planning, and therefore of town building, has arisen: one which should be observed in every new settlement or extension of existing settlements. For traffic engineering and practical reasons no change is to be expected in the basic values of speed and cycle length. Junctions should not any longer be located anywhere the planner fancies. Only if this new rule is followed can a town plan be called 'adapted to traffic'.

6. Parking areas

(a) Need

Parking areas are the terminal stations of road traffic. Their location can have a marked effect on the movement of traffic streams in the overloaded sections. Since more and more on-street parking spaces must be removed in order to gain additional areas for moving traffic this question must be examined with precision.

The remaining parking spaces must be husbanded. The basic principle that short-period parkers (customers) should have priority over long-period parkers (workers) is generally recognized. Anyone who parks his car for eight hours and more on a city street is taking more than his share of scarce space. He could put up with a longer walk to and from a parking space.

Whether parking meters are used to obtain better utilization of space, or whether a so-called 'blue zone' (disc system) is introduced is immaterial for planning. Parking meters permit a more reliable supervision and grading according to urgency of parking need. They bring in revenue to the city which are best applied to the provision of additional parking places. But they are not ornamental and they take up footway space. They are by far the best solution as regards traffic control.

There are several ways of estimating demand for parking space. As a first approximation it can be estimated by applying the rule of thumb that the peak accumulation of parked cars in the central area of a town will amount to 12 per cent of the cars domiciled in the town, and sometimes up to 18 per cent in special cases and in small towns; and that the peak accumulation at the main railway station will amount to 1·2 to 1·5 per cent of the same total. Where a town has several large railway stations this last percentage should be apportioned between them. Although the central area is defined differently in different towns, there is remarkably little variation in these percentages.

More precise calculations can be made on the basis of the town's population or of traffic counts. In a town with 250 cars per 1,000 inhabitants the demand will be as follows:

Residential areas:

Single-family houses	1 or 2	} parking spaces per dwelling
Residential blocks	0·7–1	

Workplaces

Banks, insurance companies	0·5–1 car spaces per employee
Public authorities, adminis- trations	0·4–1 car spaces per employee
Business offices	0·3–0·8 car spaces per employee
Shops	0·3–0·7 car spaces per employee
Industry	0·2–0·6 car spaces per employee

Other land uses:

Big stores, shops	1–3 m^2 of parking space/m^2 of sales floor space
Hotels, boarding houses	0·3–1 parking spaces per bed
Restaurants, cafes, bars	0·2–0·3 parking spaces per seat
Assembly rooms	0·15–0·4 parking spaces per seat
Churches	0·1–0·2 parking spaces per seat
Sports stadia	0·1–0·15 parking spaces per seat
Hospitals	0·2–0·4 parking spaces per bed
Schools	1–2 parking spaces per classroom
Colleges	as for assembly rooms

The demand is not equally great in all districts and all professions and trades. When many employees live within walking distance or are well served by public transport it is smaller. Not all employed persons are long-period parkers. Some of them use their cars several times a day. The number of cars per 1,000 inhabitants is not the same in all parts of the town. It is greatest in outlying districts without public transport, where well-to-do people live. An accurate breakdown of vehicle registrations between different parts of a town is usually not obtainable.

In mixed residential and business areas parking demands overlap. By day the employees require parking space, while at night only the inhabitants require it. It is difficult to evaluate all influences reliably. For this reason parking space demand should only be determined by this method in the case of new developments or for comparison. In all other cases it is better to use values based on traffic surveys (Fig. 225).

A survey of trip destinations will show how many trips begin and end in a certain area. Usually the peak parking accumulation occurs just before the beginning of the peak hour for moving traffic. More vehicles can be parked on a car park within an hour than there are parking stalls, because

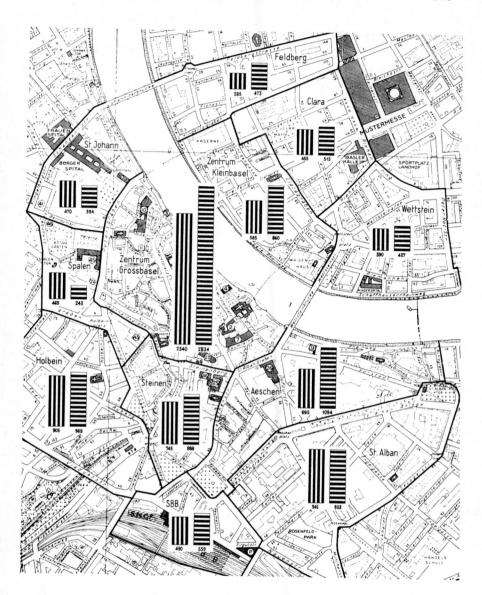

Figure 225: In Basle the future parking needs were determined on the basis of
traffic counts and figures for population and employment. In most areas the
survey gave lower figures because the same parking space is used by workers
by day and by residents by night. But in the West the figures are considerably
higher because drivers who can find no parking space in the city centre go to
these fringe areas to park. The vertically-striped bars represent the observed
numbers; the horizontally-striped bars represent the calculated demand.

some stalls are used successively by several cars. Observations made in the business cores of many cities in Holland, West Germany, Switzerland and Austria have shown that the average parking duration on public car parks in the late afternoon, when the peak accumulation occurs, is 40 to 45 min. Thus every parking stall can be used 1·4 times within the hour; and for every 100 cars with trip origins or destinations within the area concerned during this hour 70 parking stalls will be sufficient. The average parking duration during this critical hour is not likely to alter within the planning period, i.e. within the next twenty-five years.

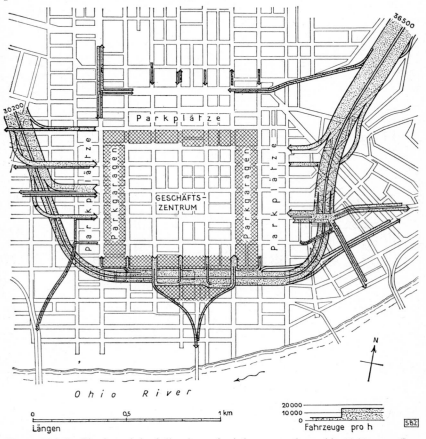

Figure 226: In Cincinnati the following principles were adopted in 1948 regarding the provision of parking space:
1. Parking spaces should be provided outside the Central Business District, but immediately adjacent to it.
2. Within the C.B.D. the existing parking spaces should be gradually removed and the building of new garages prevented.
3. An inner ring of garages and meter parking, to serve short-period parkers, should be provided at the edge of the C.B.D.
4. Further out there should be a ring of parking lots on cheap ground, permitting cheap rates for long-period parkers.

(b) Meeting the need

It was shown in detail above that traffic volumes in the city centre can be influenced by the number of parking stalls. It follows therefore that urban transportation policy must promote the provision of new parking facilities or in congested parts of the city prevent such provision. It may even be necessary to remove existing parking space (Fig. 226).

On no account must the parking problem be considered in isolation

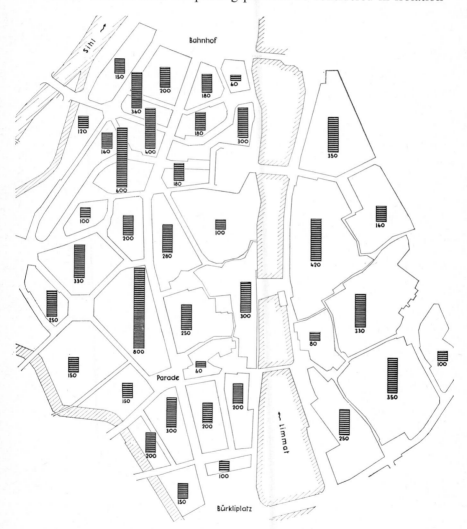

Figure 227: Future parking demand in the central area of Zürich. The number of spaces required for each street block is shown. Within a few years 9,000 spaces will be required. But there would have to be a matching increase in street capacity.

M

from the traffic problem as a whole. The effects of increasing or decreasing the amount of parking space on private and public transport as a whole, and beyond that on the economic health of the city, must be carefully studied before decisions are taken. The policy adopted can retard or promote the economic progress of the city centre. The new groups of shops in the outer areas, with their big parking areas, attract not only traffic but also customers away from the older parts of the city. The authorities must consider to what extent such a diversion of trade is desirable.

In new settlements as in old ones the city administration must make up its mind on this question. It is possible for them to make the side streets and residential streets very wide, or alternatively provide parking areas, so that frontagers can park their cars permanently on public land. The garages will then remain empty. Or the city may confine itself to providing the minimum road widths which are absolutely necessary for moving traffic and for servicing buildings. Provision of parking facilities (land and pavings) will then be the responsibility of frontagers.

Traffic planners can only lay down the amount of parking space to be provided on public land. They have no power to compel landowners to surrender their land for use as parking space. Compulsory purchase can only be used in many countries to acquire land needed for moving traffic. Landowners can also not be compelled to use their land for parking lots or garages.

The planning engineer must therefore confine himself to dividing up the future demand as accurately as possible (Fig. 227), and indicating the approximate position of the parking facility within a certain area. All further steps are the responsibility of the authorities, especially the purchase or exchange of suitable sites.

(c) Car parks

Parking needs can be met by either:
> Parking lanes on streets
> Off-street car parks
> Parking garages

Continuous parking lanes are not desirable on main streets, since moving traffic can be disturbed and endangered by parking and unparking manoeuvres along the whole length of the parking lane. Segregated frontage roadways are better from the traffic engineering point of view. But they are uneconomic and are usually under-utilized. Off-street car parks are more suitable.

Parking lanes for parking parallel to the kerb are 2·50 m (8 ft) wide, or 2·00 m (6 ft 6 in) in cramped conditions. It is advisable to demarcate them either by a distinctive road surface, a special colour or a continuous, sunken kerb. A length of 7 m (23 ft) should be allowed for each car, so that drivers can park and unpark easily. In Central Europe parking meters

are also spaced this distance apart where they are needed, in the U.K.
meter bays are normally 20 ft long.

On wider parking lanes or on car parks cars can be parked at a right-
angle or an oblique angle to the roadway or parking aisle (Figs. 228, 229).
The most popular angle is 45°. The stalls are usually 5·50 m (18 ft) long
and 2·30 m (7 ft 6 in) wide. In the U.K. the length is 16 ft. Different
dimensions for big and small cars are very seldom used. The individual
stalls are marked out on the ground.

Parking aisles with one-way traffic in the car park and a parking angle
of 45° are usually 4·5 m (14 ft 6 in) wide, and 6 m (20 ft) wide with
parking at 90°. With two-way traffic a width of at least 5·5 m (18 ft) is
necessary.

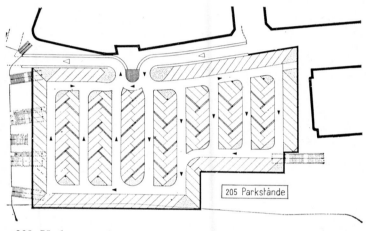

Figure 228: Underground garage underneath a square. Entry and exit are at the
same point for ease of comprehension. With a parking angle of 45°, 205 cars
can be parked.

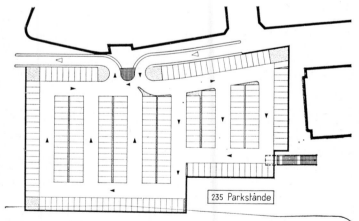

Figure 229: With parking at 90° the same garage would hold 235 cars.

For purposes of a first approximation, the area of a parking stall including access aisle can be calculated as:

> Car stall   25 sq m
> Bus stall   140 sq m

With a good layout somewhat smaller areas are sufficient for cars down to 18 sq m.

(d) Parking garages

In central business districts the demand for parking space is so great that it cannot be met on one level. High land values make multi-level parking facilities essential. These require a cubic space of 65 cu m (1,430 cu ft) for every car stall. Building costs per stall (exclusive of land cost) average 7,000 to 9,000 DM (£600 to £750) for above-ground structures, and much more for underground garages. The latter can under certain circumstances serve as air raid shelters, which is not generally true of facilities for moving traffic (underground tramways and roads). But the requirements of traffic and air raid protection are so different that it is best to divide the functions. Traffic facilities would then only serve as accesses to shelters.

There are many possible types of parking garage, some with lifts, some with ramps. Lifts are only to be recommended on cramped sites, because there is a danger in big facilities of queues forming at the entrances and exits where demand is heavy. A ramp can carry 12 to 15 entering or exiting cars in a minute. Details of layout will not be considered here.

The location and size of car parks and parking garages must be carefully chosen. They must be correctly located in relation to several networks: the street network, the network of pedestrian links and the public transport network (Figs. 230, 231). It is not good enough just to use any site of the right size which happens to be offered.

Local street congestion must be avoided. If at the beginning or end of the working day 75 per cent of the cars want to enter or leave a parking garage within 20 min, the resulting traffic volume in one direction will be at an hourly rate of $3 \times 100 \times 75$ per cent $= 225$ cars/h for every 100 cars parked in the garage. In the city centre, where the average parking duration is 40 to 45 min, there will be 130 to 150 in and out movements in the hour for every 100 stalls. Car parks and garages in urban areas should therefore as a rule not have more than 600 stalls, since otherwise the full capacity of a traffic lane will be exceeded. And the individual parking facilities should be far enough apart that the traffic streams starting from them can distribute themselves. With garages for more than 1,000 employees' cars special care must be taken to ensure a balance between the capacity to accept cars and the capacity of the access streets.

Access to a parking garage should be by a right turn out of the roadway. The exit should if possible lead out into a side street so that no additional disturbance and danger arises on the main street. At the first main road junction the dense stream of vehicles leaving the garage will already branch out in different directions.

Parking facilities are interchange points at which car occupants transform themselves into pedestrians or public transport passengers. It is, therefore, not enough to locate them favourably solely in relation to the main

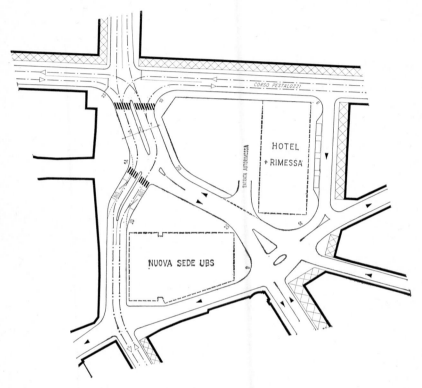

Figure 230: A parking garage is to be erected at the entry to Lugano from the Gotthard direction. It will be prominently located at a main crossroads so that visitors will recognize it at once. But the entry is deliberately located in a side street so that traffic on the main street will not be disrupted. The cross street forks into two streets, one of them reserved for buses and the other used primarily by private vehicles. In order to emphasize this forking the cross street, which formerly ran straight across, has been bent.

streets. Thought must also be given to how people are to proceed after parking their cars. Pedestrians should be given short and if possible straight and comprehensible routes. Interchange between parked car and tram or bus must equally be made as comfortable as possible for 'park-and-ride' customers in big cities. There should be no main roadways between car park and bus or tram stop.

A parking garage is a magnet for many people and improves the

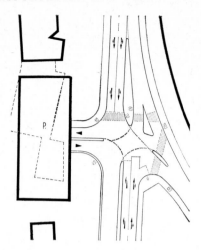

Figure 231: A garage is deliberately located in such a way that the entry and exit form the fourth arm of a crossroads.

business situation of its surroundings. Consideration must therefore be given, when locating a garage, to the town-planning consequences.

As regards the correct layout of filling stations, reference may be made to the carefully prepared 'Standards for the layout of filling stations' published by the German Road Research Society.

7. Interchange points

(a) Main-line stations and their environs

Railway stations and airports are especially important interchange points. They must provide sufficient space for the parking of public transport vehicles, taxis, private cars, and heavy and light goods vehicles (luggage and express freight). The distance covered by people and goods should be short. Entering and exiting traffic must not hinder each other.

There is no 'standard' layout for vehicular access areas at railway stations and airports. Local requirements and traffic conditions are too different. The interchange area and the parking area—the latter is often right in front of the building—should not be located on a main traffic route. But in many cities heavily-loaded roadways pass directly in front of the station building—e.g. in Berne, Basle (S.B.B. and Badisch stations), Constance, Munich, Wiesbaden, Luxemburg, Utrecht, Essen, Dortmund and Leipzig (Fig. 232). On the other hand it is not a good idea to have the station access in the form of a cul-de-sac, as is the case in Linz (Austria), Zug (Switzerland), Wanne-Eickel, Wittenberg and Potsdam (Fig. 233).

Unfortunately in the boom period of railway building the main streets of cities were often laid out directly in line with the ticket halls, e.g. the Bahnhofstrasse in Zürich and that in Biel, the Königstrasse in Stuttgart,

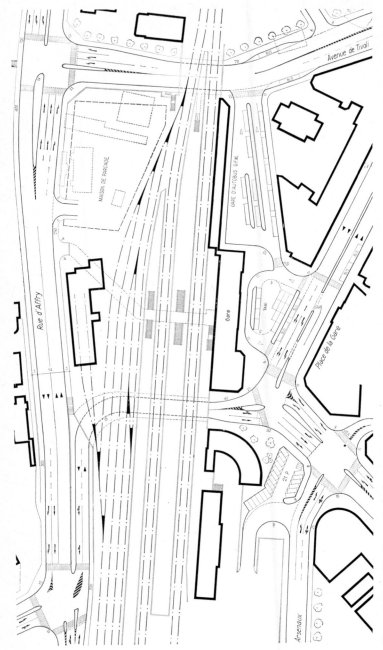

Figure 232: In Freiburg, Switzerland, the Place de la Gare is to be relieved by a new link running eastwards. Cars visiting the railway station will be served by a parking garage on the opposite side of the tracks from the ticket hall and station forecourt. The latter will then be large enough to handle taxi traffic and the many long-distance bus lines which call at the station without the need to demolish any buildings.

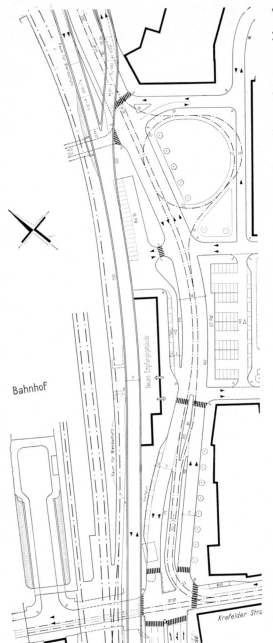

Bahnhof

Figure 233: The ticket hall at Neuss station is to be moved from the cul-de-sac between the tracks to the town side of the tracks. Here there is very little space available. At a later stage a two-lane flyover is to be provided for the heavy traffic parallel to the railway. The tram stop is to the south of the station entrance, a small taxi setting down and loading point to the north of it, and a car park for 57 cars opposite the entrance on the other side of the street. The tram tracks are separated sufficiently to provide a median island for pedestrians using the crossing outside the station entrance. Thus the northbound tram track enters the northbound roadway before the latter curves to the left, so that this danger point can be recognized in good time, and a 'hidden funnel' is avoided.

the Kaiserring in Mannheim and the Kaiserstrasse in Frankfurt (Figs. 234, 235). As a result difficult junctions have arisen—usually T-junctions lacking in capacity—which are now congested. This unfortunate state of affairs can hardly be altered. Thus expensive relief measures cannot be avoided. These must often be two-level solutions, as in Rotterdam (Fig. 236), Brussels Nord and Midi, and Duisburg. In Düsseldorf the through traffic has been deliberately diverted to other streets. In Hagen/Westfalen the through traffic has been diverted to a parallel street a block away from the station.

Sufficient space must be provided for vehicular access. The demands are large and getting larger. Even really big areas such as those in Strasburg and Bremen are no longer big enough. The areas outside the

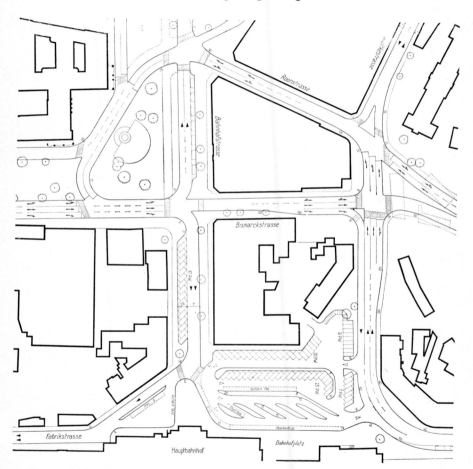

Figure 234: In Trier the Bahnhofstrasse is directly in line with the centre of the ticket hall. Traffic through the station forecourt will in future be one-way. Many local and long-distance bus lines terminate here. All through traffic will be diverted to the Bismerckstrasse.

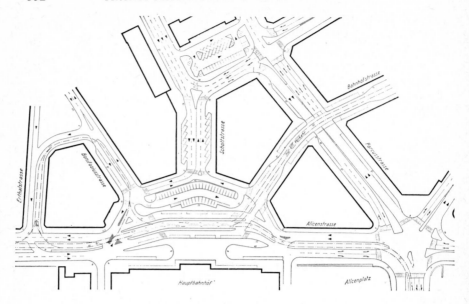

Figure 235: In Mainz several streets radiate star-fashion from the entrance to the railway station. The through street is to be bent away from the station entrance to provide sufficient space for pedestrians. On either side of the pedestrian peninsula will be setting down bays for luggage and taxis. The tram stops are placed in the centre of the space outside the station; and what is left over is used as a car park. The Bahnhofstrasse becomes a 'tram street' open only to public transport and pedestrians. In this way its intersection with the Parcusstrasse, which reduced capacity because of its proximity to other junctions, ceases to be important.

long-distance stations in Vienna, Dresden, Berlin, Hamburg, Copenhagen, Stockholm, Paris, London, Madrid and New York are quite inadequate. But in general these areas cannot be enlarged. The only way out is to use a second level, as in Berne, or to create a second access area on the 'wrong' side of the station, free of through traffic, as has been done in Bochum and Cologne (Fig. 237).

The access areas must be designed in relation to the interior layout of the ticket hall and the way the ancillary functions are arranged. They therefore look different in a long-distance station in comparison with sub-urban stations. They can seldom be laid out symmetrically. Ideally the setting down points of the various means of transport bringing passengers to the station should be laid out fanwise around the main entrance; this will give the shortest distance to the entrance for people and goods and is the most comprehensible layout. As a rule one side of the area is used for public transport and the other for private transport. Sometimes one side is reserved for passenger traffic and the other for goods traffic. The two sides are separated by a pedestrian peninsula, which should point in the direction of the main route to the city centre or alternatively towards the stopping place for local buses or trams.

The ticket hall must also be carefully planned from the traffic engineering point of view. The most important principle is to have short, comprehensible routes with few conflict points. The classical station entrance hall of imposing dimensions is called by the French 'la halle des pas perdus' (hall of lost steps). There should be not a yard longer distance than is

Figure 236: A model of the new railway station forecourt in Rotterdam, which is very successful from both traffic engineering and architectural points of view. The traffic on the main street is taken through an underpass in one direction, so that trams, buses and cars turning into and out of the forecourt cross only minor traffic streams. On either side of the ticket hall are a large car park and a bus station for long-distance buses. (Cf. Figure 166).

strictly necessary, and not a step more to be climbed. Entrance halls should therefore be but not deep. The ticket office, baggage registration and express parcels office should be on the right, the waiting rooms and ancillary rooms on the left. In conformity with this internal layout the setting down point for parcels should be at the right-hand end of the access area, the stopping places for trams or buses in the centre or also to the right. The left-hand side will be primarily for private traffic. Further details must be developed according to the particular local situation (Figs. 238, 239).

Many railway goods stations still have dimensions dating from the days of the horse-cart. Modern goods vehicles need more room because they usually have to back up to the railway wagons or goods platforms rather

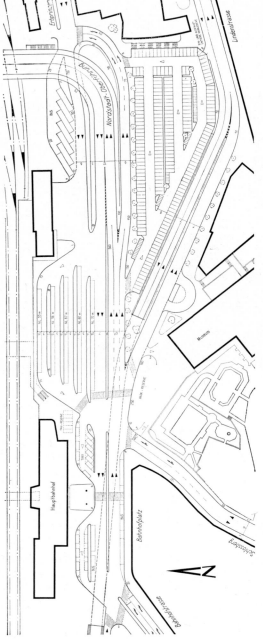

Figure 237: At Pforzheim it is proposed to provide parking space for cars and motorcycles on the far side of the street from the station; and to build a two-lane two-way underpass for traffic parallel to the railway to free the area outside the station. Apart from westbound traffic using the underpass the Lindenstrasse will be one-way, paired with the Erbprinzenstrasse. The land falls away towards the east (which favours the underpass), and advantage is taken of this to provide parking on two levels. Access to the upper level is from the surface street near the station entrance; access to the lower level is from the Lindenstrasse. There are separate setting down points for cars and taxis either side of the station entrance. East of these is a terminal for long-distance buses. Access to this from the west is via a loop passing under the bridge over the railway (the Nordstadt-Überführung), either direct or via a bus parking lot for 7 buses.

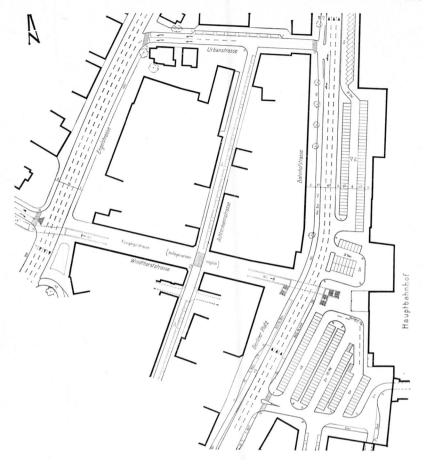

Figure 238: Proposed treatment outside the station in Münster in Westfalen. The narrow street opposite the station entrance would become a pedestrian street (with frontage traffic perhaps permitted), thus eliminating the T-junction outside the entrance. The Bahnhofstrasse and the Engelstrasse become a one-way couplet (to simplify the problem at neighbouring junctions); but a southbound bus lane is provided in the Bahnhofstrasse so that buses in both directions can pass directly in front of the station. In traffic engineering terms this bus lane is in the centre of the one-way couplet.

than drawing up alongside them. Since however, the vehicular access is part of the internal layout of goods stations they are dealt with in the author's book *Railway passenger and goods stations.*

(b) Vehicular access areas at airports

Vehicular access areas at airports should be laid out in basically the same way as access areas at long-distance railway stations. The main streets should be at a sufficient distance and should not be in line with the

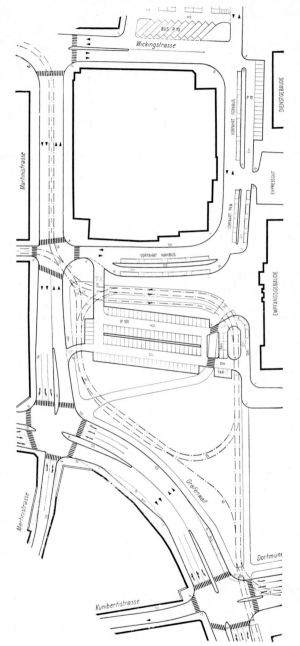

Figure 239: An unusual treatment outside the station in Recklinghausen, carried out in 1960/62. The stopping places for trams and local buses are at right-angles to the ticket hall. The stopping place for long-distance buses is to one side, and further to the right, on the other side of the Wickingstrasse, is a parking place for cars and 10 buses. The landscaped area alongside the Grafenwall is left largely intact, and pedestrians are led diagonally across it from the station entrance to the Martinistrasse, which leads to the city centre.

terminal building. But the mistakes made with the older railway stations are being frequently repeated, both outside and inside the buildings, because too much value is placed on grandiose halls.

In the last few years arriving and departing passengers have been placed on two separate levels, one above the other, at certain airports, e.g. Zürich, Frankfurt, Rome and Istanbul. This means that passengers and their luggage must gain height unnecessarily, and strangers find it hard to orientate themselves. This is nonsensical since at airports there is sufficient room available to accommodate arrivals and departures alongside each other at the same level.

In view of the rapid increase in air traffic, large parking areas must be provided in good time for coaches, cars and goods vehicles in the immediate proximity of the terminal buildings. They should not be separated from the buildings by a main road—as at Zürich airport.

(c) Other interchange points

Passenger interchange takes place at every transfer point on urban public transport networks. Passengers change between lines or between trams and feeder bus services. Here again the requirement for short distances free of conflict points applies. Ideally the transfer passenger should not have to cross over any roadway (Fig. 240). This can be achieved by placing all the stopping places on a large central island between the roadways (Figs. 241, 242). Well-known examples of such treatment are to be found in Vienna at the Südtirolerplatz (interchange between suburban railway, tram and long-distance coaches) and at the Ringturmkreuzung and the Hietzinger Brücke. At the terminals of tram routes tram loops and bus lanes can be dovetailed with each other to one side of the main road so as not to interrupt the alignment of the latter.

Truck terminals for the transfer of goods from long-distance trucks to smaller units need extensive parking areas. The basis for the layout of such terminals should be the traffic lanes. All such terminals have a great similarity to vehicular access areas at railway stations. They must serve various means of transport, are heavily loaded and require much space (Fig. 243).

It must be emphasized that there are no standard solutions in the whole wide field of urban transport planning, and there never can be any, because in each task different conditions must be met with regard to traffic, economy, operation, construction and appearance. Nearly always every possible solution has big advantages and certain drawbacks. The various pros and cons must be carefully weighed against one another. It would be wrong to give undue emphasis to particular points of view. Nearly always there remains a considerable task of evaluation for the developers and engineers responsible for any scheme. It is the most favourable solution that must be sought, not the ideal solution.

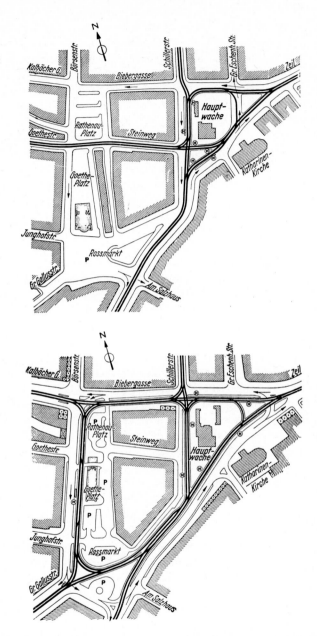

Figure 240: The tram interchange at the Hauptwache in the centre of Frankfurt am Main is a pedestrian area surrounded by one-way streets. Above is the small junction of 1945; below is the much larger present-day area. Construction of an underground tram station began in 1966, and was completed in 1969.

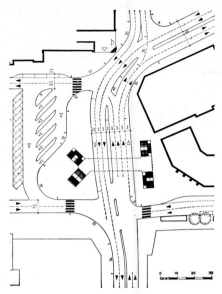

Figure 241: Proposed treatment outside the station in Lucerne, with bus lanes on either side of the main street, separate bus station for the long-distance buses.

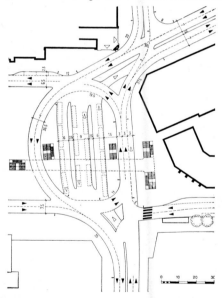

Figure 242: An alternative treatment with all bus stops brought together within a central island. In the centre are three stops in each direction for local buses, flanked by four stops in each direction for the terminating long-distance buses. This arrangement is more convenient for the many interchange passengers and more comprehensible for strangers. Before this interchange point was designed the question had to be considered to what extent radial bus routes should be linked together to form diametrical routes. Geometric design is not the beginning but rather the final stage in dealing with traffic problems.

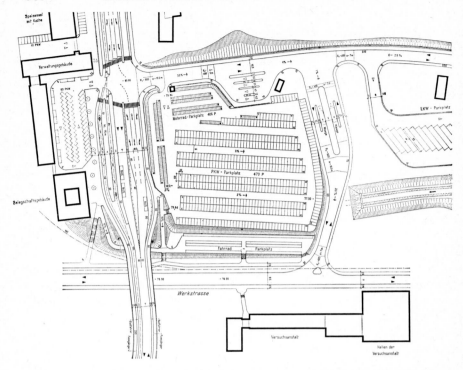

Figure 243: Treatment of the area outside a factory employing 9,000 people. The
following had to be provided as close as possible to the main entrance: tram
stopping place (with inverted flow to save space), bus stops, pedestrian and
pedal-cycle access (led under the main street), parking places, filling station
and big weighbridges for the heavy tractor-trailer combinations entering and
leaving the works.

V. COMPREHENSIVE TRANSPORT PLANS

(a) The planning unit

Every city and every conurbation needs a comprehensive transport plan.
Without one no up-to-date town planning is possible. Indeed the transport
plan must be given a certain priority, both in importance and in time. But
unfortunately it often happens that settlements are designed or areas ear-
marked for certain purposes without the means of servicing them being
made clear or land being reserved for the transport channels which are
needed to serve the entire urban area.

The comprehensive transport plan must cover all means of transport
over the entire urban area. This objective cannot be attained if the three
elements of the network—stretches between junctions, junctions, parking
areas—are handled separately. The interaction between public and private

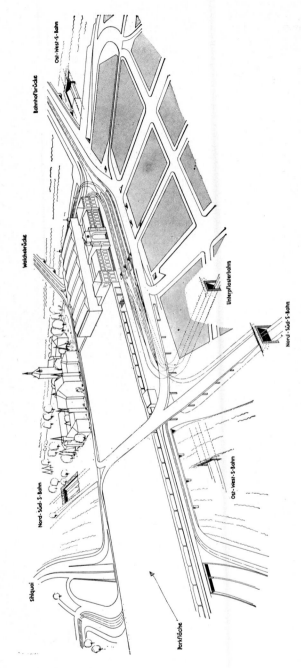

Figure 244: The comprehensive transportation plan for a city or a region forms an indivisible unity. Under the 1953 transportation plan for Zürich roads, trams and underground suburban railways were to cross each other at different levels in the area of the main station. Special levels were to be provided for pedestrians and for parking. Individual elements cannot be wantonly altered either at a complex of this kind or in a whole urban or regional transportation network.

transport becomes more and more important. They use to a large extent the same roadways. It is impossible to plan for either in isolation from the other since they move within the same road space (Fig. 244).

In the publications of the last few years much space has been devoted to private motor traffic because it was developing especially rapidly and posing new problems. But traffic engineers who do not know just as much about public transport are not capable of performing the task that faces them. Water and air transport must also be taken into account.

Figure 245: A model of the Rhine bridgehead layout at Mannheim carried out in 1958/61. Models, like drawings, are however, best considered not from a bird's-eye viewpoint but from a human-eye viewpoint—i.e. from a few millimetres above the 'ground'. (Cf. Figure 13.)

For traffic planning the support of the political powers that be is indispensable. The authorities must lay down the financial limits within which transport facilities must be planned. Likewise they must provide the key to the distribution of costs between various authorities. The administrations must provide the necessary contacts with neighbouring authorities and other districts.

They must also keep themselves informed about the way the plan is being formed, and about all its stages from traffic survey to final scaled designs, which proves the feasibility of the plan and permits cost estimates to be made for land acquisition and construction with a certain degree of accuracy. Scale models can give good service in this respect as a supplement to written and oral explanations (Figs. 245, 246, 247).

Figure 246: A model of the proposed treatment in the Heuwaageviadukt–
Elizabethenanlage–SBB station area of Basle. (Cf. Figure 194.)

Figure 247: A model of the Tegelbacken junction in Stockholm, with the town
hall on the left and the main station in the centre

(b) Construction stages

The plan ought not to be rigid and unalterable in all its details. And it must be divided into comprehensible construction stages (Fig. 248). Possible extensions beyond the design year should be envisaged. Each construction stage can be designed in detail, decided on and carried out one after the other over the years. There would be little sense in taking binding decisions at once concerning the carrying out of works, their sequence and their costs over the entire planning period of twenty-five to thirty years.

In each interim condition the urban environment must be livable and the traffic engineering installations must have sufficient capacity, so that no disadvantages will follow from any interruption of the programme

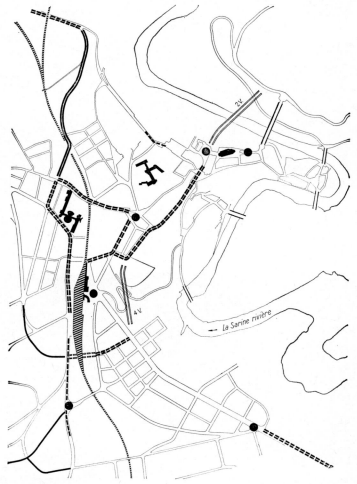

Figure 248: The general transport plan for Freiburg, Switzerland, can be divided into a series of separate projects which can be decided on, financed and carried out separately. Black points are intersections to be rebuilt.

caused by any events of a political or economic kind. For these interim conditions capacity calculations should be made for streets, junctions, parking areas, public transport and pedestrian links. On heavily-loaded streets road and tram traffic can only be interrupted for a matter of hours, so that construction work may have to be spread over long periods of time.

If economic activity, population or traffic volume should increase more rapidly than had been expected, the carrying out of the programme of works should be compressed into a shorter period of years. If there is an economic boom tax revenues will increase, so that the necessary means will be available to the authorities sooner; if there is a recession the opposite applies.

Dividing the programme into construction stages facilitates execution hereof (Fig. 249). If for example the reconstruction of a stopping place, of

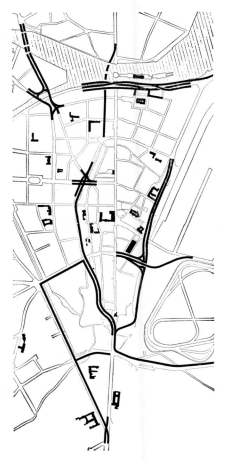

Figure 249: The individual elements in the transport plan for Neuss can be carried out independently. Each measure on its own will bring measurable benefits, but each fits into the overall plan.

a street and of a group of buildings are mutually interdependent, or if the reconstruction of a junction requires the removal of a tram line or its replacement by a bus service, the decisions of all concerned, the financing and the construction work would all have to be dovetailed together. It is certainly simpler to carry out each of these tasks independently of the others. Otherwise unfortunate delays can arise.

(c) Objective

A comprehensive transport plan must not follow a revolutionary path. This requirement does not mean that new types of solution, and large-scale solutions, are ruled out. But it is advisable to proceed warily, since mistakes once turned into concrete can hardly be reversed. The existing situation must be gradually adapted to meet new needs. The new must grow step by step. All individual measures must fit into an overall plan.

If a comprehensive transport plan is laid down and decided on as a standard, the framework for the years ahead is staked out. The misdirection of means is eliminated. But the work is by no means over. Traffic planning must be carried on as a permanent function, keeping track of developments which affect it. It must continually work out all individual questions; deal with neighbouring authorities on more far-reaching transport questions; and prepare designs for dates beyond the design year of the plan. And it must test the plans continually on the basis of new surveys carried out every few years, and improve them so that they will not be overtaken by events. In this context new scientific knowledge must be thoroughly evaluated and social, economic and technical changes taken into account.

In this way we shall gradually succeed in mastering traffic congestion and creating a modern method of town building.

BIBLIOGRAPHY

BENDTSEN, P. H., *Urban and Suburban Railways* (Danmarks Naturvidenskabelige Samfund, Copenhagen 1938).
- *Byplanlaegning* (Politeknish Forening, Copenhagen 1955).
- *Town and Traffic in the Motor-age* (Danish Technical Press, Copenhagen 1961).
BERGER, R., *Untergrundbahnen und ihre Einsatzgrenzen* (Wilhelm Ernst und Sohn, Berlin 1951).
BJORKMAN, BO, *Vägstandard, Kapacitet och Trafikekonomi* (Stockholm 1961).
BLUM, O., *Städtebau*, Berlin 1937).
- *Die Entwicklung des Verkehrs* (Springer, Berlin 1940).
BLUM, O., POTTHOFF, *Strassenbahn und Omnibus in Stadtinnern* (Fischer, Jena 1942).
BLUM, O., LEIBBRAND, *Personen- und Güterbahnhöfe* (Springer, Berlin/Göttingen/ Heidelberg 1961).
BRANDT, L., *Stadtverkehr heute und morgen* (Droste-Verlag, Düsseldorf 1953).
- *Untersuchungen zur inneren Verkehrslage grosser Stadtkreise* (Droste-Verlag, Düsseldorf 1953).
BRUNNER, K., *Städtebau und Schnellverkehr* (Springer, Vienna 1955).
EGLI, E., *Geschichte des Städtebaues* (Rentsch, Zürich 1959).
FISCHER, A., *Neue Weltstatistik* (Freytag-Berndt und Artaria, Vienna 1951).
FITZPAYNE, *Urban transport and city planning*. Report to the International Union of Public Transport, Edinburgh (Brussels 1951).
FORDHAM, J., *Parking Legal, Financial, Administrative* (Eno Foundation, Saugatuck, Conn. 1956).
GÖDERITZ, RAINER and HOFFMANN. *Die gegliederte und aufgelockerte Stadt* (Wasmuth Tübingen 1957).
GRABE, H., *Strassenverkehrsknoten, ein Beitrag zur Leistungsermittlung und Beurteilung von ungeregelten Strassenverkehrsanlagen* (Diss. TH. Hannover 1952).
- *Leistungsermittlung von nicht lichtsignalgesteuerten Knotenpunkten des Strassenverkehrs* (Kirschbaum, Bielefeld 1954).
GREENSHIELDS, SHAPIRO, ERICKSEN, *Traffic Performance at Urban Street Intersections* (Eno Foundation, Saugatuck, Conn. 1947).
GYLDENSTEIN, G., *Stockholms Tunnelbanesystem* (Stockholm 1952).
HARBOUR, B. H., *Priority for public transport* (I.U.P.T. Review, Brussels 1963).
HARLAKOFF, N., *Die wirtschaftliche Erschliessung von Wohngebieten unter besonderer Berücksichtigung eines nichttrennenden Strassenverkehrs* (Dresden 1960).
HOOVER, E., and VERNON, R., *Anatomy of a metropolis* (Harvard University Press, Cambridge/Mass. 1959).
HOUNSFIELD, *Traffic Surveys* (London 1949).
- *Engineering Aspects of the Transport Problem of London* (Euston Press, London 1951).
KORTE, *Strassenverkehrsplanung* (Bauverlag, Wiesbaden/Berlin 1960).
KREMER, PH., and LEIBBRAND, K., *Generalverkehrsplan für die Stadt Zürich* (Zürich 1953).
LAMBERT, W., *Nahverkehrsbahnen der Grossstädte* (Springer, Berlin/Göttingen/ Heidelberg 1956).

LANGEVIN, M., *Les Transports Urbains* (Paris 1954).

LEHNER, F., *Der öffentliche Nahverkehr in den Innenräumen unserer Städte* (Arnold, Dortmund 1957).

– *Menge, Arbeit, Leistung und Wirkungsgrad im Verkehr* (Verkehr und Technik).

– *Public transport within the framework of urban general traffic plans.* Report to the International Union of Public Transport, Copenhagen (I.U.P.T. 1961).

LEIBBRAND, K., *Verkehrsingenieurwesen* (Birkhäuser, Basle 1957).

– *Das Verkehrswesen als Glied der Landes-, Regional- und Stadtplanung* (Carl Heymann, Cologne/Berlin 1957).

– *Postkartenzählung (Biel)* (Strasse and Verkehr, Solothurn, Heft 8/1955).

– *Die jährliche Fahrleistung der Motorfahrzeuge im Kanton Zürich* (Schweiz. Archiv für Verkehrswissenschaft, Berne 1957).

– *Studie über die Entwicklung des Flughafens Zürich* (Verlag der Zürcher Handelskammer 1956).

– *Zürcher Luftverkehr 1970* (Verlag der Zürcher Handelskammer 1958).

– *Gesamtverkehrsplan Basel 1958.*

– *Gesamtverkehrsplan Münster/Westfalen 1962.*

– *Gesamtverkehrsplan Memmingen 1963.*

LEIBBRAND, K., PHILIPP HOLZMANN AG, WAYSS & FREYTAG KG, HOCHTIEF AG, ALWEG-FORSCHUNG GMBH, *Stadtbahn Frankfurt am Main, Planerische Gesamtübersicht* (Frankfurt 1961).

LILL, E., *Das Reisegesetz und seine Anwendung auf den Eisenbahnverkehr* (Vienna 1891).

MAESTRELLI, R., *L'impiego delle Metropolitane* (L'impresa pubblica, Rome 1959).

MATSON, SMITH, HURD, *Traffic Engineering* (McGraw Hill, New York 1955).

MAY, E., BOESLER, F., LEIBBRAND, K., *Das neue Mainz* (1961).

MITCHELL and RAPKIN, CH., *Urban Traffic, a function of land use* (Columbia University Press, New York 1954).

MÜLLER, W., *Fahrdynamik der Verkehrsmittel* (Springer, Berlin 1940).

– *Eisenbahnanlagen und Fahrdynamik* (Springer, Berlin 1950/53).

OWEN, W., *The Metropolitan Transportation Problem.*

PAMPEL, F., *Zur Frage der künftigen Verkehrsmittel für den öffentlichen Personennahverkehr* (Schmidt, Bielefeld 1959).

PATRASSI, A., *Trasporti rapidi di persone in un'area urbana o metropolitana* (Ingegneria ferroviaria 1960).

POTTHOFF, G., *Gleisentwicklungen* (VEB Verlag Technik, Berlin 1955).

– *Die Wartezeiten beim Umsteigen* (Wiss. Zeitschrift der Hochschule für Verkehrswesen Dresden, 1955).

– *Verkehrsströmungslehre* (Verlag für Verkehrswesen, Berlin 1962).

RAPP, H. J., *Die Leistungsfähigkeit von ungesteuerten Verkehrsknotenpunkten* (Birkhäuser, Basel 1954).

REAL, W., *Erfahrungen und Möglichkeiten bei der Aufstellung von Richtlinien für die Stadtplanung* (Buri, Berne 1950).

REICHOW, H. B., *Die autogerechte Stadt* (Maier, Ravensburg 1959).

RICKER, E., *Traffic Design of Parking Garages* (Eno Foundation, Saugatuck/ Conn. 1957).

RISCH/LADEMANN, *Der öffentliche Personennahverkehr* (Springer, Berlin/ Göttingen/Heidelberg 1957).

RÖPKE, W., *Jenseits von Angebot und Nachfrage* (Rentsch, Zürich 1958).

SAMUELSON, ST., *Der Ausbau der öffentlichen Verkehrsmittel in Gross-Stockholm* (I.U.P.T. Review, Brussels 1952).

SAWHILL, R., and FIREY, J., *Predicting fuel and travel time consumption of motor transport vehicles* (Highway Research Abstracts 1961).

SCHLUMS, J., *Die Problematik der Verkehrsentfaltung der Grossstädte* (Duisburg 1952).

SCHRAMM, W., *Der Gleisbogen* (2nd edition, Elsnerverlag, Darmstadt 1954).

SEDLMAYR, H., *Der Verlust der Mitte* (Otto Müller, Salzburg).

SILL, O., *Die Parkraumnot* (Schmidt-Verlag, Berlin/Bielefeld/Munich 1951).

– *Parkbauten, Handbuch für Planung, Bau und Betrieb der Parkhäuser und Tiefgaragen* (Bauverlag, Wiesbaden/Berlin, 2nd edition 1967).

SMITH, W., and LE CRAW, C., *Parking* (Eno Foundation, Saugatuck, Conn. 1946).

– *Parking Lot Operation* (Eno Foundation, 1948).

STEIN, *Kultur-Fahrplan* (Herbig, Berlin 1954).

STEINER/GUTHER/LEIBBRAND, *München, Stellungnahme der Planungsberater* (Munich 1960).

STRAMENTOW, A. (Moskau), *Ingenieurfragen der Stadtplanung* (Berlin 1958).

SZABO, D., *Városi közlekedés* (Derstädtische Verkehr), (Tankönyvkiadó, Budapest 1962).

UMLAUF, J., *Vom Wesen der Stadt und der Stadtplanung* (Werner-Verlag, Düsseldorf 1951).

VAHLEFELD, R., and JACQUES, F., *Garages and service stations* (Leonard Hill 1963).

VAN TRAA, C., *Rotterdam, der Neubau einer Stadt* (Donker, Rotterdam 1958).

WALTHER/LEIBBRAND, *Strassenverkehrsplanung der Stadt Bern* (Berne 1954).

VAN WISSELINGH, *Weg en Verkeer* (van Holkema & Warendorf, Amsterdam).

Deutsche Forschungsgesellschaft für das Strassenwesen, *Richtlinien für die Anlage von Stadtstrassen* (Kirschbaum, Bielefeld 1953).

– *Richtlinien für die Anlage von Tankstellen* (Cologne 1951).

Untersuchungen für einen Generalverkehrsplan der Stadt Düsseldorf (1960).

VÖV, *Moderne Nahverkehrsplanung* (Bielefeld 1961).

Arbeitsgemeinschaft Stadtentwicklungsplan München, *Grundzüge des Gesamtverkehrsplanes* (A. Innenstadt, Munich 1961).

Deutscher Städtetag, *Die Verkehrsprobleme der Städte* (Kohlhammer, Stuttgart/Cologne 1963).

Völker, Staaten und Kulturen, ein Kartenwerk zur Geschichte (Westermann, Braunschweig 1956).

Regionalplanung im Kanton Zürich (Direktion der öffentlichen Bauten des Kantons Zürich, 1960).

Hochbauamt der Stadt Zürich, *Garagenverordnung* (Hefte I–IV, 1958–1960).

Vereinigung schweizerischer Strassenfachmänner, *VSS-Vorschriften und Richtlinien* (1952 ff.).

Parkeerrapport 1958, Nader Onderzoek naar Parkeerduur, Dienst van Stadsontwikkeling en Wederopbouw (Rotterdam 1959).

Generalplan för Stockholm (Stockholms Stads Stadsplanekontor 1952).

Svenska Kommunal-Tekniska Föreningen (Gatan, Eklunds Tryckeri, Stockholm 1953).

Storstadens Trafikproblem, Ingeniörvetenskapsakademiens Transport-Forskningskommission (Stockholm 1955).

Busstationer, Ingeniörvetenskapsakademiens Transport-Forskningskommission (Stockholm 1958).

Ministry of Transport, *Report of the Working Party on Car Parking in the Inner Area of London* (London 1953).

Public Administration Service, *Traffic Engineering Functions and Administration* (Chicago 1949).

Public Roads Administration, *Uniform Traffic Control Devices* (Washington D.C. 1948).

American Automobile Association, *Parking Manual* (Washington D.C. 1948).
Parking Guide for Cities (US Department of Commerce, Bureau of Public Roads, Washington D.C. 1956).
Automobile Facts and Figures 1959–1962 (Automobile Manufacturers Association, Detroit 1960 ff.).
Annual Report of the Commissioner for Government Transport 1958–1962 (Sydney N.S.W. 1958 ff.).

SOURCES OF
ILLUSTRATIONS

SUBJECT INDEX

(See also Index of Places and Names)

INDEX OF PLACES
AND NAMES